BLOOD AND SAND

BLOOD AND SAND

SUEZ, HUNGARY, AND EISENHOWER'S CAMPAIGN FOR PEACE

ALEX VON TUNZELMANN

HARPER

An Imprint of HarperCollins*Publishers*

Maps © MLDesign

HarperCollins books may be purchased for educational, business, or sales promotional use. For information, please email the Special Markets Department at SPsales@harpercollins.com.

FIRST EDITION

Library of Congress Cataloging-in-Publication Data has been applied for.

ISBN 978-0-06-224924-1

16 17 18 19 20   RRD   10 9 8 7 6 5 4 3 2 1

FOR MIKE

CONTENTS

MAPS

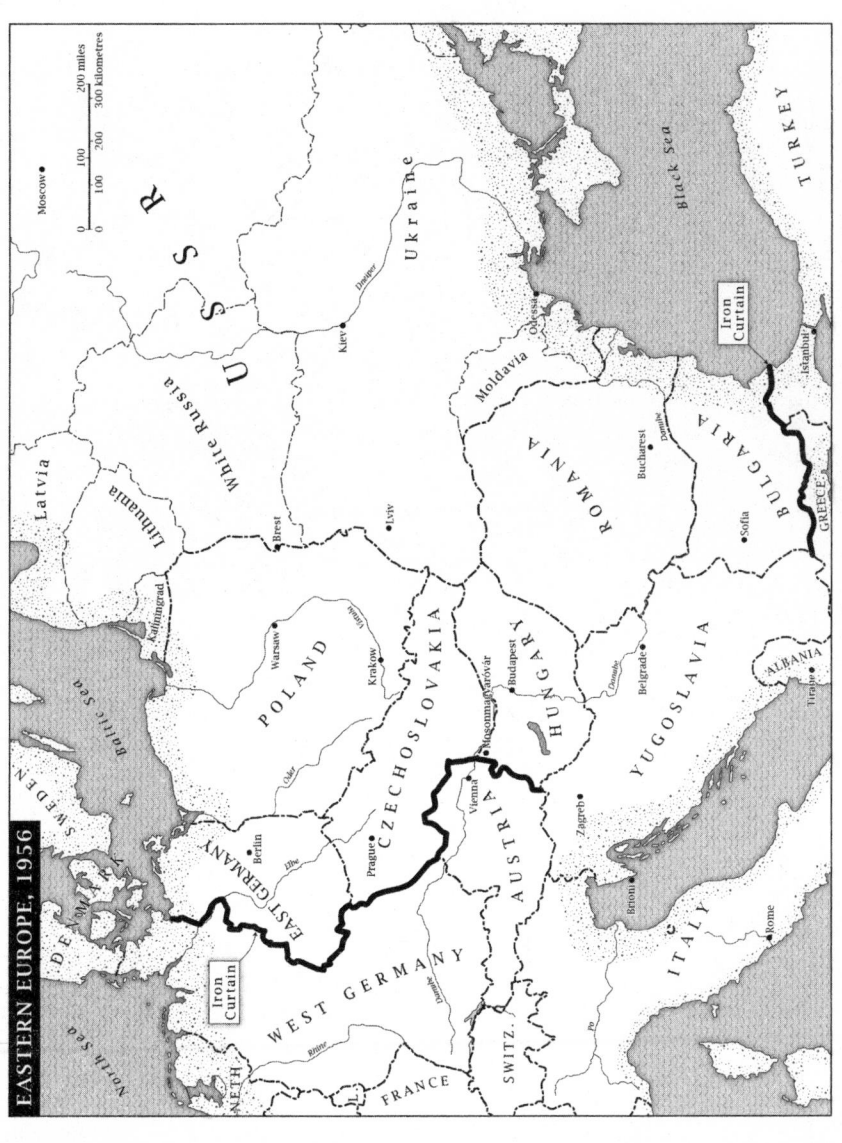

EASTERN EUROPE, 1956

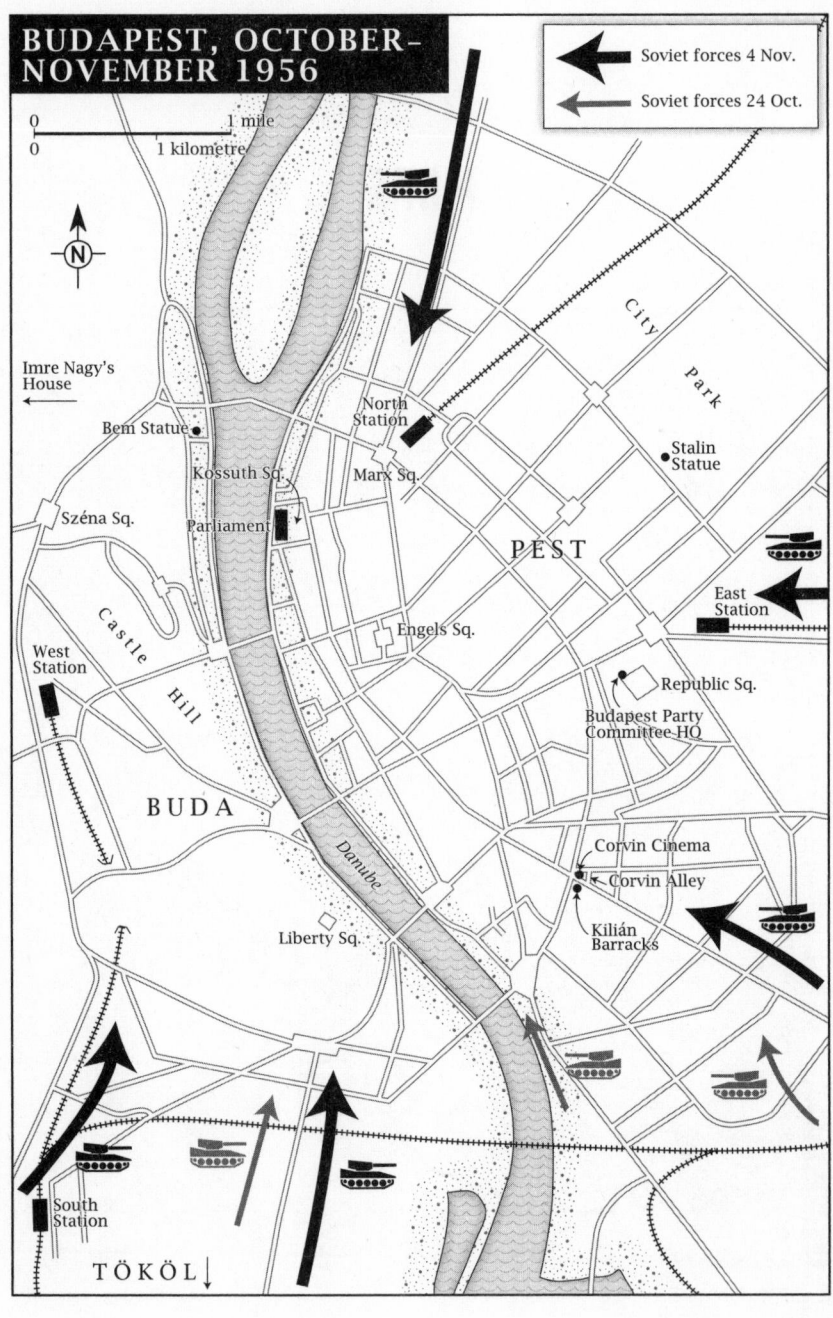

BUDAPEST, OCTOBER–NOVEMBER 1956

Soviet forces 4 Nov.

Soviet forces 24 Oct.

0   1 mile
0   1 kilometre

N

City Park

Imre Nagy's House

North Station

Bem Statue

Stalin Statue

Kossuth Sq.   Marx Sq.

Széna Sq.   Parliament

PEST

Engels Sq.

East Station

West Station

Castle Hill

Republic Sq.

Budapest Party Committee HQ

BUDA

Corvin Cinema
Corvin Alley

Danube

Kilián Barracks

Liberty Sq.

South Station

TÖKÖL

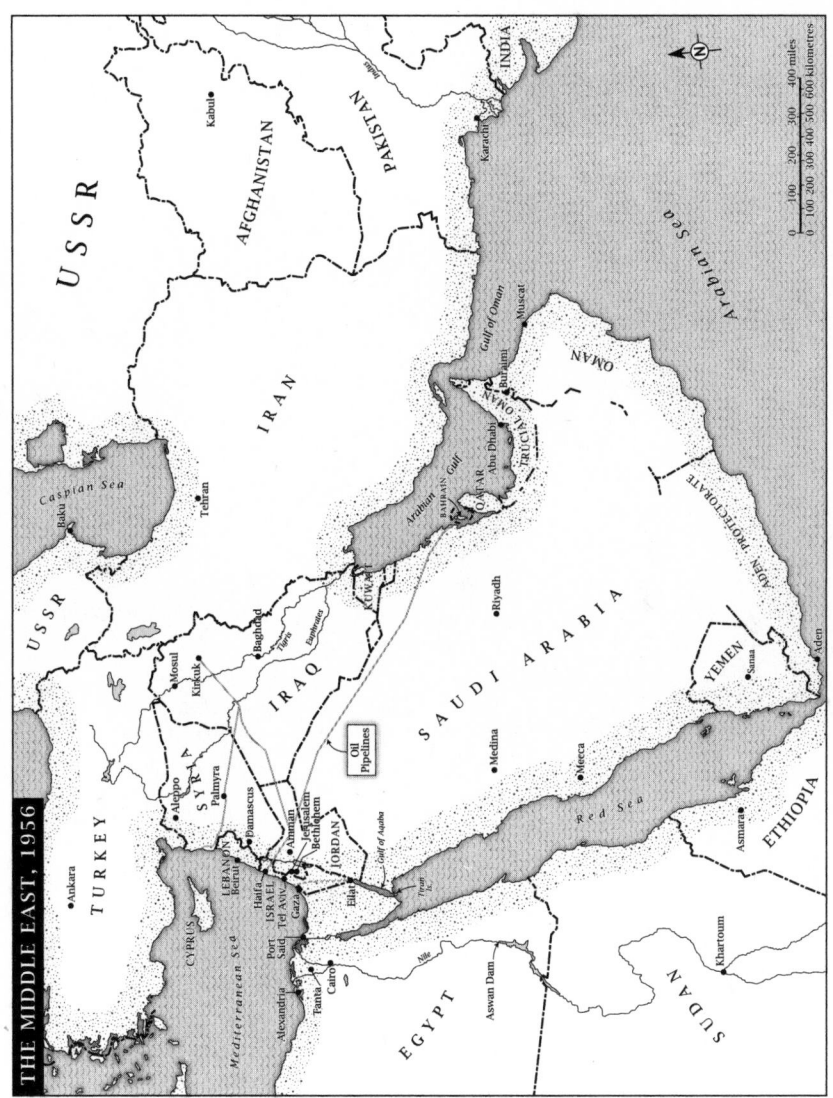

THE MIDDLE EAST, 1956

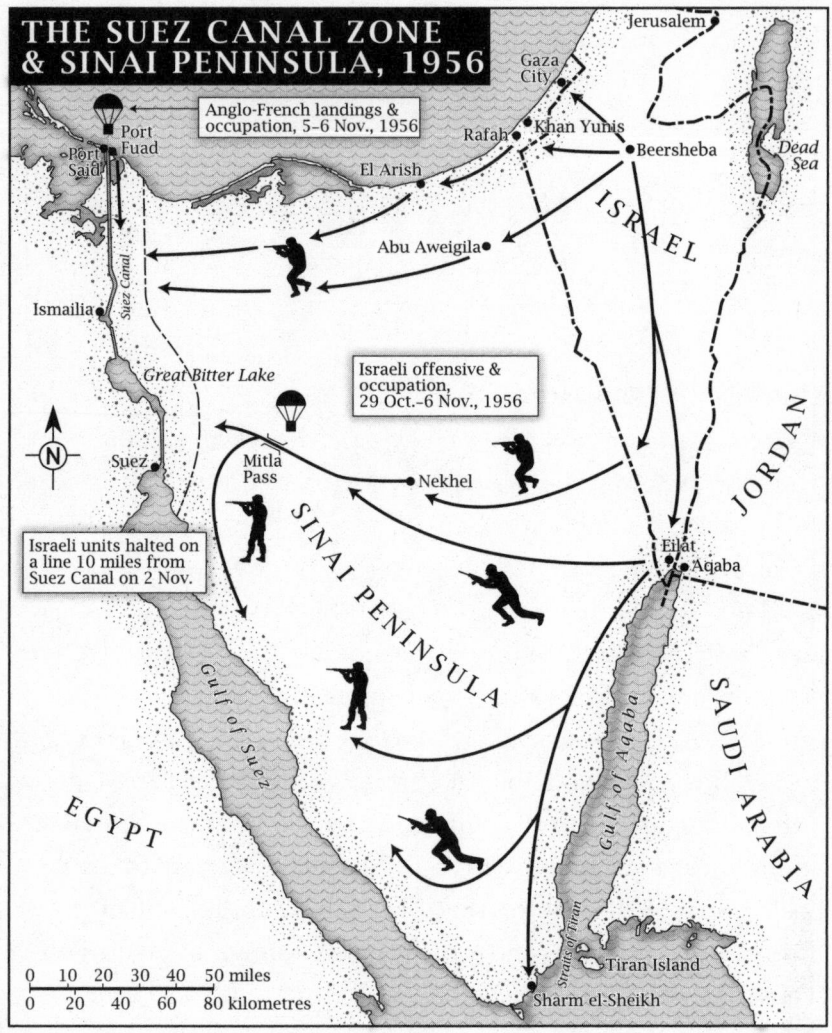

THE SUEZ CANAL ZONE & SINAI PENINSULA, 1956

Anglo-French landings & occupation, 5–6 Nov., 1956

Israeli offensive & occupation, 29 Oct.–6 Nov., 1956

Israeli units halted on a line 10 miles from Suez Canal on 2 Nov.

Jerusalem

Gaza City

Port Fuad
Port Said

Rafah   Khan Yunis

Beersheba

Dead Sea

El Arish

ISRAEL

Abu Aweigila

Ismailia

Suez Canal

Great Bitter Lake

JORDAN

Mitla Pass   Nekhel

N

Suez

Eilat
Aqaba

SINAI PENINSULA

Gulf of Suez

Gulf of Aqaba

SAUDI ARABIA

EGYPT

0   10   20   30   40   50 miles
0   20   40   60   80 kilometres

Straits of Tiran

Tiran Island

Sharm el-Sheikh

AUTHOR'S NOTE

Multiple transliterations exist of Russian, Chinese, Arabic, Hebrew, Persian, and other place and personal names. Gamal Abdel Nasser may be written as Gamal Abd el-Nasr, Gamal 'abd-an-Nasir, and further variations. It is Jamal Abdul Nassir in some texts, though "Jamal" is misleading for English speakers: the Arabic letter *jīm* (ج), pronounced like an English *j* by many Arabic speakers, is pronounced in Egypt as a hard *g* (as in "get"). Places in Israel or the Palestinian territories often have different transliterations reflecting usage in Arabic and Hebrew: Qibya/Kibbiya, Kafr Qasim/Kfar Kassem.

It is impossible to be entirely consistent, so the transliterations most common in 1956 English-language sources have been preferred. Some of these have now fallen out of use—for instance, Peking is now universally known as Beijing. It is hoped that the forms used, even if outdated, reflect the tone of the time and are more consistent with the sources quoted. Where quotes use a different spelling, it has not been changed.

The "Arabs" and "Arab world" referred to in this book are defined as they commonly were in 1956, though many people living in those areas then and now are not Arabs. The Arab world was broadly defined linguistically but formed a diverse cultural and political entity. It included the Arabic-speaking territories of North Africa and the Middle East. Iran and Turkey, where Persian (Farsi) and Turkish are spoken respectively, are not and were not Arab, though they do comprise part of the Middle East. Pakistan is neither Arab nor part of the Middle East, but joined the regional defense alliance known as the Baghdad Pact along with Turkey, Iraq, Iran, and the United Kingdom.

Hungarian names are written with the surname before the first name: Nagy Imre rather than Imre Nagy. When writing in English, Hungarians usually reverse this to conform with Western conventions. This book follows their lead.

When researching a book that covers history one day at a time, it soon becomes clear that sources disagree on the precise dates and times of events. Wherever possible, the dates given in this book have been verified with archival documents and daily newspapers, but sometimes different witnesses have conflicting memories that are impossible to resolve.

BLOOD AND SAND

"I WANT HIM MURDERED"

March 1956 // Savoy Hotel // London, United Kingdom

It had been a busy Monday for Anthony Nutting. As part of his ministerial duties at the British Foreign Office, he had completed a plan for a United Nations police force takeover of British military positions on Israel's border. At the same time, Britain would increase military and economic aid to its Arab allies.

As the spring day shaded into evening, Nutting left his Whitehall office for the more sumptuous surroundings of the Savoy Hotel on the north bank of the Thames. He was to dine with a visiting American member of the United Nations disarmament commission.

Halfway through dinner, they were interrupted. Nutting was told there was an urgent telephone call for him on the hotel switchboard. He excused himself. Out of earshot, he took the call.

"It's me," said the agitated voice at the other end. "What's all this poppycock you've sent me? I don't agree with a single word of it."

Caught flat-footed, Nutting explained that the plan he had submitted earlier that day was designed to rationalize Britain's position in the Middle East. The aim was to reduce the influence of Gamal Abdel Nasser, the president of Egypt and the most irritating of all the thorns in the British side.

"But what's all this nonsense about isolating Nasser or 'neutralising' him, as you call it?" shouted the voice. "I want him murdered, can't you understand?"[1]

The threat shocked Nutting, but he kept his cool. Nasser could not be removed, he said, unless a preferable alternative were ready to replace him. Otherwise, Egypt might descend into anarchy.

"But I don't want an alternative. And I don't give a damn if there's anarchy and chaos in Egypt," snarled the voice, which belonged to the prime minister of the United Kingdom of Great Britain and Northern Ireland. There was a click on the line, then silence. Sir Anthony Eden had hung up.[2]

July 26, 1956 // Alexandria, Egypt

The thermometer hit 110° Fahrenheit as Gamal Abdel Nasser stepped up to speak in Alexandria's Mansheya Square. He was thirty-eight years old, broad-shouldered, confident, and ambitious. Since the beginning of the decade, he had been a rising star in Egypt's military. He had won important admirers— most notably inside the American Central Intelligence Agency (CIA)'s operation in Egypt. Nasser made it clear he was open to American overtures—potentially to the cost of Britain's long-standing influence in Egypt: "America can win our friendship by acting in accordance with the principles of the American liberation revolution," he said.[3]

Nasser had already overthrown a king and a president. He had been behind the dethroning of King Farouk in 1952. He had ousted Farouk's successor, President Mohamed Neguib, in 1954. This was not a man who would quail at taking on an empire, or even two.

In another age, Nasser could have been the sort of Arab leader favored by the West. He was pro-American, anti-Communist, and secular, yet blessed with almost unlimited credibility throughout the Middle East. He was, according to one CIA agent, "a magnificent-looking man," witty and personable, with an excellent command of English.[4] He was fiercely opposed to Israel, but so were all Arab leaders; the CIA believed he had more potential for making peace than most of them. Though Egypt and Israel had engaged in an arms race against each other, he had consistently tried to avoid open war. With American encouragement, he had even allowed secret channels for communication to open between Cairo and Tel Aviv. He could be ruthless with his own people, but much of his ruthlessness was directed toward fighting the Muslim Brotherhood—whose leading ideologue, Sayyid Qutb, would go on to become the intellectual father of al-Qaeda. Less than two years earlier, Nasser had been speaking on the same spot in Mansheya Square when a Muslim Brother had slipped through the crowd and, from a distance of just twenty-five feet, fired eight shots at him. All eight had missed. Nasser had enhanced his public image by appearing unruffled.

The estimated quarter of a million people filling the elegant park of Mansheya Square on July 26, 1956, were crammed in under the palm trees between neoclassical facades leading down to the Mediterranean Sea. Nasser's speech was broadcast over his Voice of the Arabs radio station to listeners throughout the Arab world and was simultaneously translated into English and French for those farther afield. For half an hour, he described imperialist crimes committed over the centuries by Britain and France, and—in a comic, knockabout style that the crowd enjoyed—his own recent negotiations with Eugene Black, the president of the World Bank. "Mr. Black suddenly reminded me of Ferdinand de Lesseps," he said.[5] He seemed to get stuck on this theme, and conspicuously mentioned the name several more times. "De Lesseps," he kept repeating. "De Lesseps."

The name was familiar to his audience, even if they were not sure why he kept saying it. Ferdinand-Marie de Lesseps had been a nineteenth-century French aristocrat from a diplomatic family. He had befriended Mohamed Said, the fourth son of the pasha of Egypt, when both men were youths. Said ran to fat; his strict father, Mohamed Ali Pasha, put him on a regime of diet and exercise. The miserable Said appealed to de Lesseps, who passed him secret bowls of macaroni.

That was fateful pasta. As an adult, de Lesseps developed one of the most ambitious engineering projects of the age: the Suez Canal. From ancient times, the rulers of East and West had dreamed of cutting a canal through the Sinai Peninsula. The slender neck of land just over a hundred miles wide, separating Africa from the Middle East, blocked a direct sea route from Europe to Asia. Ships were obliged to spend weeks circumnavigating the African continent. De Lesseps realized his dream with land and loans granted by his grateful childhood friend, Mohamed Said Pasha, who was by then ruler of Egypt and could be as fat as he liked.

The opening of the canal on November 17, 1869, was one of the grandest parties in history. The harbors of Alexandria and Port Said were clogged with royal yachts. Empress Eugénie of France cut a striking figure on the hot sands of Ismailia, riding a camel sidesaddle with her frothy underskirts billowing in the breeze. Accompanying her were the emperor of Austria-Hungary and princes of Prussia, Russia, and Holland. Thousands of Europe's and the Orient's most celebrated personalities dined in the desert under silken tents. The evening was, according to one French journalist, "like something out of the Arabian nights."

Like many good parties, Egypt's opening of the Suez Canal was followed by a long and unpleasant hangover. The canal transformed Egypt into a conduit for world trade. Egypt's rulers had believed this would make their nation rich. Instead, it made them vulnerable. The canal was coveted by the British, then approaching the height of their power. Britain's bloated eastern empire helped it account for more than half of Suez Canal traffic before 1914.[6] Britain and France were far stronger than Egypt—and Egypt had something they each wanted to control.

Egypt was a province of the Ottoman Empire until 1867, when the sultan bestowed a degree of independence upon it and raised the status of Egyptian monarchs from pasha to khedive. The first official khedive of Egypt was Mohamed Said Pasha's nephew, Ismail Pasha. Ismail Pasha mired himself in a lengthy, expensive war with Ethiopia. During his first twelve years on the throne, his country's debts increased from £3 million (by share of GDP, about £3.5 billion today) to £100 million (£117 billion).

Britain's prime minister, Benjamin Disraeli, had his eye on the khedive's 44 percent share in the Suez Canal Company, the private company that had exclusive license to operate the canal until the distant future date of 1968. In 1875, the khedive put his shares up for sale. The British Parliament was not in session at the moment they went on the market, so Disraeli could not put the deal through the legislature. Instead, he borrowed £4 million (£4.75 billion) personally from the banker Lord Rothschild on Britain's behalf to buy the khedive out.

The physical structure of the canal was owned by Egypt. Britain's new 44 percent share in the operating company—not the canal itself, though it was often assumed they were the same thing—was afterward said to be the best investment the British government ever made. Yet it was not secure enough. Overreacting to rumors of Egyptian unrest, British forces invaded Alexandria and Port Said in 1882.

De Lesseps, a patriot who had done his best to keep Britain

out of the canal project all along, was hysterical with rage. "The English shall never enter the Canal, never," he telegraphed to Ahmad Arabi, the Egyptian minister of war. "Make no attempt to intercept my Canal. I am there."[7] There or not, he could do nothing to stop them. Nor could the Egyptians. The British took Cairo, and installed a "representative" with the powers of a viceroy. Though it was not technically colonized, Egypt's sovereignty was abrogated. In Constantinople, the great European powers—along with Russia and with Egypt's imperial master, the Ottoman Empire—agreed to internationalize the canal. Egypt's opinion was not sought.

"We do not want Egypt," the British prime minister Lord Palmerston had once said, "any more than a rational man with an estate in the north of England and a residence in the south would wish to possess the inns on the north road. All he could want would be that the inns should be well-kept, always accessible, and furnishing him, when he came, with mutton-chops and post-horses."[8] From 1882, Britain operated what became known as the "veiled protectorate." The khedive's family remained on the Egyptian throne, but with a British agent and British advisers pulling the levers behind the scenes— furnishing British visitors with all the mutton-chops and post-horses they required. The protectorate became official only in 1914, when the Ottoman Empire, still theoretically the sovereign power above Egypt's khedive, supported Germany against Britain in World War I. After the protectorate's unveiling, the British tendency to treat the canal as their own property became increasingly difficult for Egyptians to ignore.

In the late nineteenth and early twentieth centuries, there was a literary, cultural, and ultimately political movement in the Middle East which became known as al-Nahda (the Awakening). This Arab renaissance developed senses of identity and purpose. It was both religious and secular, unifying and regionally diverse, bringing in ideas from the West as well as the East. From it were born ideas of pan-Islamism and the more secular pan-Arabism. The independence movements of many parts of the Arab world against the Ottoman Empire and European imperialism had their roots in al-Nahda.

The Arab renaissance coincided with the industrialized world's shift from coal to oil as its main energy source and with the discovery of vast reserves of oil in the lands around the Persian Gulf. The oil industry originated in the United States in 1865, when a twenty-six-year-old businessman named John D. Rockefeller won an auction for a Pennsylvania company that would become Standard Oil. Within fifteen years, he was the richest man in the United States.[9] Britain was then heavily dependent on a domestic coal industry to fuel energy-guzzling resources like the railways and the Royal Navy. Even so, a British oil company, Shell, was founded at the end of the nineteenth century. It later merged with another European company, Royal Dutch. To the fury of imperial Russia, Britain secured exclusive oil concessions in Persia from the shah. The Anglo-Persian Oil Company went public in 1909.

Black blood flowed in ever greater quantities through the veins of the Middle East to sustain the industrializing economies and militaries of Europe. While World War I was horrific for millions of ordinary people, to the oil industry it presented an unmatched opportunity for profit. The years from 1914 to 1918 saw a decisive shift away from the horse to horsepower. The land and air vehicles of war—trucks, motorcars, motorcycles, airplanes, and, from the Battle of the Somme onward, tanks—multiplied exponentially, demanding ever more oil. Moreover, the British Royal Navy was finally persuaded to switch from coal to oil. At the end of 1917, the French prime minister Georges Clemenceau wrote to the American president Woodrow Wilson that gasoline was "as vital as blood in the coming battles," and warned that an acute shortage of oil might "compel us to a peace unfavourable to the Allies."[10] In 1918, a senior admiral advised the British prime minister David Lloyd George that the British must "obtain the undisputed control of the greatest amount of Petroleum that we can" if Britannia meant to continue ruling the waves.[11]

With the Ottoman Empire collapsing, the British and French moved in. Lloyd George coveted the oilfields of Mosul in Mesopotamia (now Iraq), and would soon decide that he also wanted Palmyra, which was on a potential oil pipeline route from Mosul to the Mediterranean. He also toyed with giving Palestine and Syria to the Americans to keep the French out, and later for the same reason became interested in independent Arab rule for Syria.

Days before the war ended, Britain pressed France into releasing a joint declaration dedicating themselves to establishing freedom and democracy in a Middle East liberated from Ottoman rule. They also pledged to support the setting-up of independent governments and free enterprise. Yet the negotiations around the Versailles treaty saw Britain and France fight bitterly over who got what. The League of Nations awarded France a mandate over Syria and Lebanon, and Britain a mandate over the new nation of Iraq as well as Palestine. Britain chose a king for Iraq in Emir Faisal, son of the grand sharif of Mecca. Faisal had been a leader of the Arab revolt and close colleague of T. E. Lawrence before becoming king of Syria in 1920. The French had swiftly ousted him. He went into exile in Britain, where—thanks in part to Lawrence's lobbying—it was decided he might do as king of Iraq instead. He was installed on his new throne in Baghdad in 1921.

After the war, the rise of the car and other gasoline-fueled vehicles ensured that the world's thirst for oil kept growing. Egypt did not have Iraq's oil, but it did have a supply route from the Gulf to Europe: the Suez Canal. In line with Lord Palmerston's pronouncement about mutton-chops and post-horses, Britain still did not want to colonize Egypt fully. Following a rebellion in 1919, its appetite for taking responsibility for the day-to-day running of the country decreased yet further. In 1922, the government in London granted Egypt theoretical independence—while reserving direct control over communications, defense, the protection of foreign interests and minorities, and the administration of the Sudan. A nationalist party, the Wafd (meaning Delegation), was allowed to form.

With many nationalist leaders in exile, the sultan, Fuad, declared himself king of Egypt and the Sudan. Fuad had wide-ranging political powers: he could dismiss his ministers, dissolve parliament or even suspend the constitution as he wished. Britain sometimes acted with him; sometimes with parliament against him. He was succeeded by his son, King Farouk, in 1936. That same year, the British foreign secretary Anthony Eden helped negotiate a new Anglo-Egyptian Treaty of Friendship and Alliance, telling the House of Commons when he was recommending it, "Because of the Suez Canal the integrity of Egypt is a vital interest of the British Empire as well as of Egypt herself."[12] British troop numbers in the Canal Zone were to be reduced to ten thousand plus support; Britain would train and supply Egypt's army. If Egypt were threatened by war, the British military would be entitled to return. This allowed Egypt to look more independent, while allowing Britain to focus its resources on the part of Egypt it really cared about.

The treaty was supposed to last for twenty years, to be renegotiated or reaffirmed in 1956. Eden openly assumed it would last in perpetuity.[13] In recognition of his role in negotiations, his face appeared on an Egyptian postage stamp.[14]

Anthony Eden was a product of the landed gentry, Eton,

Oxford, and World War I. After his war service on the western front, he had married and produced two sons. He became a member of Parliament in 1923, went to the Foreign Office in 1931, and became foreign secretary four years later. He fell out with Neville Chamberlain and resigned in 1938. There were political considerations behind this resignation—yet the chancellor of the Exchequer, Sir John Simon, thought Eden was "both physically and mentally ill." Eden denied this on the record, but privately confided to fellow MP Malcolm Mac-Donald that he was indeed "physically unwell and mentally exhausted."[15] He took the noncabinet post of secretary of state for dominion affairs in 1939—and, after Winston Churchill became prime minister in 1940, returned to his former position as foreign secretary. Initially his relationship with Churchill was strong, though the demanding and increasingly erratic prime minister gradually wore him down. He developed a duodenal ulcer within two years of returning to the foreign office.

The Second World War again magnified Egypt's strategic importance, and Britain's promised troop reductions and withdrawals from non-canal areas did not come to pass. In 1941, Churchill declared that the "loss of Egypt and the Middle East would be a disaster of the first magnitude to Great Britain, second only to successful invasion [of Britain] and final conquest."[16] When Nazi troops under Field Marshal Erwin Rommel moved on Alexandria, some Egyptians—including a young Gamal Abdel Nasser and his associate Anwar Sadat—came to believe Rommel might do more for their liberation than the British ever had. Yet Allied troops defeated Rommel's forces decisively at El Alamein in 1942, driving the Nazi threat away from the Suez Canal.

Britain's postwar Labour government wanted to remove troops from Egypt entirely. The prime minister, Clement Attlee, proposed in 1946 to abandon the Suez base. Churchill, then leader of the opposition, exploded at this idea, calling it a "scuttle"—which was what he usually said about any retreat from empire, however measured.[17] By 1948, the British had finally fulfilled their promise to restrict their troops to the Canal Zone, though progress on full withdrawal was stymied by complicated negotiations and mistrust on both sides.

In 1951, Churchill was returned to power as prime minister and Eden became foreign secretary yet again. He had suffered personal tragedy at the end of the war: his elder son was killed in Burma, and his marriage disintegrated. Churchill had implied that he would let him take over as party leader—yet in the event decided to stay in control.[18]

By now, Eden was a senior figure on the international stage. Yet he was still not well, suffering attacks of appendicitis and jaundice as well as alarming physical collapses. A colleague remembered him fainting twice—literally pitching forward and landing flat on the grass—while attempting to make a speech at a United Nations rally at Warwick Castle in 1950.[19] His flashes of temper and fragile nerves led some to wonder about his genetic inheritance. His baronet father had been such an extreme eccentric—complete with episodes of "uncontrolled rages," falling to the floor, biting carpets, and hurling flowerpots through plate-glass windows—that even the Wodehousian society of early twentieth-century upper-class England had noticed something was up.[20]

At the same time as the Conservative Party returned to power in Britain, Egypt's discontent with its British semi-overlords found expression. The Wafd government abrogated the 1936 treaty and a separate Anglo-Egyptian Condominium on the Sudan, signaling that Egypt no longer considered Britain's presence in the Canal Zone or the Sudan to be legitimate. Britain hit back by pouring eighty thousand troops into the

Canal Zone—eight times more than it was permitted under
the 1936 treaty—and setting up a cordon around it.

Faced with what they saw as an occupation, nationalist
Egyptians and the Muslim Brotherhood attacked British nationals and property. A general strike was organized against
British companies. Ninety percent of Egyptian workers em-
ployed by them went on strike, with the Wafd offering them
jobs in the civil service instead.[21]

By the beginning of 1952, thirty-three British servicemen
and around one hundred Egyptians had been killed. Churchill wanted to mount an aggressive response. A full British
battalion with six tanks and armored cars attacked an Egyptian police station at Ismailia, inside the Canal Zone, on January 25, 1952. There was a six-hour battle. Somewhere between
fifty and seventy Egyptians were killed, about another seventy wounded. The following day, there was a rising in Cairo
against European interests, known as Black Saturday. British
properties in Cairo—and several other properties that seemed
foreign enough to be suspect—were set on fire by mobs, including the famous Shepheard's Hotel, Thomas Cook, BOAC,
Barclay's Bank, the Turf Club, the British Council, the French
chamber of commerce, the consulates of Sweden and Lebanon,
and dozens of cinemas, bars, and restaurants.

Even the most ardent British imperialists were now losing
faith in King Farouk's ability to keep order. Those Conservative MPs making up the "Suez Group" in Parliament—a
group that considered the canal integral to the future of British world power—tended to share Churchill's instinct to impose Britain's will by force rather than rely on Farouk as a
client-king. Yet one problem for such imperial enthusiasts in
the early 1950s was that Britain no longer had the funds to run
a full empire, as the Treasury sharply reminded Churchill's
government in 1952. The Second World War had left British

finances in a disastrous state. Encouraged by the "special relationship" Churchill had described between Britain and the United States, the likes of Anthony Eden now believed it might be possible to reassert British control with American muscle. "Our aim," Eden wrote, "should be to persuade the United States to assume the real burdens in such organisations while retaining for ourselves as much political control—and hence prestige and world influence—as we can."[22]

The United States had not up to this point shown much interest in Egypt. Under President Harry S. Truman, American involvement in the Middle East was limited mostly to private oil assets in Saudi Arabia and its attachment to Israel. Beyond that, the United States had been content to let Britain hold sway. The Soviet Union had not seen much opportunity in the region either. According to Nikita Khrushchev, then first secretary of the Moscow Regional Committee of the Communist Party of the Soviet Union, King Farouk appealed to Stalin to send arms for Egypt to force Britain out. Stalin refused. "Stalin said in my presence that the Near East was part of Britain's sphere of influence and that therefore we couldn't go sticking our nose into Egypt's affairs," Khrushchev remembered. "Not that Stalin wouldn't have liked to move into the Near East—he would have liked to very much—but he realistically recognized that the balance of power wasn't in our favour and that Britain wouldn't have stood for our interference."[23]

This was all about to change. In March 1952, the CIA operative Kermit "Kim" Roosevelt was in Cairo. The American Department of State was at the time wrongly predicting that there would be a popular revolution in Egypt; the CIA was correctly predicting a military coup linked to the mysterious Association of Free Officers, an organization of around eighty soldiers. The Free Officers adhered to no particular ideology, though they had contacts with most groups in Egypt, from the Wafd to the Muslim Brotherhood to the Communists.

One of those Free Officers the CIA thought might be influential was a young colonel, Gamal Abdel Nasser. Roosevelt had a series of secret meetings with Nasser and established that he was acceptable to American interests: motivated by frustration at the lack of effective government, the privileges of the upper classes, the supine state of the army, and the continuing presence of the British. He was open to communication with the United States and did not seem excessively hostile toward Israel. "Nasser explicitly admitted to Roosevelt that he and his officers had been 'humiliated' by the Israelis," remembered Roosevelt's fellow CIA officer Miles Copeland, "but he insisted that their resentments were 'against our own superior officers, other Arabs, the British and the Israelis—in that order.'"[24] Roosevelt reported to his superiors in Washington that a coup was going to happen whether they liked it or not; the men involved seemed reasonable; and the United States could not really help except by letting them get on with it.

On the night of July 23, 1952, it came to pass. The ringleaders of the Free Officers formed a fourteen-member Revolutionary Command Council. The Ras el-Tin palace in Alexandria was surrounded. King Farouk sent desperate messages to the American ambassador and to the British commander in the Canal Zone, asking them to rescue him. Neither the United States nor Britain had any intention of doing so. The Free Officer Ali Maher turned up at the palace with an abdication document.

"Is not mine the supreme will?" Farouk pleaded.

"The will of the people is supreme, Your Majesty," said Maher.[25]

Farouk signed. He had one afternoon to pack, meaning he had to leave with a mere couple of hundred trunks of his belongings. Among the things he left behind, according to the American diplomat Chester Cooper, was "the world's largest royal collection of dirty pictures."

"In ten years," Farouk said as he stood on the deck of his yacht, sailing into exile, "there will be five kings left: Hearts, Clubs, Diamonds, Spades, and England . . ."[26]

The new regime was headed by Mohamed Neguib, a prominent general, with Nasser and other more junior officers keeping a low profile. The Muslim Brotherhood was constrained. Though the new government itself promoted left-wing policies—redistributive land reform, social justice, and anti-imperialism—it also clamped down on the Communists. "Once Nasser confided to me that the Communists were his greatest opponents because they appealed to the masses in the same manner, and advocated the same cause, as he did," recalled the Sudanese politician Muhammad Ahmed Mahgoub.[27]

Any potential Nasser had for Communism was not obvious to the Soviets, though. "We were inclined to think that Nasser's coup was just another one of those military take-overs which we had become so accustomed to in South America," said Nikita Khrushchev. "We didn't expect much new to come of it." To Moscow, Neguib's supposedly revolutionary government appeared bourgeois, its leaders attached to privilege and property. The Soviets were disappointed that no serious efforts were made by the new rulers to restrain banks or capitalists. Stalin had long doubted the potential for the Third World to be converted to the Soviet cause. He had disbanded the Comintern, the organization set up by Lenin to promote Communism internationally, in 1943. Since the end of World War II, the Soviet Union's efforts had been focused on creating and consolidating allies in Eastern Europe. The fate of one of these Eastern Bloc nations, Hungary, was to intertwine—coincidentally, but momentously—with that of Egypt during the Suez Crisis.

The Soviets felt Nasser lacked the requisite Marxist-Leninist theoretical background. According to Khrushchev, "He talked about Socialism in such a way as to make us uncertain whether he really understood what he was saying."[28] Conversely, the Americans in Cairo were impressed. "During the period when he was consolidating his position his attitude toward his American friends was, 'If you don't like the way I'm doing it, show me a better way. At least I'll listen,'" wrote Copeland. "We never tested his sincerity because at no point along the line could we think of a better way."[29]

In London, Winston Churchill was still inclined to take a hard line on Egypt. Anthony Eden advocated complete military withdrawal. For personal reasons, it was an impolitic time for the prime minister and foreign secretary to disagree. Shortly after the coup in Egypt, Eden married his second wife: Clarissa Spencer-Churchill, twenty-three years his junior and the niece of his boss. Any coziness between the two men implied by this marriage was undercut by what one of Eden's biographers called "an element of sadism" in Churchill's behavior toward the neurotic Eden. Churchill's joint principal private secretary, Sir John Colville, described it as "cold hatred."[30] The prime minister seemed to take pleasure in needling Eden and playing him off against other colleagues. Messages from Churchill frequently provoked panic: "My nerves are already at breaking point," Eden told his civil servants. So often did Eden end telephone calls to Churchill's office with the words "And tell Winston that I'm at the end of my tether!" that his private secretaries developed an abbreviation: "The Foreign Secretary's at the E. of his T. again."[31] When the American secretary of state Dean Acheson met the two of them, Churchill commented approvingly on his strong, healthy looks and bearing. "Dean looks like you are supposed to do," he scolded the ailing Eden.[32]

The tension between Churchill and Eden peaked over Egypt. On January 30, 1953, Eden's private secretary Sir Evelyn Shuckburgh wrote in his diary: "Jock [Colville] tells me that the PM is very bellicose against A.E. [and says] 'If he resigns I will accept it and take the Foreign Office my-self.'"[33]

Crucially, at this point, Eden enlisted the help of the new American president, Dwight D. Eisenhower, who had developed a firm friendship with Churchill. Brought up in an ordinary Midwestern family without high-society connections, Eisenhower had joined the top ranks of the army relatively late in his career. Following a stint with the irascible General Douglas MacArthur in the Philippines in 1935, he gained a reputation for being able to work with the most difficult of men. This skill served him well with Churchill.[34] Eisenhower had been posted to London in 1942 and was made supreme Allied commander in Europe the following year.

British politicians were sometimes wary of anti-imperialist feeling on the part of Americans, suspecting them of being motivated less by a moral desire to free the oppressed and more by a strategic interest in eroding British influence. Yet Churchill, whose mother was American and whose admiration for military men was profound, had genuine respect for Eisenhower. "I admired and liked him," Eisenhower wrote of Churchill just after the war. "He knew this perfectly well and never hesitated to use that knowledge in his effort to swing me to his own line of thought in any argument. Yet in spite of his strength of purpose, in those instances where we found our convictions in direct opposition, he never once lost his friendly attitude toward me when I persisted in my own course, nor did he fail to respect with meticulous care the position I occupied as the senior American officer and, later, the Allied commander in Europe."[35] If there is a note of strain in this generous passage—the hint that Churchill may have used Eisenhower's goodwill to manipulate him, the pulling of rank—that may be because the two men often fought, sometimes violently. Even so, their affection for each other endured.

Together, Eden and Eisenhower eased Churchill into a more moderate position on Egypt. The foreign secretary managed to persuade his prime minister that British power might even be strengthened by moving troops to other British bases in the Middle East, including Jordan and Cyprus. Meanwhile, Eden's health took another knock. In April 1953, he was diagnosed with gallstones. Two unsuccessful operations made things worse. He flew to the United States to have a third and was out of politics for six months, recuperating. Two months later, Churchill suffered a serious stroke—yet still refused to relinquish power.

Eisenhower's government began to seek more overt links with Egypt in 1953, offering to sell arms to Neguib's government. Though Eden had hoped the United States might get involved in the Middle East, he was horrified at the prospect of this deal. He sought a guarantee from the American ambassador in London that no weapons would be supplied while relations between Britain and Egypt were still shaky, for American weapons might be used to kill British troops. He received assurances from the ambassador, but remained frustrated that the Americans would not do more to persuade their new friends in Cairo to negotiate with Britain.[36]

"American policy in general seemed to be conditioned by a belief that Egypt was still the victim of British 'colonialism', and as such deserving of American sympathy," Eden noted in his memoirs. This view, along with an American fear of unpopularity and lust for influence, he thought, "resulted in the Americans, at least locally, withholding the wholehearted support which their partner in N.A.T.O. had the right to expect."[37]

Eden had believed it might be possible for British brains to run the world with American muscle. He had not expected the Americans to develop ideas of their own.

*   *   *

Between February and April 1954, there was a power struggle in Cairo. Neguib was removed from the presidency and prime ministership, and Nasser became prime minister; then Neguib was restored and Nasser dropped down to the level of deputy prime minister; King Saud arrived from Saudi Arabia to mediate. It was confusing, but the direction of events was plain to see. "President Naguib was being edged out as coolly as if he had been a Paramount executive in the whirling 1920s," remarked the Hollywood director Cecil B. DeMille, who was in Egypt at the time preparing to film his biblical epic *The Ten Commandments*.

DeMille had hoped to meet Neguib but was instead directed to meet Nasser, whom he found to be sincere, impressively masculine, and "by no means unfriendly to America." Nasser endeared himself to DeMille with his love of Hollywood movies: "The young Gamal Abdel Nasser's fellow-officers had nicknamed him 'Henry Wilcoxon'!" wrote the director.[38] In his youth, Nasser bore a striking resemblance to the brooding Wilcoxon, one of DeMille's leading men—especially in his 1934 role as Marcus Antonius, lover of the Egyptian pharaoh Cleopatra.[39]

On April 17, 1954, Neguib resigned for good and Nasser became prime minister again. He would ultimately become president, too, confirmed in that position by election on June 23, 1956. One of Nasser's first priorities as leader of Egypt was to conclude negotiations with Britain for the complete departure of British troops from the Canal Zone. He had been involved in these negotiations since May 1953. The final agreement was signed by Nasser and the British Foreign Office minister Anthony Nutting on October 19, 1954. Under its terms, all British troops would be evacuated from the Canal Zone by June 18, 1956, and their bases handed over to the Egyptian army. British interests in the Canal Zone would thereafter be maintained by civilian contractors only. The agreement was set to last for seven years from the date of signing. During that time, if there was an attack by an "outside Power" on Turkey or any member of the Arab Collective Security Pact (Egypt, Iraq, Jordan, Lebanon, Saudi Arabia, Syria, or Yemen), Britain had the right to reenter the Suez base with its military and operate from there.[40]

As the existing quasi-colonial presence in Egypt, the British knew they were not liked but were nonetheless sensitive to any confirmation of that fact. Judiciously, Nasser had tempered his statements on the British presence around the canal by emphasizing his admiration and even affection for Britons. "I am not against the British people, but I am opposed to the British forces' occupation of the Canal Zone," he told the *Daily Mirror* in 1953. "If this question were settled, a great friendship would exist between us."[41] After the 1954 agreement, Nasser was positive—genuinely positive, according to those who knew him well—about the prospect of moving smoothly into a new phase of Anglo-Egyptian friendship.[42]

This conciliatory tone seemed to chime with Anthony Eden's attitude. Eden meant to make British foreign policy more affordable in the Middle East. By removing tens of thousands of men from active duty, the Suez Base Agreement certainly did that. He wanted to reaffirm British influence, hoping it would now appear to be based on cooperation rather than colonialism. Yet Britain remained the largest single shareholder in the Suez Canal Company. Control over the running of the canal appeared essential to many Britons if their nation were to move on from the old imperial model to a new, prosperous future within the Commonwealth. By 1956, the canal was carrying 115 million tons of shipping a year and making clear profits of £11 million—of which Britain's share was £4.5 million. The British Treasury estimated the value of its assets in the Canal Zone to be £500 million.[43] But the Canal's real and growing importance concerned oil. For Britain in particular, the shortcut to the Persian Gulf was essential: the Gulf was where British oil companies operated, and therefore was where the oil priced in sterling came from. Oil from the Americas was priced in dollars, making it much less convenient or affordable for the British to buy.[44]

The Suez Canal meant power: oil power and global power. And global power was being rebalanced. Across a world map that had once been tinged in every corner with British imperial pink, different colors had begun to return.

Much effort had been put into presenting the end of the British Empire as a positive development. The style was set by Lord Mountbatten in India, with a focus on friendship and equality between Britain and its former colonial possessions—even if this was quickly overwhelmed by horrific violence. The partition of India was a disaster in human terms, and in most other terms—but Mountbatten's great achievement, from a public relations point of view, was reconciling a positive imperial narrative with the lowering of a flag. As historian David Cannadine observed, this "sought to present the *end* of the British Empire as the whole *point* of the British Empire."[45] The story was carefully constructed to imply that Britain's motives had always been benign.

"The United Kingdom has, for a century or more and in an increasing degree, applied herself to the trustee conception of her responsibilities towards colonial territories," Eden wrote in 1959. "As a result, we have for years past fostered and

admired the growth of countries which were once colonies and
have since become part of the Commonwealth. Great nations
like Canada and Australia, countries growing apace like New
Zealand and the Union of South Africa, are the earliest examples. More have followed."[46] All four of the examples he gave
were "white dominions": countries where people of European
heritage had assumed control at the expense of the indigenous
population. By the 1950s, even the staunchest of British imperialists accepted the granting of self-determination to other
white people.

Following the independence of India and Pakistan, it became feasible inside the British establishment to consider
people who were not white potentially responsible. Recently,
a form of this rosy-tinted paternalism had been extended to
Africa. "The end of 134 years of foreign rule in the Sudan
could not have been more civilised," wrote Mohamed Ahmed
Mahgoub, who was foreign minister of Sudan during the Suez
Crisis and later its prime minister. "The British handed over
the Khartoum barracks to the Sudanese at a cocktail party."
Sudan achieved full independence on January 1, 1956, being,
Mahgoub claimed, the first nation in Africa proper to exit
imperial rule in what he called an "orderly" fashion.[47] Yet
while the South Asian ex-colonies of Burma, Ceylon, India,
and Pakistan had been offered Commonwealth membership,
Sudan—like its regional neighbors Egypt, Iraq, Transjordan,
and British Palestine—was not. Though Britain had managed
the fiscal, foreign, and military affairs of these Middle Eastern
and North African territories, they had operated as mandates
or protectorates rather than colonies. Now they were held at a
distance.[48]

Not everyone in Britain was sold on a comforting view
of the end of empire. For many—especially, but not exclu-
sively, on the political right—Britain appeared to be losing its

divinely and racially ordained place at the top of the world. This induced a kind of desperation, growing ever more urgent and angry, to cling to the rotting reins of Britannia's imperial chariot. It was impossible for some Britons to imagine a world that they did not control and did not want to control. If they could no longer dominate their colonies openly, they must at least try to foster a secret British Empire club: not the Kumbaya-ing Boy Scout jamboree of the Commonwealth, but a powerful hidden empire of money and control.[49] For oil was the future, they knew, everyone knew: and the canal was the lifeline to what was by imperial right Britain's oil, inconveniently situated 3,500 miles off the white cliffs of Dover in the Persian Gulf.

Access to oil had already sparked conflicts. In 1951, the Iranian government had nationalized the Anglo-Iranian Oil Company. The British foreign secretary Herbert Morrison had warned that as a result "Egypt might be emboldened . . . to bring the Suez Canal under Egyptian control."[50] Iran's prime minister, Mohamed Mossadegh, was ousted in 1953 by a CIA-orchestrated coup, ordered by the British secret intelligence service, MI6. The Suez Canal was an even bigger deal than Anglo-Iranian Oil. Two thirds of Europe's oil was transported through it, a situation Eden characterized as giving Nasser a "thumb on our windpipe."[51] Half of all the oil imported by Western Europe was consumed by Britain.

Otto von Bismarck, the great nineteenth-century chancellor of Germany, once described the Suez Canal as the "spinal cord" of the British Empire, "which connects the backbone with the brain."[52] To neo-imperialist Britons, it also came to look like the route to the future. For Egyptians, though, the canal remained a sore: the justification of outside control of their government, the excuse for foreign presences in their country, and the source of riches to which they were not entitled.

April 1955–March 1956 // London

In April 1955, Winston Churchill finally stepped down, allowing Anthony Eden to take over the British prime ministership. Eden had by then served as foreign secretary or shadow
foreign secretary for twenty years, on and off, and was widely
considered to have been a success. Yet his premiership started
poorly. Trade figures declined. The balance of payments became unbalanced. Fears grew about speculative runs against
the pound. The chancellor, Rab Butler, adopted a program of
austerity and rises in indirect taxation. "By the end of August
[1955] our gold and dollar reserves were falling by over $100
million a month," Eden wrote in his memoirs.[53] The story of
the Cambridge Spies broke and reflected poorly on the Foreign
Office. Though the key period of the spies' operation had been
while Eden was in opposition, his association with the Foreign
Office was so strong and the criticisms of its culture were so
broad that inevitably he was tarnished. Hugh Gaitskell was
elected as Labour leader. He was sharp, clever, and ten years
younger than Eden. Conservative support slumped.

The press bubbled with criticism of Eden's supposedly skit-
tish and incoherent leadership—notably in a series of stinging
articles written by Winston Churchill's son and Eden's own
wife's cousin, Randolph Churchill. The phrase "control freak"
would not come into use for another decade, but it would have
characterized Eden's habits—which included telephoning
ministers in the middle of the night to ask if they had done
a certain task or read a particular newspaper article. Members of Eden's own party described him as "highly strung" and
suffering "a lack of confidence." One claimed that "no one in
public life lived more on his nerves than he did."[54]

On March 1, 1956, Eden received a piece of news that seems
to have triggered a decisive abandonment of rational thought.

It was about John Bagot Glubb, a British soldier who had for thirty years commanded the Arab Legion, the British-fostered army of Jordan. It was generally assumed in London that Glubb Pasha, as he was known, was adored by the Arabs, a successor to Lawrence of Arabia. This was not true. As a man known to serve two masters, Britain and Jordan, he was in a sticky position. He was widely rumored to be a British agent, and was blamed—unfairly, perhaps, but forcefully—for giving land away to Israel during its first war in 1948.

That day, Eden's foreign secretary Selwyn Lloyd was in Cairo dining with Gamal Abdel Nasser. During the dinner, the British ambassador to Egypt, Sir Humphrey Trevelyan, received a telegram informing him that King Hussein of Jordan had sacked Glubb Pasha and ordered him to leave the country immediately. He did not tell Lloyd—but he did notice that Nasser also received a note during the party, which he assumed contained the same information. On their way back to the British embassy, Trevelyan told Lloyd what had happened. "He was greatly upset," Trevelyan remembered. "He was convinced that Nasser had known of General Glubb's dismissal and half convinced that Nasser had planned it to coincide with his visit."[55]

One of Eden's pet projects was the Baghdad Pact, a Middle Eastern defensive alliance in British interests. He had hoped Glubb would persuade King Hussein to join, and now he thought Nasser must have schemed to oust the British commander so Jordan would not join the pact. At this point, Anthony Nutting said, "the Prime Minister of Great Britain declared a personal war on the man whom he held responsible for Glubb's dismissal—Gamal Abdel Nasser, President and Prime Minister of Egypt."[56]

Though the move to oust Glubb undoubtedly suited Nasser, cooler heads pointed out that King Hussein had made the

choice himself. Jordan had been riven by riots since the end
of 1955, which Glubb and the Arab Legion had failed to control. Anti-British feeling was an element in these riots. Glubb's
constant advice to Hussein could have been interpreted as interference.[57] "I often had to stop the King doing silly things,"
Glubb later said, "like promoting people who I knew were dis-
honest or incompetent."[58] It is easy to see how the fifty-eight-
year-old British commander might have seemed patronizing
to the twenty-year-old king.

In his memoirs, Eden put a different spin on their personal
relationship: "I thought at the time, and I am convinced now,
that part of the King's sentiment towards Glubb was based on
jealousy of a younger man for an older one long established in
a position of authority in the country."[59] Bearing in mind that
Glubb was unpopular in Jordan at the time and that Hussein
was in a position of considerable authority by virtue of being a
king, this seems unlikely.

Nasser denied that he had anything to do with Glubb's
sacking. This was a little disingenuous—he had sent his most
important colonels to persuade Hussein to do just that[60]—but
he did not know it was going to happen at that precise point.
"I thought that this was a move by the British Government,"
he later said. "And to my understanding this was a very good
move and a very progressive move, because Glubb was aggravating the hatred of the Arabs in Jordan against Britain."

The next morning, Lloyd met Nasser briefly on the way to
the airfield. Nasser congratulated him on getting rid of Glubb.
"He thought that I was joking, about him," remembered
Nasser. "The reaction of Mr Selwyn Lloyd was nervous, and
I was surprised about his nervousness. Then he left without
telling me anything."[61]

Lloyd went on to Bahrain, where he was greeted by anti-
British rioters throwing mud and stones. Both Lloyd and Eden

chose to believe that Nasser had organized this too. In fact, the rioters had just emerged from a soccer match and may have been acting spontaneously. Nasser assured the British ambassador that he had no organization in Bahrain.[62] Nevertheless, this was the point at which Eden telephoned Nutting at the Savoy to tell him he wanted Nasser murdered.

The Tory MP Nigel Nicolson remembered Eden addressing a meeting of Conservative backbenchers at the time. "He looked tired and worried," Nicolson remembered. "He painted a haunting picture of what would happen if our oil supplies were cut off. We were obliged to suffer constant humiliations, sucking up to Egypt's President Nasser, all for the sake of 'oil, oil, oil', and he spat the words out like cherry stones."[63]

Somehow, Eden seemed to have made the Egyptian leader a scapegoat for all his problems: the sinking empire, the sluggish economy, the collapse of his reputation within his party, and his dwindling popularity in the country at large. Lord Home, who was Commonwealth secretary in 1956, remembered that Eden saw Nasser as a man "who cheated in public affairs. That was really what it was. It was a blatant cheat, it was, and he was a nasty bombastic fellow."[64] Nasser can hardly have imagined that a man he had met once (at a dinner in February 1955) would have developed such a vendetta against him. Yet on Eden's side, at least, this conflict would be intensely personal.[65]

July 19, 1956 // Washington DC

Out of context, the decision taken by John Foster Dulles, American secretary of state under President Dwight D. Eisenhower, on July 19, 1956, sounded humdrum. It involved the financing of foreign exchange costs for a development project to build a new dam on the Nile at Aswan.

Nasser considered the Aswan Dam essential to the modernization and industrialization of Egypt. It was ambitious: the

Americans estimated that it would take twelve to sixteen years to build and would cost $1.3 billion.[66] It would allow Egypt to control its annual flooding, increase its agricultural land by an estimated 30 percent, store water for planned irrigation projects, and generate hydroelectricity.

Neither the Americans nor the British much liked the dam project as Nasser planned it. The Americans thought it too expensive, while the British preferred other schemes. But then, in the autumn of 1955, Nasser made an arms deal with Czechoslovakia—part of the Soviet bloc. Foster Dulles declared angrily that Egypt was, with this deal, "jeopardizing its ability to remain a fully independent member of the free world,"[67] but he opposed any drastic response. If the United States did anything overt, he feared, "the entire Arab world might be aligned against us, which would make it more susceptible to Communist penetration."[68]

It had been British policy to exclude Russia from the Mediterranean since the Crimean War, and this policy had not softened now that the Suez Canal existed and the Russians had become Soviets. "On no account must we let the Russians into the Nile Valley," Anthony Eden told one of his ministers.[69] When the Soviets hinted they might pay for Nasser's dam as well as sell him arms, the Americans, the British, and the World Bank offered to stump up foreign exchange costs for the project to keep them out. The initial grant included $56 million from the United States, £14 million from Britain, and $200 million from the bank.[70]

According to American diplomat Chester Cooper, Dulles had another motive: he hoped to use the dam as a bargaining chip in a plan to end the seven-year-old Arab-Israeli conflict. He was trying to push the reluctant nations of Israel and Egypt together to settle political and territorial questions, yet neither the Israelis nor Nasser wanted to talk about such sensitive issues alongside an industrial development project. "So much for the secretary [of state]'s attempt to tie aid for the dam to an Arab-Israeli treaty," wrote Cooper. "And so much for whatever dreams he may have had of winning a Nobel Peace Prize."[71]

During the first half of 1956, Britain and the United States turned against the dam. Nasser's resistance to British influence in the Middle East was making relations with London difficult, while his recognition of Communist China in May upset Washington. "For the secretary, recognition of China had come to assume almost religious significance," wrote Cooper; "it was just short of devil worship."[72] The Soviets floated the possibility that they would loan Nasser the full $1.3 billion cost of the dam at 2 percent interest over sixty years. Though Dulles thought the Soviet offer was probably a bluff, Nasser did not immediately reject it. By July it looked increasingly as if the United States would back out of the deal.

Foster Dulles was due to see the Egyptian ambassador, Ahmed Hussein, on the afternoon of July 19. At 3:20 p.m., forty minutes before Hussein was due to arrive, he telephoned his brother Allen Dulles, the director of the CIA. Foster told Allen that he was canceling the offer to finance the dam.

The secretary of state was under domestic pressure to make this decision, for Congress was demanding deep cuts to the foreign-aid budget. The trenchant attitude of some American politicians was summed up in a line from Otto Passman, the conservative Democratic congressman from Louisiana: "I don't smoke and I don't drink. My only pleasure in life is kicking the shit out of the foreign aid program of the United States of America."[73] There was fierce opposition to aiding Egypt from pro-Israel and anti-Communist lobbies. The Senate Appropriations Committee had unanimously passed a resolution declaring that none of the 1957 funds could be used for the Aswan Dam. As Foster told Allen Dulles in that telephone call,

"Congress will chop it [the funding] off tomorrow and the Sec. [Foster Dulles] would rather do it himself."

Foster Dulles suggested to his brother that the Soviets stepping in might even help the American cause within the nations of the Soviet bloc: "If they [the Soviets] do make this offer [to Egypt] we can make a lot of use of it in propaganda within the satellite bloc. You don't get bread because you are being squeezed to build a dam." Foster told Allen that he had informed the British ambassador of his decision that morning. He had the impression that the British agreed with the policy of withdrawing support: "They would have liked more time but in view of Congressional situation, they understand." Though the withdrawal of finance from the dam project was "hazardous," the brothers agreed, the minutes stated that Allen Dulles "is inclined to think it wise in the long run."[74] It was Foster Dulles's decision: Eisenhower was at this moment incapacitated following an emergency operation for ileitis. According to the president's son John, this was "the only instance in which Dulles made a policy move without consulting Dad first."[75]

At four p.m., Ahmed Hussein turned up for his meeting. "Don't please say you are going to withdraw the offer, because"—Hussein patted his pocket—"we have the Russian offer to finance the dam right here."[76]

"Well then, as you already have the money, you have no need of our support," Dulles snapped back. "The offer is withdrawn."

Hussein asked him to confirm that the decision was final. "I am speaking for the President," Dulles said, "and I am sure that I am also expressing the feelings of Congress and the country."[77]

As Hussein left the meeting, a State Department official remarked, "He looks as if he's had a kick in the pants."[78]

"Did you make a decision to cancel the offer of aid on the Aswan Dam in order to force a showdown with the Soviet Union in the Middle East?" a journalist asked Dulles some months later.

Dulles replied ambiguously: "I think that question could be answered in the negative."[79]

At 5:10 p.m., right after the meeting with Hussein, Senator William F. Knowland telephoned Dulles. Dulles told him what he had done. "The Secretary [Dulles] said it would be interesting to see what happens," the minutes of the call recorded. "In all probability when Nasser goes to Moscow he will sign up some agreement with the Russians. The Sec. said that the Egyptians, he told the Amb., having just won their independence, ought to be pretty careful."[80]

That evening, on his way out of the office, Dulles stopped by the desk of his special assistant, William Macomber. Stopping for a social chat was not Dulles's style—indeed, this was the only time he had ever done it. Macomber leaped awkwardly to his feet.

"Sit down, Bill," said the secretary of state. "Well, this has been quite a day."

"Yes, sir," replied Macomber.

"Well," said Dulles, "I certainly hope we did the right thing."

"I hope so," said Macomber.

"Yes, I certainly hope we did the right thing," Dulles said again. He turned and left.[81]

Though the timing of Dulles's decision may have been ordained by his domestic political situation, it was a shock to his colleagues and allies. "The secretary of state has gone mad!" exclaimed Miles Copeland, one of the key CIA agents dealing with Egypt. He predicted Nasser would react violently.[82] In London, Anthony Eden's press secretary raced upstairs in

Downing Street to give the prime minister the news in his bedroom. "Oh good, oh good for Foster. I didn't really think he had it in him," said Eden. There was a pause, and he added, "I wish he hadn't done it quite so abruptly."[83]

Dulles issued a carefully worded press release affirming friendly intentions toward the people of Egypt. It was not worded carefully enough. "We in the CIA had nothing to do with that statement," wrote Copeland, "and when Allen Dulles asked Kim Roosevelt later what he thought of it Kim was almost as enraged as Nasser."[84] Allen Dulles asked how they thought Nasser would react. Copeland and Roosevelt's immediate boss, Frank Wisner, suggested that Nasser might nationalize the Suez Canal Company. "Kim and I both kicked him under the table," remembered Copeland. The prospect of nationalization seemed so unlikely that his fellow agents were trying to dissuade Wisner from making "a fool of himself" by mentioning it.[85]

At that moment, Nasser was at the summer residence of the Yugoslav leader Marshal Josip Broz Tito on a picturesque island in the Brioni Archipelago in the Adriatic. Tito had invited him there for talks that would form the basis of the Non-Aligned Movement—a group of nations attempting to tread a neutral path between the capitalist and Communist extremes of the Cold War. It had been a convivial few days, with Tito serving wine from his own vineyard; nonalcoholic grape juice had been provided for Nasser.[86] Tito's other guest was Nasser's closest political ally outside the Arab world, Indian prime minister Jawaharlal Nehru.

Nehru and Nasser sat in the front seats of a Viscount plane back to Cairo with Nehru's quietly ambitious daughter Indira Gandhi and Nasser's foreign minister Mahmoud Fawzi. The pilot and one of Nasser's secretaries, who were listening to BBC radio news in the cockpit during the flight, sent messages back.

Nasser told Nehru the news from Washington. "There is no end to their arrogance!" exclaimed Nehru. "These people are arrogant! Arrogant!" He turned to Nasser: "My dear friend, I know that you have much on your mind. But you will have to think about it carefully."[87]

The plane landed in Cairo in the small hours of July 20. Dulles's statement had gone down as poorly as the CIA had feared. According to Nasser's friend and confidant Mohamed Heikal, Nasser felt it went far beyond the mere cancellation of some development funding: "The studied offensiveness of the language made it clear that Dulles' action was also a deliberate snub, a political challenge to Egypt's dignity as well as to her aspirations."[88] The next day, Eden, too, canceled his nation's support for the Aswan Dam project.

Nasser's anger was apparent at a reception he attended that day for foreign diplomats in Cairo. He had a good personal relationship with the American ambassador Henry Byroade, but now he took him aside. "You know, I've had a lot to do with the Russians, and I don't like the Russians," said Nasser. "I've had a lot to do with your people, and basically I like your people. This action of Mr. Dulles is an action against me by a great power, and no great power can take action against me without taking into account the necessary consequences of it." He jabbed a finger against Byroade's chest. "And the necessary consequences are that you fellows are out to kill me. And all I can do is protect myself. I tell you this. I am not going to be killed."[89]

Nasser and his aides spent that day working out a formal response. The strategy they came up with was designed to hit right at the most visible symbol of foreign influence in their nation. They would nationalize the Suez Canal Company. Later, the British ambassador Sir Humphrey Trevelyan suspected that Nehru—who had led his own nation to independence a

decade earlier—had put Nasser up to this plan. The evidence
from those close to Nehru suggests that Nasser's action came as
a complete surprise to him.[90]

Nasser's motivation was in part suspicion about the true purpose of Anglo-American policy. "It was the manner of the withdrawal which upset them [the Egyptians], since it appeared to
conceal some other purpose directed at them," Trevelyan remembered.[91] Nasser later told Chester Cooper that the decision
to nationalize was taken because he believed Britain and the
United States were trying to use the dam funding issue to push
him to make concessions to Israel—perhaps even to agree to
an Arab-Israeli peace on unfavorable terms. This was not a suspicion without foundation, for it was exactly what Dulles had
tried to do the previous year. "The purpose of his [Nasser's] dramatic reaction had therefore been to show that Egypt was not
going to be pushed around by the West," Cooper wrote.[92]

July 26, 1956 // Alexandria // London // Washington DC

Back in Mansheya Square on July 26, 1956, Nasser said "De
Lesseps" a final time. Only one person knew what the signal
meant: his trusted friend, Colonel Mahmoud Younis. When
Nasser mentioned the name of the man who had designed
the Canal, Younis mobilized his men. They stormed into the
headquarters of the Suez Canal Company, guns drawn. In Alexandria, Nasser paused for a moment—then announced to
his audience: "Today, in the name of the people, I am taking
over the company. Tonight our Egyptian canal will be run by
Egyptians. *Egyptians*!"[93]

The crowd erupted with joy: embracing each other, shouting *"Mabrouk!"* ("Congratulations!"), letting off fireworks,
and firing guns into the air. Revelers celebrated around a float
depicting the Egyptian Sphinx devouring a British soldier, the
Union flag sewn on his backside.[94]

In 10 Downing Street, London, the news came through at around ten forty-five in the evening. Anthony Eden was hosting a dinner party. The guest of honor was the twenty-one-year-old King Feisal II of Iraq, along with his uncle Crown Prince Abdulillah and Nuri es-Said, Iraq's prime minister. Iraq was a solid British ally: Nuri detested Nasser. The Iraqis were easy company for Eden, who had read Oriental languages at Oxford and had taken first class honors in Persian and Arabic.[95] Nuri had been a friend of his almost since that time. His Anglophilia earned him the scorn of some: Nikita Khrushchev, the leader of the Soviet Union, dismissed him as "a puppet of British imperialism and a faithful dog of the colonialists."[96] Also present were Hugh Gaitskell, leader of the opposition; the French ambassador; and the American chargé d'affaires. Striking a classically imperial note, everyone was clad in full evening dress and decorations, with Eden and the Marquess of Salisbury in Order of the Garter sashes and knee-breeches.[97]

Nasser's nationalization of the Canal Company was not illegal, as Eden's own advisers would point out. Eden argued that it was "an international asset,"[98] but it was a privately owned and run company. Other countries, including Britain, had nationalized those. Egypt offered financial compensation to the shareholders. Eden based his objection on two elderly treaties, the Constantinople Convention of 1888 and the Concession to the Canal Company of 1856. The former guaranteed "at all times and for all powers the free use of the Suez Maritime Canal," yet Nasser was not planning to limit the operation or use of the canal—merely to change the ownership of its operating company. His government had prevented Israeli ships from using the canal since 1949. Eden tried to argue that Britain would be acting in defense of Israel's rights, though the obvious question was why the British government was only now impassioned by the abrogation of those rights after an interlude of seven years. (In practice, between 1951 and 1954, Egypt had allowed canal passage to more than sixty ships carrying Israeli cargo, as long as they were not under the Israeli flag. Nasser relaxed the rules similarly during 1956.)[99] Anthony Nutting found this argument spurious in any case, remembering that only a couple of years before Eden had admitted that Egypt had a right under the Constantinople Convention to deny passage to the ships of a nation with which it was at war.[100] Yet to those in 10 Downing Street that night, Nasser's nationalization appeared a hostile act. Eden titled the chapter dealing with it in his memoirs "Theft."[101]

"Hit him hard," Nuri advised Eden. "Hit him soon, and hit him by yourself."[102] According to Anthony Nutting, Nuri claimed specifically that he had warned Eden against any alliance with France or Israel against Nasser. The indignant response of the Iraqis to Nasser's Suez decision cemented the hope in Eden's mind that the British had solid support in the Arab world.[103] He was conscious, though, of the difficulty of moving immediately against Egypt. British troops were already engaged, fighting colonial rebels: EOKA in Cyprus, the Communist Malayan National Liberation Army in Malaya, and the Mau Mau revolt in Kenya. A substantial part of the armed forces was assigned to the North Atlantic Treaty Organization (NATO), based in Germany, and could not be pulled out.[104] There was nonetheless a lust for war in London and Paris that night.

On the other side of the Atlantic, Britain and France's most important ally felt differently. The European leaders had a tendency to underrate the president of the United States. "Despite his military prestige, Eisenhower is a weak man," sneered Christian Pineau, the French minister for external affairs; "Dulles is his backbone."[105] Eden and many in his cabinet—along with some American officials—also believed

Eisenhower had little interest in foreign policy and left it to his secretary of state, the calculating Foster Dulles. In this presumption they were mistaken. Though Eisenhower took Dulles's counsel on foreign affairs, he would drive Suez policy personally.

When the news of Nasser's nationalization reached Washington, Dulles was away on a visit to Lima. Eisenhower met with the acting secretary, Herbert Hoover Jr., and with Allen Dulles. The notes of the meeting reveal Eisenhower's response as measured and cautious, correctly predicting that "the British would want action in this matter" but reserving further judgment until more could be ascertained about Nasser's legal position and whether any Americans would be caught up in it.[106] Within forty-eight hours, with Foster Dulles still absent, the opinions of Eisenhower and Hoover crystallized into strong opposition to any military action against Nasser. According to Hoover, Eisenhower agreed that he "must adopt a firm policy but at [the] same time not jeopardize our long-term position by precipitate action."[107]

"Neither the sure prevention of war, nor the continuous rise of world organisation will be gained without what I have called the fraternal association of the English-speaking peoples," Winston Churchill had told an audience in Fulton, Missouri, on March 5, 1946. "This means a special relationship between the British Commonwealth and Empire and the United States."[108] The "special relationship" was easy to believe in when it was presided over by Eisenhower and Churchill, two old war heroes and friends. It had withstood American intervention in Korea, which Britain reluctantly but loyally joined. It had faltered slightly when Britain had refused to go into Indochina. Now, with a British government under Anthony Eden preparing for what looked like a colonialist initiative in the Middle East, that relationship would be tested to its limit.

The crisis that spiraled from Suez would drag in much of Europe, Asia, North America, and the Commonwealth as well as the whole of the Middle East and North Africa. Furthermore, the high point of the Suez crisis—from October 22 to November 6, 1956—would coincide precisely with the biggest rebellion yet against Soviet power, which took place in Hungary from October 23 to November 4. The fact that the Suez War and the Hungarian uprising happened simultaneously would ratchet up tension between the major Cold War players to its highest level since the end of World War II. With the United States, the Soviet Union, and Britain all then holding nuclear weapons, this was a moment of unprecedented danger. It would test the limits and the mettle of the United Nations as never before.

Though many in Eden's generation blamed him personally for Suez, later historians have instead set the British and French government's actions in the context of the complicated, oil-fueled politics of the Middle Eastern region. This context is vital. Some of the triggers for action in the Canal Zone were related to oil or to the military and political demands of treaties. Moreover, the Hungarian rebellion and the Soviet response to it would affect the progress of events in Egypt; events in Egypt would likewise rebound on Hungary. Yet it would be a mistake to assume that everything that happened over the sixteen acute days of crisis in October and November 1956 had a sensible or rational basis. The crisis would be intensely emotional for the nations involved. For Hungary and Egypt, it would be about freedom. For Israel, it would be about survival. For France, it would be about saving territory it considered integral to the republic. For the Soviet Union, it would be about resistance to Western colonialism as well as reasserting and extending its own influence. For the United States, it would be about decency and the trustworthiness of its allies. And for Britain, as the then leader of the House of Commons Rab Butler admitted in his memoirs, it would be about the "illiberal resentment at the loss of Empire, the rise of coloured nationalism, the transfer of world leadership to the United States."[109]

For each of the state and individual actors in this drama, the 1956 crisis felt fundamental—even existential. This was the reason they were prepared to take it to the brink of what many at the time would call World War III.

I

"WE *MUST* KEEP THE AMERICANS REALLY FRIGHTENED"

0300 Washington DC // 0800 Rabat; London // 0900 Paris // 1000 Cairo

Wearing neat blue lounge suits, five Algerian rebels gathered at the airfield in Rabat, Morocco, to await the arrival of the sultan. Their leader was Ahmed Ben Bella: a farmer's son, a former football star, and a war hero. He had won the Croix de Guerre for his bravery during the German bombing of Marseilles and later the Médaille Militaire, the highest honor in the Free French forces. A grateful General Charles de Gaulle had presented him with his medal.

VE Day, May 8, 1945, was a turning point. A victory parade in the northeastern Algerian town of Sétif turned into a protest against French rule. There were rapes, mutilations, and murderous attacks on Europeans, leaving over 100 dead and a similar number injured. It was five days before the authorities could restore order. When they did, it was with unprecedented brutality. Muslim villages were bombed from the air and sea by French forces; 5,000 peasants from the Sétif region were forced to grovel on their knees in front of a French flag and plead for forgiveness.[1] Summary executions were carried out by the military, and many Algerians were lynched by European vigilantes. An official French report suggested that 1,020 Algerian Muslims were killed. Far greater figures were quoted throughout the Arab world, up to 45,000.

Many politicians in Paris, much of the population in France, and much of the European population living in Algeria (known as *pieds-noirs*, literally "black feet"), argued that Algeria was an integral part of France: an equal, not a colony. Much of the political elite in Algeria—some Muslims as well as Europeans—believed strongly that Algerian nationhood was an artificial construct. Before French unification, they argued, the territory had been culturally, linguistically, and politically disparate. Their pride expressed itself not in advocating for independence but in achieving their full potential as free citizens of democratic France. Yet many indigenous Algerians outside the political elite did not feel free or equal, observing the generally greater wealth of Europeans, the disproportionate political representation of Europeans, and the fact that European farmers had settled in the most cultivatable parts of the land. Increasing numbers began to consider themselves under French occupation.

Ben Bella left the French army and joined the Algerian political opposition. The French tried to have him assassinated, so he went into hiding. He was found and imprisoned in 1950 but escaped two years later in a plot that seemed to have fallen out of a cartoon. A loaf of bread was delivered to him in prison with a metal file hidden inside. He used it to saw through the bars on his window, then fled to Cairo and to Gamal Abdel Nasser.

Nasser welcomed Ben Bella and other members of the nascent Algerian National Liberation Front (FLN) to Egypt. In 1954, the FLN began an armed uprising against French colonialism in Algeria. Ben Bella remained in exile, coordinating international relations from Egypt and Tunisia and attempting to involve the United Nations on the FLN's side.[2]

In February 1956, Guy Mollet—the new socialist prime minister of France, who had been in office for only a week—visited Algeria. He was ambushed by a mob who pelted him with rotten fruit and vegetables. This incident was described by the French and Algerian press as *la journée des tomates*, the Day of the Tomatoes. In the aftermath of the tomatoes, Mollet assumed a firm position. Describing the rebels as "a handful of maniacs and criminals who take their orders from outside Algeria," he stated, "The Government will fight, France will fight to remain in Algeria, and she will remain there. There is no future for Algeria without France."[3]

Mollet and his government had no doubt who they thought was giving the rebels orders from outside Algeria. An internal French government report on June 13, 1956—six weeks before the nationalization of the Suez Canal—accused Nasser of "a resumption of Egyptian interferences in the affairs of North Africa; outrageous propaganda on 'Voice of the Arabs'; training commandos under the aegis of Egyptian officers . . . according hospitality to Algerian rebel military staff."[4]

Anthony Eden was not the only man in Europe who had decided Nasser was his personal nemesis. According to C. Douglas Dillon, the American ambassador to Paris, Mollet "had almost a fixation about President Nasser." The French prime minister believed that Nasser "was going to control oil and, therefore, control the world. . . . He was violently concerned about this."[5]

Senior figures in the French government were open about their discomfort with Arab and African self-rule. "According to the most reliable intelligence sources we have only a few weeks in which to save North Africa," Christian Pineau told Foster Dulles on August 1. "Of course, the loss of North Africa would then be followed by that of Black Africa, and the entire territory would rapidly escape European control and influence."[6] The director-general of the French Defense Ministry told the prime minister of Israel, "Black children in Equatorial Africa already bear flags with Nasser's picture."[7] Canal nationalization affected the situation between France and the Algerian rebels, according to a CIA report: "Suez has hardened attitudes on both sides and dispelled the more favorable atmosphere for negotiations that had been developing."[8]

The Algerian rebels had been staying in Morocco as guests of the sultan. The sultan, along with the Tunisian prime minister, Habib Bourguiba, was encouraging them to continue peace talks with the French. These had been going on in secret for a year. Mollet's government had been pursuing a tough policy of "pacification"—heavy policing—alongside limited social and economic reforms. It was unpopular with the French public, for the cost of keeping the Algerian population subdued was steep. By the autumn of 1956, a blunt CIA memorandum determined that French policy in Algeria "had failed."[9] The talks with the FLN appeared to represent a different approach. The French government promised Ben Bella and his delegation safe conduct by air to meet Bourguiba in Tunis.

As they waited, word came from the palace that owing to a lack of space the Algerians could not share the sultan's plane and would have to fly in a separate Air Atlas DC-3. "I was very upset by this news," said Ben Bella afterward. But there was no time to reschedule. As the DC-3 took off from the airfield, Ben Bella carefully stashed his revolver in his seat pocket.

The plane's route had been planned to avoid flying directly over French-controlled Algerian territory. It made a scheduled stop in Palma de Mallorca in the Mediterranean. Soon after it took off again, Ben Bella began to fear that they were flying too far south. He asked the stewardess what was going on.

"Maybe we're taking a more direct route," she replied.

Ben Bella started with alarm. "What do you mean, more direct?" he said. "We're still not flying over Algerian territory, are we?"

"No, no," she said hastily.

The plane entered Algerian airspace. As soon as it did, French fighter jets scrambled to meet it. They were not there as an escort. Instead, they forced the plane down.

Ben Bella went for his revolver. "Leave your weapon where it is," said one of his comrades. "You're not going to give them this wonderful pretext . . ."

The plane touched down in Algiers. "Then the interior lights went out and we could see armoured cars with spotlights and truckloads of gendarmes with submachine guns following us as we taxied to a halt," wrote Thomas F. Brady of the *New York Times*, who was traveling with the rebels.

"All right," said Ben Bella, as a gendarme with a tommy gun burst into the cabin. "We will come out." Ben Bella and his companions were taken off the plane, arrested, and hand-cuffed. "This is how you can trust the French!" Ben Bella exclaimed.[10]

Two journalists, Brady and a colleague from *France-Observateur*, were also arrested and questioned—though Brady would soon be released.[11] They were packed in a secure van with policemen and escorted away by motorcycles and tanks.[12]

News of this kidnapping began to spread throughout the Arab world that day, provoking outrage and an immediate demonstration in Tunis against the French. Habib Bourguiba "said that the arrest of the Algerian leaders risked hurling all North Africa into a trial of strength with France," noted the *Times* of London.[13]

On an airfield outside Paris that same damp and misty morning, almost no one's attention was on another plane: a

French DC-4. The scene, Christian Pineau later wrote, "was worthy of a James Bond sequence."[14] The plane touched down on the wet asphalt, and a huddle of men disembarked. Among them was a distinctive figure, his cloud of white hair squashed under a broad-brimmed hat. One of the airfield workers did notice: he thought the figure looked like David Ben-Gurion, prime minister of Israel, and dashed off to tell a journalist friend. The journalist replied that he must have been mistaken. Such a visit was wholly implausible.[15]

Their cover unblown, Ben-Gurion and his Israeli delegation—Shimon Peres, Moshe Dayan (wearing large glasses instead of his trademark eyepatch), and Lieutenant Colonel Nehemia Argov—got into unmarked black cars and drove to Sèvres. Under Ben-Gurion's arm was a copy of the *History of the Wars of Justinian* by the sixth-century Byzantine historian Procopius. It was a hint as to why he was there. The history mentions an island at the southern end of the Gulf of Aqaba, where the tip of what is now Saudi Arabia stretches toward the Sinai peninsula. This island was, according to Procopius, the site of an ancient Jewish community.

Ben-Gurion settled pragmatically on the island of Tiran as the site of the ancient community. His reasons were not entirely drawn from Procopius. Tiran was a strategic point on the sea approach to Eilat, Israel's only southern seaport, linking it to the Red Sea and opening up potentially valuable trade routes to the Arabian Sea, the Persian Gulf, and beyond. The importance of the Straits of Tiran and the port of Eilat would become plain in 1957, when the Israelis would broker a secret deal with the National Iranian Oil Company to build an oil pipeline known as the Trans-Israel Pipeline, or Tipline, from Eilat to Ashkelon. This could bring Iranian oil through Israel to the Mediterranean and thus to the European market without using the Suez Canal, avoiding potentially hostile Arab territory. It had the potential to make Israel's security vital to European interests.[16] The possibility of this pipeline was discussed by the Israeli ambassador with British politicians as early as July 1956.[17] Egypt, which controlled the Straits, had closed them to Israeli shipping in October 1955.[18] Since then, Ben-Gurion had been putting together a plan to take Tiran by force.[19]

At Sèvres, a summit convened in a private villa belonging to a friend of the French minister of defense, Maurice Bourgès-Maunoury. Representing France were Bourgès-Maunoury; Christian Pineau, the minister of foreign affairs; General Maurice Challe; and other senior French military officers. A British representative was to arrive later. The objective was to plan a secret war.

This was a huge moment for Israel: a possible alliance, even in secret, with two major world powers. The Israel of 1956 was a very different state than it is today: physically smaller and militarily far weaker. For its Jewish inhabitants, the Nazi Holocaust was a sharply recent trauma.

The history of Israel and its future hinged at this point on the political maneuverings of David Ben-Gurion. He had been born David Grin (sometimes spelled Grün) in Poland in 1886, at a time when antisemitism was on the rise throughout Europe. He was nine years old at the beginning of 1896, when the Hungarian Jewish writer Theodor Herzl published *The Jewish State*—suggesting that Jews leave Europe and set up their own country, perhaps in Palestine or Argentina (Uganda later came up as an alternative, but was quickly dropped). "The real, the only, Zionism is a colonization of Palestine," David wrote to his father; "everything else is just eyewash, blah and a waste of time."[20] Some Zionists did not see the colonization of Palestine as essential to the project of creating a Jewish state. Some Jews continued to reject Zionism altogether, as they had for many years before Herzl revived the idea. As for Palestine itself, it had a population of around half a million people at the time, the great majority of whom were Arabs and Muslims. There was a small minority of Christians and an even smaller minority of Jews, though this soon began to grow as a result of Zionist immigration.

At twenty, David left Poland on a fake passport and made his way to Odessa. From there he took a Russian cargo ship to Jaffa, arriving on September 9, 1906. Palestine was then under the rule of the Ottoman Empire. Life was hard for the European Zionists who turned up. Few could cope with the climate, the unsanitary conditions, the hard labor, or the cool welcome they received from indigenous Palestinian Jews. David became a jobbing farmhand and contracted malaria. In 1912, he went to study law at Istanbul University. Around this time, he chose a Hebrew name: David Ben-Gurion. He returned to Jerusalem but, when World War I broke out, the Ottoman Empire decided that foreign national Jews in Palestine might constitute a fifth column. He and many others were expelled.

Ben-Gurion went to New York City. His prospects and those of Israel changed dramatically in November 1917, when the British foreign secretary, Arthur Balfour, wrote a letter to Lord Rothschild of the Zionist Federation of Great Britain and Ireland (the son of the Lord Rothschild who had lent Benjamin Disraeli the money to buy a stake in the Suez Canal Company). The full Balfour declaration read:

"His Majesty's Government view with favour the establishment in Palestine of a national home for the Jewish people, and will use their best endeavours to facilitate the achievement of this object, it being clearly understood that nothing shall be done which may prejudice the civil and religious rights of existing non-Jewish communities in Palestine, or the rights and political status enjoyed by Jews in any other country."

The British government had no authority over the land or people of Palestine at this point. Its conversion to Zionism was opportunistic. The prime minister, David Lloyd George, "does not care a damn for the Jews or their past or their future," remarked his predecessor as prime minister, H. H. Asquith, "but thinks it would be an outrage to let the Christian Holy Places—Bethlehem, Mount of Olives, Jerusalem &c—pass into the possession of 'Agnostic Atheistic France!'"[21]

Official British Zionism was a response to the top-secret Sykes-Picot agreement of 1916. When the British diplomatic adviser Mark Sykes and the French diplomat François Georges-Picot planned to carve up the Middle East between areas of British and French control, they could not agree who should get Palestine. Eventually, both reluctantly accepted that if the Ottomans were pushed out in the course of World War I, it would be placed under international control.

Without Palestine, though, Sykes felt there would be a hole in British defenses. Herbert Samuel, the British home secretary (who was both Jewish and a Zionist), argued that a Jewish colony east of Suez would be loyal to Britain—plugging that hole. He also argued that the small Jewish population in the United States—then around two million—might prove powerful advocates for British interests if Britain were seen to favor a Jewish state.

When the United States entered the war in April 1917, President Woodrow Wilson specifically warned against further imperialism by any European powers. Six months later, British troops under General Edmund Allenby were on the verge of conquering Palestine. This put the British government in a quandary. The terms of the Sykes-Picot agreement meant Britain would have to hand Palestine over to international control—which it did not want to do. If the British took it for themselves, though, the Americans would see that as imperialism. The cabinet therefore chose this precise moment to declare in favor of Zionism. If Palestine were ostensibly ruled by Jews, they might be able to persuade the Americans it was not a colony.

Allenby launched the third British attack on Gaza in Palestine on October 31, 1917. By the morning of November 2, he was heading for victory. Balfour wrote his declaration that same day. It was published in the *Times* of London on November 7, just as Allenby's troops marched into Gaza and found that the Ottomans had fled.[22]

The British cabinet had embraced Zionism because it presented an opportunity to stitch up the French and shut up the Americans. The fallout from this decision was disastrous. Britain had vital Arab allies. It would come to depend on the oil they supplied more and more as the century wore on. The diplomat Evelyn Shuckburgh thought, from the moment Balfour made his declaration, it was inevitable that British power would decline. "Palestine was the burial ground of our hopes for maintaining the British position in the Middle East," he wrote some years later.[23] For Zionists, though, it was a signal moment: a leap in the international legitimacy of Jewish claims for statehood. In the wake of the declaration, Ben-Gurion signed up for the Jewish Legion of the British army, which fought to liberate Palestine from the Ottoman Empire. By the time he got there, that liberation had already happened.

From 1920, Palestine was administered by the British, legitimized by a mandate from the League of Nations after 1922. The mandate was intended to be a temporary arrangement. During the 1920s and 1930s, enthusiasm for the Zionist cause began to falter within the British government, as the difficulty of balancing its Arab and Jewish interests became apparent. Jews in Palestine realized they were going to have to fight their own battles. The Haganah, a paramilitary organization, was set up to defend Jewish communities against Arabs. In 1931, a Haganah splinter group, the Irgun, formed to move from defense to attack. During that decade, Ben-Gurion vied with Ze'ev Jabotinsky for leadership of the Zionist movement and won.

In 1939, a White Paper from the British government backed off the idea of creating a Jewish state in Palestine or partitioning the territory between Arabs and Jews. With oil now indispensable to the British economy and armed forces, and the threat of another war looming, any sentimental attachment to the Balfour Declaration vanished. The prime minister, Neville Chamberlain, explained to his cabinet the "immense importance" of its alliances in the Muslim world. "If we must offend one side," he said, "let us offend the Jews rather than the Arabs."[24] The White Paper placed strict limits on the immigration of Jews into Palestine at the point when they were facing a meticulously planned genocide at the hands of the Nazis in Europe. It also placed limits on Jewish acquisitions of land from Arabs. It proposed a jointly ruled successor state to be governed by Arabs and Jews in proportion to their populations. Zionist Jews generally saw the White Paper as an abject betrayal. An armed terrorist insurrection began against the British.

The full horror of the Holocaust began to be uncovered in the last stage of World War II. When the United Nations Special Committee on Palestine (UNSCOP) arrived in the Middle East in 1947, it was clear from the testimony of the Zionist leaders that the appalling revelations had made their demands urgent. "Not a few thousands, not tens of thousands, but millions, six millions were put to death. Can anybody realise what that means?" Ben-Gurion asked in his statement to the Special Committee. "Can anybody realise—a million Jewish babies burned in gas-chambers? A third of our people, almost as

many as the whole population of Sweden, murdered?"[25] UN-
SCOP recommended partition. The United Nations drew up a
map dividing the territory into three tracts of Arab state and
three tracts of Jewish state, intersecting at crossing points, with
Jerusalem preserved separately under a Special International
Regime. On November 29, 1947, the United Nations General
Assembly passed a resolution in favor of partition of the ter-
ritory. A Jewish state was given international legitimacy by
this United Nations resolution, as was an independent state for
Palestinian Arabs.[26]

At one minute past midnight on May 14, 1948, the British
Mandate ended. The following day, the brand-new state of
Israel was invaded by expeditionary forces of Egypt, Jordan,
Syria, and Iraq. Lebanon joined later. Saudi Arabia and Yemen both sent troops. The fighting continued for almost ten
months. At the end, Israel retained all the territory it had
been allocated under the United Nations partition plan, and
took more than half of what was to have been the Palestinian
Arab state. Jordan occupied the West Bank; Egypt occupied
the Gaza Strip. These two tiny and compromised parcels of
land were all that remained of any kind of Palestinian territory.

For the Palestinian people, this was the climax of al-Nakba,
the Catastrophe. Seven hundred thousand people were displaced, many crammed into refugee camps in the West Bank
and Gaza. Devastated, occupied, overcrowded with traumatized people, and divided physically from each other by hostile
Israeli territory, the West Bank and Gaza had little prospect of
forming a coherent or stable state.

Israel may have won its first war, but the fighting left many
Jewish Israelis—and Ben-Gurion particularly—feeling that
their struggle for survival was far from over. "We have beaten
the Arabs, but are they likely to forget it?" asked Ben-Gurion.

"Are they going to take that insult? They must certainly have some self-esteem. We shall try to bring peace, but two are needed to make peace. Let's be frank—it wasn't because we were able to perform miracles that we won, but because Arab armies are rotten. What will happen to us if an Arab Mustapha Kemal [Atatürk] makes an appearance one of these days?"[27]

The years 1950–55 saw militarization in the supposedly demilitarized zones along the borders with Syria and Egypt, and infiltration raids into Israel by small bands of fighters and civilians. But these skirmishes did not appear to be building toward full-scale war. In Egypt, according to one of Nasser's senior associates, there was no plan to attack Israel: "We did not even mention Israel," he remembered. "We didn't even realise that we didn't mention it. . . . It wasn't even in our agenda. . . . We did not ever think to attack Israel because we know that if we attack Israel we are attacking the whole world."[28] Indeed, so peaceable were the early 1950s that the Israeli chief of the general staff disbanded the Israeli Defense Force (IDF)'s Southern Command on its borderlands with Egypt.[29]

But an Arab Mustapha Kemal Atatürk did emerge: a charismatic visionary from a middle-class family with a strong military background, who had an ambition to create a modern, industrialized, secular state.[30] That man was Gamal Abdel Nasser.

Uri Avnery was perhaps Israel's most prominent critical journalist, editor of the magazine *HaOlem HaZeh* (*This World*). His family immigrated from Nazi Germany in 1933, when he was ten years old. He joined the Irgun when he was fifteen; he fought as a commando in the 1948 war. He became interested in ideas of Semitic unity: a joint initiative between Jews and Arabs to resist colonialism in the Middle East. In the 1950s he became a strong voice for peace with the Arabs—and an outspoken critic of Ben-Gurion.

"Ben-Gurion could not stand Abdel Nasser from the beginning," Avnery said. "When Abdel Nasser came to power,
Ben-Gurion developed a complex. He was by then an old
man." Ben-Gurion was sixty-seven when Nasser became prime
minister in 1954. "And there was for the first time a young
Arab leader, progressive, tall, good-looking—everything Ben-
Gurion was not! He was not a good speaker, he was short, he
was old—he was afraid. Abdel Nasser was inspiring a new generation of Arabs. . . . This was one of the real hidden motives of
the [Suez] war—there was a new style of pan-Arab nationalism
and Ben-Gurion wanted to destroy it." Avnery compared the
Egyptian leader not to Atatürk, but to a historical figure perhaps even more powerful: "Nasser looked like a new Saladin."[31]

Since the end of 1955, Israeli intelligence services and the
IDF had been predicting that Egypt might attack Israel.
Moshe Dayan, a charismatic ladies' man who had worn a black
eyepatch since World War II, was chief of the general staff.
He noted in February 1956 that nine of Egypt's sixteen bri-
gades were in Sinai, compared to just one a few months before.
Dayan encouraged Ben-Gurion to consider a preemptive war
against Egypt, with the aim of seizing the Gaza Strip and the
Straits of Tiran. The more moderate foreign secretary Moshe
Sharett wrote in his diary, "The press is covered with screaming headlines about Egyptian troop concentrations 'on the border.' . . . The impression left is that we are actually on the brink
of war, but the sceptical reader can understand that we have
artificially exaggerated [this impression in order to] buttress
our demand for arms."[32] But Dayan's enthusiasm for such a
war was genuine, and he had Ben-Gurion's attention. Mindful of the potential reaction of the international community,
the prime minister had so far held back. Yet in October 1956
everything changed, for the Israelis found themselves at a negotiating table with Britain and France.

The plan discussed at the secret Sèvres meeting was so fool-hardy that many in the British and French establishments would subsequently find it impossible to believe. Israel would invade Egypt. Britain and France would publicly condemn this action—though covertly they would support it. The two imperial nations would intervene under the guise of peacekeepers, interposing themselves between the Israeli and Egyptian forces for the "protection" of the canal. The canal would be given over to "international" control, and Israel would be confirmed in much of its territorial gain. Following a psychological warfare campaign, Nasser would be removed and Egypt handed over to a more obedient viceroy. The identity of the viceroy was undetermined, but the British had drawn up a list of candidates—including the former president Mohamed Neguib, former foreign minister Muhammad Salah al-Din, former prime minister and Axis sympathizer Ali Maher, and former interior minister Ahmed Mortada al-Maraghi. "Everything our colleagues in SIS [MI6] and the Foreign Office said to us showed that they had no information that made any sense at all on which Egyptian officers or civilians might constitute a new government if Nasser were to be eliminated," remembered CIA agent Miles Copeland. "And they didn't seem to care. They thought they should get rid of Nasser, hang the practical consequences, just to show the world that an upstart like him couldn't get away with so ostentatiously twisting the lion's tail."[33]

"The British were still under the illusion that, even after the withdrawal from Egypt, they could organise the Arab world in their interests against Egyptian opposition," wrote the British ambassador in Cairo, Humphrey Trevelyan, who repeatedly warned his own government against interfering in Egypt's internal affairs. "Our actions were designed for a situation which no longer existed."[34]

1500 London // 1600 Paris

Monday, October 22, 1956, was a day of bad news in London. Results from a general election in Jordan indicated that candidates who opposed the defense treaty Jordan maintained with Britain had done well. Many new representatives favored closer links with Gamal Abdel Nasser. "The trend against the West was clearest on the west bank of the Jordan River, in territory formerly part of Palestine," reported the *New York Times.* "All three candidates elected from Jerusalem are considered strongly anti-Western." One of them "generally is called a Communist."[35]

Anthony Nutting requested a meeting with his superior, the British foreign secretary, Selwyn Lloyd. He was told Lloyd had a bad cold. He offered to telephone instead. Lloyd's office replied that he was not taking calls, either.

Nutting thought this extremely strange.[36] But then Lloyd was a strange foreign secretary. He was not a dynamic man; neither his intelligence nor his imagination was rated highly by colleagues. He had risen through the ranks politically by being unthreatening, diligent, loyal, and ready to take on tasks no one else wanted.

In 1951, when the Conservative Party returned to government, Lloyd had been summoned to Winston Churchill's country house at Chartwell. He had assumed he might be made attorney general or solicitor general owing to his background as a lawyer. Instead, Churchill asked him to join the Foreign Office. "I was flabbergasted," Lloyd admitted in his memoirs. "I wondered whether it was a case of mistaken identity."

"But, Sir, I think there must be some mistake," he said. "I do not speak any foreign language. Except in war, I have never visited any foreign country. I do not like foreigners." (This, he added hastily in his book, was "a view which I very soon changed.") "I have never spoken in a Foreign Affairs debate in the House. I have never listened to one."

"Young man," said Churchill (Lloyd was forty-seven at the time), "these all seem to me to be positive advantages."[37]

With the ailing Churchill as prime minister and the ailing Eden as foreign secretary, both frequently absent from their desks, Lloyd was exposed to more than his expected share of responsibility. He was promoted to minister of defense in April 1955, when Eden became prime minister, and foreign secretary that December. He had by then visited some foreign countries and met some foreigners. He even liked a few of them, such as United Nations Secretary-General Dag Hammarskjöld. He had dutifully plodded his way through any number of briefings and meetings. But he still could not be said to have a natural feel for his subject. He was easily influenced by the opinions of others, principally Eden's. He referred almost every decision he was required to make back to the prime minister. "It becomes daily more apparent that we have no Secretary of State," his officials were heard to remark.[38]

At the moment Nutting asked for him, Selwyn Lloyd was not in bed with a cold. He was in an RAF plane landing near Paris. In Lloyd's official Foreign Office diary, everything on October 22 was crossed out. His assistant private secretary, Donald Logan, wrote on the page, "A day marked, among other things, by a nearly fatal car accident—for which my driving was not responsible!"[39] This was a private code. There had been no nearly fatal car accident, just a near miss on the drive from the airfield to Sèvres. Logan later admitted that he wrote the cryptic clue to remind himself "of our clandestine visit to Sèvres. I had no idea that this scrap of paper would get into the public archives. I ought not to have been so flippant."[40]

At Sèvres, the first session began at four p.m. with just the French and the Israelis. Ben-Gurion was on strong form, even though he was coming down with influenza. Israel, he said, faced a sea blockade to the south and terrorism from the Arab states, especially Egypt. He feared the Soviets were pouring armaments into Egypt. This was why his country wanted an offensive, which he described as: "More than a raid, less than a war." France agreed to Ben-Gurion's request for French air squadrons and warships to protect Israeli towns.

Then Selwyn Lloyd arrived. "His face gave the impression of something stinking hanging permanently below his nose," wrote Ben-Gurion's military assistant Mordechai Bar-On.[41] Ben-Gurion felt Lloyd talked down to him; Lloyd found Ben-Gurion arrogant. "He did his best to put the British case, but I agree with the Israeli accounts of the conversations that his heart wasn't in it," remembered Donald Logan.[42] "Moshe Dayan, with his black eye patch, gave the impression of a Caribbean pirate trying to board a vessel of Her Britannic Majesty," noted Christian Pineau.[43] It was perhaps not an auspicious image.

Though Eden was keen to work with the Israelis, Lloyd was not so sure. "Selwyn Lloyd was a modest man and was not very confident in his own judgement, I think," said a Foreign Office civil servant. "Eden, of course, had a great reputation as an expert in foreign policy and I think Selwyn felt that he ought not to challenge Eden's judgement."[44] There was a sticking point. Ben-Gurion wanted a simultaneous attack by Israel on Sinai, and by France and Britain on the canal. Eden wanted the British and French to attack two days after Israel, so that it looked as though the European powers had a pretext for intervention. But Ben-Gurion feared that plan would give the Egyptians two days in which to retaliate with their new Soviet arms, perhaps bombing Israeli cities.

In Washington, Dwight D. Eisenhower was nearing the climax of his campaign for a second term as president. While

Eisenhower shared the instinctive anticolonial sentiment of many of his countrymen, he had noted in his diary just before his inauguration as president in 1953 his concern that "immediate independence would result in suffering for people and even anarchy" if it were rolled out carelessly throughout the Third World. He understood that nationalism, anti-imperialism, and opposition to racial inequality ran high in colonized nations, and he was sympathetic. His fear was about how these sentiments might find expression if First World powers failed to listen: "Moscow leads many misguided people to believe that they can count on communist help to achieve and sustain nationalistic ambitions." To avoid losing Third World countries to the Soviet bloc, Eisenhower believed the old imperial powers must distance themselves from colonialist ways: "Western powers must not appear before the world as a combination of forces to compel adherence to the status quo."[45]

Despite his military background, and to a considerable extent because of it, Eisenhower based his reelection appeal on his ability to make peace—most recently demonstrated by bringing the Korean War to a close. His slogan was "Peace, Prosperity, and Progress." He told the nation: "The only way to end World War III is to prevent it." His television advertisements showed the same young men who had struggled and fought on Heartbreak Ridge in Korea now enjoying the relatively controlled violence of an American football game. Eisenhower's mother had been a strong pacifist on religious grounds. Having experienced so much war as a soldier and commander, her son's feelings against taking the United States into another armed conflict were just as passionately held. "The sum of our international effort should be this," he told the nation in his State of the Union address in January 1956: "the waging of peace, with as much resourcefulness, with as great a sense of dedication and urgency, as we have ever mustered in defense of our country in time of war. In this effort, our weapon is not force. Our weapons are the principles and ideas embodied in our historic traditions, applied with the same vigor that in the past made America a living promise of freedom for all mankind."[46]

Americans were due to go to the polls to give their verdict on this message in just two weeks. Never did Eisenhower imagine that his British and French allies were capable of launching a bellicose folly such as the Suez plot at this acutely sensitive moment. He was not expecting to have his credentials as a peacemaker tested before the votes were cast.

1200 Washington DC // 1700 London // 1800 Paris // 1900 Cairo

The American secretary of state, John Foster Dulles, was imposing, vain, clever, cool, and sometimes awkward of manner. Winston Churchill called him "Dull-duller-Dulles."[47] An American diplomat once described him with a phrase worthy of Raymond Chandler: "Foster looks as succulent as a hunk of Vermont marble."[48] He liked pragmatism and efficiency, defined on his own terms. "Handsome as a young man, Mr. Dulles in later years assumed the characteristics of a stern church elder," his *New York Times* obituary would one day read.[49] His father had been a stern church elder: a Presbyterian pastor who had instilled in his eldest son a powerful sense of right and wrong. His maternal grandfather, John W. Foster, and uncle, Robert Lansing, had both served as secretaries of state. His younger brother, Allen Welsh Dulles—a warmer personality, though ultimately an even more guarded man—was director of the CIA.

"Seven years younger than Foster, Allen Welch [*sic*] Dulles had little in common with him except the constant affliction of gout," wrote Allen's colleague, CIA agent Wilbur Eveland. "Fond of drink, rich food, and pretty women, Allen Dulles had in fact been the first to court Foster's faithful wife, Janet, but had rejected her as dowdy and unexciting."[50]

Foster Dulles's sense of right and wrong expressed itself most clearly in the struggle he perceived between America—freedom-loving, enterprising, God-fearing land of opportunity—and Communism, which he saw as antithetical to all those things. Senator Joseph McCarthy had lent his name to McCarthyism, the crusade against Communism in the domestic arena. Dulles advocated a similarly febrile anti-Communism in the international sphere. "I think that Mr. Dulles had a certain strong religious streak in him which he brought to bear on the Communist problem," said Charles Bohlen, the American ambassador to Moscow, "and he seemed to feel that it was black and white."[51]

The Dulles brothers did have a couple of things in common aside from their gout. Both believed that the United States had to root out Communism wherever it sprouted. Both believed in taking an active yet highly secretive role in this struggle. When Foster became secretary of state and Allen director of the CIA, there had been fears inside the Washington establishment—expressed, among others, by the heads of armed services intelligence and by the head of the FBI, J. Edgar Hoover—that the CIA's mission would creep from passive intelligence gathering to off-the-books political action.[52]

It did. In 1953, Allen Dulles's CIA engineered a change of government in Iran, ousting the democratically elected president and replacing him with a pro-Western absolute monarch. In 1954, it overthrew the democratically elected government of Guatemala and replaced it with a right-wing military dictatorship. These escapades were regarded within the CIA as successes.[53] For Foster Dulles even more than for his brother, the world lined up into "with us" or "against us." Those who refused to line up—notably the Non-Aligned Movement, which included Jawaharlal Nehru of India and Gamal Abdel Nasser of Egypt—could be tolerated and worked with but remained politically suspect. "He felt that neutrality was immoral," remarked Charles Bohlen, "and . . . there became a slight public difference with the President over that."[54] Foster also felt strongly against alternative power blocs, such as the old European empires. The Europhile Allen was more forgiving of them.

Foster Dulles faced the complicating factor that his principal allies in the struggle against Communism were Britain and France—old European empires. Britain and France were the United States' partners in the North Atlantic Treaty Organization (NATO), which had been carefully curated by the United States since 1949. The western European leaders, Dulles had told Eisenhower at the White House early in his administration, were "shattered 'old people'" who "want to spend their remaining days in peace and repose." They acted too casually, he thought, as if the "Soviets, like Ghenghes Khan, will get on their little Tartar ponies and ride back whence they came."[55]

Both Britain and France reassured the United States regularly that they were on its side in the Cold War against Communism. Yet in the Arab world—which to Dulles's mind was one of the most vulnerable fronts in that war—they seemed to be making strange decisions, and they did not seem to be telling him the whole truth.

When Nasser had nationalized the Suez Canal Company in July, the immediate reaction of the British and French prime ministers, Anthony Eden and Guy Mollet, had been to call for an invasion of Egypt. Eden assumed the Eisenhower administration would back him: ideally by sending troops, or at least by supporting Britain's case. He had no evidence for this assumption. On the afternoon of July 30, just after the nationalization, the British ambassador Sir Roger Makins met Foster Dulles in

Washington. Dulles was adamant that the United States government would have no sympathy for the use of force against Egypt. "While he agreed that our attitude should be a firm one," wrote Makins, "his view was that so long as there was no interference with the navigation of the canal, and no threats to foreign nationals in Egypt, there was no basis for military action." Dulles explicitly ruled out any possibility of American intervention.[56]

In Paris, though, according to the British ambassador, "the mood was one of extreme urgency, since it was thought that the effect of Nasser's action in Algeria would be so serious if counter-measures were not taken immediately that the whole position there might well collapse. The French were ready to go all the way with us. They would be prepared to put French forces under British command if this were necessary." The French were considering a land and air response, as well as naval operations, and even declared themselves ready to take troops from Algeria to use against Egypt.[57]

The following morning, July 31, Eisenhower heard that the British and French had decided to go in. He wrote a strong letter to Eden expressing his horror at the prospect "of your decision to employ force without delay or attempting any intermediate and less drastic steps." The letter left no room for doubt: "I have given you my own personal conviction, as well as that of my associates, as to the unwisdom even of contemplating the use of military force at this moment." He asked Eden to rethink his position and sent Dulles to London to put pressure on in person.[58] Yet Eden did not want to hear what Eisenhower was saying. His analysis of this letter, made some years later in his own memoir, was: "The President did not rule out the use of force."[59]

The French minister for external affairs, Christian Pineau, also went to London to meet Lloyd at the House of Commons.

He argued that they should "not allow themselves to be held up by United States waverings and reluctance." Extraordinarily, he also suggested that a widening of the issue into a global conflict might be a good thing: "In a way the U.S.S.R. might be a sort of guarantee of safety. If they came in the Americans could not stand aside." Lloyd recommended leaving the Soviet Union and the United States "on the side-lines," adding an observation that "The Americans often followed where others took action."[60]

When Dulles arrived in London, he found the British bristling for war. This was precisely the impression they had planned to give. "I think he [Dulles] was quite alarmed; for he had hoped to find me less extreme, I think," wrote Harold Macmillan in his diary. "We *must* keep the Americans really frightened. . . . Then they will help us to get what we want, without the necessity for force. But we must have a) international control of the Canal b) humiliation and collapse of Nasser."[61] This attitude could hardly have been calculated to annoy the Americans more. "Eden's arguments that Nasser had 'grasped at the throat' of the imperial lifeline, and that it was 'a matter of life and death' for the British Empire, explained so patronizingly to Americans as though we were a lot of backward children, cut no ice with us at all," wrote CIA agent Miles Copeland. "Rightly or wrongly, we just didn't take them seriously."[62]

Neither the British nor the French government liked Americans to express contrary opinions, but in Eden's case it was personal. Eden and Dulles had taken a dislike to each other when they first met in 1942. During the negotiations for the Japanese peace treaty of 1951, Eden felt Dulles behaved duplicitously. Dulles thought Eden went too soft on Communism; Eden thought Dulles was a manipulative hard-liner and anti-British. When Eisenhower became president, Eden had specifically asked him not to make Dulles his secretary of state on the grounds that he could not work with him.[63] Eisenhower had gone ahead anyway.

Then, in 1954, Eden and Dulles had been thrown together again at the Geneva Conference, attempting to end the war in Korea. According to Chester Cooper, "it was at Geneva that Dulles's disdain for Eden blossomed into loathing." Evelyn Shuckburgh, a Foreign Office civil servant, agreed: "There is no doubt that Dulles and A.E. have got thoroughly on each other's nerves, and are both behaving rather like prima donnas," he wrote in his diary. "Dulles is said to be irritated by the 'imprecision' of A.E.'s mind." Cooper added that Dulles was backed up by many in the State Department: "Under Secretary Herbert Hoover, Jr., could not abide the prime minister, and another senior official had said of Eden that he 'had never met a dumber man.'"[64]

This situation did not improve while Dulles was in London trying to talk Eden out of military action against Nasser. The American diplomat Robert Murphy, who was present, remembered that "there was an obvious lack of rapport between the two of them [Eden and Dulles], which didn't help matters at all."[65]

In London, Dulles did a considerable disservice to his own nation's position, which would haunt the rest of the crisis. At a meeting with the British and French foreign secretaries on August 1, he appeared to speak in favor of "international" control of the canal and seemed not to have closed his mind to a military option. "A way had to be found to make Nasser disgorge what he was attempting to swallow," he told them, and noted, "It should be possible to create a world opinion so adverse to Nasser that he would be isolated. Then if a military operation had to be undertaken it would be more apt to succeed and have less grave repercussions than if it had been undertaken precipitately."[66]

These words seemed to contradict Eisenhower's stated opposition to the use of force. "I should say that Mr. Dulles was a lawyer—this is very important to remember—and that everything was a brief to him," explained Charles Bohlen. "And he could be pleading a brief before one audience and forgetting the effect on the other."[67] Dulles often talked to allies as he had to clients: framing things in their own terms to make them feel he was on their side. His mind was flexible and unemotional; he did not realize the extent to which Eden and Mollet were dead set on one course and were profoundly emotional. The British and French premiers listened to him—and heard what they wanted to hear. "The judgment carried by Mr Dulles on Colonel Nasser's decision and on Colonel Nasser himself is very severe," noted a French diplomat.[68] "These were forthright words," wrote Eden. "They rang in my ears for months."[69] Following the meeting with Dulles, Eden formed the impression that it did not matter what Eisenhower said on the record: the United States was on his side and would support whatever he did.

Dulles persuaded Britain and France to agree to a conference of international powers, to be held in London from August 16 to 23. They consented—paying lip service to Dulles's argument that every diplomatic method had to be exhausted before force was used, while at the same time believing incontrovertibly that force would have to be used. They continued to plan a joint invasion of Egypt.[70]

Nasser was invited to the London conference but was unsure whether to accept. On his own initiative, Eisenhower at this point considered an extraordinary intervention. He floated the idea that he could go to Rome before the conference and meet Nasser there. Then the two of them would travel to London together. He hoped that he could work in tandem with Jawaharlal Nehru. For Nasser, appearing flanked by two of the world's great statesmen would allow him to attend the conference with his head held high. As leaders of postimperial nations themselves, Eisenhower and Nehru were in potentially ideal positions to mediate between the old guard of Europe and the nations emerging from colonial domination.

This was a thrilling and bold idea, reflecting Eisenhower's instinctive sympathy with the postcolonial predicament. In a meeting with both Dulles brothers, the joint chiefs of staff, and others on July 31, Eisenhower had strongly disagreed with the suggestion that the United States should support Britain if it tried to oust Nasser, arguing, "Nasser embodies the emotional demands of the people of the area for independence and for 'slapping the white Man down.'"[71] He seemed to understand this demand much more clearly than his colleagues and did not appear threatened by it, as some of them were. He also knew full well that appearing with Nasser would induce apoplexy among his fellow white men in London and Paris. Yet he was prepared to stand shoulder to shoulder with two of the world's most influential Asian and African men to achieve peace.

It might have been a signal moment in world history. But Foster Dulles talked Eisenhower out of it on August 8, telling him that Nehru would probably not go to the conference. Instead, India would be represented by his favored emissary, Krishna Menon. Menon was a clever man: founding editor of Pelican Books and a Labour Party councilor in London before Indian independence. He was rabidly disliked by almost every diplomat with whom he ever negotiated. One British diplomat described him as Nehru's evil genius; Eden called him the Hornet.[72] Eisenhower balked at the prospect of dealing with Menon. Dulles flattered the president that he "had greater prestige throughout the world than any single man had ever had before," not even pausing to exclude Jesus of Nazareth, before adding the kicker: "I recalled how [Woodrow] Wilson had dissipated his prestige at the [1919] Paris Peace Conference."[73] It was settled. Eisenhower would not go. Dulles would, and he would most certainly not be standing shoulder to shoulder with Nasser and Nehru.

At nearly the same moment this was happening, on the other side of the Atlantic, Eden made a public broadcast in which he called Nasser a "megalomaniacal dictator." "The pattern is familiar to many of us, my friends," he said. "We all know this is how fascist governments behave and we all remember, only too well, what the cost is in giving in to fascism."[74] Eden had been foreign secretary in 1936, when Nazi Germany remilitarized the Rhineland. He had participated in the British government's decision not to challenge Hitler's action at the time. Afterward, he deeply regretted his stand. This experience fueled his enthusiasm for an early strike against Nasser.

In 1951, the political philosopher Leo Strauss coined the term *reductio ad Hitlerum* to describe the often misleading comparison of an opponent's views or behavior to those of Adolf Hitler or the Nazi Party. The reductio ad Hitlerum, applied to Nasser, became a trope of British and French political language in the summer of 1956. Eden wrote to Nehru that Nasser's actions in nationalizing the canal were "dictator methods reminiscent of Hitler and Mussolini," but toned it down for Eisenhower, to whom he wrote, "I have never thought of Nasser as Hitler, he has no warlike people behind him. But the parallel with Mussolini is close."[75] In his memoirs, he would compare Nasser to Hitler, Mussolini, and Goebbels.[76] Harold Macmillan wrote in his diary that Nasser spoke like "an Asiatic Mussolini."[77] Guy Mollet told the American ambassador to Paris that "Nasser's deal with the Soviets for arms is the parallel to the Hitler Stalin pact of 1939," and claimed that his book *The Philosophy of the Revolution* was "a perfect parallel" to *Mein Kampf.*[78]

Christian Pineau and Selwyn Lloyd repeatedly told American diplomats that Nasser was a new Hitler: Pineau arguing that the nationalization of the Suez Canal Company was a direct parallel to the remilitarization of the Rhineland, Lloyd insisting to Foster Dulles that "Nasser was a paranoiac and had the same type of mind as Hitler."[79]

The problem with all this was that Nasser was not like Hitler. So irritated were the Americans by having this theme constantly blasted at them that the Bureau of Intelligence and Research draw up a three-page memorandum, systematically debunking it: "In manner, Hitler was noted for ranting and raging at visitors. Nasser tends to a relaxed and rational attitude. . . . Nazism was the extreme of reactionary totalitarianism in Germany. Nasser stands far from the conspicuous right-wing Moslem Brotherhood which indeed shows strong fascist elements. . . . Persecution of indigenous minorities, notably antisemitism, was the essence of Nazism. Nasser has not molested native Jews, despite the tension over Israel, and has even made addresses in synagogues, as well as in Coptic churches. . . . The master-race was proclaimed by Hitler as a justification for expansion. Nasser has produced no such concept."[80] And so it went on: there was no basis for any reasonable comparison in appearance, in personal life or habits, in the two men's self-appraisal, in philosophy, in their attitudes to allies or opponents, in their styles of leadership, in their political organizations, nor in their actions.

Eden's former chancellor of the exchequer, Rab Butler, was listening despairingly to the prime minister's broadcast on August 8 at his home in Stanstead. "Nasser was not in politics for the good of our health, but he was no Hitler, no incarnation of evil, no megalomaniac who had to be toppled before free men could rest easy in their beds," he wrote in his memoirs.[81] Eden's insult, he said, "virtually made it impossible for Nasser to attend" the London conference.

Accordingly, Nasser canceled his plans to come to London, sending an associate instead—not to attend formally on behalf of Egypt but to receive briefings from the Indian and Soviet delegations and report back to Cairo.[82] Following a week of negotiations, the conference agreed by a majority of eighteen out of twenty-two nations to set up an international association to run the canal, made up of interested countries, including Egypt.

Sir Robert Menzies, the prime minister of Australia, was sent to announce this decision to Nasser in Cairo. Nasser was not inclined to accept the pronouncements of the conference in any eventuality, for Menzies had not been sent to negotiate on any substantial points; accepting outside proposals in their entirety would mean, the British ambassador to Egypt admitted, "destroying his position in Egypt and the rest of the Arab world."[83] Menzies managed to appear insensitive to the Egyptians, conveying the impression that the entire rest of the world thought they were incompetent to run the canal and that Nasser himself was untrustworthy. Personally, Menzies considered Nasser "in some ways a likeable fellow" but "rather gauche. . . . I would say that he was a man of considerable but immature intelligence."[84]

The same day, Eisenhower answered a question at a press conference about Suez by saying that the United States was "determined to exhaust every possible, every feasible method of peaceful settlement." He implied that peaceful negotiations might continue if Nasser rejected the Menzies mission—removing the threat of military action. "How could the West deal with a man like Nasser," Menzies fumed, "if they throw their trump cards into the wastepaper basket?"[85] The mission loitered in Cairo until September 9 and achieved nothing.

Part of Eden's motivation at this point—and of his chancellor, Harold Macmillan's—was to save the pound. Eden's government had presided over a weakening economy. International confidence in sterling had fallen low by the middle of 1956. In 1955, the currency had effectively returned to convertibility—making it easy for investors to dump. British wages had been creeping up, which worried the markets. The nationalization of the Canal Company might, some feared, be the penultimate straw on the camel's back. Were Britain unable to trade freely, especially in oil, it might take only one more event to collapse sterling altogether. The sort of event they had in mind seemed all too feasible, if Nasser continued in power: for instance, he might unite the oil-producing states against Britain.

So serious was the pressure on sterling that Macmillan and officials at the Treasury and the Bank of England were concerned that the currency might have to be devalued again. The pound had already been devalued by 30 percent in September 1949, from $4.03 to $2.80. A second devaluation only seven years later might, it was feared, terminate the use of sterling as a reserve currency. The plight of sterling—and the possible mortal threat the currency faced from Nasser—was repeatedly used by Eden and Macmillan to justify their preference for military action.[86] "If Middle Eastern oil is denied to us for a year or two, our gold reserves will disappear," explained a Foreign Office civil servant just after the Menzies mission failed; "if our gold reserves disappear, the sterling area disintegrates."[87] Eden and Macmillan did not seem to anticipate that an attack on Nasser might itself unite the oil-producing states against Britain, thus bringing their worst fears to life, for they did not seem to imagine that a plan to topple him might fail.

"We are wasting our time talking to the Americans," Christian Pineau told the British ambassador. "Our two countries should now go firmly ahead on our chosen path."[88] Foster

Dulles realized that the British and French would take the failure of Menzies's mission as an opportunity to gear up for battle. He had to find another monkey wrench to throw into their works, and the one he came up with was an internationally governed Cooperative Association of Suez Canal Users (CASU). The Dutch foreign minister pointed out that this recalled the phrase *in casu belli*, "the cause of war," referring to an act intended to provoke war. His suggestion for an alternative acronym, CASCU, was rejected by the Portuguese, in whose language that sounded like "something which is really not mentioned"—a vulgar term for testicles—and by Pineau, who heard it with a French ear as *casse-cul*, or "assbreaker." Selwyn Lloyd suggested ASCU, but the Portuguese pointed out that this still sounded rude in Portuguese and in Spanish as well. All of the potential implications of these names were far too apt. The version finally settled upon was the Suez Canal Users' Association, or SCUA.[89]

Neither Britain nor France cared for SCUA. Pineau thought it was a ruse to delay military action until after the American election. Eden complained again to Eisenhower, explicitly now comparing Nasser to Hitler.[90] Eisenhower and Dulles stood firm and again refused to see the parallel. Eventually Mollet and Eden agreed, despite Pineau's and Lloyd's reservations, to give SCUA a whirl. Though they did not believe it would resolve anything, they were keen to keep the Americans on their side. "The more we can persuade them of our determination to risk everything in order to beat Nasser, the more help we shall get from them," wrote Harold Macmillan in his diary. "We shall be ruined either way; but we shall be more inevitably and finally ruined if we are humiliated. . . ."[91] To the CIA agents who knew Egypt, SCUA "seemed to be the nuttiest idea of all," remembered Miles Copeland: "A series of dignitaries were to fly to Cairo to explain to Nasser how his nationalization of the

Canal was unacceptable to the rest of the world and how, now that he'd had his fun, he should turn the whole thing over to adults who knew how to manage such things."[92]

On September 11, Eisenhower was again asked at a press conference whether he might back Britain and France if they used force in Egypt. "I don't know exactly what you mean by 'backing them,'" he replied. "As you know this country will not go to war ever while I am occupying my present post, unless the Congress is called into session and Congress declares such a war." Another journalist pressed him further. "I think this," Eisenhower said. "We established the UN to abolish aggression and I am not going to be a party to aggression if it is humanly possible."[93]

Eden declared himself shocked by what he considered to be a change in Eisenhower's opinion in early September. "Hitherto he and his officials had always given us to understand that the United States would not take exception to the use of force, if all peaceful means of settlement had been exhausted," he wrote.[94] There are sheaves of documents in the British and American archives that prove Eisenhower's position against force had been solid from the beginning. It seems almost impossible to credit how powerfully the British were able to deceive themselves about the potential for American support—but it was because they chose to listen to Dulles rather than Eisenhower. The British ambassador to Washington, Sir Roger Makins, later said that there was a feeling that Anglo-American friendship had been unbreakable since the Second World War and that, when it came to a crunch, Eisenhower would go along with whatever Dulles said, "and of course that was a fundamental misunderstanding because Eisenhower was a very much stronger and more dominant President than people have given him credit for. He was the man who ran American foreign policy, not Dulles."[95]

The American ambassador to Paris, C. Douglas Dillon, said the British had "read into what he [Dulles] had said . . . the sense that all right, let's make a real attempt here, and if Nasser won't behave, then, if you want to go clobber him, you're free." When Dulles kept trying to solve the problem with new diplomatic ideas, "they felt sort of double-crossed by Mr. Dulles."[96]

Eden went to the House of Commons the next day and announced SCUA, adding that the British government reserved its right, if Egypt failed to comply with this plan, to "take such further steps as seem to be required." He was booed and jeered by members of Parliament crying out "You are talking about war" and "Nonsense!"[97] The Egyptians responded that, as far as they were concerned, the imposition of a Users' Association would be an attack on their sovereignty. Nasser was thoroughly confused as to the messages coming from Washington. "I don't know what America's stand is," he said. "The American President speaks of peace. The American Secretary of State makes proposals which mean war."[98] Yet he made sure that the Americans knew that he was prepared to negotiate. So conciliatory was he that Dulles had to warn Eden to tone the aggression down: "Egypt is striking a note of sweet reasonableness," he pointed out.[99]

Most non-Egyptian pilots who had worked for the private Suez Canal Company, piloting ships through the canal, left by September 15. The newly nationalized operation replaced them with Egyptians and a handful of foreigners, including Russians and Yugoslavs. The British had arranged to back fifty ships up at both ends of the canal, deliberately causing chaos for the new pilots. This would, they hoped, demonstrate that Egypt was incompetent to run the canal and create a justification for intervention. In the event, the new pilots managed the excessive traffic without any problem. A jubilant Nasser bestowed the Order of Merit on each of them.[100] "This argument [about Egyptian incompetence] just faded away," remembered Eisenhower, "because the British faces were really quite red about the proof of the Egyptians' skill."[101]

From September 19 to 21, another London conference attempted to formalize SCUA. Dulles's emphasis on cooperation with the Egyptian government impressed several of the non-Western countries involved. By the same token, though, Britain and France lost what little enthusiasm they had had for the plan. Selwyn Lloyd waited until Dulles was on a flight back to Washington, then undercut all his efforts by referring the question of the Egyptian government's behavior to the United Nations Security Council.

At the United Nations, Britain and France were pressed into talks with the Egyptians by Dulles and the secretary-general, Dag Hammarskjöld. There was another upset at the beginning of the process when Dulles gave a press conference on SCUA. "There is talk about teeth being pulled out of the plan," he said, "but I know of no teeth: there were no teeth in it, so far as I am aware." This repeated disavowal of force, plus a couple of quite gentle references to "the problem of so-called colonialism" in Egypt, set Eden off again. "It was I who ended the 'so-called colonialism' in Egypt," he told a journalist, exaggerating his role considerably. "And look what Britain has done all over the world in giving the colonies independence." He went on: "We have leaned over backwards to go along with him. And now look. How on earth can you work with people like that? It leaves us in a quite impossible situation. We can't go on like this."[102]

In fact, Egypt showed itself ready to compromise at the United Nations. Talks began on October 9. Selwyn Lloyd laid down his Six Principles on October 13:

1. There should be free and open transit through the canal without discrimination, overt or covert.

2. The sovereignty of Egypt should be respected.

3. The operation of the canal should be insulated from the politics of any country.

4. The manner of fixing tolls and charges should be decided by agreement between Egypt and the users.

5. A fair proportion of the dues should be allotted to development.

6. In case of dispute, unresolved disagreements between the Suez Canal Company and the Egyptian government should be settled by arbitration.

Nasser's foreign minister, Mahmoud Fawzi, agreed to all of these, and was prepared to discuss the possibility of having the canal run jointly by a committee of Egypt and its users—which was, in effect, SCUA.

"I felt that there was now little chance that force would be used against Egypt," remembered the British ambassador to Egypt, Humphrey Trevelyan. "Nasser was giving no provocation and there was a clear division of opinion on the use of force in Britain."[103] The United Nations Security Council unanimously accepted Lloyd's Six Principles on the same day he proposed them.[104]

Dwight D. Eisenhower addressed his nation on television, telling Americans, "It looks like here is a very great crisis that is behind us."[105] The Suez Canal dispute could have been neatly resolved through diplomacy on October 13, 1956, saving everyone a lot of trouble.

It was not, and one reason it was not was that significant actors in the conspiring governments of Britain, France, and Israel did not want it to be. Back in March, months before the nationalization of the Canal Company, Eden had spoken privately of his wish to have Nasser murdered. The French government had decided at around the same time that Nasser was responsible for the trouble they were having in Algeria. As far as these two powers were concerned, nationalization was no more than a hook to hang their case on. Resolving that did not resolve their problem. They wanted Nasser gone. Both nations began to behave as obstructively as possible at the United Nations, insisting on more and more impossible concessions from Egypt. As they hoped, this stalled talks.

1644 Washington DC // 2144 London // 2244 Paris // 2344 Cairo

Even though Dulles had no idea that British, French, and Israeli representatives were meeting secretly at Sèvres that day, he knew the French wanted a war with Egypt. He did not expect them to move immediately, though. At 4:44 p.m., he took a telephone call from Henry Cabot Lodge Jr., the American ambassador to the United Nations, in New York. According to the minutes, Dulles told Lodge that he had "quite a bit of info from the Fre. [that] they are willing to stall until after [the American presidential] elections and then are not disposed to delay the use of force." He was unhappy about Britain and France slowing things down in the United Nations. The minutes concluded firmly: "The Sec[.] feels this delay is very bad."[106]

"I have the impression from your cables . . . that [the] French government feels that our opposition to the use of force in connection with Suez results from an election situation and that we might not be as strongly opposed after election," he wrote in a top-secret telegraph to the American embassy in Paris that day. "I can assure you the views of the President and myself on this point are basic and fundamental and I do not see any likelihood of their being changed after election."[107] In fact, according to David Ben-Gurion's diary, Christian Pineau's whole strategy had been to go ahead with an attack on

Egypt *before* the presidential election. "What position will the U.S. take? Pineau's opinion is that they will be angry, but if the operation takes place before November 6, no actions will follow," he wrote on October 18. "What about Russia? Pineau thinks they will not intervene."[108]

It was nearly midnight in Paris by the time Selwyn Lloyd left the villa at Sèvres, heading back to London. But the talks he had had with Ben-Gurion and Pineau had not gone well, and the mood among those he left behind was low. Pineau attempted to cheer the Israelis up by promising that he would fly to London himself the next day, to convince Anthony Eden to join the plan. Nobody trusted Lloyd to achieve this on his own.

"We'll see what will happen tomorrow," wrote Ben-Gurion. "I fear that Pineau's trip will be in vain."[109] In London, though, Sir Anthony Eden was keenly awaiting his chance to go to war against his nemesis: Gamal Abdel Nasser.

2

TUESDAY, OCTOBER 23, 1956
THE HAMMER AND SICKLE TORN OUT

0400 Washington DC // 0900 London // 1000 Paris; Budapest
During the Cold War, Europe was said to be divided by an
Iron Curtain: the border between Western-aligned and Soviet-
aligned nations. The Soviet Union had surrounded itself with
Communist countries—Albania, Bulgaria, Czechoslovakia,
East Germany, Hungary, Poland, and Romania (plus until
1948 Yugoslavia). These were collectively known as the Eastern Bloc, the Soviet bloc, or the Soviet satellites—or as the
"captive nations" by anti-Communists like John Foster Dulles.
In 1955, when NATO admitted West Germany and allowed it
to rearm itself, the Soviets reacted by formalizing the Soviet
bloc with the Warsaw Pact, their own treaty of mutual defense
and cooperation.

In the time of Stalin, Hungary had been controlled by
Mátyás Rákosi. The Hungarian people were inclined to refer
to him as Baldy or Asshead, though not within his earshot.[1]
Under Rákosi's leadership, Hungary became a repressive
Stalinist state, terrorized by the interrogation and torture ex-
perts of the State Security Authority (Államvédelmi Hatóság,
AVH).[2] Many were imprisoned arbitrarily. "Then aged 23, I

was locked up in a camp near Budapest as an alleged Trotsky-
ite, although I had not read a single volume of Trotsky's
works," remembered the Hungarian journalist Paul Lendvai.
His fellow prisoners included a farmer who had failed to supply enough grain to the authorities, a fascist count who had
worked in military intelligence, a Jewish doctor accused of
Zionism, and a chess grandmaster who had defected to the
West then unwisely returned. The ideologist of the Nazi-style
Arrow Cross party, which had ruled Hungary from 1944 to
1945, was in the camp alongside Lendvai; so was the judge
who had sentenced the ideologist.[3] Talk of the repression and
dissatisfaction at all levels of Hungarian society found its way
back to the Soviet Union.

After Stalin's death in 1953, the Soviets summoned Rákosi
to Moscow and told him to resign as prime minister, though he
was permitted to stay on as leader of the Communist Party. If
there was any impulse to liberalize in this decision, there was
also pragmatism—and antisemitism. Rákosi had been born
into a Jewish family. Like other Communists, he renounced
his family's religion. But the Soviets officially considered Jew-
ishness a nationality as well as a religion—and that could not
so easily be renounced. Believing that ex-Jews inevitably retained loyalties to Judaism, they considered them unreliable.
Despite the killing of 565,000 Jews—around two thirds of
Hungary's entire Jewish population—during the Nazi occupation in World War II, Jewish people were still a substantial presence in the nation's political life on all sides. Rákosi's
deputy, Ernő Gerő, and another of his powerful inner circle,
Mihály Farkas, were of Jewish backgrounds and were hard-
line Stalinists. At the same time, estimates suggest that most
active anti-Stalinist intellectuals in Hungary were of Jewish
heritage.[4]

The Soviets were not comfortable with any of this. "What

we're saying is that there must not be three Jews [Rákosi, Gerő, and Farkas] in the leadership," the chairman of the Council of Ministers, Georgy Malenkov, told Rákosi. Lavrenty Beria, Stalin's former secret police chief, added a threat: "As an old Bolshevik, you, Rákosi, must know that we really know how to break someone's back."[5]

The Soviets replaced him with a non-Jewish figure, Imre Nagy. Nagy was a Communist, but a reformer rather than a Stalinist. He had stood out from the beginning of his political career, when in the 1920s he had been sent to prison for his Communist beliefs and had arrived there wearing a bowler hat. "A Communist with bowler hat!" exclaimed the Hungarian journalist Tibor Méray. "He must be a different kind of Communist."[6] Later, he got into trouble with his party for refusing to stand at attention when "The Internationale" was played. It had been suggested in the press and in American State Department documents that he could be a Hungarian version of Josip Broz Tito, the charismatic president of Yugoslavia: unique among Eastern Bloc leaders for publicly splitting from Stalin's Soviet Union.

Nagy had a skeleton in his closet. In the 1930s, he had lived in Moscow and acted as an informant for two predecessor organizations of the KGB: the OGPU and the NKVD. This may have been a survival strategy. Like other Muscovite Hungarians he was subject to constant intimidation, including arrest and the threat of much worse. "These Muscovites lived in a curious mental state that combined permanent anxiety and boundless idealism," wrote the Hungarian journalist and historian Charles Gati. "Their Communist faith blinded them to the realities they were experiencing, because they believed in the promise of a Communist paradise with all their heart."[7] Nagy's dubious past was unknown to the public in the 1950s. Had it been, he might have been a lot less popular. By the time he got into power, there was no doubt he was sincerely a reformer. Yet his brushes with the dark side of the Soviet system may hint at why he was such a cautious one.

Nagy was chairman of the Council of Ministers—effectively, leader of Hungary—from July 1953. He began a "New Course" of limited but significant reforms, including rehabilitating some Hungarian politicians and thinkers who had been imprisoned. In 1955, Rákosi convinced the Soviets that Nagy was a right-leaning anti-Soviet, beloved of Western imperialists. The Soviet leaders summoned Nagy to Moscow to fire him. The American radio station Voice of America, Khrushchev told Nagy during that painful interview, was hoping he would "become a traitor . . . Churchill is rubbing his hands now."[8] Though he was removed from power, Nagy was allowed to live freely in Budapest. He continued to be regarded by many as a man of courage and commitment to liberalizing Hungary, though he remained personally reluctant to join, let alone lead, any revolution.[9]

In February 1956, Nikita Khrushchev denounced Stalin and Stalinism in what became known as the Secret Speech. Though Khrushchev himself emphasized the need for secrecy during the speech, he meant its message to get out: he ordered edited copies to be distributed and read out to millions throughout the Soviet Union. "Now those who were arrested will return," remarked the poet Anna Akhmatova, "and two Russias will look each other in the eye: the one that sent people to the camps and the one that was sent away."[10]

The Secret Speech was thrilling but dangerous. It promised hope and some relief from the most repressive aspects of Stalinism. It also opened the door to a plurality of ideas, which could destabilize the whole Soviet revolution. In its wake, there were protests both for and against Stalinism. In some parts of the Soviet Union, Stalin's statues were defaced, while in others—notably his native Georgia—there were enormous demonstrations against Khrushchev for insulting his legacy. The Soviet system struggled with the new concept of accommodating dissent. Its instincts were to shut it down—yet Khrushchev wanted political prisoners to be freed and limited forms of open debate to be permitted. The difficulty many Soviet officials had in reconciling these conflicting urges to repress and to conform goes some way toward explaining what a mess they were about to make of things in Eastern Europe.

Rákosi had finally been removed from the Hungarian party leadership in the summer of 1956 by his Moscow overlords and replaced by Ernő Gerő. This did not quell Hungarian dissent, for Gerő was Rákosi's closest political ally. Large political meetings had taken place in mid-October. The American ambassador reported that there was a "stormy atmosphere" and students were chanting "Go home!" at Soviet troops. Demands were also made for the freer expression of religion in a nation where that had been repressed for a long time.[11] The leader of the Catholic Church in Hungary, József Mindszenty, was imprisoned during World War II by the Nazi-aligned Arrow Cross regime and had been imprisoned again by the Communist government since 1948, becoming an international cause célèbre (though some Hungarian dissenters considered him a reactionary of limited intelligence).[12]

On October 21, 1956, Władysław Gomułka was elected first secretary by the Polish United Workers' Party, making him leader of Poland. Gomułka was not a radical anti-Soviet, but he was a strong believer in Poland's right to determine its own economic and political policy—and an opponent of Soviet military presence in Poland. In Washington, Foster Dulles declared that the world was "seeing the beginning" of Poland's liberation.[13] The Soviets had been accusing the Poles for at least six months of "wanting to go West." It looked as though that could be about to happen.

"In Moscow the meeting of the Polish Central Committee and the election of Gomułka has produced something like a state of panic," wrote Yugoslav ambassador Veljko Mićunović in his diary for that day. Soviet leaders Nikita Khrushchev, Anastas Mikoyan, Vyacheslav Molotov, and Lazar Kaganovich flew to Poland—uninvited—to bring the Poles back in line.[14] Gomułka refused to be intimidated.

As the Soviets knew, rebellions spread. Hungarian students had been demonstrating since Gomułka's election, and specifically cited his rebuff to the Soviet leaders as an inspiration for their big demonstration on October 23.[15]

On the morning of October 23, news spread throughout Budapest that those students (in collaboration with professors, writers, and even some party leaders) had drawn up a list of demands to present to the government. They had occupied the Red Spark printing plant and ran off leaflets, which were now being distributed throughout the city, calling among other things for the withdrawal of Soviet troops, free elections, free expression, the reconstitution of political parties, and a new caretaker government under Imre Nagy. Nagy was not leading the students, nor was he even aware of their demands; he was that morning on a train returning from a trip to the countryside. When student representatives went to his house to invite him to join them, he had not yet returned. His wife answered the door and appeared anxious at the prospect that her husband might be roped into an uprising.[16]

The Hungarian Ministry of the Interior attempted to ban demonstrations in Budapest that morning. An hour and a half later, it realized it could not stop them and issued permission. Citizens assembled that afternoon around a statue of national hero Jószef Bem, a Polish general who had joined Hungarian forces in 1848 to fight in a previous Hungarian revolution. The crowd swelled until it numbered in the thousands. Factory workers and some uniformed soldiers were seen alongside the students. The demonstration was, according to the American legation, "orderly but highly emotional." An old Hungarian national flag, with the coat of arms of nineteenth-century hero and patriot Lajos Kossuth, was fixed to Bem's sword buckle. Students carried the current flag—a red, white, and green tricolor with a Communist hammer, wheatsheaf, and red star crest in the center—with the Communist emblem torn out to leave a gaping hole. "We vow we shall no longer be slaves," they chanted. Older Hungarians watched with tears streaming down their faces.[17]

Gerő telephoned Nikita Khrushchev to report all this.

"You must come to Moscow urgently for talks," said the Soviet leader.

"The situation in Budapest is serious," replied Gerő. "I would rather not go to Moscow at this time."

Just a couple of minutes later, Khrushchev received almost simultaneous communications from Marshal Zhukov, his minister of defense, and from Yuri Andropov, his ambassador in Budapest, both advising that Soviet troops would be required in Hungary soon. In his replies to both men, Khrushchev indicated that he was inclined to send the Red Army.[18]

0900 London // 1000 Sèvres

After failing to see Selwyn Lloyd the day before, Anthony Nutting was shown into the foreign secretary's room.

"How's the cold?" he asked as he walked in.

Lloyd paused and then, looking (according to Nutting) "like a schoolboy caught in some mischief," said, "Oh! the cold! Yes. Well, I never had one. I went to see Ben Gurion outside Paris."

Nutting did not have time to reply before he continued. "And you, my dear Anthony, will no doubt be delighted to hear that it doesn't now look as if the French plan will come off."[19]

Lloyd told Nutting that the Israelis were sticking on the point that they needed early British and French airstrikes to eliminate the Egyptian air force so that Israeli cities would not be threatened. They were mistrustful of British commitment, believing the British to be too pro-Arab and in particular too bound up with Jordan and Iraq.

Nutting asked Lloyd what he would do.

"I really don't know," said Lloyd. "I am so confused and exhausted that I honestly have no advice to offer any more."[20] He added that he hoped someone else would make the decision. Nutting replied, with a sharpness he later regretted, that he had never in his life thought he would hear a British foreign secretary say something so weak.

In later weeks, months, and years, as the real story of Suez began to seep out and became increasingly embarrassing, some British ministers claimed that the full cabinet had never been made aware of what was going on with France and Israel. Yet on October 23, minutes of a meeting of the entire cabinet state that "from secret conversations which had been held in Paris with representatives of the Israeli government, it now appeared that the Israelis would not alone launch a full-scale attack against Egypt."[21] It seems the cabinet knew of the talks at Sèvres, even if it was not fully informed of what action might be taken.

At Sèvres, the conversations continued—more cordially in the absence of Lloyd. The French and the Israelis tried to work out how they could create a believable motive for Britain to step in. There was an awkward moment at lunchtime when General Challe, the French deputy chief of staff, suggested that Israel could stage a fake "Egyptian" bombing raid on the

Israeli town of Beersheba—historically an Arab-majority city but one that since 1948 had seen huge growth in its Jewish population.

"As the General explained his idea, Ben-Gurion's face visibly darkened," remembered Shimon Peres. Ben-Gurion replied, "There are some things that I cannot do, and that I cannot advise my Government and my country to do. One of them is to lie to the world . . . to lie to the world in order to make things more convenient for England!"[22]

In the end, Moshe Dayan suggested the plan that was adopted as a front—which, as he put it, would allow Britain and France to "wash their hands in the waters of purity."[23] It would be claimed that the Israelis were undertaking an operation to eliminate fedayeen bases in the Sinai, creating the appearance of a reprisal raid. The fedayeen (literally meaning "those who sacrifice themselves") were armed groups of Palestinians and/or other Arabs who attempted to carry out guerrilla attacks in Israel. They usually infiltrated from bases in the Gaza Strip (which was under Egyptian control), the West Bank (under Jordanian control), or the borderlands of Syria. They were considered terrorists by Israel and resistance fighters by much of the Arab world. Fedayeen raids were happening almost weekly in 1955–56.[24] Under Ben-Gurion's direction, Israel's policy was to answer the fedayeen with reprisals: for each attack, the IDF would retaliate with great force. The theory was that this would have a deterrent effect.

Technically, staging a reprisal into the Sinai still involved lying to the world. As Ariel Sharon admitted, "in fact there were no terrorist bases in the Sinai."[25] Still, this plan was preferable, for it did not involve bombing an Israeli town. IDF paratroops would land at the strategically important Mitla Pass in the Sinai Peninsula, close to the canal, and from there work their way backward toward the Israeli frontier through the mythical fedayeen bases. As Shimon Peres put it, "We would start our war from the end."[26]

Ben-Gurion let Dayan and Peres work out the details with Christian Pineau in private. Dayan drew up a list of Israel's conditions for participation. These included its desire for "permanent annexation" of half of the Sinai Peninsula: the entire area east of a line drawn from El Arish to Abu Aweigila to Nekhel to Sharm el-Sheikh, to secure the Straits of Tiran and "free herself from the scourge of the infiltrators." Perhaps not entirely coincidentally, Ben-Gurion was aware that oil had recently been found in Sinai. "Britain and France are required to support or at least to commit themselves not to show opposition to these plans," Dayan said. "This is what Israel demands as her share in the fruits of victory."[27]

If Britain's motivation in the Suez crisis was about controlling oil and trade, and France's was about ending the troubles in Algeria, Israel's motivation was intimately connected to the Arab-Israeli conflict. And the Arab-Israeli conflict was now connected to Britain, France, and the United States. In 1950, those three nations had issued the Tripartite Declaration. This was intended to freeze the conflict in the Middle East in the hope that, if the status quo could be allowed to settle in, peace might become a realistic long-term goal. Britain, France, and the United States agreed to maintain a balance in arms sales between the Arab states and Israel to avert an arms race. They agreed not to supply arms to any country in the region intending an act of aggression against another. They also agreed to "take action, both within and outside the United Nations," if any state in the region violated frontiers or armistice lines.

Though the Arab-Israeli conflict did quiet down for the first few years of the 1950s, it was impossible to freeze for long—especially after a strong Arab leader arrived on the scene. Since Nasser had come to power, he had worked to create international connections: not only within the Middle East, but beyond that to the Non-Aligned Movement and the United States, and to some extent with the Soviet Union. He was also easing Britain out by the diplomatic means of negotiating full withdrawal from the Canal Zone. When he came to power, Nasser perhaps hinted subtly at his own hopes for future allegiances by changing the three packs of cigarettes he smoked every day from the British Craven A to the new American brand L&M.[28] He maintained links with the United States overtly through its embassy and covertly through the CIA. The small CIA team in Egypt was run by James Eichelberger and more distantly overseen by Middle East specialists Kermit ("Kim") Roosevelt and Miles Copeland. The CIA men liked Nasser personally and appreciated his potential as a strong leader—perhaps even strong enough to push through a settlement of the Arab-Israeli conflict.[29] CIA agent Wilbur Eveland arrived in Cairo just after Nasser had assumed the presidency and found his colleagues in a jubilant mood. "Copeland hinted that Roosevelt had 'invented' Egypt's new president and conducted high U.S. policy discussions with him much as he did with the shah of Iran," Eveland remembered. "Kim, he [Copeland] said, as I no doubt knew, had staged King Farouk's ouster and had now moved up Nasser to run the country." In conversation with Eveland some years later, Roosevelt was more modest about his role.[30]

Though he liked the CIA men, Nasser was initially wary of the potential for more substantial support from the United States. As he told the American ambassador, he believed it "always sides with Britain"[31] and that it was attached to Israel to an extent that was dangerous for the Arabs.[32]

The Tripartite Declaration of 1950 was still in place, with the aim of balancing the Israelis' and Arabs' arms. In the past, Egypt had bought most of its arms from Britain, but Egypt's relations with Britain had deteriorated in the early 1950s. The British had proven increasingly obstructive, supplying guns with no ammunition and holding up exports of obsolete aircraft on bureaucratic grounds.[33] The Egyptians worried that Israel would soon outgun them. In 1954, Nasser turned to the United States for arms. He felt this would help him maintain Egypt's balance against Israel, with the added benefit of cementing his nascent relationship with American agencies. When the terms of the deal were made clear, though, the Americans offered him only $20 million worth of weaponry, less than a fifth of what he had hoped for. Furthermore, American legislation meant he was required to welcome a military mission of American soldiers to supervise the arms. Kermit Roosevelt and the CIA tried to sweeten the pill by offering a suitcase containing $3 million in cash, euphemistically described as being for the purchase of "certain morale-building items of military equipment such as uniforms and staff transportation." Deeply insulted by this bribe—for one thing, it was not very much—Nasser used the money to build the decorative but functionless Cairo Tower on Gezira Island. Locals in the know soon nicknamed it *el wa'ef rusfel*—Roosevelt's Erection.[34]

Relations between Egypt and Israel worsened in the later half of 1954. Kermit Roosevelt tried to coax Nasser back into secret talks. "It appears to many of us in Washington you are in danger of walking into some well laid Israeli traps . . . which will handicap seriously the ability of your friends in the United States to counter Zionist pressures here," he wrote to Nasser at the end of the year. "As you are aware, these pressures are steadily mounting."[35]

At that time, Anthony Eden set in motion two policies for the Middle East intended to reaffirm British influence after the Canal Zone withdrawal. The first aimed toward a NATO-style defensive union of friendly Middle Eastern states oriented toward Western interests and designed to keep the Soviets out of the region. Its effective figurehead would be Eden's friend and Nasser's rival Nuri es-Said, prime minister of Iraq. This would become known as the Baghdad Pact and later as the Central Treaty Organization (CENTO). Britain persuaded only one Arab nation, Iraq, to join, building on an existing agreement Iraq had with Turkey. Iran and Pakistan were also roped in. Eden hoped the United States would come in, too, but Foster Dulles, despite having an enthusiasm his colleagues called "pactomania" for international treaty organizations, dragged his feet.[36]

French Ministry for External Affairs documents reveal that the French were discomfited by this organization "where they [the British] are the only representatives of a western power."[37] They also noted that the signing of the Pact had "the most unfortunate consequences," namely, "Britain lost, in Egypt, the benefit of the sacrifices it made in evacuating the Suez Canal. It awoke the distrust and increased the concerns of Syria and Lebanon. It discouraged Israel. It seriously alienated Saudi Arabia. Finally it compromised its good relations with Jordan."[38] Many Arab nations saw the pact as a hostile move by Britain against their interests. It presented a direct challenge to Nasser's unofficial leadership of the Arab world and his prestige in the Muslim world.

The second policy, a project devised by Eden and Foster Dulles in the utmost secrecy, was known as Alpha. It aimed to resolve the Arab-Israeli conflict—and explicitly acknowledged that the only Arab leader powerful enough to achieve that was Nasser. Britain and the United States would have to influence him, and in order to do so, they would have to work with him.

These policies could not sit together. For Alpha to work, Nasser needed to be strengthened and had to trust Britain and the United States. Yet the Baghdad Pact was aimed at undermining him.[39]

On February 22, 1955, Eden and Nasser met for the first and only time, at the British embassy in Cairo. Eden brought his young wife, Clarissa. He seemed, Nasser thought, to be trying to impress her. He began by greeting Nasser in Arabic—which "astonished" the Egyptian president, according to his friend Mohamed Heikal—and then rolled out a lengthy monologue on the Quran, Arabic poetry, the nobility of the desert Bedouin, and so forth. Next, he attempted to move smoothly from romantic orientalism to the subject of Egypt's defense.[40] He told Nasser that he should not consider the Baghdad Pact a crime.

"No, but it is one," replied Nasser with a laugh.[41]

Faced with resistance to his charms, Eden became testy. He asked why Nasser would not ally with people like Nuri es-Said and the Hashemite family.

Nasser tried to explain that the Baghdad Pact was dividing the Arab world while he strove instead for Arab unity. According to Mohamed Heikal, "Eden said that he knew enough about Arab unity, after all it was he who initiated the idea of the Arab League."[42] Nasser tried to explain that Eden had not in fact invented pan-Arabism himself with one speech in 1942. Yet Eden would not listen, said Heikal; he "was completely convinced of the correctness, the justice and the strength of his line of thought."[43]

"Eden tried rather insensitively to lecture Nasser on what his defence arrangements should be," said Ralph Murray, a member of the Foreign Office team who was there with him. "It produced rather a bad effect on Nasser, who didn't like being lectured." Nasser, for his part, felt Eden talked to him as if "he was talking to a junior official who could not be expected to understand international politics."[44]

The week that followed Eden and Nasser's meeting on February 22, 1955, dramatically changed the Egyptian leader's outlook. Just two days later, the Baghdad Pact was officially signed. Just four days after that, Israel launched a massive raid on the Egyptian-held Gaza Strip. This raid—known as Operation Black Arrow or the Gaza raid—would be the most serious yet of Israel's reprisals and the most substantial engagement between Egypt and Israel since the 1948 war. It was led by a twenty-seven-year-old officer, Ariel ("Arik") Sharon. "Few, if any of his superior officers over the years had a good word to say for him as far as human relations and integrity were concerned," remarked Chaim Herzog, who commanded the Jerusalem District during the Suez Crisis and would later become president of Israel, "although none would deny his innate ability as a field soldier."[45] Sharon had already gained considerable notoriety—and, in some important quarters, approval—for his efforts, notably the Qibya raid of 1953.

On October 12, 1953, a grenade was thrown into an Israeli house in Yehul. A woman and her two children were killed. Two nights later, Sharon's forces crossed the border into the Jordanian-held West Bank and blew up forty-five buildings in the village of Qibya. Fifty-three people were killed. The wounded were abandoned to die, raising the number of dead to sixty-six. This was a far greater toll than the politicians who had ordered the reprisal had intended. Ben-Gurion claimed publicly that the reprisal was not an official Israeli action, but rather a spontaneous response to Arab harassment by Israeli citizens.[46] The international community did not believe him. CIA agent Wilbur Eveland was sent to investigate on behalf of the American ambassador to the United Nations. Appraising the evidence, he wrote that it "left no doubt that Israeli troops had waged an unjustifiable attack on a defenseless village."[47]

Sharon, writing many years later, admitted that it had been

an official action but argued that it was intended to cause only military damage: "I was to inflict as many casualties as I could on the Arab home guard and on whatever Jordanian army reinforcements showed up. I was also to blow up every major building in the town. A political decision had been made at the highest level. The Jordanians were to understand that Jewish blood could no longer be shed with impunity. From this point on there would be a heavy price to pay." Sharon maintained that his forces had rescued a little boy and girl they had found in the buildings and that the civilian deaths were accidental. "In those big stone houses where three generations of a family might live together, some could easily have hidden in the cellars and back rooms, keeping quiet when the paratroopers went in to check and yell out a warning," he wrote. "The result was this tragedy that had happened."[48]

Israel was strongly censured by the UN Security Council.[49] Foster Dulles announced that the United States would withhold $60 million of economic aid from Ben-Gurion's government.[50] The campaigning Israeli journalist Uri Avnery published a piece criticizing Sharon's actions in his magazine, *HaOlem HaZeh*. Soon afterward, he was attacked by unknown assailants who broke both his hands. "I asked Arik about Qibya once," Avnery said. "There was a short while when we were friendly after he left Likud. He assured me that they did not know people were in the houses. This whole story"—he laughed dryly at the memory—"it was a lie from beginning to end."[51]

Despite all of these reactions, Ben-Gurion appeared satisfied. A few days after Qibya, he invited Sharon to Jerusalem to meet him for the first time. "It doesn't make any real difference about [*sic*] what will be said about Kibbiya around the world," the prime minister said. "The important thing is how it will be looked at here in this region. This is going to give us the possibility of living here."[52] Even so, after Qibya, the IDF altered its policy to attack what it considered to be Arab military rather than civilian targets.

Fedayeen raids against Israel continued. Some Palestinian activists in the Gaza Strip, then administered by Egypt, believed their best tactic was to harass Israel in the hope of provoking an all-out attack by the IDF on Gaza. If that happened, they thought Nasser would be drawn into a war—which might improve their lot or at least wreak some kind of revenge. It was a desperate strategy and unlikely to work. Nasser attempted to restrain these activists, without much success.[53] He visited Gaza in early 1955 and spoke of peace. Neither he nor the Israelis, he told his Palestinian audience, wanted the borderlands to become battlegrounds. It is true that the Egyptians did not: Nasser knew he could not win a war against Israel. Owing to the slowdown in arms sales in the early 1950s from Britain and the United States, the Egyptian armed forces were in a parlous state. It was estimated that the army had only enough tank ammunition to last for an hour of battle.

Ben-Gurion returned to the Israeli government as minister of defense on February 21, 1955, the day before Eden met Nasser and three days before the Baghdad Pact was signed. Israeli intelligence services assured him that the Egyptians were incapable of a large-scale military attack on Israel. They presumed this meant Israel could attack Gaza without fear of the consequences.[54] On February 23, a group of fedayeen from Gaza traveled far into Israel, reaching the outskirts of Tel Aviv. There was some suggestion that they may have been sent by Egypt on an intelligence mission. That day, they murdered an Israeli civilian.[55] Ben-Gurion made his decision. Sharon was unleashed again on February 28 to undertake Operation Black Arrow, a raid on Egypt's military camp in Gaza. Thirty-six Egyptian and Palestinian soldiers were killed and twenty-nine wounded. Two Arab civilians were also killed. CIA agent Miles Copeland judged that the Gaza raid was "an atrocity by anyone's definition."[56]

Israeli intelligence had been right to predict that Egypt would not strike back. It could not and did not. Those Palestinians who had hoped Egypt could be drawn into a war on their behalf were disappointed. There were violent protests against Egypt in Gaza, especially by Communists and Islamic fundamentalists. Nasser was denounced; Egyptians were accused of being in thrall to "American agents." Twenty-five-year-old Yasser Arafat led a demonstration at the Arab League headquarters in Cairo.[57]

Yet Israeli intelligence had been wrong to imagine that this raid would be without consequence. It was, as the historian Avi Shlaim said, "a turning point in the history of the Middle East."[58] The Gaza raid reignited the Arab-Israeli conflict with extraordinary force and made a future war between Egypt and Israel inevitable.[59] The focus of Egypt's military policy shifted from relations with its fellow Arab states to active conflict with Israel.[60]

After the raid, Nasser "spoke of his sleepless nights and increasing tension," and described himself as being in "constant fear of an Israeli attack," wrote Humphrey Trevelyan, the British ambassador to Egypt at the time.[61] His fear was not unrealistic: Ben-Gurion proposed to the Israeli cabinet in April 1955 that they attack Gaza again, aiming to push all Egyptian forces out. Moshe Sharett warned against it on the grounds that such an action would violate the Tripartite Declaration, potentially obliging Britain, France, and the United States to join the fighting on the Egyptian side. It would give the United States cause to stop all economic aid to Israel. According to the American embassy in Tel Aviv, Sharett "gave the impression of a man under great emotional strain who had been subjected to strong pressures from his colleagues" after the meeting. He won the vote against Ben-Gurion: nine cabinet members to four.[62] That time, Gaza was left alone.

Another result of the Gaza raid was that Nasser's enthusiasm for entertaining American overtures cooled. Disappointed by the failure of his American arms deal, he wondered, according to aides, whether the United States was deliberately using Israel to pressure him into accommodating its own defense needs. He resented Foster Dulles's continued attempts to persuade him to make peace with the Israelis.[63] Now he felt he must look elsewhere to buy weaponry. The United States had been trying to convince him for some time that the greatest danger to Egypt was the Soviet Union, but there was no chance he would accept that now. He saw his greatest enemy as Israel and believed he must to buy more arms to protect Egypt against it. At the Bandung conference of non-aligned nations, he asked China's Chou En-lai whether China could supply him. Chou told him China was itself dependent on the Soviets and pointed him in the direction of Moscow.[64]

On September 19, 1955, a panicked American cable from Cairo reported talk of a "Soviet arms offer [to Egypt] . . . said to be almost embarrassing in size."[65] On September 27, the news became public: Nasser had made an arms deal with the Soviet satellite state of Czechoslovakia. For Israel, this particular unintended consequence of the Gaza raid spelled potential disaster. Arab armies may have been "rotten," as Ben-Gurion had said after the 1948 war, but Arab armies backed by unrestricted Soviet military supply might be a very different prospect.

Egypt's deal was not without precedent. Israel had bought arms from Communist Czechoslovakia when its American arms supply was stopped in 1948.[66] This, too, had caused consternation in London and Washington, though not on the scale of the British and American reactions to Nasser's deal in 1955. A crucial difference was that this new deal undercut the Tripartite Declaration. If the Egyptians bought arms from the Soviets, the Western powers could not even know what they had, let alone regulate the situation. So serious was this that one senior British civil servant commented darkly, "We may have to get rid of Nasser, especially if he becomes committed to the [Soviet] contract."[67]

The CIA men in Cairo still backed Nasser. Kermit Roosevelt and Miles Copeland had helped him draft his announcement of his arms deal; according to Copeland's recollection, it was Roosevelt who advised him to say the arms had come from Czechoslovakia rather than ultimately from the Soviet Union itself.[68] Now they tried to explain that by getting involved with Moscow he was endangering his position with the United States. According to Mohamed Heikal, Kermit Roosevelt told him, "[Foster] Dulles was behaving like an agitated ox and was determined that the deal had to be stopped." The Egyptian ambassador to Washington, Ahmed Hussein, warned Nasser not to upset the Americans, nervously repeating, "Guatemala, Mr. President, Guatemala." He was referring to the recent CIA overthrow of Jacopo Arbenz's left-wing government on skimpy evidence that it was cooperating with the Soviets.

"To hell with Guatemala," growled Nasser.[69] He kept his Soviet deal. Kermit Roosevelt tried to convince Allen Dulles at the CIA back in Washington that they should not pull a Guatemala on Nasser: "Our conviction . . . is that Nasr remains our best, if not our only, hope here."[70]

A few days after the Czech deal, Nasser met the American ambassador, Henry Byroade, who read him a stern letter from Foster Dulles.[71] "I have been through a nightmare . . . which your Secretary of State may not be able to realize," Nasser replied. He explained that he had tried to buy arms from France first, but they had not been delivered; he felt he had no choice. "In summary he said that in all frankness he had the conviction that [the] US Government was trying to keep Egypt weak and that this resulted from Jewish influence in the US," Byroade reported to Washington.[72]

Nasser still tried to work with the Americans. In November 1955, he agreed again—in extreme secrecy—to pursue a settlement of the Arab-Israeli conflict.[73] The CIA operatives in Egypt were not optimistic. "Although we would work at trying to bring about peace between the Arabs and Israel, we did so largely for the benefit of our domestic audience," wrote Miles Copeland, "while fully realizing that a continuing state of hostility was something we just had to live with."[74] Foster Dulles, though, may still have thought he had a shot at that Nobel Peace Prize that his colleagues believed he craved. It suited Nasser to be seen to play along with Western interests, and in any case he found some evidence for hope on November 9. Anthony Eden gave a speech at the Guildhall in the City of London that day on possible solutions to the Arab-Israeli dispute. The British prime minister called for Israel to make territorial concessions to the Arabs, notably in the Negev desert, to create a land link between Egypt and Jordan and to bring the map of the Middle East closer to the 1947 United Nations partition plan. Eden's speech found a predictably poor reception in Israel. Golda Meir, then minister of labor, railed against the demand that Israel should "serve this peace to Nasser . . . on a platter of the Negev," and stated that the Israelis would give up "not one grain of sand—not one."[75] Nasser saw Eden's speech as a distinct improvement in Britain's attitude.

Concerned that Nasser might outgun them with his new Soviet weapons, the Israelis asked the United States for a new arms deal which they hoped would rebalance their defenses against Cairo's under the terms of the Tripartite Declaration.

Moshe Sharett and the diplomat Abba Eban—both moderates within the Israeli administration, preferring political solutions to war—were attempting to negotiate this deal in December 1955. As they did so, Ben-Gurion again sent forth Sharon. This time, he went to Kinneret, where, in reprisal for the harassment of Israeli fisherman, he attacked Syrian emplacements around the Sea of Galilee.

"The next day there was an outbreak in Kinneret in which our forces killed 73 Arabs in retaliation for an Arab attack on our fishing vessels which had scraped the paint off the vessels and had not caused any casualties," Eban recalled. "This was, of course, an appalling international situation, because the gulf between the effects of the retaliation and the thing which had brought it about was greater than any engagement that had happened before or since. It is no secret that Mr. Sharett finally protested Mr. Ben Gurion's decision nor of [sic] the furls and flurries of letters that I exchanged with Mr. Ben Gurion then."[76] The Americans were furious. Dulles halted Israel's arms deal. But if Israel could not get arms cleanly through the Tripartite Declaration, it, too, would have to try to work around it.

From an Egyptian point of view, it looked as though the Americans were trying to play both sides of the Arab-Israeli conflict. They also seemed to be in cahoots with Britain, which was trying to divide and rule the Arab nations with the Baghdad Pact. "We think you have been conducting a comic opera in the Middle East," Nasser told a CIA agent in a meeting in Cairo on February 22, 1956. British and American activities in support of the Baghdad Pact, he explained, were creating "internecine warfare" among the Arab states. He also felt the British were running a propaganda campaign against him. Nasser refused point-blank to meet with Israelis, though the agent hopefully reported to his superiors that "we may have as much as one out of five chances of changing his mind."[77] Though the situation between Israel and Egypt calmed down with a formal cease-fire from April 18, 1956, it would not stay quiet for long.

In 1954, the date for Britain to withdraw its troops from the Canal Zone had been set as June 18, 1956. As that date approached, there were rumblings in some quarters of the Conservative Party that this had been too hasty. Glubb Pasha was sacked in March, and Eden's dislike for Nasser rocketed into an expressed wish to have him murdered. The Arabs and the Israelis were at each others' throats, and the Tripartite Declaration was no longer preventing a Middle Eastern arms race. The security of the region was precarious. Yet the Suez Base Agreement stood. The last British soldiers left the Canal Zone as agreed. Nasser felt able to be magnanimous. "In regard to Britain, she has fulfilled her obligations under the Evacuation Agreement," he said in a broadcast speech on June 19. "Britain had 80,000 troops in the Canal Zone. They have all left. In connection with Britain we have no aggressive aims against them at all."[78]

Soon afterward, Egypt's relations with Israel took another dive. On July 11, 1956, Israeli military intelligence delivered a bomb disguised as a book to Colonel Mustafa Hafez, the head of the Egyptian intelligence service and the man they held responsible for coordinating fedayeen attacks. Hafez was killed and was celebrated in Gaza as a martyr.[79] Dulles's withdrawal of the Aswan Dam funding just days later, followed by Nasser's nationalization of the Canal Company, changed the international atmosphere. The CIA agents on the ground had been supporters of Nasser; Dulles was not. After the nationalization, he removed two key American diplomats who were sympathetic to Nasser—Ambassador Byroade and Assistant Secretary George Allen—from Egypt, replacing them with more pliant State Department officials. "Foster Dulles was now clearing the deck of any independent thinkers and would take complete personal charge of the Middle East," wrote the CIA's Wilbur Eveland, despairingly.[80] Dulles, agreed Miles Copeland, was "making moves that gave Nasser little choice but to escalate the conflict."[81]

Nasser's response was to work on his own regional alliances throughout 1956, in an attempt to shore up his influence against Nuri es-Said and the Baghdad Pact and as a defensive move against Israel. By October 23, 1956, these alliances were bearing fruit. That very day, two Russian-made transport aircraft landed in Amman, Jordan. From them emerged Major General Abdul Hakim Amer, the Egyptian minister of war and chief of staff, and thirty Egyptian military men, including more than a dozen pilots. At almost exactly the same moment, the Syrian chief of staff, Major General Tewfik Nizameddin, arrived in Amman, having driven from Damascus. The Egyptians and Syrians were there to meet King Hussein and Jordanian military commanders to talk about greater cooperation. Saudi Arabia was also involved. Their schedule included a visit to the border with Israel. The *Times* of London fretted that this visit coincided with Egypt and Syria's introduction of Soviet-made equipment in their frontline forces, meaning Egypt and Syria's plan could well be to sell off their old Western-made arms to Jordan on the cheap. "Each item supplied in this way would in effect bear the message 'Look what help we are giving! What have Iraq or your western friends provided?'" the correspondent wrote.[82] Only a week before, an Iraqi military delegation had visited Jordan to encourage it to join the Baghdad Pact, without success. There seemed to be a serious danger of Britain losing its influence in Jordan altogether.

In the wake of France's kidnapping of the Algerian rebels the day before, anti-Western feeling was running high throughout the Middle East on October 23, 1956. There was a general strike in Tunisia that day, and anti-French demonstrations and rioting throughout North Africa: French flags were torn down, cars were torched, and three Frenchmen were killed in a riot in Meknes, Morocco.[83] Demonstrators in Casablanca shouted "Free Algeria!" and "Lacoste to the gallows!" (Robert Lacoste was the French minister residing in Casablanca.[84]) French prime minister Guy Mollet again accused Egypt of arming the Algerians, withdrew his ambassador from Cairo, and ordered the French fleet to patrol the whole North African coast in case Nasser attempted to ship more weapons to rebel forces. According to an internal CIA memorandum, "Morocco and Tunisia . . . tried without success to obtain US and British intervention."[85] Thanks to the French action, NATO countries looked at best unhelpful—at worst villainous—just as Nasser was putting the finishing touches to his Arab anticolonial alliance. The omens did not portend peace.

1200 Washington DC // 1700 London // 1800 Budapest

By six o'clock that evening in Budapest, the crowd of protesters had crossed the Danube and congregated with other citizens outside parliament on the Pest side of the city. A United Nations report later estimated their numbers at an extraordinary two hundred thousand to three hundred thousand. The crowd shouted for Imre Nagy, who had by now returned from his trip. A group of writers and intellectuals had spent much of the afternoon at his home trying to persuade him to speak to the people. Sticking to his belief that reform must be orderly, though, he refused—waiting for the Communist Party itself to summon him. Finally, a close friend of his pleaded that hundreds of thousands of people had been waiting for him for hours. He gave in and went to parliament.

Nagy encouraged the crowd to trust the party to reform

itself. He said little and could not be heard well. He addressed them as "comrades," which provoked a chorus of booing. After just a few sentences, he asked them to disperse peacefully and let change proceed at a natural pace, which was not what they had hoped to hear.[86] "Crowd hardly listened and Nagy said 'you called me here to give my opinion and I'm giving it,'" reported the American legation. The American officer was disappointed: "Legation sternly urges media refrain from taking any kind of stand on Imre Nagy for the time being."[87]

"Only when I perceived the mood in the square did it become clear to me that what was called for was quite different from what I had prepared, for that would not satisfy the crowd," Nagy admitted later.[88] He cheered them somewhat at the end of his speech by singing the Hungarian national anthem.[89]

After Nagy had gone, a speech recorded earlier that day by Ernő Gerő, the first secretary of the Central Committee of the Communist Party, was broadcast. Gerő's speech had been greatly anticipated by the protesters, for he had that day returned from a visit to Tito. It was hoped that some of the Yugoslav leader's liberalism might have rubbed off. Yet Gerő's speech made no move toward liberalizing anything. Instead, he enraged the crowd by insisting in heavily Soviet tones that they were "a mob attempting to make trouble," reactionary and chauvinist riffraff.[90] As Tito later put it, Gerő had "insulted almost an entire nation. . . . That in itself was enough to put a match to the fire."[91] Shouts of "Down with Gerő!" and even "Death to Gerő!" echoed throughout the city.

The terms in which Gerő dismissed the protesters—accusing them of being counterrevolutionaries—were significant. During the middle years of the twentieth century, a tendency developed in the United States to view any foreign movements opposed to American involvement in their countries through the polarizing lens of the Cold War. Communists were anti-American, and anti-American feeling was Communist. This conflation was disastrous and frequently counterproductive. In Cuba, for instance, the 1959 revolution began as a nationalist movement, and the first administration installed by Fidel Castro was right of center politically and economically. Only after his repeated attempts to cooperate with the United States were rebuffed did Castro and his revolution become socialist, then eventually Communist.[92] In the Soviet Union, the understanding of dissent was no more sophisticated. Khrushchev, whose liberalizing instincts offered a ray of hope after the gruesome years of Stalinism, still tended to assume that dissatisfaction within the Soviet bloc was stirred up by fascist quislings or outside provocateurs. The rest of the Soviet leadership felt the same. When rebellion broke out in Hungary, Kliment Voroshilov, the chairman of the presidium (effectively, the Soviet cabinet), immediately claimed that "American secret services" were active in it.[93]

Since the CIA-orchestrated coup in Guatemala two years earlier, it was far from impossible to believe that the United States was behind movements to oust left-wing governments. But Hungary under Communism was a brutal and repressive society, nothing like, for example, the relatively moderate left-wing democracy presided over by Jacopo Arbenz in Guatemala. The CIA, which along with the State Department had consistently underestimated the potential for Hungarian rebellion, had no Hungarian speakers in its nearest operation, in Vienna, only one Hungarian-speaking agent in Budapest itself, and "seven or so" more in the country at large. It was as surprised as anyone by the uprising on October 23.[94] It was certainly not responsible.

Nonetheless, a feeling that the Hungarian rebellion must be the result of outside interference was rife among the Soviets.

At an emergency meeting in the Hungarian interior ministry, a new Soviet adviser was introduced. His name was not mentioned, but it was Ivan Serov, the head of the KGB. This would be the first time a KGB chief had taken charge personally of an operation outside the borders of the Soviet Union. Serov was furious about the demonstration: "The fascists and imperialists send their shock troops into the streets of Budapest and there are still comrades of your armed forces who hesitate to use arms."

"Clearly, the comrade counsellor from Moscow hasn't had time to inform himself of the situation in our country," replied Sándor Kopácsi, Budapest's chief of police. "He should know that it is not fascists and other imperialists who are planning the demonstration. These are university students, sons and daughters of peasants and workers, very carefully chosen, the pride of our intelligentsia who demand their rights and want to manifest their sympathy for the Poles."[95]

Serov lost his temper, but Kopácsi was right. Few of these rebels were the "fascists" of Soviet nightmares; they were ordinary and diverse Hungarians, exhausted by years of hardship under a Stalinist regime. The leaders of rebel groups in the city included Gergely Pongrátz, a twenty-four-year-old agricultural engineer; János Szabó, a fifty-nine-year-old bus driver and former soldier of peasant origins; and László Nickelsburg, a thirty-two-year-old factory worker who was Jewish and a Communist, whose mother and three siblings had died in a Nazi concentration camp.[96] The British journalist Peter Fryer, who was in Budapest for the Communist *Daily Worker* newspaper, described it as a spontaneous uprising: "A city in arms, a people in arms, who had stood up and snapped the chains of bondage with one giant effort."[97]

The United States and the Soviet Union were two nations themselves formed by revolution, each of which revered its revolutionary forebears. Yet now that their founding revolutions had settled into power and were beginning to expand, neither seemed able to imagine that new revolutions might spring up against them. They believed they were different from the old European empires. They believed they were exceptional.

"On every appropriate occasion, the Secretary [Foster Dulles] would recount the fact that the United States was once a colony itself, and that it became a nation by freeing itself from colonial domination," said Herman Phleger, a legal adviser to the Eisenhower administration. "He frequently, in speeches and otherwise, expressed the view that one of the missions of the United States in the world was to see that every people, all people, were free to choose their own method of government."[98] In a very frank speech that April, Foster Dulles had argued that the old empires were falling. "You take the British," he said. "They feel that they are on the downgrade; they are just desperately grasping almost at straws to find something that will restore their prestige and influence in the world. And France is the same. Most of our Western Allies are in the same position. Their colonial areas are melting away, and with it [*sic*] many of their reserves in terms of raw materials, and so forth, and they feel in a quite desperate position." By contrast, he claimed, "the United States is, I suppose, the only country in the world which has foreign policies which are not primarily designed for its own aggrandizement. Almost every other country in the world is thinking primarily on how it can develop itself, generally at the expense of somebody else."[99]

The Soviet leader Nikita Khrushchev echoed Dulles's sentiments—though he felt they applied to the Soviet Union. "It wasn't that we wanted to replace England as an exploiter of Egypt and other Arab countries," he remembered. "We weren't motivated by self-centred, mercantile interests. Quite the contrary, we wanted only to help these peoples to cast off the yoke of their servile dependence on their colonialist masters. Ours has been a noble mission."[100] Sometimes the peoples "helped" either by the Soviets or the Americans found that their experience diverged significantly from the noble stated aims of those powers.

At nine p.m. in Moscow, the presidium met. "Hungary is coming apart," said Vyacheslav Molotov. Lazar Kaganovich agreed. Georgy Zhukov advised sending troops, declaring martial law, and imposing a curfew.

"There's no alternative but to send in soldiers without delay," Khrushchev said.

Anastas Mikoyan was the only man present who disagreed. "We should get Imre Nagy into the Hungarian leadership and let him try to restore order," he suggested. "It's cheaper for us that way. What are we losing? If our troops go in, we will ruin things for ourselves. The Hungarians will restore order on their own. We should try political measures and only if they fail then send troops."[101]

Khrushchev compromised somewhat. Mikoyan would be sent to Budapest, along with Mikhail Suslov. Nagy would be given a chance. But Soviet troops would be mobilized—just in case.

1500 Washington DC // 2000 London // 2100 Budapest

Christian Pineau arrived in London from Sèvres with the details of the plan Moshe Dayan had designed. He dined with Selwyn Lloyd, who (as he had indicated to Anthony Nutting earlier) did not think the plan would come off. Lloyd was now inclined to let the United Nations set up an Egyptian-operated canal-management authority under international control, along the lines Dulles had been suggesting.

Pineau sensed the opportunity slipping away—until Anthony Eden arrived after dinner. Eden was much more enthusiastic about Pineau's plan than Lloyd, and the opportunity seemed to have returned. Eden decided to send another British representative to Sèvres the next morning.

While the British and French politicians were talking in London, the mood in the streets of Budapest was growing explosive. The protesters had decided to enforce one of their demands themselves and spent four hours attempting to topple the enormous statue of Stalin on Heroes Square. They attacked it with blowtorches and hauled it with winches attached to cars and trucks. When finally, at 9:37 p.m., it pitched over and lay in the street, protesters went at it with hacksaws, knives, and axes, and stood upon its colossal head.[102] Only Stalin's boots remained rooted to the plinth.

"It was such an eerie sound," recalled one of the students there to see it fall, "several thousand people sighing with joy. I think we all had a sense of making history."[103] Red Stars were chiseled off buildings. Some students attempted to enter the Radio Building. They were teargassed, then shot at, by the AVH.[104] Rumors on the streets suggested dozens had been killed. Two officers from the American legation saw the body of a young man in the street. He had been shot in the face.[105] Troops of the Hungarian army were also sent in to subdue protesters. Faced with fighting their countrymen, many defected to the rebel side. The United Nations investigating committee afterward reported one striking story. At ten p.m., an army unit was stopped by protesters. An old worker climbed upon a truck and recited a famous poem: "Shoot not, my son, for I shall also be in the crowd." At this the soldiers, with just a quick glance at their commanding officer, leaped from their vehicles and joined the rebels.[106]

Large numbers of workers were now driving into the center of town to join the uprising, supported by soldiers and police who joined them and distributed arms. Pitched battles raged at the Radio Building and at the offices of the Communist Party newspaper. In the offices of the Communist Party, Gerő and Nagy had a fight in front of their comrades.

"You instigated the riots," shouted Gerő. "Now you can stew in your own juice."

"I have instigated nothing and you know it," Nagy shouted back. "Everything that is happening now could have been prevented if you had handled the situation better during the day."[107]

In the middle of the night, the presidium's instruction came through from Moscow: Nagy was prime minister again. On Khrushchev's request, he was told to sign an appeal for Soviet troops to enter Budapest and restore order. Shortly afterward, such an appeal was made to the Soviet Union in the name of Imre Nagy.[108] It is now clear that Nagy did not sign this appeal himself, though there was confusion about this at the time. He did, on the other hand, impose martial law and a curfew.[109] Here was his chance: if he could pacify Hungary fast, he might be able to install a government the people could tolerate.

2000 Washington DC // 0100 London // 0200 Budapest

In Washington, Eisenhower had a long talk in the afternoon with Foster Dulles and Lewis L. Strauss, the chairman of the Atomic Energy Commission. "One highlight of the discussion came with another display of Eisenhower's pacifist fervor—and the World War II soldier's view of nuclear war as 'unthinkable,'" remembered the president's aide and speechwriter, Emmet Hughes.

The reason for their discussion was that Nikolai Bulganin of the Soviet Union had on October 17 called for the United States to support an international ban on nuclear testing. The United States had increased its nuclear capacity under Eisenhower, but the president himself had a profound fear of the power of nuclear weapons. Nor was he confident in the policy of mutual assured destruction, which assumed that neither side would dare use nuclear weapons first in case the other side struck back.

"I do not fully share your conclusion that an end to nuclear war will come about because of realization on both sides that by using this weapon an unconscionable degree of death and destruction would result," he wrote to Winston Churchill in April 1956. "I do think it might tend to reduce very materially the possibility of *any* war; but I think it would be unsafe to predict that, if the West and the East should ever become locked up in a life and death struggle, both sides would still have sense not to use this horrible instrument."[110]

Eisenhower was wary of how such a ban could be enforced when the vastness of Soviet territory made it relatively easy for them to hide nuclear test sites. His advisers decided to issue a cautious statement along those lines. Yet the president himself was inclined to agree with Bulganin's basic principle: that the weapons both the United States and the Soviet Union now possessed were so dangerous that they had to be controlled.

"My God, we have to simply figure a way out of this situation," said Eisenhower. "There's just no point in talking about 'winning' a nuclear war." He waved an arm in the direction of the Atlantic. "You might just as well talk about going out and swimming that ocean."[111]

Eisenhower could not have realized how close the danger was. The Soviets were poised to take action that could pit the nuclear-armed superpowers against each other. Though Bulganin may have been sincere about disarmament when he wrote his letter to Eisenhower on October 17, by October 23, Hungary was in rebellion. At two a.m. Budapest time, six thousand Soviet troops, with armored cars, tanks, and cannon—which had been waiting southeast and southwest of the city—rolled toward Budapest at top speed. They powered through the city in the middle of the night, spraying machine-gun bullets into apartment blocks and office buildings. Order would be reimposed. If Imre Nagy could not or would not do it himself, the mighty Red Army would do it for him.[112]

3

WEDNESDAY, OCTOBER 24, 1956

A PLAN ON A CIGARETTE PACKET

**0213 Washington DC // 0713 London // 0813 Budapest //
1113 Moscow**

Hungarians woke in a city filled with Red Army soldiers and tanks. At 8:13 a.m., the news was broadcast over Budapest Radio that Imre Nagy was now in charge. In reality his power was limited. "Fascist and reactionary elements have launched an armed attack against our public buildings and against the forces of law and order," announced the official radio station. "The Soviet soldiers are risking their lives to protect the peaceful citizens of Budapest and the tranquillity of the nation. . . . Workers of Budapest, receive our friends and allies with affection."[1]

Within twenty minutes of the announcement of Nagy's premiership, two Soviet tanks opened fire near Marx Square, killing two civilians who had perhaps failed to receive them affectionately enough. Others fired on members of the public near the Western Station and in People's Park. Budapest's police chief Sándor Kopácsi had been fighting from his headquarters, which were under attack by rebels looking for weapons. "The bullets were crashing against the walls like hailstones," he remembered.[2]

In London, the Foreign Office assistant undersecretary Patrick Dean was asked to come to 10 Downing Street before breakfast. Dean was also chairman of the Joint Intelligence Committee and, until August 29, had been the Foreign Office's adviser in MI6. Anthony Eden explained to him the broad strokes of the secret Suez plan that was emerging in Paris and told him to go to Sèvres to complete the negotiations. The prime minister said that Britain, France, and Israel all felt it was essential to stop Nasser inflicting further disasters on the Middle East. There was a concern that the Suez Canal would be threatened in the event of conflict between Israel and Egypt.

This was hardly the full story, but the meeting lasted only fifteen minutes—leaving little time to explain all the intricacies of the secret negotiations and to give Dean full instructions on how he should proceed. And so the intricacies were not explained. Dean assumed that what was being discussed was a contingency plan rather than something to be enacted immediately, and further assumed that Eden must have already approved it with his cabinet. Eden drew one clear red line: Britain could not act unless Israel had already invaded Egypt and the canal was in danger. He also told Dean to keep the meeting absolutely secret. A military plane would take him to Paris that afternoon.[3]

1000 Sèvres

That morning, Ben-Gurion summoned Moshe Dayan and Shimon Peres to talk under the trees outside the villa at Sèvres, going over the precise plan for the invasion of Sinai so that he could make Israel's final decision on whether or not to go ahead. Moshe Dayan wanted to sketch out the military maneuvers, but no paper could be found. Instead, Peres offered him a cigarette packet. Dayan sketched a map of Sinai with arrows to show troop movements. When it was finished, he and Shimon Peres signed it; Ben-Gurion, with much laughter, did too. Thus the Israeli plan for the invasion of Egypt was literally drawn on the back of a cigarette packet, a historical document that would be carefully preserved.[4]

It was significant that all the Israelis negotiating at Sèvres were committed Ben-Gurionists, for this represented the victory of a militant type of Israeli politics. The Mapai (Workers' Party of the Land of Israel), the leading political force in Israel's early years, was more divided than has often been thought as to how to deal with the Arab world. Though there were many different opinions, the mainstream of Mapai formed two broad blocs: one behind David Ben-Gurion, another loosely aligned to Moshe Sharett.

Moshe Dayan defined the difference between the two men's approaches as he saw it: "'Ben-Gurionism' expressed firmness, activism, leadership, concentration on vital matters and going forward fearlessly even when doing so involves many risks and difficulties. 'Sharettism' symbolized accommodation, recoiling from action and acceptance of what is available at the expense of what is desirable."[5] A critical view of Dayan's definitions might suggest that Ben-Gurionism was firm to the point of inflexibility, obsessed with pushing the Palestinians out rather than finding a way to live alongside them, and so aggressive that it isolated Israel and prevented neighboring Arab states from making any move toward peace. Nuri es-Said, Iraq's prime minister, complained of Ben-Gurion that "he explodes all the time." It was impossible for any of the Arab leaders, even those like Nuri who were keen to serve Western interests, to negotiate with him.[6]

Sharettism's "acceptance of what is available at the expense of what is desirable" may have looked to some Israelis like weakness, but to others it was pragmatic. Sharett himself, speaking in 1957, characterized Ben-Gurionism and Sharett-tism respectively as "the military school" and "the political school."[7]

Sharett was much more familiar with Arab people than Ben-Gurion. He immigrated to what was then Ottoman Palestine from Russia with his family when he was just twelve, grew up partially in an Arab village, spoke Arabic, and knew some Arab history. He was no Arab sympathizer: after the war of 1948, he argued for Israel to keep its territorial gains and did not want the Arab refugees who had fled to return.[8] Yet he believed two things that Ben-Gurion did not: that a negotiated peace was possible and that a negotiated peace was desirable.

The reprisals carried out by the IDF at Qibya, Kinneret, and many other places, as well as the Gaza raid, had not sprung out of nowhere. They were the result of a long buildup of tension and the ascendance of the military school in Israeli politics. In the uneasy peace after 1948, Israel felt under threat from Palestinian refugees and its Arab neighbors. There were frequent infiltrations into Israeli-held territory. On many occasions these resulted in violence against Israeli civilians, including murders. Many of these infiltrations may have been made out of desperation by displaced people returning to harvest crops from their old farms or retrieve their lost possessions, but violent infiltrations were nonetheless a real and frightening fact for Israeli civilians. The question was not whether Israel should take action to stop fedayeen attacks. It was what sort of action would prove most effective: outright war, reprisal, diplomacy, outreach, or even—among the most radical thinkers—integration of Jews, Muslims, and Christians into one egalitarian community.

Even after taking considerable tracts of Arab land in the 1948 war, Israel was a small and fragile country. At the end of the previous century, Max Nordau—a founder of the World

Zionist Organization alongside Theodor Herzl—had proposed a new culture of "muscular Judaism." Crude antisemitic depictions of Jews in European culture sometimes caricatured them as weak but crafty intellectuals: too clever by half, cowardly, and sneaky. To counter this, Nordau suggested the "new Jews" focus on physical culture, outdoor activities, and sport. These new Jews, he believed, would be better placed to counteract stereotypes and fight for Zionism.

As Jewish settlements expanded in Palestine during the early twentieth century, this focus on physical culture became a survival strategy. Settlers had to be hardy enough for constant active labor and strong enough to defend themselves against attack. Ben-Gurion's lifelong devotion to making the rocky wastes of the Negev desert bloom was in part about proving that if Jews were tough enough, they could achieve anything. His kibbutz, Sde Boker, still functions today, with his modest house immaculately preserved; his dream of cultivating the Negev never entirely blossomed. Even so, as Israel formed, some of the ideals of muscular Judaism were taken up. These included compulsory national service, kibbutz living, and the idolization of strong, uncompromising men like Moshe Dayan and Ariel Sharon (and, to an extent, strong, uncompromising women like Golda Meir).

Muscular Judaism was a natural fit with the doctrine of *ein brera* (in Hebrew, "no alternative"). This meant that if Arabs aimed at the destruction of Israel, Israel had no choice but to fight back as powerfully as possible.[9] *Ein brera* was simple, strong, and uncompromising; undeniably muscular, even macho. "In retrospect, one might ask whether the deterrence policy that Israel pursued for three straight years [up to 1956] had failed," wrote Ariel Sharon in 1989. "Might some other approach have brought peace and security rather than a spiral of violence? At that time I was utterly convinced that there

was no alternative. I am even more convinced of that today."
Without his reprisal raids, Sharon believed that Israelis living
in border and desert settlements would have been forced to
evacuate. Israelis would have abandoned their periphery and
clustered in the center of the country, "and with that would
have come national demoralization and a ruinous contraction
of the nation's economic life." He did concede, though, that "it
was also true that deterrence had not stemmed the violence,
and that the actions had become larger and more costly for
ourselves as well as for the Arabs."[10]

Ben-Gurion stepped down from government in 1953, retir-
ing to Sde Boker. He was replaced by Moshe Sharett, in what
the American State Department regarded as a "potentially encouraging development": Sharett was more moderate and inclined toward peace.[11] The new president of the United States,
Dwight D. Eisenhower, was concerned about Ben-Gurion personally "because he was an extremist who might go the whole
way even to war to achieve his goals," as he explained to his
friend, the economist Eli Ginzberg.[12]

In February 1954, there were two dramatic developments
in the Arab world. The president of Syria was overthrown in
a coup, and it began to look as though Gamal Abdel Nasser
would oust Mohamed Neguib in Egypt. Sharett met with Ben-
Gurion, Dayan, and his militant defense minister, Pinhas Lavon, to discuss how to respond. Lavon and Ben-Gurion both
favored opportunistic military responses. Lavon wanted to
sever the Gaza Strip from Egypt. Ben-Gurion wanted to break
up Lebanon, carving a Christian-Maronite state out of its
southern territory, which he thought would be friendly to Israel. Both wanted to send troops into the demilitarized zone
in the north, along the border with Syria, on the pretext of
protecting Israeli settlements. Sharett, who at that stage had
some authority as prime minister, shut all of these ideas down.

Instead, he managed to open several secret channels for talks with Nasser's government, some through British and American intermediaries and some direct. (One of these channels was the British Labour MP Maurice Orbach, who claimed that in a personal letter Nasser warmly addressed the Israeli leader as "My brother Sharett.")[13] These contacts did not, over the course of 1954, get very far. Even so, they were an attempt—and, according to Egyptian sources, a genuine one—to move toward a diplomatic solution.[14]

While Sharett was trying to make peace, Pinhas Lavon allegedly took matters into his own hands. Israel had been organizing an information network in Cairo and Alexandria since 1951. Concerned that Britain was on the verge of signing its agreement to get out of Egypt—thus removing what some Israelis hoped was a restraint on Nasser—somebody in the Israeli administration, possibly Lavon, ordered a covert terrorist campaign. The Israeli network was to plant bombs in civilian targets such as stations, cinemas, and libraries, especially places linked to British and American interests. These attacks, it was hoped, would be blamed on the Muslim Brotherhood. The aim was to demonstrate to Britain that its interests would not be safe unless military occupation continued.

Israel's secret services were nowhere near as sophisticated in 1954 as they would later become. Operation Susannah, as it was codenamed, was a disaster. The first bombs went off on July 2, in a post office and a railway cloakroom. There were more on July 14, at the American information centers in Cairo and Alexandria, the American consular offices in both cities, and the American embassy. The United States was furious with Israel, which confused the Israelis—who had not realized that their top agent in Egypt was also working for the Egyptians and had leaked the plan. On July 23, a young man of European appearance attempting to bomb a Cairo cinema

accidentally set himself on fire instead. He was arrested and
was found to be an Egyptian Jew. He survived and revealed
his network. On October 5, several suspected spies were arrested in Egypt. They were tried in December and January:
one committed suicide in prison, one either committed suicide
or may have been killed by his interrogators, two were hanged,
and the rest were imprisoned. Within the Israeli government,
there was a fight about responsibility. Sharett had not known
about Operation Susannah. Ben-Gurion's diary indicates that
he had not either.[15] Lavon denied it and blamed Peres. Peres
and Dayan blamed Lavon. "Lavon developed obsessive suspicions," remembered Shimon Peres. "He suspected Dayan and
me of constantly conspiring against him."[16] Lavon eventually
resigned, though the question of his guilt or innocence would
surface again in the 1960s.[17] But the damage to Israel's reputation had been done in Washington and London, as it had in
Cairo.

Ben-Gurion returned to the government as defense minister after Lavon's resignation in early 1955, telling Sharett that
he wanted a "coalition" between the two of them. It would
not be a happy one. The factions lined up: Sharett controlling
the Foreign Ministry versus Ben-Gurion controlling Defense,
which he believed should take priority over all other foreign
policy considerations and be free of any "interference" from
the Foreign Ministry.[18] "Israelis don't respect Foreign Ministry types," observed the veteran Israeli journalist Uri Avnery.
"They respect Defense Ministry types." There was little in
the world of Judaism more muscular than the Israeli Defense
Ministry. Within less than a week of starting his new job,
Ben-Gurion had allowed the Gaza raid to go ahead. Egypt's
attitude to Israel transformed into one of outright aggression.
Though Sharett managed to hold Ben-Gurion back from some
of his most bellicose plans during the immediate aftermath

of the raid, his support in cabinet began to peel away. "Poor guy," remembered Avnery with a wry chuckle. "No influence whatsoever. Everybody despised him."[19] As fedayeen attacks increased, the fear felt by ordinary Israelis grew; Ben-Gurion's muscular line became more appealing.

When the Mapai lost five seats in Israel's 1955 general election, the loss was blamed on Sharett's weakness. Ben-Gurion told the party that Sharett was concerned only about "what the Gentiles will say," meaning the United Nations and foreign powers like Britain and the United States.[20] It took until November for the new government to be formed with Ben-Gurion back at its head. Against his better judgment, Sharett was persuaded to stay on as foreign minister. Gradually, over the course of the next few months and into the summer of 1956, Israel dropped attempts toward dialogue with Arab or international bodies and instead concentrated on the possibility of preventive war.

In early 1956, Eisenhower sent his close friend and deputy secretary of defense Robert Anderson to the Middle East in an attempt to push the Egyptians and the Israelis back into talks. Anderson explained the Alpha plan to Nasser, who nodded politely. Anderson left buoyant, imagining that Nasser had just agreed with everything he had said. But the Egyptian leader asked Kermit Roosevelt, accompanying Anderson, to stay behind.

"What was Mr. Anderson talking about?" Nasser asked. It turned out he had not understood anything Anderson had said, owing to the deputy secretary of defense's heavy Texas drawl.

"I think he believes that you've agreed to meet with Ben-Gurion to resolve all your differences," admitted Roosevelt.

"I could never do that. I'd be assassinated," Nasser exclaimed. "Go stop him. Don't let him send that cable!" Roosevelt hurried back to Anderson to withdraw any agreement

that had been accidentally implied.[21] Anderson had no more
luck with Ben-Gurion. If anything, his mission—and another
he tried a few weeks later—confirmed the sense already widespread in the military school of the Israeli government that
the Americans were of limited use. "Britain remained firmly
committed to the arms embargo that it had proclaimed with
the creation of the state [of Israel]," wrote Shimon Peres, "and
despite its political support, the United States never wavered
from the embargo it had imposed upon us at the height of the
War of Independence, when it stolidly denied us even the most
basic weapons." Israel shifted away from its alliance with the
United States and sought a new, more enabling friend: "Of all
the major arms producers in the world, France was the only
one that was not hostile to us and did not boycott us."[22]

The French government's interest in an Israeli alliance was
provoked by their loathing of Nasser for his involvement in
the Algerian rebellion and their hope that Israel might attack
him.[23] "The French asked, 'Who is the enemy of my enemy?'—
and it was Israel," explained Uri Avnery, who was no fan of
Peres. "So they invited Shimon Peres, a young man who had
no suit to go there. [He] had to order one quickly which did not
fit very well. The French called him 'the Fellow with the Blue
Suit.'"[24] Peres remembered: "I worked hard at our French connection, at times actually commuting between Tel Aviv and
Paris."[25]

Sharett finally resigned from the Israeli government in the
middle of June and was replaced as foreign minister by Golda
Meir, who was unquestioningly loyal to Ben-Gurion. It is impossible to say whether a Sharettian approach, had it prevailed,
would have led to anything like peace with the Arabs and a
resolution to the Arab-Israeli conflict. He was able to pursue his
strategy for less than eighteen months, and even during that
time was repeatedly undermined by his own Defense Ministry.

The men in charge of Israel's destiny in October 1956 were all of the muscular strain. They had wanted a preventive war with Egypt, and now they were going to get it. Their French friends would be at their back—and, they hoped, the French would hold the flightier British to their part in the production.

1200 Budapest

At midday, Imre Nagy broadcast over the radio to the people of Hungary. Again, he urged them to unite behind the government and allow it to reform itself. Again, even people who usually considered themselves his supporters were dismayed. "We had accumulated over the years a measure of moral and political capital," said Miklos Vásárhelyi, a Communist journalist dedicated to reforming the party, "but now Nagy had accepted the role of Prime Minister in a government which was otherwise the same as two days earlier—the government against which we had been fighting."[26] Nagy was, according to the Hungarian journalist Charles Gati, who glimpsed him at points during the revolution, "dazed, tired, and out of touch." He was also being sent conflicting messages from Moscow, as the Soviet leaders fumbled for a coherent policy.[27]

On one side, Soviet troops and the Hungarian AVH fought with Red Army resources; on the other, workers, students, and miscellaneous insurgents—including young children—fought back, mostly with equipment supplied by the sympathetic regular police. At the police headquarters, two Hungarian tanks arrived to secure the arsenal. To the horror of police chief Sándor Kopácsi, the inexperienced tank commanders started firing on everything they could see—including the British embassy, its Union flag now fluttering under machine-gun fire.

The telephone rang. "Sir, I am speaking to you lying down on the floor beneath a table in the salon," said the secretary of the British embassy to Kopácsi. "For the love of God, what's going on?"

"Listen, tell the ambassador that the men in those tanks are bumpkins from the boondocks who don't know what they are doing," Kopácsi explained. "Please relay our apologies and tell the ambassador that we do not wish to provoke the British Empire."[28] Eventually, he was able to signal the tanks to stop.

The rebels had occupied several buildings in Budapest and turned them into strongholds, including the Corvin Cinema and the Kilián Barracks. Substantial groups formed at Baross Square and Práter Street in Pest, and Széna Square in Buda. The Corvin had a gasoline store on its premises, which the rebels used to make Molotov cocktails to throw at tanks. "You know there were these Russian war movies that were on in the cinemas all the time those days," remembered Pál Kabelács, who was a nineteen-year-old rebel fighter at the time. "Those taught us what we should do and how to do it. Bottles filled with gasoline, Molotov cocktails, and so on."[29] In the old, narrow, and winding streets of Budapest, guerrilla tactics hampered Soviet heavy weaponry and vehicles. During the course of Wednesday, large fires were started all over the city.[30]

Colonel Pál Maléter, a senior Hungarian army officer, saw Soviet tanks fire on people near Corvin Alley. "I was horrified and deeply upset by what I saw," he said. "It didn't seem to me that these were fascists or counter-revolutionaries. All I saw were the bodies of kids lying in the street—and tanks being shot up by rifle fire." He blocked the entrance to the Kilián barracks with his own tank until the Soviets withdrew. When they did, he remembered looking "at a scene that might have been the end of a battle in a major war. Bodies lay all over the place, the wounded were screaming." Maléter's men took the doors off nearby houses to make stretchers, and carried the injured inside the barracks. The scene made Maléter rethink his own position: "As a result I informed the Minister of Defence that I was going over to the insurgents."[31]

At two p.m., Anastas Mikoyan arrived at the Communist Party headquarters in Budapest in an armored car. Though he and his fellow Soviet representatives had driven through shoot-outs on the journey, they reported back to Khrushchev the impression that everything was under control. "All the hotbeds of the insurgents have been crushed," they telegraphed that afternoon; "liquidation of the main hotbed, at the radio station, where about 4,000 people are concentrated, is still going on." They claimed the radio station group would not hold out beyond that evening.[32] It was a strange message—but perhaps Mikoyan had been sincere about delaying military action to give Imre Nagy his chance.

1500 Sèvres

At three p.m., Christian Pineau arrived back at Sèvres after his trip to London. He told the Israelis that Eden had seemed to him sturdy and keen to act. The British prime minister was ready to accept most of Israel's demands, and British representatives were on their way.[33] An hour and a half later, Patrick Dean arrived from London with Donald Logan, Lloyd's private secretary. They discussed the operation with the Israelis in vague terms: Dayan did not want to reveal everything he had drawn on the cigarette packet. "We will carry out such an operation that you will be able, without any doubt, to claim that there is danger to the Canal," Dayan promised. "We won't make a declaration [of war]. We'll simply smash 'em."[34] Dean and Logan went over the various issues again, as they had been directed.

The Israelis adjourned the meeting in the early evening. Shimon Peres disappeared with Guy Mollet and Maurice Bourgès-Maunoury for a private discussion. According to

Peres's memoirs, "It was here that I finalized with these two leaders an agreement for the building of a nuclear reactor at Dimona, in southern Israel . . . and the supply of natural uranium to fuel it."[35] The Israelis had been pushing for a nuclear reactor for some years. Thanks to the new leverage the collusion gave them with France, they got it. Israel's nuclear age had begun.[36]

During the adjournment, Dean and Logan could hear a typewriter clacking in the next room. At seven p.m., they were presented with a document in French to sign: the Protocol of Sèvres.

The British civil servants had a private word at this point. Eden had not told them that there would be anything written down and had not mentioned signing anything. On the other hand, he had not told them *not* to sign anything—and he had been concerned to hammer out the precise details of the plan. The protocol was only a summary of the discussions that had taken place over the past three days. Dean and Logan agreed that it would be useful to have such a record. Furthermore, they feared that if they refused to sign it, their behavior would look suspicious. And so it was signed by Pineau, Ben-Gurion, and Dean, with Dean emphasizing that his signature was subject to the approval of the British government.[37]

Clarissa Eden mistakenly believed Dean had been explicitly told not to negotiate or sign any text. "The Israelis' more high-powered representatives unfortunately, or fatefully, ran rings around us, and our representatives signed in the belief that the document was a record of the meeting—an *ad referendum*, subject to the approval of our government," she wrote later. "We were committed. The French and Israelis popped champagne in relief once Dean and Logan had departed."[38]

Ben-Gurion's military assistant Mordechai Bar-On remembered his boss receiving his signed copy of the Protocol of Sèvres, a secret treaty which put Israel on a level of diplomatic parity with Britain and France. "He folded the document with emphasized care and put it, almost with a ritualistic gesture, into his waistcoat pocket," Bar-On wrote. "His face was grave but shining with deep satisfaction."[39] After the British left, the French and the Israelis signed a second document. This agreed that the French air force could use Israeli airfields, and the French navy could use Israeli harbors. This would, of course, make the collusion plain to see, but the French and the Israelis were less concerned about secrecy than the British. Eden did not know the second agreement existed.[40]

Dean and Logan arrived back in London and presented the protocol to Eden. The prime minister was horrified. Lady Eden was wrong in thinking that Dean's signature on the protocol committed Britain to war. Had her husband disagreed with the plan—which Dean had made clear was subject to government approval—he could have withheld his approval or simply stood Britain's military forces down. He did not. Instead, Patrick Dean reported to a meeting at 10 Downing Street at eleven p.m., with Eden, Butler, Macmillan, Head, and Mountbatten present. All of them agreed to recommend the plan made in the Protocol of Sèvres to the full cabinet the next day.[41] The problem with the protocol was not its substance but the fact that it was a smoking gun. Eden demanded that all copies of the protocol, and the English translation the Foreign Office had rather efficiently already made, be brought to 10 Downing Street and destroyed.[42] He told the unfortunate Dean and Logan that they would have to get straight back on another plane to Paris the next day and tell the French and Israelis to destroy their copies, too.

There can be no doubt that Eden wanted to start a war. He just did not want anyone to know he had started it.

1130 Washington DC // 1930 Moscow

In the past couple of weeks, Foster Dulles's carefully constructed plans for SCUA and, beyond that, peace in the Middle East had begun to unravel—creating a distraction just as the anti-Soviet liberation movement he had for years hoped would emerge was bubbling up in Poland and Hungary. Britain and France were not cooperating publicly with him at the United Nations. Their diplomats were being uncommunicative in private, too. Israel and Jordan were bristling at each other. Egypt, Syria, and even the United States' preferred Arab nation, Saudi Arabia, were throwing their lots in with Jordan. And the government of France had taken to kidnapping Algerians. At least, the CIA called it a "kidnapping" in a National Security Council briefing, though someone crossed that word out by hand and replaced it with the apparently less controversial "seizure" (later in the same document, the author got away with "abduction"). The kidnapping, seizure, or abduction, the CIA judged, "has sharply worsened the French position throughout North Africa and has diminished the prospects for a political settlement in Algeria."

Ahmed Ben Bella and his FLN associates were now being interrogated, as Ben Bella himself put it, "by all the police there were in Algeria at that time," then by the military. The CIA believed he was "talking freely."[43] Anger at the kidnapping of the Algerians was still being expressed in violent street protests in Morocco (where, according to CIA sources, sixty people, mostly French, had now been killed) and Tunisia, as well as Algeria itself.

The CIA did not believe that Guy Mollet himself had been party to the kidnapping, "but felt forced to uphold it" once it became public in France.[44] Ben Bella, too, believed his capture was carried out by the military without Mollet's knowledge, but noted that his government "had the weakness to accept it."[45] When Christian Pineau found out, he went to see Mollet and found him—most unusually—in a fury.

"Whoever ordered this bullshit," Mollet said, "will lose us the war in Algeria." But the prime minister did not know who had ordered it.

"What can we do?" asked Pineau.

"We must not hesitate!" Mollet replied. "The prisoners must be released. We have no choice!" Mollet questioned his cabinet, but no one would admit to giving the order. Yet the cabinet was split, while wider parliamentary and public reaction in France to the kidnapping was overwhelmingly positive. Mollet felt he had to go with the tide. "I do not believe that in the current state of public and parliamentary opinion, we can afford to release the prisoners," he admitted to the cabinet after some consideration. "If we do that, the government would be overthrown tomorrow. The damage is done. We cannot go back."

Mollet and Pineau were roundly lauded for the action they had not ordered. A right-wing member of parliament pulled Pineau aside in a corridor at the National Assembly. "I'm sorry, I took you for a coward." he said. "I was mistaken."[46]

Perhaps, as Pineau suggested in his memoir twenty years later, this praise was painful for him and Mollet to accept. At the time, both men gave convincing impressions of supporting France's action vigorously. Impassioned representations were made to the government in Paris by the shocked Habib Bourguiba of Tunisia and the abjectly embarrassed sultan of Morocco, who had known nothing of the kidnap plot. The prime minister and foreign minister of Morocco flew to Paris and pleaded with Guy Mollet in person for an hour to release the Algerians.[47] If Mollet was moved, he did not show it.

Dulles was concerned about French actions and suspicious

of what the British might be up to. That morning, he had received a cable from Winthrop W. Aldrich, the United States' ambassador in London. Aldrich had been at a cocktail party with Walter Monckton, who had a few days before resigned as Britain's minister of defense. Monckton had drawn him aside and said his resignation was not prompted solely by physical exhaustion—his public excuse. Rather, he had gone because there was a chance Britain would use force against Egypt. This, Monckton felt, would be a "great blunder."[48] If it came to war, he could not be a part of it.

At eleven thirty a.m., Dulles went to tell Eisenhower about the French kidnapping. "I expressed great concern lest the British and French commit suicide by getting deeply involved in colonial controversies in an attempt to impose their rule by force on the Middle East and Africa," he wrote in his notes afterward. "The President indicated that he fully shared my concern in this respect."[49]

"Commit suicide" was the language that came to Dulles, and yet he did not know the worst of it. He did not know that the British and French were planning to collude with Israel in an invasion plan that had been drawn up on the back of a cigarette packet that morning. Yet the phrase "commit suicide" is notable for, ultimately, this is what Dulles hoped would happen. British and French power in the Middle East and North Africa had been so strong that it had been difficult for the Americans to gain a foothold. If the British and French were to destroy themselves in a flurry of retrograde imperialist brio, they would leave a vacuum. For Dulles, what was aggravating about this situation was not the breaking of British or French power, but the fact that this breakdown might come at a point when the Soviets were more ready and able to fill the vacuum than he was.

At seven minutes past six o'clock that evening, Foster Dulles telephoned Henry Cabot Lodge, the American ambassador to the United Nations, about the reports of fighting in Budapest. He raised the possibility of bringing the question of the Hungarian rebellion to the United Nations Security Council. Dulles described himself as being "worried that it will be said that here are the great moments and when they came and these [Hungarian] fellows were ready to stand up and die, we were caught napping and doing nothing."

Lodge compared the situation to Władysław Gomułka's defiance in Poland a few days earlier, but Dulles replied "that was different and there is more excuse to take this to the SC." Dulles considered asking the British and French to join in the condemnation of the Soviet Union. Both men agreed their European allies would be "reluctant," though Dulles thought the two NATO members could be prevailed upon to vote with the United States.[50]

As Budapest burned, Gomułka was addressing a crowd of more than a quarter of a million people outside the Palace of Science and Culture in Warsaw, Poland. There, the Soviets had decided to be conciliatory. Gomułka told the crowd that Soviet troops in Poland were now returning to their bases. He was cheered as he exhorted the people to go back to their jobs and work hard for a better future. Yet international correspondents noticed Hungarian flags among the banners in the audience. Thousands of youths marched through Warsaw that night to the Hungarian embassy, shouting anti-Soviet slogans. "Witnesses said that as the youths approached the Embassy, men in civilian clothes wearing red arm bands dashed into the procession and broke it up," reported the *Times* of London. "The demonstrators said the men punched and kicked them and beat them with rubber and wooden truncheons."[51]

The Soviets were under pressure. A delegation had arrived from Mao Tse-tung's China the day before, led by Liu Shao-chi, to consult on the Polish crisis. Mao believed Khrushchev had moved too quickly in recanting Stalinism. The mushrooming uprisings in Eastern Europe seemed to indicate that he was losing control. That day, the Soviet leadership were treated to a lengthy and blistering speech in the Kremlin by Liu, detailing scores of mistakes the Chinese thought the Soviets had made. "It was right to abandon the sword of Stalin since it was already useless," Khrushchev protested to Liu.[52] The Chinese were not convinced. In Moscow that evening, American ambassador Charles Bohlen attended an art exhibition. Both Khrushchev and Bulganin were present. "I had no opportunity to talk to either of them but both were grim and unsmiling," Bohlen reported, adding "more so than I have seen at any time previously."[53]

Khrushchev was now receiving reports contradicting Mikoyan's earlier message that the Hungarian rebellion had been contained. Fires and skirmishes continued in Budapest: twenty Soviet soldiers and around eighty Hungarians were dead, and protests had spread to other industrial cities around Hungary. These included many places that the Soviets, who saw themselves as the natural allies of factory workers, had imagined would be loyal.[54]

Yugoslav ambassador Veljko Mićunović saw Khrushchev at nearly midnight. "The principal and practically only subject of conversation was Hungary," he wrote in his diary. "Khrushchev looked very worried, to put it mildly." To Mićunović, Khrushchev blamed the Western powers for mischievous covert intervention in Hungary. "He alleges that the West is seeking a revision of the results of World War II, has started in Hungary, and will then go on to crush each socialist state in Europe one by one," Mićunović wrote. "But he claims that the West has miscalculated. He told me to take a message to Tito about the Soviet view of the situation and the readiness of the

Soviet Union to answer force with force. Khrushchev assured me that the Soviet leadership was completely unanimous on this." Khrushchev added that the Soviets would of course seek a political solution, but "gave the impression that he had no faith in such a solution."[55] In Moscow, just as in London, Paris, and Tel Aviv, the war hawks were gathering.

4

THURSDAY, OCTOBER 25, 1956
BLOODY THURSDAY

0800 Paris // 0900 Jerusalem; Cairo; Amman; Damascus

From Amman, it was officially announced that Jordan would join the Egyptian-Syrian military command, placing its Arab Legion forces under Gamal Abdel Nasser as commander in chief. Nasser had been trying to secure this alliance since the Baghdad Pact was signed in February 1955. It came together at this moment because, like the United States, he believed Israel was gearing up to attack Jordan.

Secretly, the Jordanian general Ali Abu Nuwar told the Egyptian general Abdel Hakim Amer that, based on the Israelis' positions, he thought they might be aiming at Egypt. Amer doubted this.[1] Publicly, Abu Nuwar confirmed reports that Egypt and Saudi Arabia had offered to replace about $30 million a year in financial aid to Jordan if Jordan dropped its defense treaty with Britain.[2] In reality, though, neither Britain nor Jordan wanted to let the treaty drop. The Jordanians reassured the British ambassador that they intended to continue their friendship with Britain alongside their friendship with Egypt. The British were keen to prop Jordan up, for fear that if the monarchy there fell, Iraq might be next.[3]

For those who knew about the conspiracy between Britain, France, and Israel, the new Arab alliance appeared potentially useful. The military consolidation of these Arab states under Egyptian direction would give the British and French evidence to back up their claim that Nasser's influence was growing and threatening regional peace.[4] The alliance would also give the Israelis a pretext to justify their mobilization.

Though the new agreement with Jordan was an achievement for politicians in Cairo, the predominant mood there remained tense. The Egyptian government knew that momentum was being lost in the discussions about the Suez Canal at the United Nations. Despite Egypt making every possible concession, Britain's commitment to negotiations seemed weaker and less sincere. There was concern that London might be trying something else, the American ambassador in Cairo reported, perhaps related to the tension between Israel and Jordan or the unreliable alliance between Jordan and Iraq. These, it seemed to him, might be "an alternative to the Suez Canal dispute which the British may no longer consider an effective means of 'getting Nasser.'"[5]

At the United Nations, the Israeli ambassador Abba Eban—who did not know what had been agreed at Sèvres—spoke at length on the tension between his nation and Jordan. Eban declared that the government of Israel had no belligerent intentions toward its Arab neighbors: "It will start no war. It will initiate no violence." All of the violence so far, he argued, was in response to acts by Jordan. "Not once have the Israel forces taken up arms except in reaction to prior Jordanian aggression, and, even then, only after patiently suffering death and destruction for months on end without any response." While pledging not to start a war, though, he made it clear that Israel would defend itself: "If we are not attacked we shall not strike; if we are attacked we fully reserve the inherent right of self-defense."[6]

In Israel, Ben-Gurion returned to his home. After the stresses and strains of the previous few days, he took to bed with a high temperature and fever. But he made sure to give his favored young commander Ariel Sharon his orders in person. "I could almost feel the wings of history brushing the air," remembered Sharon.[7] Moshe Dayan went to the army headquarters to retune the plan for the invasion of Sinai along the lines decided at Sèvres. The IDF began to mobilize.

1000 London // 1100 Paris; Budapest

The British chief whip, Edward Heath, arrived at the cabinet room shortly before the meeting was due to start. Anthony Eden was already there. He was standing by his chair, "bright-eyed and full of life."

"We've got an agreement!" the prime minister said. "Israel has agreed to invade Egypt. We shall then send in our own forces, backed up by the French, to separate the contestants and regain the Canal."

Eden admitted that the Americans would not be informed about this plan. "He concluded, somewhat unnervingly, that 'this is the highest form of statesmanship,'" Heath remembered. According to his own recollection, he tried to change Eden's mind. The prime minister "simply reiterated that he could not let Nasser get away with it."[8]

The cabinet meeting went ahead at ten a.m. Eden told his colleagues that the Israelis were massing their forces to attack Egypt: "They evidently felt that the ambitions of Colonel Nasser's Government threatened their continued existence as an independent State and that they could not afford to wait for others to curb his expansionist policies." If Israel did invade Egypt, an Anglo-French force could issue an ultimatum and require both parties to withdraw ten miles from the Canal. If

Egypt failed to comply, he noted, "there would be ample justification for Anglo-French military action against Egypt in order to safeguard the Canal." He also admitted, "We must face the risk that we should be accused of collusion with Israel." He brushed this off on the not especially convincing grounds that Israel might have become involved anyway, had Britain and France gone ahead with an attack on Egypt earlier that summer.

Four objections were immediately raised by members of the cabinet. First, intervention might offend the United States and damage the special relationship. Second, if both sides were asked to withdraw ten miles from the canal, that meant the Egyptians would have to withdraw farther into their own territory while the Israelis would still be on Egyptian soil, far in advance of their own border. Third, Britain and France might be accused of breaking the Tripartite Declaration. Fourth, it might undermine the United Nations.

Each of these four points would prove significant, yet all four were overridden at the meeting. One of the conclusive arguments in favor of action with the French was simply that it had already been planned. "A crisis in the Middle East could not now long be delayed," said the minutes. "If . . . force might ultimately have to be used, would it not be used more effectively and with more limited damage if we acted promptly now when an Anglo-French operation was already mounted?" The cabinet agreed to Eden's war.[9]

Afterward, Selwyn Lloyd returned to the Foreign Office. His face, Anthony Nutting remembered, showed strain.

"When is it to happen?" Nutting asked.

"October 29: next Monday," Lloyd replied. "And now, I must call a meeting to draft the ultimatum which we shall be sending out. You are welcome to stay and help us if you'd like to." The British government would afterward maintain that the ultimatum Lloyd was already drafting had been issued in response to Israel's "surprise" action four days later.

"You seem to have forgotten our talk of last week," Nutting replied. "Or perhaps you did not take me seriously. But I meant what I said. I cannot stay in the Government if this sordid conspiracy is carried out. You can draft your own ultimatum without me."

Lloyd told him he had discussed Nutting's threat to resign with Eden. "He's very put out, of course," he said, "but he doesn't want to lose you, and if you feel you cannot stay at the Foreign Office, he'd be very willing to give you some other department."

Nutting refused the offer. He agreed to continue coming into the Foreign Office for the meantime to avoid embarrassing or exposing the government.

Later, at the Commons, he met an old friend, Walter Monckton. "He made no bones about his view that Eden was a very sick man," Nutting remembered. "He had always been excitable and temperamental, but in the last few months he had seemed to be on the verge of a breakdown."

Looking for an explanation for Britain's behavior during the crisis, many at the time seized on the idea that Eden's ill health had affected his judgment. When official documents were released, though, it became clear that members of the cabinet, as well as others in political and military circles, had known of the Suez plot—and some, such as Harold Macmillan, had been far more bullish about it than they had wanted to admit later. Whatever Eden's mental difficulties were at this point, they cannot explain other men's enthusiasm for the plan.

Yet the question of Eden's health cannot be written out of the story entirely, for so many of his friends and critics at the time insisted it was a factor. At the very least, it does provide one possible explanation for why a man who had been a stalwart public supporter of the League of Nations and the United Nations from the beginning, who was considered a master of diplomacy, who had a long history of sympathy for Arab causes and of moderate and respectful behavior toward Egypt in particular, might over the course of a few months in 1956 pursue a course of action that seemed designed to undermine all his life's work. "Who can wonder that in the present crisis he was so edgy and indecisive?" wrote the military historian Correlli Barnett. "His were the dithers of a bishop nerving himself to enter a brothel."[10]

Eden had been acting irrationally toward Nasser and Egypt since Jordan's dismissal of Glubb Pasha in March. His level of tension alarmed colleagues then; his grip on his physical and mental health appeared to be loosening. He gave a weak performance in the House of Commons in early March discussing the Baghdad Pact and Egyptian policy. "Eventually Eden sat down and everybody was saying after it that he really could not last much longer," the leader of the Opposition, Hugh Gaitskell, recorded in his diary. "He looked thin and tired and ill and one could not help feeling really rather sorry for him."[11] In late March, Foster Dulles had a meeting with Eisenhower, Prime Minister Louis St. Laurent of Canada, and Lester Pearson, the Canadian secretary of state for external affairs. "I said I had felt some concern because of the rather jittery attitude evidenced by the British," Dulles wrote in his memorandum on the meeting. "Mr. Pearson said that he was very much concerned and particularly worried about Sir Anthony Eden. He said he had great admiration for Eden. On the other hand, he felt that he was not reacting very well to the strains and pressures of the present situation. He referred to the fact that his father had been quite eccentric."[12]

"Eden seemed to alternate between phases of sublime confidence and dreadful misdoubt [sic] during the months of crisis and trauma," wrote Chester Cooper of the American embassy in London. "He was acutely sensitive to everything that was happening, but seemed sometimes unaware of and sometimes excessively obsessed by the dire consequences that dogged his every move. Eden appeared to be functioning on a level 10 percent removed from reality. It was a critical 10 percent and virtually guaranteed that his Suez policy, flawed as it was, would turn into a grave national and personal tragedy."[13]

Just three weeks earlier, with the British case for war foundering, the Americans refusing to support him, and criticism piling up on all sides, it had all become too much. On Friday October 5, Eden had been visiting his wife, Clarissa, who was in University College Hospital for a dental examination, when he had suffered a sudden collapse and needed to be admitted himself. "I suddenly felt chilled to the bone," he remembered. "In a few minutes a severe ague fell upon me and I was put to bed, somewhat ignominiously, in a neighbouring room. I did not know much more after that for a while, but I was told later that my temperature had risen to 106°."[14] Though he stayed in the hospital only from Friday to Monday, his health took a serious knock. He was thereafter, according to one biographer, "in constant need of drugs."[15] One of his closest aides later claimed that he used amphetamines as well as heavy painkillers, while a senior Whitehall official confirmed that he was "practically living on Benzedrine."[16]

Harold Macmillan destroyed his diaries from the high period of the Suez crisis, but wrote afterward that "Eden was a very sick man" by the time of his resignation.[17] Eden's doctor told Rab Butler that "Anthony could not live on stimulants any more."[18] Eden himself denied all of this in his memoirs. "My critics wrote that I was calm under the strain," he claimed. "I felt at ease; there was a reason for this. From the first I was convinced that the course on which we had decided was the only acceptable one in a grim choice of difficulties. I did not expect it to be popular, but my colleagues and I had been grappling with the deteriorating situation for months and we were confident in our cause. That makes for calm."[19]

Eden's 1959 memoirs are an extraordinary read, often betraying a disconnection from the truth so profound as to indicate that he must have been engaged in a deliberate project of denial, whether conscious or unconscious. He refused to admit any collusion with Israel; he insisted his own motives stemmed purely from concern for international trade, for Arab-Israeli peace, and to prevent Nasser from becoming Hitler. He blamed the United States for everything that had gone wrong for him at Suez. He repeated throughout that public opinion in Britain was with him, at one point pathetically quoting in his own defense a fan letter written to his wife by a London transport worker: "If a bus driver agrees—he must be right—I personally thank God we've got one man who's not afraid to do the right thing."[20] His colleagues attempted to dissuade him from publishing. "I think it will damage his own reputation so much," wrote Selwyn Lloyd, who read a draft of the manuscript. "Many of the things said in it seem rather petty and to indicate personal malice and resentment of criticism. . . . I feel that to publish the book in anything like its present form is a mistake from his personal point of view."[21] Rather than providing a counterargument to the suggestion that Eden's mental health may have been on the rocks during the Suez Crisis, Eden's memoirs paint a picture of a man who was still, three years later, unwilling or unable to engage with reality.

After Nutting had seen Monckton, he considered dragging the Suez affair into the light himself: "I was seized with a sudden wild desire to make straight for the American Embassy and there to tell the Ambassador everything I knew in the hope that this would bring Eisenhower to weigh in and prevent us and the French from going ahead." The Americans, he knew, already suspected collusion between France and Israel. It would take only a few words to whisk the veil off the whole operation. That might, he knew, save his country's reputation. (Monckton, as the American archives show, had already hinted to the Americans the previous evening that there would be a war. It is not clear whether Nutting knew this.)

Nutting could not do it. To blow the whistle might save his country, but it would betray his government. "Yet, looking back on that fateful October afternoon, I wish in more ways than one that I had yielded to my first impulse. No one can tell how we should have then ended up; but that we should have lost less than we did in reputation and influence cannot be denied."[22]

Meanwhile, Patrick Dean and Donald Logan arrived back at the Quai d'Orsay in Paris, to ask Christian Pineau to destroy the remaining two copies of the Protocol of Sèvres. Pineau was unimpressed with the request and pointed out that the Israelis had already taken theirs back to Tel Aviv. He said he would make inquiries, and he had Dean and Logan shown into a grand reception room.

Dean and Logan waited for some time, but Pineau did not return. At lunchtime, they decided to venture out—to find they had been locked in. Aware that they were there on a secret mission, they did not dare shout for help or hammer on the door in case somebody unauthorized came to rescue them.[23] So they sat in the room and waited.

1200 Paris; Budapest

While Dean and Logan were twiddling their thumbs, shocking things were happening in Budapest. Overnight, Soviet forces had occupied much of the city. The loyal Radio Kossuth had been announcing since dawn that "Soviet troops liquidated the counter-revolutionary putsch attempt on the night of October 24."[24] The rebels had not been liquidated, for incidents of fighting broke out intermittently across the city in many places throughout the morning. The Soviets on the ground—Anastas Mikoyan, Mikhail Suslov, and the head of the KGB, Ivan Serov—were in the Communist Party head-quarters on Academy Street that morning and could hear the gunfire. They lashed out at Ernő Gerő.

"You stampeded us into an ill-advised commitment of So-viet troops through an exaggerated and distorted picture of the situation," Mikoyan told Gerő.[25] Suslov ordered him to re-sign. János Kádár—a loyal Communist, but not one tainted by too close an association with the old Stalinists like Rákosi and Gerő—was brought in to replace him.

Gerő's fall was not made public immediately. At the same time as he was being given the sack, a crowd of unarmed demonstrators marched through the city, demanding his resignation. Among them were some Russian speakers, who addressed the Soviet troops: "Russian friends. Do not shoot! They have tricked you. You are not fighting against counter-revolutionaries. We Hungarians want an independent, demo-cratic Hungary. You are not shooting at fascists but at workers, peasants and university students."[26] The police chief in Buda-pest, Sándor Kopácsi, saw Soviet troops get out of their tanks and talk to these Hungarians—even embrace them.[27]

The protesters, estimated at between three thousand and twenty thousand in number, assembled in Kossuth Square, op-posite a line of Soviet tanks guarding parliament. It seemed to some observers that Soviet vehicles and troops deliberately "shepherded" various protesters from around the city into Kossuth Square. The crowd that gathered was, by all reports, peaceful.

Eyewitness reports of what happened next are confused and

contradictory. Some reported the Soviet tanks fired straight into the crowd, and others reported that AVH snipers began shooting first from the windows of the Ministry of Agriculture and Ministry of Defense, as well as from the rooftops. It has been suggested that some Hungarian border guard units also fired on their compatriots. There were reports of counterfire, including some Soviet forces attempting to defend the crowd. The firing went on for about fifteen minutes. Then, as the survivors were trying to flee or to help the injured, they were shot at again, for another fifteen minutes.

"Am typing on floor," began an unsigned teletype message to Washington DC from the American legation, just a couple of streets away from Kossuth Square. "A big battle has just took [*sic*] place in front of Legation seems to have gone towards Parliament seems all Americans still OK and safe. Street fighting again flaring up with tanks fighting it out at present." The writer reported heavy firing and the presence of large numbers of Soviet tanks and troops. The officers of the legation, he wrote, were "all in TELEX room huddling on floor to avoid gunfire."[28]

The variance in estimates of the number killed in Kossuth Square and its surroundings on what would become known to Hungarians as Bloody Thursday are considerable. The subsequent Soviet-authorized government investigation suggested a mere 22, and even that was not admitted publicly: for thirty years after Bloody Thursday, no atrocity was officially acknowledged. Some eyewitnesses put the total casualties lying in the square in the hundreds, which was probably accurate, and the total dead, including those who later died of their injuries, at 1,000, which is probably far too high. The journalist John Mac-Cormac, reporting from Budapest for the *New York Times*, saw a dozen bodies in Kossuth Square and estimated total casualties at 170.[29] The British embassy observed that twelve trucks were brought in to take the bodies away, but it would have been difficult for its witnesses to establish how many of these bodies were dead and how many were merely injured.[30] Recent archival research by the Hungarian Institute for the History of the 1956 Revolution has suggested 60 to 80 were killed and around 100 to 150 wounded.[31] As for who ordered the massacre, it has been suggested by former Soviet security officers that the man responsible was the head of the KGB himself, Ivan Serov.[32]

The Soviets could suppress official mention of the Bloody Thursday massacre, but they could not stop news spreading among the people. As it did, more and more Hungarians decided to fight. An estimated two thousand people besieged the American legation, appealing for intervention. A similar crowd gathered outside the British embassy.[33] Imre Nagy spoke on the radio, emphasizing his commitment to reform and a more broadly based government—and pledging that he would "initiate negotiations" with the Soviets, "including the question of withdrawal of Soviet military forces."[34] This did not wholly convince the people of Budapest. Another three divisions of the Red Army—twenty thousand men—arrived in the Hungarian capital from Romania and the Soviet Union that afternoon.

At four p.m. Paris time, half an hour after Nagy's broadcast, Christian Pineau finally returned to liberate Patrick Dean and Donald Logan from the reception room at the Quai d'Orsay. Both the French and Israeli governments, he informed them, declined to destroy their copies of the Protocol of Sèvres. Dean and Logan's hours of waiting had been in vain. They returned to Eden with the news that two copies of a document proving Britain's guilt still existed somewhere in the world.[35]

1500 Washington DC // 2000 London // 2100 Paris

That evening, Guy Mollet's government called and won a vote of confidence in the French parliament prompted by events in Algeria and Suez. His administration had faced two resignations over the kidnapping of the FLN rebels: those of the undersecretary of state for Moroccan and Tunisian affairs and of the ambassador to Tunisia. Mollet took an assertive line on the arrest of the rebels. He recognized, he said, that there would be serious repercussions in countries like Tunisia and Morocco, but this was not France's fault.

The town of Meknes in Morocco was still in a dire state. Two French policemen and five European civilians were killed, taking violent deaths of Europeans there in the previous forty-eight hours to a total of forty-one. A crowd of Europeans demonstrated outside the French police headquarters, demanding weapons. The Moroccan government refused to send its troops to protect French lives. In Tunisia, there were clashes between Tunisian troops and a French military convoy trying to cross the border from Algeria. Habib Bourguiba, the prime minister, was defiant in his address to parliament, saying: "We prefer death to degradation, and battle to servitude." The impassioned parliamentarians rose to sing the Tunisian national anthem.[36]

The Egyptian minister of state, Anwar Sadat, wrote, "France, a rotten, decrepit state, has become a third-class country which wants to make a show of force at the expense of the Arabs." He added a comment that would only confirm French suspicions that Nasser was involved in Algeria, arguing that the rebellion there "is closely linked with the struggle about the Suez Canal and that in the Jordan-Israel border region."[37] Meanwhile, the Moroccan government recalled its ambassador to France and turned to the United States, with the usual implication that its next option would be to go to the Soviet Union. An "authoritative Moroccan" was quoted by the *New York Times* saying, "The United States can save North Africa for the West if she helps us now. France is pushing us towards the East."[38]

At the same time Mollet was defending himself in Paris, Anthony Eden was hosting a dinner party in London for the American general Alfred Gruenther, NATO's supreme Allied commander in Europe. Among the guests was the first sea lord, Lord Mountbatten, who harangued Eden about the planned war. "He started on the doorstep," remembered Clarissa Eden, "and Edwina [Lady Mountbatten] interrupted him and said, 'You are being very foolish, Dickie,' although she presumably agrees with him." Mountbatten wrote a few days later to Eden of their conversation: "You told Edwina and me that you realised how much I hated making the preparations which had been ordered." A stalwart defender of her husband, Lady Eden thought she knew the reason for Mountbatten's objection to the planned operation: "The Chiefs of Staff are very reluctant to have the Israelis as allies."[39]

Conversation beyond the doorstep must have been more discreet, for there were Americans present. The American ambassador, Winthrop Aldrich, was among the guests and had a chance to talk both to Eden and Lloyd. "Eden was in mellow, relaxed mood in contrast [with] recent occasions on which I have seen him," Aldrich cabled to Foster Dulles in Washington. "He expressed [the] view that Israel-Jordan situation and Egyptian involvement therein is of more fundamental importance even than Suez problem. On latter, Lloyd said there have been relatively few new developments." Lloyd was frustrated at what he perceived as the Americans' lack of support: he felt "that this course is driving him into closer alliance with France and away to some extent from us, which he deplores. Among other things, he believes the French are politically inept and may be counted on to make major political blunders, such as the arrest of the five Algerian leaders."[40]

All these tidbits of information that Eden and Lloyd were feeding to the American ambassador were designed to throw Dulles off the scent, distracting him from Suez with the new situation between Israel and Jordan and falsely claiming that the British were reluctant to get into any action with the French.

In Washington, though, attention was focused on Hungary. The minutes of a meeting of the Special Committee on Soviet and Related Problems at the State Department that day note: "We're considering UN action"—first through the Security Council, then possibly the Human Rights Committee or the General Assembly.[41] Just after five p.m., Foster Dulles telephoned Eisenhower (who was in New York) to discuss whether to circulate a letter in the United Nations Supreme Court about Hungary. Circulating a letter was a procedural move to raise the issue without putting it on the agenda or inscribing a resolution: a low-profile way to make a fuss. Allen Dulles also raised this possibility in a conversation with his brother and suggested it might be worth trying to team up with India's Jawaharlal Nehru. Though he knew Nehru was committed to remaining nonaligned, he suggested that "if he [Nehru] gets consulted and feels he is in things, he would operate differently."

The president and secretary of state were of different minds as to how to operate in the United Nations. Eisenhower wanted to "act in deliberate fashion," and bring in other NATO countries. Dulles thought the other NATO countries "will be reluctant to come along with us—as they will interpret it as being an election move" by Eisenhower with less than two weeks to go until the presidential election. Dulles was also concerned about the United States alone condemning Soviet repression in Hungary at the United Nations, because "it might look as though we were in the back of it."

The thought that it might then look as if the Americans had provoked the Hungarian rebellion did worry Eisenhower. "The worst thing, said the Pres., would be to be thought of as guilty of spurious interest."[42] An essential truth about Eisenhower and Dulles's policy on the Soviet Union is revealed in these minutes. Though they talked tough for American voters, both men tacitly accepted a state of coexistence with the Soviets. Eisenhower was consistently more concerned than Dulles about human rights violations and the cost of violent conflict, but he was also mindful of the global picture.

That night, Eisenhower spoke at an election rally in New York. "Twenty thousand roaring partisans inside Madison Square Garden and 10,000 relatively quiet ones who stayed outside, unable to get in, far surpassed the crowd attracted two nights earlier in the same arena by Adlai E. Stevenson, the Democratic Presidential nominee," noted the *New York Times*. The fire department had to order the doors closed. Eisenhower's speech called for a strong military—but a policy of peace. Owing to the tight schedules of radio and television broadcasts and the fact that he was interrupted forty-eight times by cheering, Eisenhower had to dump large chunks of his speech as he spoke. One of the lines he dropped had said that it was the purpose of the United States "to strengthen the love of liberty everywhere—and to do all within our peaceful power to help its champions." Some journalists, who had received copies of the speech beforehand, noticed this omission and queried whether the line had been removed because the word *peaceful* appeared to rule out American military intervention in Hungary. Eisenhower's press officer said the president stood by the pre-prepared draft of his speech.[43]

In reality, Eisenhower was not considering intervention, for the reasons he had discussed with Dulles. If something could be done through the United Nations—with the involvement of allies such as Britain and France, and better still the support of nonaligned nations like India—joint action might be a possibility. But the United States would not go it alone. What the Soviets were doing in Hungary was bad. The fallout from a Soviet-American war could be much worse.

5

FRIDAY, OCTOBER 26, 1956
THE TWO MUSKETEERS

1000 London

In London that morning, Eden received a report from the chiefs of staff suggesting that the consequences of Britain and France invading Egypt would be terrible. The Egyptian economy, infrastructure, communication, and civil administration would be in disarray; public health would be threatened, and "an unpredictable proportion of the Egyptian people would be hostile." It warned of guerrilla action and labor strikes. It pointed out that an uncooperative government might still be in power: "In this case it would first be necessary to overthrow such a government and create conditions favourable to the setting-up of one prepared to co-operate." Occupying only the Canal Zone, it suggested, was not feasible: "We should be prepared to occupy Cairo and possibly Alexandria." The commitment of British military power required by such an operation was so large—three or four divisions, naval and air force units, plus administrative and other support—that Britain would not be able to meet any other emergencies if they arose, except by pulling troops out of NATO. Furthermore, national service and reservist levels would have to be maintained. The Chiefs of Staff recommended that occupation of Egypt should be avoided altogether or restricted to a minimum. Beyond that, it was airily hoped that Britain would not have to cope with strife in the rest of the Arab world on the grounds that "the reaction of the oil-producing states to the Suez crisis [so far] suggests that their governments are well aware of the need in their own financial interest to maintain the flow of oil to Europe." It did, however, acknowledge that these governments might struggle against internal dissent.

Eden was upset by this memorandum. Even though it was signed by Dickson, Mountbatten, Templer, and Boyle, on the front page a hand added in pencil, "Spoken to Gen. Stirling. This was written by the Staffs who were not in the picture."[1] The picture, presumably, would have included full details of the planned collusion with Israel. But all the Chiefs of Staff had put their names to it, indicating the concern among them about invading Egypt under any circumstances. The fact that the potentially enormous consequences of ousting Nasser were only just being considered in late October indicates how unrealistic some of the military planning that summer had been.

The British and French armed forces had been planning a joint military operation against Egypt since Nasser's nationalization of the Canal Company in July, under the name Operation Musketeer. Eden and Mollet had wanted to invade immediately, but were told that neither of their nations' militaries was in a position to launch anything other than an air attack on such short notice. "Unless we could fly all the forces needed, they [would have] had to swim" to Egypt, Eden wrote. "The nearest place from which to swim was Malta, a thousand miles away."[2] He was not serious about making them swim. The operation would require landing craft, which could be launched only from Malta's harbor. The British base in Cyprus

was much closer to Egypt—250 miles away—but had no suitable harbor.

In the first hours after Nasser's nationalization, there was
hope in London that the United States might join an invasion.
Remembering this some years later, Eisenhower remarked:
"And of course, the British themselves, only two years earlier,
had refused to touch the Indochina affair, and so we thought
now their excuse for trying to get us to participate in an attack
on Nasser was just thin. It wouldn't work." Eisenhower made
it clear from the beginning that he could not support an attack on Egypt: "We said, 'We don't believe there's any legal or
moral grounds that will stand up before world opinion or the
World Court, for any interference with that thing by force.'"[3]
To the dismay of the French, the British could neither logistically nor, under pressure from the United States, politically
invade in August.

Yet the British did want to go ahead. As Foster Dulles com-
menced his long summer of negotiations, Britain and France
planned their joint operation in secret (or at least in semi-
secret: troop, equipment, and naval moves could not be hidden
entirely). Working together was not easy: Britain and France
had been rivals for centuries. While Agincourt, Yorktown, and
Waterloo may have been distant memories, their fierce competition in the Middle East over oil and territory was a live issue.

Control of Operation Musketeer planning was centered
in Britain. There was, from the beginning, friction among
the chiefs of staff there. "They all argue with one another,"
complained civil servant Evelyn Shuckburgh. He complained
about the chairman of the chiefs of staff committee, Marshal of the Royal Air Force Sir William Dickson, in his diary,
writing that he "has an ulcer and talks too much." Dickson
himself admitted that he had taken the job only because he
thought it would be easy. "I was told that Defence would be

a piece of cake, a rest cure."[4] According to Shuckburgh, Louis
Mountbatten, Earl Mountbatten of Burma—first sea lord and
chief of the naval staff, who was promoted to admiral of the
fleet on October 22—"is full of undigested bright ideas and is
really a simpleton though very nice."[5] Air Chief Marshal Der-
mot Boyle was less objectionable. The least ineffective of them
was General Sir Gerald Templer, chief of the Imperial General Staff, but he had blighted his record in the Middle East
the previous year with a catastrophic visit to Jordan. During
an official meeting, he had lost his temper with King Hussein and his ministers, shouted at them, and ended up punch-
ing a table.[6] For reasons not connected to the table but very
much connected to Templer's visit, anti-British riots broke out
throughout Jordan. The prime minister of Jordan had to resign.[7] "The British never had any sense in the Middle East,"
mused Eisenhower on hearing of the disaster.[8] Furthermore,
Templer loathed Mountbatten, once saying to him across a
dinner table, "Dickie, you're so crooked that if you swallowed
a nail you'd shit a corkscrew!"[9]

These fractious old men were supposed to coordinate a plan
with General Charles Keightley, the appointed commander in
chief of Operation Musketeer, and General Hugh Stockwell,
the appointed land force commander. The outline plan for an
operation would take weeks or months to set up. Forces had to
be moved within striking distance of Egypt before an ultimatum would be issued. If Nasser did not accept the ultimatum,
there would be a maritime blockade and air bombardment.
If this did not break him, there would be an assault on the
north end of the Suez Canal and on Alexandria. The Joint Intelligence Committee warned as early as August 3, 1956, that
this needed to be a major operation: "Should Western military
action be insufficient to ensure early and decisive victory, the
international consequences both in the Arab States and else-

where might give rise to extreme embarrassment and cannot be forecast."[10]

The plan was hampered by a triple objective: to destroy the Egyptian army, to bring down Nasser, and to secure the canal under international control.[11] If the assault began at Alexandria, it would threaten Nasser but not secure the canal. If it began at Port Said, it might secure the canal but not threaten Nasser. The British cabinet had trouble deciding which of these things it wanted more, and Eden reacted angrily when he was asked for clarification of the operation's objectives by Mountbatten and Keightley, so they remained confused.[12] In August, the decision was made that it would begin at Alexandria, and a psychological warfare component was added to debase Egyptian morale. D-Day was set for September 15.

Viscount Montgomery of Alamein, formerly the chief of the Imperial General Staff and one of the most distinguished commanders of World War II, was then in Paris. Eden asked him to return to Britain to discuss Musketeer.

"Will you tell me what is your object?" Montgomery asked. "What are you trying to do?"

"To knock Nasser off his perch," replied Eden.

"I said that if I were his military adviser—and I made it very clear that I was not—that object would not do," remembered Montgomery in 1962. "I should need to know what was the political object when Nasser had been knocked off his perch, had been 'hit for six,' because it was that which would determine how the operation was best carried out, what was the best position for our Forces, and so on. In my judgment, it was the uncertainty about the political object of our leaders which bedevilled the Suez operation from the beginning."[13]

In the first flush of anger about Nasser's nationalization of the Canal Company in July, there was considerable support from the British press and public, and from the Labour opposition, for military action against Nasser. As tempers cooled, this dissipated. The leader of the opposition, Hugh Gaitskell, warned Eden off attacking Egypt in August in a series of private letters and meetings, stating that the Labour Party would not support any use of force unless Nasser were first condemned by the United Nations.[14] Gaitskell's concerns about intervention in Egypt arose despite his long-standing support for Israel. At the time, Zionism was popular on the democratic left internationally; as a result of his sympathies for it, Gaitskell was not always well received in the Arab world. "I accuse the leader of the British Labour Party of being a puppet and hireling of world Zionism," Anwar Sadat had said on Voice of the Arabs radio in April 1956, after Gaitskell had criticized Eden for allowing the sale of British tanks to the Egyptians. "It is well known to all of us that he is married to an ardent Zionist Jewess. . . ."[15] Gaitskell's wife, Dora, had been born in Latvia into a Jewish family.

Musketeer preparations continued despite the lack of political support. British reservists were called up, obliged to abandon their civilian lives to wait for a war to begin. "Most of the reservists bore up cheerfully and without complaint," Eden claimed. "A few became restive."[16] Yet by August 10, opinion polls were showing only around one third of Britons interviewed favored military action even if diplomacy failed.[17] Moderate Conservatives, such as Walter Monckton, expressed queasiness at the prospect of a war. So increasingly did Mountbatten, though he was advised by the political chiefs at the Admiralty that it would be unconstitutional to say this to Eden directly. He was obliged to restrict himself to expressing his opinions loudly and repeatedly in the joint chiefs of staff committee. There, he claimed that the Egyptian people were solidly behind Nasser, that there was no workable plan for a new government in the event of Nasser being overthrown, and that Operation Musketeer would create long-lasting disorder throughout the Middle East.[18]

Nonetheless, as the politicians and diplomats of twenty-two nations negotiated in London during the week of the first Canal Conference in August, Eden and Lloyd put pressure on Dulles to speed things up by telling him that British and French military action—suspended during the conference—"could not long be delayed." Dulles replied that he "had encountered a general feeling that the British public would not support the use of force," adding that the Soviet negotiator had noticed it too. According to Dulles's assistant William Macomber, the secretary of state was frequently recognized when they drove through London: "Every time we stopped at a red light people would bang on the window. . . . They would say, 'God bless you Mr. Dulles, keep us out of the war.'"[19] Eden and Lloyd denied there was any such feeling among the public, Eden insisting that "when the chips were down, the Government would have the full backing of the public in any military operation." The Labour Party, he claimed, would fall in line too. Dulles was not convinced.[20]

Even within the British government, the question was being raised as to whether public opinion really was on the side of the interventionists. Members of the cabinet began to consider more conspiratorial methods of justifying force to a skeptical public. Harold Macmillan suggested in his diary that they might need to arrange some sort of fake provocation and attribute it to Egypt. "Of course, if an 'incident' took place, that w[oul]d be the way out," he wrote. "We must secure the defeat of Nasser, by one method or another. If not, we sh[oul]d rot away."[21]

By September, though, conditions had changed. The operation was repeatedly delayed beyond its original D-Day: to September 19, then to September 25. The planners warned that it

could not be mounted beyond the first week of October owing
to the unreliability of the Mediterranean weather. With political negotiations still going on, an attack on Nasser personally
was looking risky. General Keightley warned that it was vital that "our moral case [should be] unassailable" before Arab
countries and the wider world, yet it was unlikely this case
could be made convincingly in just a few weeks before military action began. He recommended delaying the operation
to "a much later date." Eden responded that the French would
not accept delays.[22]

Major practical difficulties with Musketeer became apparent. Beginning the assault at Alexandria would likely cause
a very high level of civilian casualties, which would do little
to help Britain and France win the psychological war or international support. Lord Hailsham, the new first lord of the
Admiralty, admitted, "There is one thing in this that I simply
cannot stomach and that is the bombardment from the sea by
the British fleet of the open city of Alexandria."[23] Mountbatten
told Eden that it would take at least two, perhaps three months
to fight from Alexandria to the Canal Zone, during which time
Egypt would surely haul them up before the United Nations.
Eden did not believe him, arguing that "the Egyptians were
yellow and would crumble immediately," and suggesting that
it would take only five days to get from Alexandria to Cairo.
For once, though, Templer, Mountbatten, and Keightley were
in agreement.[24] Musketeer would not work.

Musketeer was redrafted as Musketeer Revise. The new operation ditched the assault on Alexandria and focused on Port
Said. The psychological warfare plan was intensified with the
aim of debasing Nasser's reputation with his own people. There
were now three phases. First, the Egyptian air force would be
destroyed by air strikes. Second, there would follow at least
ten days of an air war campaign alongside psychological oper-

ations. Third, the landings would take place. By that point, it was hoped they would not face much resistance.

Musketeer Revise still failed to impress the commanders who were supposed to carry it out. General Stockwell later wrote that Phase Two "produced considerable apprehension in the minds of the Joint Task Commanders." British intelligence sources in Egypt were woeful, he admitted: the military commanders would not know to what extent the psychological campaign had worked, so troops would have to land without a clear sense of the opposition they might face. Furthermore, he did not believe air strikes alone would destroy the Egyptian army, the national guard, and any armed civilian resistance.[25] Air Marshal Sir Denis Barnett added that Musketeer Revise "was dictated to the Force Commanders as a result of political limitations and was never considered by them to be a sound military operation." He concluded that the entire operation "was coloured and limited by political considerations from start to finish."[26] Air Chief Marshal Sir David Lee, secretary to the chiefs of staff committee, remembered extensive opposition to any military action at all: "Lord Mountbatten was the strongest opponent of the operation, but I think the other Chiefs of Staff, if not quite so vociferous about it, were very anxious that it was an operation which might lead us into very considerable difficulties, and, for example, get us bogged down again in Egypt, a country which we'd only left six months beforehand."[27]

On the other side of the Atlantic, Eisenhower—himself a five-star general—considered any plan to occupy Egypt untenable. "I remember the President saying that, if you went in to topple Nasser, you would have to contemplate occupying Cairo," remembered his adviser Herman Phleger, "and that occupying a city of a million or two million people, if they were putting up a fight, was an almost impossible task—

because they fought from house to house and block to block—
and that it would take many, many thousands of troops. Then
the question of ever getting out was one that was appalling.
They [*sic*] felt that if you got militarily involved in Egypt,
you would have to occupy the country and you probably never
could get out."[28]

The CIA formally assessed the prospect of British and
French military success if they invaded Egypt. It did not have
access to their plans, but even so it predicted that in the event
of invasion, the Egyptians would block and close the Suez Canal, other Arab nations would sabotage oil pipelines, and the
invaders would face "widespread anti-Western rioting" and
"substantial guerrilla activity." The CIA believed this might
be suppressed "within a few weeks," but there would still be
major problems: "sabotage and terrorism and manifest Egyptian restiveness under military occupation would continue.
Nasser would probably set up a government-in-exile to direct
this activity and furnish a basis for UN action." It also believed
that no new Egyptian government would survive long without the support of the British and French militaries: "As a result the occupation would have to be prolonged."[29] Some in the
British armed forces recognized this, too. As the commander
in chief of the Royal Air Force in the Middle East put it, "Even
with a puppet regime in Egypt favourable to us I believe we
shall have to face a basically hostile and uncooperative population."[30]

Musketeer Revise had a Latin motto, *Nec tenui ferar penna*:
"Nor shall I be borne on a fragile wing." As it turned out, a
fragile wing was built into the operation at the last minute: the
element of collusion with Israel. When Britain agreed to the
Protocol of Sèvres on October 24, there was no time to design a
new operation. Musketeer Revise had been devised as an overt
invasion of Egypt, not a peacekeeping mission. Now, with a

matter of days to go before its launch, it had to be made to fit a different situation: to look like a spontaneous response to an Israeli attack with the aim of separating two warring nations. "The British generals' ignorance of the secret alliance with Israel contributed to the problem [of bad military planning]," wrote the London-based American diplomat Chester Cooper. "Not until October 26, on the very eve of the Israeli invasion, did Eden tell his commanders what had been arranged."[31]

The only person in the British military who seems to have been told the full extent of collusion with Israel was Lord Mountbatten. General Keightley alerted his troops to be on ten days' notice for Musketeer Revise on October 24, fewer than ten days before the operation was to begin. He seems to have been told that Israel was likely to launch an attack and Britain would respond with Musketeer Revise, but it is not clear how much he was told about the Protocol of Sèvres, if anything.[32] On October 26, he summoned the acting quartermaster general of the forces, and told him, "The PM has decided that the landing at Port Said must take place as soon as possible but has also said that no one is yet to know." The armed forces were told that they were participating in an exercise rather than preparing for war. General Stockwell found out that Israel was preparing to launch an attack on Egypt in three days when he landed in Paris on his way to Malta on October 26—and he was told by his own deputy, the French general André Beaufre. "The English General Stockwell, commanding aviation [sic— land forces], seems devoid of any imagination; he is in any case very badly informed," wrote Christian Pineau.[33]

Once he arrived in Malta, Stockwell told the four British admirals running the naval operation about the Israeli attack. Admiral Manley Power looked up from a chart of the Mediterranean. "My dear old boy," he said, "we'll have to start tomorrow."

Power recalled a conversation afterward with his fellow admiral Guy Grantham. "The Government must have gone raving mad," he said. "If we are in any way mixed up with Israeli action we shall upset the whole Muslim world and I think we shan't have the rest of world opinion behind us either. It's daft."[34]

As Power had realized, the new fact of collusion with Israel meant endangering one of Britain's most important priorities. Apart from the significant blip of the Balfour Declaration, British interests in the Middle East had rested on good relations with the Arabs. With the appetite for oil still growing, it seemed to many in the Foreign Office that these good relations would be even more essential to British interests in the future. On no account, then, must the invasion of Egypt seem like a broader anti-Arab move—and that meant it must not appear to aid Israel in any way.

"Anglo-French action in the Canal Zone will probably be misrepresented, to our damage in the Arab world, as part of an imperialist plot hatched with Israel," predicted a paper composed by a British Foreign Office committee in the first stage of planning on August 3, long before any possibility of collusion was raised in London. "It is, therefore, important that we and the French (and the Americans) should agree to use our influence to keep Israel right out of the dispute." The Foreign Office paper even considered adding a component to the operation that would go against Israel's interests, suggesting that Britain could in the course of an invasion of Egypt push Israel back beyond its "existing boundaries."[35] The British cabinet was united over the summer on the point that Israel should be kept out of the operation—with the exception of the chancellor of the exchequer, Harold Macmillan, who had convinced himself that Israel could be a useful ally.[36] In the political directive prepared by the cabinet office for General Keightley in

September, there was another strong warning against cozying up to the Israelis: "It is possible that Israel may take advantage of the situation and attack Egypt. . . . It is politically most important that . . . there should be no association or appearance of association between your forces and Israeli forces."[37] The French cabinet was told by the British that Israel must neither be involved nor even informed of the plans. The French cabinet was not especially concerned with keeping such things secret. This directive was leaked swiftly to Shimon Peres in Tel Aviv.[38]

Given that Ben-Gurion and many others in Israel nurtured long-standing resentments toward Britain and knew that Britain saw them as toxic allies, it may seem curious that the two nations embraced collusion with each other that autumn. The emulsifier was France. The French had been planning to collude with Israel from the start. On July 27, the day after Nasser had nationalized the Canal Company, interior minister Maurice Bourgès-Maunoury had asked Shimon Peres to an urgent meeting.

"How long, he asked, would it take the IDF to fight its way across the Sinai and reach the canal?" remembered Peres. Peres stated in his 1995 memoirs that he had guessed about two weeks; in a 1990 article, he remembered saying about six or seven days.

Bourgès-Maunoury asked Peres straight out: "Would Israel be prepared to take part in a tripartite military operation, in which Israel's specific role would be to cross the Sinai?"

To the astonishment of a more cautious colleague, Peres replied, "Under certain circumstances I assume that we would be so prepared."[39]

The cordial relationship between France and Israel had begun in the early 1950s, thanks to France's willingness to sell Israel arms and Israel's willingness to assist France with its nuclear program. Israeli scientists developed procedures for uranium separation and heavy-water manufacture, which France bought in 1953. After Nasser came to power, the two nations found they had even more in common. The French government, increasingly convinced that Nasser was wholly responsible for unrest in Algeria, wanted Israel to act as a counterweight and a distraction to Egypt. Israel, frustrated by American and British condemnation of its reprisals policy and the consequent withholding of military and economic aid, sought a new powerful ally that would be less squeamish about its actions. Though Franco-Israeli relations were supposed to be clandestine, news soon filtered out and caused trouble. "We were collaborating with the French, it was said, in their war against the FLN in Algeria," remembered Shimon Peres. "We had created 'an unclean alliance with the forces of imperialism.'"[40] The United States tacitly approved the French supply of arms to Israel: Washington hoped, a little naively, that this would satisfy Israel and put pressure on Egypt to seek Arab-Israeli peace.[41]

The pragmatic nature of the Franco-Israeli association was underpinned by genuine comradely feeling. Guy Mollet was close to Israel's socialists, particularly members of Ben-Gurion's Mapai. Many French politicians had witnessed firsthand the persecution of the Jews in World War II and were inclined to accept Israel's own assessment of its defense requirements. Foremost among these was Christian Pineau himself, who as a French Resistance leader had been imprisoned in Buchenwald concentration camp from December 1943 until April 1945, where he was traumatized by seeing Jews brought in from Auschwitz as the Soviets advanced. They had been reduced to "half frozen skeletons . . . covered in pus, dust, excrement," he wrote. All of them died in the week following their arrival at Buchenwald. The "nightmare vision," he remembered, became "ingrained in me. . . . I remain convinced that the destruction of the State of Israel would condemn the Jews to a similar fate to the one they suffered in Auschwitz and other extermination camps."[42] Well before Nasser's nationalization of the Suez Canal Company, mainstream opinion in the French government leaned toward Israel. The view is summed up by a letter sent by France's ambassador in Tel Aviv to Pineau in June. Israel, he claimed, was "a young state, the only stable and peaceable element in a tormented region," set against "an Arab bloc . . . increasingly turbulent, backward and bellicose."[43]

If anyone had a chance of convincing the lifelong Arabist Anthony Eden that he needed to align himself with Israel, it was Guy Mollet. Though Eden was a conservative and Mollet a socialist, the two got on exceptionally well. "I have never enjoyed a more completely loyal understanding with any man," Eden wrote of Mollet in his memoirs. "In the hours of strain there was never a harsh word, a reproach or a recrimination between us."[44] Mollet began to work on Eden.

Yet if in August 1956 it had seemed like a bad idea for Arab-allied Britain to be associated with Israel, the events of September and October made it much worse. On September 10, Jordanian national guards shot at an IDF unit near the border, killing six men and injuring three. An Israeli reprisal was carried out the next day, killing six Jordanian policemen and ten soldiers, as well as demolishing a police fort and a United Nations school. Another Israeli reprisal two days later killed eight Jordanians. On September 23, a Jordanian national guardsman—not acting on orders, according to his government—fired his machine gun at a group of archaeologists who were working on a site at the Israeli border, killing four and injuring sixteen. Two Israeli civilians were killed in separate incidents that day. Two days later, Israeli forces overseen by Moshe Dayan himself attacked an Arab Legion post at

Husan, near Bethlehem. There was fierce fighting; the death toll included ten Israelis, thirty-seven Jordanian police and soldiers, and two civilians.[45] "This is the first action involving deliberate Israel penetration of Arab territory to which the Israelis have openly admitted for several months," reported a British diplomat in Tel Aviv.[46]

The Foreign Office was "somewhat disturbed" by these outbreaks of violence on both sides. "If the Israel Government as a whole now considers that *fedayeen* attacks from Jordan will increase and that the Jordanian Government will lose control of the situation, we can only suppose that this is the effect which they intended to bring about by their raids," wrote the officer in London. "In other words their purpose is not to pacify the border but to create an excuse for invading Jordan." He added that the Foreign Office hoped they were wrong about this.[47]

Britain had a mutual defense treaty with Jordan. If Jordan called in British troops, Britain would have to fight Israel. Britain did have a war plan ready for fighting Israel, under the code name Operation Cordage. This could not be carried out at the same time as Musketeer Revise, logically or even logistically, for it required the same troops and equipment. On September 27, Ben-Gurion and Dayan discussed the possibility that a full-scale war with Jordan would mean war with Britain—but another option was already on the table. On September 30 and October 1, a delegation led by Golda Meir held secret meetings in France to put together a plan for invading Sinai and taking the Suez Canal—attacking Egypt, not Jordan.

Then two Israeli workers were murdered in an orange grove at Even Yehuda, near the Jordan-controlled West Bank. In a reprisal on October 10, the IDF attacked Qalqilya, in the West Bank. This was on a different scale from previous reprisals. It began with an air attack and artillery bombardment, then turned into a pitched battle. Eighteen Israelis were killed;

the Jordanian death toll was somewhere between sixty and a
hundred. As the attack went on, King Hussein called for assistance from British Royal Air Force bases in Jordan, invoking
the Anglo-Jordanian alliance. The British consul general in
Jerusalem telephoned the Israeli governor there and told him
that he had to call off the attack or Britain would have to declare war on Israel.[48] According to Ariel Sharon, who was one
of the commanders at Qalqilya, these political concerns won
out: "General Headquarters was trying to limit the scope of
the operation."[49] Sharon was furious about the restrictions on
his action and fell out badly and publicly with Moshe Dayan.
Such was the tension that the British air and naval forces
earmarked for Musketeer Revise were put on alert to enact
Operation Cordage instead. They were ready, if the situation
required, to go to war with Israel.[50] The British government
tried to squirm out of sending its own troops to King Hussein.
Eden asked Nuri es-Said to send Iraqi troops to Jordan in their
place. But this ploy created a new problem of its own: the Israelis were horrified by the possibility of a large, well-equipped
Arab army amassing just over their border.

Mollet realized at this point that he would have to let Eden
in on his plan to collude with Israel. Throughout negotiations
at the United Nations in the first weeks of October, Christian
Pineau had been meeting secretly in his New York hotel every
morning with Colonel Yehoshafat Harkabi, the Israeli chief of
army intelligence, to discuss this new plan.[51] The United Nations adopted Selwyn Lloyd's Six Principles on October 13. The
next day, General Maurice Challe, the French deputy chief of
staff, and Albert Gazier, the French foreign minister, visited
Eden at Chequers, the prime minister's official country residence. Anthony Nutting remembered that it was "a glorious
autumn day, radiant with sunshine and crisp as a biscuit." The
men talked for a while in front of a private secretary—until

Gazier indicated to Eden that he should instruct the secretary to stop taking notes. Eden did so. Then Challe presented the possibility that Israel might agree to attack Egypt, so Britain and France could invade on the pretense of "separating the combatants" and "extinguishing a dangerous fire."

"Doing his best to conceal his excitement, Eden replied non-committally that he would give these suggestions very careful thought," Nutting remembered, but he already knew that the prime minister was committed to the plan.[52] Now, though, Eden had to deal with the problem that he had already asked the Iraqi army to go to Jordan. He begged Nuri to make two concessions: first, to send a token infantry regiment instead of full forces, and second, to keep them nowhere near the border with Israel. Nuri complied. The Israelis were not mollified. "Save for the Almighty," Dayan wrote in his diary, "only the British are capable of complicating affairs to such a degree. At the very moment when they are preparing to topple Nasser . . . they insist on getting the Iraqi Army into Jordan, even if such action leads to war between Israel and Jordan in which they, the British, will take part against Israel."[53]

Eden and Lloyd flew to Paris on October 16 to meet Mollet and Pineau. According to Eden, they discussed their disappointment with the United Nations and with Dulles's SCUA, and their fears that Middle East peace was faltering owing to the "line-up between Jordan, Egypt and Syria . . . menacing [Israel] with destruction."[54] Eden did not mention in his memoir that they also discussed the details of a possible Israeli attack on Egypt and subsequent intervention.[55] Meanwhile, in Israel, Shimon Peres had to exert all his diplomatic skills to soothe Ben-Gurion, who had thought the French plan was for Israel to mount a joint invasion of Egypt with France and Britain—not to stage a feint to allow Britain to keep its image clean. "He saw in this proposal the acme of British hypocrisy," remembered

Peres. "It reflected . . . the British desire to harm Israel more than their resolve to destroy the Egyptian dictatorship."[56]

"The English plot, I imagine, is to get us involved with Nasser," Ben-Gurion wrote in his diary, "and bring about the occupation of Jordan by Iraq."[57] Relations between Britain and Israel worsened when the British representative at the United Nations, Sir Pierson Dixon, criticized the Israelis for their reprisal at Qalqilya in front of the Security Council. Eden was exasperated, complaining that Dixon "aligns himself with the Russians." Dixon did not know what was going on with the Israelis behind the scenes and could hardly be blamed for pursuing the British government's usual line of condemning reprisal raids. Eden was now terrified of scaring Ben-Gurion off: "The French warned how suspicious of us the Israelis are."[58]

"October 1956 was one of the craziest months in history," remembered Shimon Peres. With outrage over Qalqilya and the threat of a British attack on Israel happening at the same time as Egypt, Syria, and Jordan were discussing a joint military command, "Israel found itself facing a terrible situation."[59] On these grounds, Peres and Mollet managed to convince Ben-Gurion that he should go to Paris for talks at Sèvres with the British. He agreed to do so but ruled out acting ahead of Britain or France; he felt that all three must invade simultaneously. Only at Sèvres had he been persuaded to change his mind. Israel's agreement had dropped the final piece of the puzzle in place for Eden. And so, by October 26, when the commanders of Musketeer Revise made one last attempt to tell Eden that it would be a disaster, it was too late. The prime minister was determined to go ahead with his new plan.

0900 Washington DC // 1500 Budapest

In Budapest, Imre Nagy struggled to deal with the chaos following the previous day's massacre. Ferenc Donáth, a liberal member of his administration, suggested that they must meet with the rebels. "The party dare not oppose the mass movement that seeks to build socialism by democratic means," Donáth argued; "it must rather place itself at the head of that movement." Even old Stalinists like Gerő agreed. Yet Nagy was curiously distracted during this meeting, wandering in and out of the room and letting others draw up a draft resolution. Afterward, he met a group of writers and students. By this point, Nagy "appeared completely helpless and we were extremely angered," remembered university assistant István Pozsár, who was there. Nagy said vaguely that he would represent their position to the administration, then turned to leave.

"You should represent it in your role as Hungary's prime minister!" yelled one student after him.[60]

Those close to Nagy tried to shake him into action. His wife told him plainly that his own supporters were baffled by his behavior, and his daughter reported that there was a real revolution in the streets. "I know it," Nagy replied. According to a colleague, Nagy then "sank into himself, he was silent and tears ran from his eyes. . . . He gave the impression of a man who was serving his people, his country, and the cause of socialism, a man full of goodwill and good intentions, [but] a man in a very difficult situation facing events without knowing what to do."[61]

Anastas Mikoyan and Mikhail Suslov reluctantly agreed to give Nagy some real power as the leader of Hungary if he could stop the fighting. Though they considered him potentially bourgeois—calling him a kulak, after the supposedly profiteering class of farmers exterminated by Stalin—they knew Bloody Thursday had made the Soviet position difficult. Mikoyan still wanted to avoid a full invasion. As he wrote to Khrushchev that day, all-out action would be dangerous: "In that case they [the Hungarian government] will lose all contact with the peaceful population, there would be more deaths which will widen the chasm between the government and the population. If we follow that path, we will lose."[62]

The rebels were building barricades and training new recruits. "The average age didn't reach 18," admitted rebel leader Gergely Pongrátz, who was himself only twenty-four at the time, "but we had over there 12–13–14-year-old kids. Many times I sent them home, and they didn't wanted [sic] to leave."[63] Throughout Hungary, smaller towns set up their own ad hoc councils of workers. In Mosonmagyaróvár, a small town near the Austrian border, a crowd called for the removal of a colossal Red Star from the AVH headquarters on October 26. The local AVH commander was not inclined to comply and instead ordered his troops to attack the crowd with machine guns and grenades. An estimated fifty-two people were killed. Afterward, four of the AVH men who had carried out the massacre were beaten by citizens. Two survived, albeit with serious injuries; two were literally ripped to pieces.[64]

As the violence continued in Hungary, Allen Dulles returned to work in Washington following a trip to Europe. He went straight into a meeting of the National Security Council. The rebellion in Hungary, he told them, was a far bigger deal than that in Poland; it "constituted the most serious threat yet to be posed to continued Soviet control of the satellites." Dulles saw two alternatives for how Moscow might respond to Hungarian dissent: either vicious repression or democratization and a loosening of control in the satellites, which might, of course, risk losing them entirely. There was excited discussion about the possibility of "Western orientation" replacing Soviet influence.

Eisenhower asked Allen Dulles what he knew about the reaction in Czechoslovakia. Dulles was not encouraging. He knew little: "In any event, practically all the potential Gomulkas in Czechoslovakia had been pretty well slaughtered."

The president's own concern, as he had discussed with Foster Dulles the previous evening, was about how the Soviets might react if they thought the United States was involved. "In view of the serious deterioration of their position in the satellites, might they not be tempted to resort to very extreme measures and even to precipitate global war?" Harold Stassen, Eisenhower's disarmament adviser, suggested that he send a message to Marshal Zhukov assuring him that the United States had no intention of pursuing military action in Hungary. Initially, Eisenhower dismissed this. He did not believe that the Soviets feared an American invasion, but he was sure they feared American subversion. Instead, he asked for a security analysis and recommendations.[65] But the idea played on his mind and on Stassen's, for both of them continued to discuss the possibility with Foster Dulles that day. Eisenhower had a subtler message incorporated into a speech, applauding the possibility of the satellite states becoming neutral.[66]

The discomfort with Communism in the United States went back to the first "Red Scare," just after World War I, in which it was feared that Communists would organize themselves and eventually topple the government as they had in Russia. Concerns that American Communists sought violent revolution grew again before and during World War II. Despite the specific protection afforded to free speech by the First Amendment to the Constitution, new laws placed severe criminal penalties on advocating such action.

Both Winston Churchill and Franklin D. Roosevelt respected the Soviet contribution to the Allied war effort—a contribution on the Eastern Front that was decisive to victory in Europe—and both had some personal regard for Joseph Stalin. Yet the prospect of continued coexistence with a

Communist superpower became increasingly troublesome for American politicians. In 1947, President Harry S. Truman declared the Truman Doctrine, stating that the United States would intervene with political, military, and economic assistance in any struggle by a democratic nation against an authoritarian threat, whether from outside or within. The policy was aimed at Soviet expansion. Generally the Truman Doctrine had been pursued passively, though in 1949 a secret joint American-British operation had parachuted trained Albanian exiles back into Albania to start a counterrevolution. This had failed, and nothing much had been tried since, aside from propaganda, notably the broadcasts of Radio Free Europe. American agents did not start the anti-Communist uprisings in East Germany or Czechoslovakia in 1953 or those in Poland or Hungary in 1956.[67]

The United States sometimes had trouble persuading its NATO allies to see the problem of communism in the black-and-white terms that Foster Dulles preferred. Dulles felt that Eden acted "like an impartial mediator" between the United States and the Soviets, rather than taking the American side.[68] Christian Pineau (a socialist himself) complained later that Dulles never distinguished clearly between different types of left-wing politics, creating a gap between European and American opinion. "At the time, I could already feel the difference. But why? Because I had read Marx and Lenin. Because I knew communist doctrine from having studied it," he wrote. "For me, these were quite current problems: my friends and I had published numerous articles on the opposition between democratic socialism and communism. For us these were familiar things: they weren't for Mr Dulles."[69] The divisions were deep: when Khrushchev and Bulganin visited Britain in April 1956, Khrushchev found that he detested British democratic socialists, ending up in violent arguments with

Labour Party luminaries Aneurin Bevan, Richard Crossman, and George Brown. By contrast, he rather liked Anthony Eden. "Bulganin can vote Labour if he likes," Khrushchev told the British ambassador to Moscow after the trip, "but I'm going to vote Conservative."[70]

Though there was no serious appetite inside the highest circles of the United States government for taking armed action in the Soviet bloc, there was a great deal of talk—in public and in official meetings—about whether the United States might "liberate" the "captive peoples" under Soviet domination. Much of this talk came from Foster Dulles himself, who had spoken during Eisenhower's first presidential campaign of the need to move "from a purely defensive policy to a psychological offensive, a liberation policy, which will try to give hope and a resistance mood inside the Soviet Empire."[71] This was politically expedient at home. Since the Truman Doctrine, a second Red Scare had surged in the United States, pioneered by the hearings of the House Un-American Activities Committee and by the investigations of Senator Joseph McCarthy. Though McCarthy himself fell from grace at the end of 1954, Communism remained a bogeyman in domestic politics.

In Eisenhower's first term, some moves had been made toward the "liberation policy" Foster Dulles had championed— notably the coup in Guatemala. A rebellion against Soviet control in Eastern Europe was an even more thrilling prospect for some in the CIA, especially as they had not started this one themselves. But they faced strong opposition on any case for intervention from more or less the whole of Eisenhower's administration.

The Middle East preoccupied Foster Dulles and Eisenhower that morning. Since Qalqilya, the Dulles brothers had been discussing the probability of Israel escalating its attacks on Jordan from reprisal raids to an invasion. Foster had told Allen that the Israelis "think Jordan is breaking up and it is a question of grabbing the pieces." Allen had confirmed that it looked like that to him, too.[72]

On October 26, Foster Dulles learned that the IDF was mobilizing, and began to smell a rat. The American army attaché in Tel Aviv believed the mobilization was greater than anything he had seen since the 1948 war. He was hearing rumors that the French were involved and the target was the Straits of Tiran.[73] Eisenhower summoned the British chargé d'affaires to ask him what was going on. The British chargé d'affaires insisted that nothing was. This was not surprising: Eden had deliberately not informed the British embassy in Washington of his plans.

Dulles cabled the American embassy in London to ask whether anyone there knew what was happening. "We do not know their [the Britons'] intentions with reference to resuming negotiations with Egyptians nor with reference to SCUA nor do we know what are [the] understandings apparently arrived at with French," he wrote. "We have information of major Israeli preparations and suspect there may be French complicity with them and possibly UK complicity with various moves which they think it preferable to keep from us lest we indicate our disapproval."

Frankly, he continued, under the protection of top-secret classification: "We are quite disturbed here over [the] fact there is apparently a deliberate British purpose of keeping us completely in the dark as to their intentions with reference to Middle East matters generally and Egypt in particular."[74] This was exactly right: even Dulles's turn of phrase was being echoed across the Atlantic. "Nobody was kept more completely in the dark than the President of the United States," remarked British foreign affairs minister Anthony Nutting.[75]

Yet there were people in Washington who could have shed light on what was happening. There is evidence from many sources that Allen Dulles had found out about Franco-British collusion with Israel on his European trip, and possibly that he had even tacitly allowed some American involvement. According to the well-informed Israeli historian (and later politician) Michael Bar-Zohar, who interviewed Ben-Gurion extensively in the 1960s, "The head of the CIA knew the truth of the matter; he even knew that the United States Army had obligingly organized an air-lift from Florida to France in order to supply the French 'Sabres' with extra fuel-tanks."[76]

Allen Dulles called a meeting of his CIA deputies later that day. In the 1970s, journalist Leonard Mosley spoke to several people who were present, including Richard Bissell and Robert Amory. The deputies reported that the British and French had gone quiet, and that Israel's top military man, Moshe Dayan, had gone missing. He was thought to be in France. At this point, according to Mosley's reconstruction, Dulles revealed to the deputies that he had been told by a source in the French cabinet that the British, French, and Israelis were planning a joint invasion of Egypt. He added that he saw why the French would do such a thing, owing to their interests in Algeria— but he was surprised that the British would risk their alliances with Iraq, Jordan, and the Gulf states by joining up with the Israelis. Bissell then showed the meeting photographs taken by U-2 spy aircraft of French warships being loaded with supplies in the ports of Marseilles and Toulon, and British military preparations in Malta and Cyprus. According to Mosley, he "dryly remarked that they were hardly there for a regatta."

Amory said that Eden would ally with anyone who would help him destroy Nasser. He added that "almost everyone on the British General Staff was dead against a military operation in Egypt," not least because they lacked the naval resources. He had heard that Lord Mountbatten had fought with Eden about it.

Counterintelligence expert James Jesus Angleton spoke up. Angleton had intimate ties with the Mossad, Israel's national intelligence agency.

"Amory's remark may sound alarming, but I think I can discount it," Angleton said. "I've spent last evening and most of the early hours with my Israeli friends in Washington, and I can assure you that it's all part of maneuvers and is certainly not meant for any serious attack. There is nothing in it. I do not believe there is going to be an attack by the Israelis."[77]

It seems Allen Dulles did not pass the mixed messages he was getting about whether the Israelis were attacking Jordan or Egypt on to Eisenhower immediately. It is not clear if he even told his brother that day. When he was later challenged on possible intelligence failures leading up to the Suez War, Allen Dulles claimed that the CIA had warned the State Department the next morning, October 27, of a possible Israeli attack on Egypt. In the official United States collection of foreign-relations documents, his letter is annotated: "No record of this communication has been found in Department of State files."[78]

General Charles Cabell, deputy director of the CIA, later claimed, "The fact of the matter is that the intelligence community did give advance warning of this [the British, French, and Israeli attack plan] to the Secretary of State—not long in advance, but advance in a matter of days. We had given tentative warnings about it considerably earlier than just days in advance." Cabell suggested that if Foster Dulles had claimed otherwise, he may have done so because "he was feeling that it was the interests of the United States to give the impression that the policy makers did get caught completely unawares of this act."[79] Speaking in 1965, Christian Pineau agreed: "There is in any case one untrue thing that has been said, and I don't mean to implicate [Foster] Dulles. It is that the Americans were not aware of our projects. This is not correct. They were not informed by diplomatic means, but I have good reason to know that they were by secret services."[80]

Under the doctrine of "plausible deniability" favored by Allen Dulles, the president was sometimes not told things it might be inconvenient or embarrassing for him to know—assassination plots against foreign politicians, for instance. But in this case, plausible deniability for the president would not have been required, for the United States was not doing anything dubious. It looks instead as though crucial intelligence about the activities of key allies was withheld from the president during an international crisis.

Faced with the prospect of war just days before an election in which he was standing on the promise of peace, Eisenhower would surely have put pressure on Britain, France, and Israel to back down. If one or both of the Dulles brothers did not want to tell the president what was going on, it could have been because they did not want Britain, France, and Israel to back down. It is possible they wanted to see Nasser fall and thought Britain, France, and Israel might achieve that. It is possible that Foster Dulles wanted to see Britain and France—in his own phrase of two days earlier—"commit suicide" in the Middle East.

There are no clues in the archives, for Allen Dulles had many of his papers destroyed. He may have seen this as a way to keep secrets. Instead, it has encouraged conspiracy theorists to indulge in wide-ranging speculation about his role in controversial events—speculation that, owing to the absence of evidence, historians are restricted in their ability to investigate. No one can now know what was going through Allen Dulles's mind on October 26 if he did intentionally withhold this crucial information from Eisenhower. There was a conspiracy in London, Paris, and Tel Aviv to topple Nasser without informing the president of the United States. It remains an intriguing but unproven possibility that there may have been one in Washington, too.

1430 Washington DC // 1930 London // 2030 Budapest

At Kensington Palace in West London that evening, the glamorous Duchess of Kent, formerly Princess Marina of Greece, gave a cocktail party. Among the guests was Jock Colville, who had been joint principal private secretary to Winston Churchill. During the party, he had "a long talk" with Eden. Eden had been impressed by the news coming from Hungary. "He was elated by the apparent split in the Communist empire." Indeed, his mood was notably positive. "I found him cheerful and apparently exhilarated."[81]

The meeting with Colville may have given Eden an extraordinary idea. Churchill's new private secretary Anthony Montague Browne remembered that at some point in late October—he did not specify exactly which day—he was summoned to see Eden in the cabinet room. "Eden seemed a different man from my previous meetings, friendly, exhilarated, almost light-hearted," he wrote.

"You are to promise not to tell anybody except Winston until this is all over," Eden said. Montague Browne promised, and Eden revealed to him the plan for an Anglo-French assault on Suez. He sent Montague Browne to see Norman Brook, the cabinet secretary, to hear more about the military plan. Before he left, though, Eden stopped him.

"I want to ask you this," said the prime minister. "If I offered Winston a seat in the cabinet without portfolio, would he accept?"

"I was astounded," wrote Montague Browne. "I simply couldn't imagine anything less likely."[82] Churchill turned down the opportunity to serve under Eden; he had had a mild stroke while in the south of France on October 20 and was in no position to take the post even had he wanted it. Montague Browne's story hints at how concerned the prime minister was at this point to legitimize his Suez strategy. It had taken Eden years to persuade Churchill to retire and bequeath the Conservative Party to him. If Churchill returned to government now—even in a relatively junior role—he would inevitably overshadow the unpopular Eden and might threaten his leadership. It was a tremendous risk to take and indicates that Eden may have suspected that he would face opposition to his war at home.

1900 New York; Washington DC

Shortly after seven p.m., Foster Dulles telephoned Eisenhower to discuss the situation in Hungary. The minutes of the conversation reveal that both men were excited about the prospect for change. As Eisenhower saw it, "The whole European and world security would seem to be on the road to achievement." As an incentive to the Soviets to let Hungary go, Dulles suggested they imply that in the event of Hungarian independence, they "might not need to build up NATO so much or something to that effect."

Eisenhower agreed. "The Pres. said that if they could have some kind of [free] existence, choose their own government and what they want, then we are satisfied and this would really solve one of the greatest problems in the world that is standing in the way of world peace."

For all their hopes, though, Eisenhower and Dulles were not blind to the fact that Hungary was still under threat. Dulles mentioned the need to get the question before the United Nations as soon as possible, "in order to focus attention on it so the Russians will not commit vast reprisals." He was contacting Selwyn Lloyd, who he expected would support the American case at the Security Council. Eisenhower instructed him specifically "to say to Lloyd it is so terrible we would be remiss if we did not do something."[83]

After he hung up, Dulles sent a telegram to the American embassy in London with instructions for staff there to tell Lloyd they wanted to inscribe an item at the Security Council: "The [Hungarian] revolt is assuming proportions which may in turn bring Red counter-action of major proportions. Emotional reaction to this would be very serious, certainly in this country." He advised that the United Nations should be focused on Hungary and that the British and Americans should speak informally to the Soviet permanent representative there.[84]

All the worst allegations the United States government had made about the Soviet Union—its antidemocratic repression, its brutality, and its imperialism—were being demonstrated for the world to see. In Cold War terms, the iron was hot. It was the perfect time for the United States to prove its point, and to do so at the world forum of the United Nations with the backing of its strongest allies, Britain and France.

Except, of course, that Britain and France were preparing to launch something which might appear just as repressive, brutal, and imperialist as the Soviet repression of Hungary—and they were planning to mobilize for it the very next morning.

6

SATURDAY, OCTOBER 27, 1956
THE OMEGA PLAN

0600 Malta // 0700 Cairo

At dawn, British and French aircraft carriers left Malta, sailing eastward on "training exercises." More French ships, renamed and repainted to look anonymous, ferried two hundred heavy trucks to northern Israeli ports. Two squadrons of French warplanes landed in Israel. Operation Musketeer Revise was under way—cobbled hastily into a new shape so it might in a few days look like a response to Israeli aggression.

The Anglo-Israeli link in the three-way alliance remained shaky. "Although Ben-Gurion had concluded an agreement with the British, he did not trust them," remembered Ariel Sharon. "Nor did the rest of us. We remembered the treatment of the Jews during World War Two too well, as we did their 1948 evacuation of Palestine when they turned over the most strategic positions under their control to the Arabs." Moshe Dayan visited Sharon at his headquarters and told him he was concerned that the British would at the last minute refuse to put their part of the plan into action. "If that happens," Dayan told Sharon, "it will be a very complicated situation. . . . You'll have to bring back your forces. I'm confident you'll be able to find a solution to that, but you might be the only ones in Sinai."[1]

Mordechai Bar-On, who was Ben-Gurion's military assistant at the time, thought Ben-Gurion still placed the British on a pedestal—in their capacity as villains as well as heroes. "He too was a prisoner of his past," Bar-On wrote of his boss. "His greatest glory, as the man who in 1948 successfully resisted the invasion of five Arab armies, pushed him to consider Arab enmity as irreconcilable. His memories of the German Blitz over London exaggerated his fears of Egyptian air raids on Tel Aviv. But the most important distorted image was his perception of the British. He certainly overrated their enmity to Israel, he over-suspected their deviousness, overestimated their capabilities as a military power, and over-appreciated their wisdom."[2]

Evidently, there were those in the British government and armed forces who were also beginning to doubt their prime minister's wisdom. Some saw Nasser as a minor problem or no problem at all; some saw him as a problem, but one that could be dealt with without going to war. For those who thought he was a big problem and Britain should get rid of him, an obvious suggestion short of war was to have him "removed." Back in March, Eden himself had dispensed with euphemism and told Anthony Nutting that he wanted Nasser murdered. Douglas Dodds-Parker, a Conservative MP and junior minister at the Foreign Office, asked the permanent undersecretary of state, Sir Ivone Kirkpatrick, why they could not "aim at Nassir alone? I understood that this was possible, using methods that had proved successful in the past—most recently the removal of Dr. Mossadeq in Iran." Kirkpatrick replied vaguely that some politicians were opposed to capital punishment and might not like that sort of thing.

"Yet they are prepared to risk an assault which could

injure, even kill, women and children, not to mention our own troops?" Dodds-Parker asked. Kirkpatrick, as far as he remembered, did not reply.[3]

It is unlikely that MI6 would have been able to carry any covert assassination plan out. In the secret struggle for influence in the Middle East—the maneuverings of the CIA and MI6, in competition with each other as well as with the French—British intelligence was in short supply. By 1956, the Americans were overwhelmingly in the lead.

Until the 1950s, Britain had maintained good intelligence sources in Egypt, especially in the royal household and the Wafd party. In 1952, though, the monarchy fell and the Wafd was dissolved. There were no moles in the new government or military to replace the ousted sources. It did not help that the MI6 office in Egypt was staffed with bumptious imperialists of questionable competence. In 1953, they scotched the idea that the army would stage a coup against King Farouk, just before it did exactly that.[4] Once the Free Officers took power, MI6 began to consider ways to bring Neguib and Nasser down, possibly replacing them with the least unappealing member of the former royal family, Prince Abdul Monheim, or with an Islamic theologian.

A shady relationship sprang up between British agents and the far-right-wing Egyptian Islamist group, the Muslim Brotherhood. It was a curious alliance, for the Brotherhood had originally been set up to oppose the British presence in Egypt—but like the French and the Israelis, the two groups were brought together by their hatred of Nasser. Islamic fundamentalists were not then seen as a threat to Western interests and were considered a potential bulwark against Communism.

The Muslim Brotherhood had been founded in March 1928 by Hasan al-Banna. The first six members were all laborers from the British military camp at Ismailia. Banna and his followers were enraged by the foreign domination of the Suez Canal Zone. Europeans seemed to enjoy every kind of privilege, from better housing and utilities to street signs in their own languages. "We are weary of this life of humiliation and restriction," the six told Banna. "Lo, we see that the Arabs and the Muslims have no status and no dignity. They are not more than mere hirelings belonging to the foreigners."[5]

Though the Muslim Brotherhood was dedicated to religious discipline, it was also strongly anti-imperialist. It rejected the ideologies of the non-Islamic world, whether nationalist, socialist, or capitalist, though it appreciated the advances of Britain, the United States, and the Soviet Union in the fields of science and governance. It envisaged a society defined by the implementation of Sharia. The Brotherhood's interpretation of Sharia was not without room for maneuver: it claimed that unpopular aspects of the law, such as the cutting off of a hand for theft, had been "misunderstood." According to Brotherhood scholars, society had a duty to provide food, clothing, and shelter for everyone; if people were provided for, then no theft would occur and consequently no hands would need cutting off. The Brotherhood condemned Saudi Arabia's willingness to chop hands off its thieves "while the rulers swim in the gold stolen from the state treasury and the wealth of the people."[6] Banna also started an auxiliary Muslim Sisterhood, though the organization largely failed to capture the imaginations of the educated women he hoped would run it.

In October 1941, there was contact between the British embassy and the Muslim Brotherhood, though witnesses told different stories about who took the initiative. A British agent afterward claimed Banna had asked him for "forty thousand dollars and a car" to support the British cause;[7] Muslim Brothers claimed that it was the other way around, that the British had tried to buy them off. Members of the competing political group Young Egypt were convinced that the Brotherhood had taken the money, for it refused to join anti-British demonstrations in favor of the German general Erwin Rommel, which they organized in the summer of 1942. The Brotherhood kept trying to expand, and in 1944 one of its recruiters met with various discontented army officers. Among them was Gamal Abdel Nasser, who met the Brotherhood officer on the Tea Island at Cairo Zoo—more often a retreat for illicit lovers. At that early stage, Nasser had some sympathy for the Brotherhood and joined its secret military wing.[8] This sympathy would not last.

After the war, the Muslim Brotherhood became notable for its tough anti-Communist stance and links to conservative parties. It accused the Wafd of having "communist affiliations."[9] Banna ordered the Brotherhood to prepare for jihad in October 1947, when it began to look likely that a Jewish state would soon be created in Palestine. Some Brothers went on to fight in the 1948 war against Israel, as Nasser did. In 1948–49, the Egyptian Ministry of the Interior presented a case for the dissolution of the Muslim Brotherhood on grounds of multiple acts of terrorism. Banna attempted to negotiate his way out of the charges. He published a pamphlet arguing that the Brothers had suffered "persecution," claiming that the government of Egypt was under pressure from abroad and intended to negotiate with the British and the Jews. He identified in all this the designs of "international Zionism, communism, and the partisans of atheism and depravity." Soon after the pamphlet was written, on February 12, 1949, Banna was shot as he was getting into a taxi in Cairo. He lived only long enough to get to a nearby hospital.

The Brotherhood survived. By the end of 1951, it had been legally reconstituted. At the same moment, the Wafd prime minister abrogated the Anglo-Egyptian Treaty of 1936. The

Brotherhood supported this, and declared jihad against the British in Ismailia.[10] It supported the revolution that threw out King Farouk and installed Mohamed Neguib as president. The Revolutionary Command Council, perhaps under Nasser's direction, invited members of the Brotherhood to join Neguib's cabinet—but the relationship soon soured.

While the Muslim Brotherhood continued to proclaim its anti-imperialist principles, its new leader, Hasan al-Hudaybi, attracted some positive attention from those imperialists themselves. A long report from the British ambassador in Cairo asserted, "It is generally believed that he is a man of different type from the fanatical Hassan al Banna" and claimed that he was received by King Farouk, that he was a stalwart anti-Communist, and that his speeches had been "studiously moderate."[11] The British embassy even considered that Hudaybi might be suitable for office. "We might be on more solid ground with a Moslem Brotherhood Government: if they could retain power long enough, and if I am right in thinking that they could produce a fairly efficient and clean administration."[12] Yet an internal CIA briefing described the Muslim Brotherhood as "a fanatical, nationalistic, terrorist organization which has caused trouble in Egypt and Syria." The CIA blamed the Brotherhood for the assassination of the former Lebanese prime minister in 1951 and warned that it was the only terrorist organization in the region that could attract "a sizeable following." Its activities, the CIA warned, created "a formidable deterrent to those Arab leaders who wish to reach a settlement with Israel or to cooperate with the West."[13]

This did not deter the British. Hudaybi met the oriental counselor of the British embassy to discuss the upcoming evacuation of British troops from Egypt, Canal Zone incidents, an Anglo-Libyan treaty, and other matters. The French ambassador reported sniffily to Paris that Hudaybi "wants power," and had therefore "declared himself ready to accept, in the name of the Brotherhood, the terms of an agreement with Britain much more disadvantageous than those obtained by the military directorate." These terms included, apparently, giving Britain permission to reoccupy its Egyptian bases in the event of a Soviet attack on Egypt.[14]

Hudaybi went to the American embassy, too, and the officer there formed the impression that he was "an extremist and a born opportunist." The British felt, "An opportunist he no doubt is, but . . . he strikes us as more of a moderate."[15] "Although El Hodeibi [Hudaybi], the Supreme Guide of the Brotherhood, had been anxious for friendly relations with us," recalled Anthony Eden, "the majority of his followers were set against any settlement acceptable to us until after evacuation was complete."[16] On January 12, 1954, Muslim Brothers and university students clashed with a group of secondary school students and organizers from the government-approved Liberation Rally and Youth Formations. Dozens were injured; a government jeep was burned. The next day, the Egyptian cabinet again outlawed the Brotherhood.

Just a few weeks later, the government of Egypt was consumed by the drama of Neguib's fall and Nasser's rise. King Saud intervened with Nasser on behalf of the Brotherhood—which, though it had started out critical of state brutality in Saudi Arabia, increasingly found itself drawn to Saud's golden embrace.[17] Its members were released and permitted to reconstitute. It seems Nasser's strategy all along was to court the Brotherhood, hoping he could win its support rather than fighting it. But Hudaybi again made a nuisance of himself after Nasser finally took power, demanding a greater voice in government. Nasser's administration turned against him, accusing him of being in league with all the greatest villains in Egyptian demonology: imperialists, Zionists, Communists, and the British.

By October, some Brothers were plotting their revenge. They came up with a plan for a suicide bomber to approach Nasser wearing a dynamite belt and blow himself up. It was scuppered by a complete lack of volunteers. Instead, a Brother was sent to shoot Nasser on the evening of October 26, 1954, while he gave a speech in Mansheya Square celebrating the agreement he had made with Anthony Nutting to set a timetable for the British to leave Egypt. As he was talking, eight shots rang out. When they finished, he spoke up again, unharmed and undaunted.

"I, Gamal Abdel Nasser, am of your blood and my blood is for you," he said. "I will live for your sake and I will die serving you. . . . Even if they kill me, I have placed in you self-respect. Let them kill me now, for I have planted in this nation freedom, self-respect, and dignity. For the sake of Egypt and for the sake of Egypt's freedom, I will live and in the service of Egypt I will die."[18]

Conspiracy theories flourished. Some thought Nasser staged the event himself to justify cracking down on the Brotherhood. Others suggested that the CIA had done it and had issued Nasser a bulletproof vest beforehand.[19] There was no evidence for these theories, though that did not diminish their popularity. The Muslim Brotherhood leaders did have a meeting at which they discussed their plan to kill Nasser, which Hudaybi apparently attended.[20] It is true, though, that Nasser's crackdown was swift and thorough. Within weeks, six Brothers had been hanged and thousands imprisoned. The Brotherhood continued unofficially, with the imprisoned Sayyid Qutb as its chief spokesman. Qutb, a teacher and civil servant who had spent some time living in the United States and had not liked it at all, was a prominent conservative Islamic thinker. Though he remained in prison for the next decade, he spent that time writing and developing a powerful ideology. He believed the world suffered under *jahiliyya* (ignorance). The term had originally been used to describe the "unenlight- ened" state that existed before the prophet Mohammed's reve- lations. Qutb applied it to parts of the Muslim world in his own time, which he thought had been corrupted by foreign and un-Islamic ideas and had lost sight of their true path.

Qutb would be tried and executed in 1966 by the Egyptian state for plotting its overthrow. His ideas would live long af- ter his death, filtering out to influence fundamentalist Islamic movements across the world. Though Qutb himself disap- proved of violence against innocents, not all of his followers heeded that aspect of his philosophy.

Among those strongly influenced by Qutb's ideas was Egyp- tian student Ayman al-Zawahiri, who became a member of the Muslim Brotherhood when he was a teenager. Zawahiri went on to become Osama bin Laden's personal physician. Ac- cording to him, bin Laden was a member of the Saudi branch of the Muslim Brotherhood.[21] Zawahiri founded the organi- zation Islamic Jihad, which merged with al-Qaeda. After bin Laden's assassination in 2011, Zawahiri became the leader of al-Qaeda. Little did the British agents who hoped the Mus- lim Brotherhood might help them overthrow Nasser in the 1950s realize what the men they were dealing with would do in the future. Though the details of that future may not have been foreseeable, the direction of travel was—which is why the CIA disdained the Muslim Brotherhood and would not work with it.

In 1954, CIA agent Wilbur Eveland wrote, "The CIA had launched an enormous operation in Egypt, perhaps the largest of its kind since the inception of the agency." He also noted,

"What disturbed me most was the youth and apparent immaturity of the people [in the CIA operation], who seemed to have been given a free hand."[22] The inexperience of the Americans was outpaced, though, by the ineptitude of the British. MI6 barely noticed their new American neighbors and omitted to report the existence of this significant CIA endeavor to London. Eveland's fellow agent Miles Copeland described MI6 as "grossly uninformed."[23]

In the spring and summer of 1955, MI6 had failed to pick up on another crucial development: the prospect of Nasser making an arms deal with the Soviets. Consequently, Britain refused an Egyptian request for more arms in June 1955, and this refusal pushed Nasser "straight into the arms of Moscow," as one British field marshal put it.[24] After Nasser's deal with Czechoslovakia, MI6 reported that he was falling to the Communists. Though this message was eagerly received by Eden and by right-wing Conservatives in Britain, it was not true. Many at the Foreign Office doubted it, even those who disliked Nasser. "It begins to look as if Nasser is even more unreliable than he seemed, and may even be consciously handing his country to Communism," wrote Evelyn Shuckburgh in his diary. "But I do not quite believe that. I think he thinks himself supremely clever, and is playing East off against West to the last moment."[25] This was a more accurate assessment than MI6 had provided, even though Shuckburgh was in Whitehall rather than Cairo.

MI6's sources in Egypt had begun to send mysterious reports to London from an agent they called "Lucky Break." They claimed Lucky Break was close to Nasser and was working to bring him down. Lucky Break said that Nasser and most of the Revolutionary Council were in thrall to Moscow and were planning a war with Israel to begin in June 1956. This information was uncorroborated by any other evidence. The

Foreign Office soon decided it was junk. Lucky Break may have been a crank, or his testimony may have been talked up—perhaps even invented—by MI6 agents or stringers to cover up their failure to secure real information. Yet Harold Macmillan, then foreign secretary, was alarmed, writing to the British ambassador in Cairo on November 26, 1955, that the Egyptians could soon be "well in the clutches of the Communists."[26]

"I think that you will agree with me that we are faced by the most serious and urgent threat to the whole Western position in Africa," he wrote in an emergency secret telegram to Foster Dulles the same day, "and that we must do all we can without delay to prevent Russia gaining control of Egypt."[27]

Instead of accepting and rectifying its inability to influence Nasser, MI6 decided the fault must be his. If they could not predict the Egyptian leader's actions, they supposed his actions must be impossible to predict. If his actions were impossible to predict, they supposed he must be volatile and dangerous, and from that it followed that he had to be removed. Allegedly, British agents were conspiring to stage riots by militant Islamic groups in Egypt's main cities to create a pretext for intervention.[28] An MI6 agent showed the CIA's Miles Copeland a highly secret document which he claimed was a chart of the organization of the Mukhabarat, the Egyptian secret service. "I thought he was pulling my leg!" Copeland remembered. It was a chart Copeland himself had drawn up in 1953 when working for the consultancy Booz-Allen and Hamilton (and, covertly, the CIA), helping to reorganize the Egyptian interior ministry. "The interesting part was the list of the section heads, all friends of mine, some of them misspelled, some without first names, and some entirely wrong due to faulty interpretation of footnotes."[29]

The French secret service had apparently already made and

botched an attempt to kill Nasser in 1954. Both the French and the Israelis would consider further plans to have him killed in 1956.[30] Former British intelligence officers have denied that MI6 could or would have carried out a hit on Nasser.[31] Yet declassified documents prove that removing the Egyptian leader from office was discussed at the highest levels. On receiving Macmillan's fervent secret telegram about a Communist Nasser posing a threat to the whole of Africa in November 1955, Herbert Hoover asked the British ambassador in Washington if the British had "thought of finding an alternative to Nasser somewhere?" The ambassador asked him who he had in mind. Hoover replied vaguely that he would need to consult his colleagues, but mentioned that there were some officers in the Egyptian forces who "were strongly attracted to [a] Western connexion and who might form the nucleus of another regime."[32] This received an immediate and enthusiastic response from London. "We are afraid that Nasser, whether innocently or deliberately, is dangerously committed to the Communists," Macmillan wrote back the next day. "Consequently, we believe that it would be advantageous to overthrow him if possible. We suggest that this problem should be subjected to joint Anglo-American examination as soon as possible."[33]

The mood became darker yet after Glubb Pasha was ousted in Jordan. "Today both we and the Americans really gave up hope of Nasser and began to look around for means of destroying him," wrote Evelyn Shuckburgh in his diary on March 8, 1956.[34] "It is either him or us, don't forget that," Eden told Shuckburgh four days later.[35]

The deputy director of MI6, George Young, confirmed to BBC documentary makers in 1985 that plans to overthrow Nasser were considered. Had they gone ahead, he admitted, "It was easy to see that Nasser might have been killed."[36] Those who talked about ousting Nasser may not always have explicitly mentioned murder, but equally they did not seem to be making plans for him to enjoy a comfortable retirement. The accounts of CIA agents indicate Young himself went further. At the end of March 1956, Wilbur Eveland had been in London with his colleague James Eichelberger to discuss Middle East affairs. "Young said that Egypt, Saudi Arabia, and Syria threatened Britain's survival," Eveland wrote. "Their governments would have to be subverted or overthrown." At the same time, the friendlier regional powers of Iraq, Turkey, and Iran would be strengthened.

Young proposed that Syria, which he suggested was about to become a Soviet satellite, should be dealt with first, then— because the Saudis would react badly to a coup in Syria—the kingdom of Saudi Arabia would have to be brought down. Finally, before Nasser could use his new Soviet arms to bomb Israel, he would have to go too. Young imagined all these coups could be carried out in conjunction with the Iraqis and said they must start within a month. Eveland remembered thinking "that I'd entered a madhouse." When Young asked him for his impressions of the triple coup plot, Eveland had to bite his lip "to avoid saying that I thought total insanity had set in." Instead he warned that too much of the British plan depended on the Iraqis' ability to overthrow both Syria and Saudi Arabia consecutively, and that the Iraqis certainly did not have the capability to knock Egypt over as well. Young, whose politics were explicitly racist, countered that the CIA were forgetting "the snipcocks," a disparaging epithet for the Israelis.[37]

Back in Washington, Foster Dulles took some of the British ideas seriously—not on Saudi Arabia, but he was worried about Egypt's and Syria's links to the Soviet Union. On March 28, 1956, he drew up a special secret policy code-named Omega. The previous plan, Alpha—aiming at achieving peace in the

Middle East through Nasser—was supplanted. The new plan aimed to curb Nasser's ambitions and curtail his power. The point, Dulles wrote, was "to let Colonel Nasser realize that he cannot cooperate as he is doing with the Soviet Union and at the same time enjoy most-favored-nation treatment from the United States." The plan aimed to delay aid to Egypt, including delaying a decision on the funding for the Aswan High Dam. It attempted to strengthen pro-Western feeling in all Arab states, especially Iraq and Saudi Arabia. Dulles recommended that the Americans give "increased support to the Baghdad Pact without actually adhering to the Pact or announcing our intention of doing so." He added, "It is extremely important that the American position in Saudi Arabia be strengthened."[38]

The preferred State Department candidate for leadership of the Muslim world was King Saud, though the CIA disagreed. Its own internal report suggested that the Muslim nation most able to lead and simultaneously to serve American interests would be Pakistan.[39] The State Department's enthusiasm for Saud was largely based on his generous entertaining of American oil interests, for the man himself could not really be said to have represented a model leader in Foster Dulles's terms or anyone else's. Saud and Nasser regularly found themselves on the same side—and that side was often opposed to American policy, notably regarding Israel and the Soviet Union. At the same time as Dulles was drawing up the Omega plan, CIA briefings to the National Security Council in Washington complained of the Arab response to Israeli recruitment of soldiers in Europe and Latin America: "Saud and Nasr gave veiled threats of doing some recruiting of their own 'outside Arab world'—i.e., in USSR."[40]

Dulles noted that Omega "would in the main be coordinated with the United Kingdom." The CIA and MI6 would jointly be charged with weakening Nasser's regime and isolating Egypt from other Arab nations. The released part of the document ends with the ominous words: "In addition to the foregoing course of action, planning should be undertaken at once with a view to possibly more drastic action in the event that the above courses of action do not have the desired effect."[41]

As part of the "more drastic" course of action, Operation Straggle, a plot to undermine and ultimately replace Shukri al-Kuwatly as president of Syria, was drawn up with input from British, American, and Iraqi agencies. Kuwatly had tried to buy American arms but had been turned down. His rejection by the United States dismayed CIA agents in Syria, who predicted that he would be forced to turn to the Soviet Union. They were right: Kuwatly soon began to consider Soviet offers, just as Nasser had.[42]

The CIA's Wilbur Eveland, who knew Syria well, was mystified as to why the State Department would go along with British plans for a coup there. He speculated that the Dulles brothers may have been bluffing: trying to make the British think that the Americans were on board. He did not think the Dulles brothers could possibly want to go all the way with the British and overthrow Nasser. "There was, at least, too much CIA prestige invested in Nasser," Eveland wrote. "To forestall the SIS [MI6] plan to eliminate the Egyptian president, the CIA had, apparently, compromised with an offer to consider joining in a Syrian coup."[43]

After George Young had told Eichelberger and Eveland MI6's plans for Nasser, the CIA men took the information straight back to Nasser himself.[44] Nasser took note, but delayed action until the summer. Egypt's secret service raided the offices of MI6's front operation, the Arab News Agency, in August 1956, arresting some British agents on suspicion of espionage. Extensive documents were recovered from the home of James Swinburn, the head of the network, detailing Egyptian military maneuvers and contacts between Nasser's administration and the Soviets.[45] Swinburn and others were tried and imprisoned. Two officers at the British embassy linked to the MI6 network were expelled. Harold Macmillan described Nasser's behavior over the British prisoners as "getting more and more truculent," as though a president who had just discovered the spies of a hostile foreign state intent on killing him should have meekly accepted them.[46]

Sir Dick White—who was then "C," the chief of MI6—later implied to historian Peter Hennessy and biographer Tom Bower that Eden had attempted to order the assassination of Nasser, but that he, White, refused to carry the order out.[47] Other accounts suggest that some madcap plots may nearly have been put into action after Nasser smashed MI6's network. These accounts are from less impeccable sources than Dick White, though sources from the murky world of intelligence are routinely less than impeccable. The former MI5 counterintelligence agent Peter Wright alleged in his sometimes questionable memoir *Spycatcher* that MI6 had developed a plan to assassinate Nasser with nerve gas: "Eden initially gave his approval to the operation, but later rescinded it when he got agreement from the French and Israelis to engage in joint military action."

Wright claimed he had been consulted about the plan by MI6's technical services. "They told me that the London Station had an agent in Egypt with limited access to one of Nasser's headquarters," he wrote. "Their plan was to place canisters of nerve gas inside the ventilation system, but I pointed out that this would require large quantities of the gas, and would result in massive loss of life among Nasser's staff. It was the usual MI6 operation—hopelessly unrealistic—and it did not remotely surprise me when [MI6 technical services officer John] Henry told me later that Eden had backed away from the operation."[48] In 1975, former CIA officer Miles Co-peland told the *Times* of London that "Anthony Eden wanted me to shoot Nasser." He said he had frequently "but not seriously" discussed the idea of having Nasser murdered with Eden and top British intelligence officials. Eden told the paper Copeland's claim was "a load of rubbish." Copeland retracted his allegation publicly at the time, but confirmed it again to the historian Scott Lucas in 1989.[49]

Further stories abounded. One claimed that a three-man assassination squad had been sent from London to Egypt, but the men apparently thought better of it once they arrived. It has been suggested that one British plot involved sending the SAS, and one French plot involved sending frogmen.[50] Another rumor held that a BBC journalist was ordered to drop off a package from his Morris Minor at the twelve-mile post outside Cairo. It contained £20,000 sterling, apparently to pay Nasser's doctor off to kill him; the journalist accidentally gave it to the wrong man. MI6's "Q" operations department was said to have considered assembling an electric razor filled with explosives, or injecting several boxes of Egyptian Kropje chocolates with poison—though the head of the department was concerned that they might be eaten by someone else. No nerve gas canisters, murder squads, frogmen, malign doctors, exploding razors, or poisoned chocolates seem ever to have reached Nasser.[51]

There was a fire beneath all the smoke. Two MI6 officers and a British MP—Julian Amery, who was Harold Macmillan's son-in-law and had been a spy in Egypt during World War II—met Egyptian military contacts in France on August 27, 1956. They discussed the planning of a coup to assassinate Nasser and his ministers and install a new government headed by former president Mohamed Neguib.[52] The prospect of ousting Nasser was discussed by the British and the U.S. State Department throughout the summer and autumn of

1956. The British were keener on overthrowing him violently than their American counterparts. On September 22, a British diplomat told Foster Dulles that Eden had "suggested that a secret working party be established to consider how Nasser might be unseated. The Foreign Office was anxious to get under way this planning operation, as it was hoped that its objectives might be accomplished within six months." Dulles replied that "we could do more in the economic, political and propaganda fields to further deterioration" in Nasser's standing, which he believed was already occurring. "If we had a group to focus on the matter, there might be a fair chance to create a situation in which Nasser's position would be undermined." Yet he emphasized, "The use of military force was not right," and added, "He had told Mr. Eden he did not want to get into CIA type work and Eden agreed."[53] Internally, the State Department worried that there were "informal indications that the British may be thinking more in terms of a CIA type operation than the Secretary intends."[54]

The subject was brought up again in secret American talks with the British Joint Intelligence Committee chairman, Patrick Dean, at the beginning of October 1956. Eisenhower intervened. As he told Foster Dulles, "We should have nothing to do with any project for a covert operation against Nasser personally."[55] Suggestions were made to him for how the CIA could do such a thing, but according to the minutes of an Oval Office meeting on October 6, "The President said that an action of this kind could not be taken when there is as much active hostility as at present. For a thing like this to be done without inflaming the Arab world, a time free from heated stress holding the world's attention as at present would have to be chosen."[56] According to a KGB agent in Cairo at the time, the Soviets dispatched two KGB protection agents to Egypt to defend Nasser against a targeted assassination.[57]

Still, one of George Young's three coup plots was about to go into action in October 1956. The CIA and MI6 had worked up Operation Straggle (alternatively known as Wakeful). Syria's president was to be overthrown and replaced by a wealthy Christian landowner, Michail Bey Ilyan, leader of the conservative Populist Party. Ilyan had already been paid 500,000 Syrian pounds—around $167,000—and the coup was originally planned for the end of August, though it had to be repeatedly delayed.[58] By mid-October, the Syrians were still not ready. The date of the coup had then been delayed until October 29.[59]

By October 27, Operation Straggle/Wakeful was still planned to go ahead in less than forty-eight hours. The CIA was therefore preparing to help topple the government of Syria on October 29, which they did not realize was exactly the same day Israel was planning to invade Egypt. If their partners in MI6 were aware of the timing clash, they do not seem to have mentioned it.

Owing to the French kidnapping of the Algerian rebels, there was unrest in Syria—which could either help or hinder Anglo-American plans for a coup. That day, October 27, anti-French and pro-Algerian demonstrators threw bombs at the French embassy and at the Jeanne d'Arc French girls' school in Damascus, Syria, and more bombs at the French consulate in Aleppo. Windows were blown out of these buildings, but no casualties were reported.[60] Throughout North Africa, anti-French protests continued. In Tunisia, roadblocks were set up by civilians (aided, apparently, by the army) to constrain French troop movement. Tunisian reports claimed that French forces trying to pass these roadblocks fired on civilians. Fourteen people were said to have been killed, including six Frenchmen. The French army admitted only to twenty-four of its soldiers being injured and seven missing. In Morocco, a European family of five were murdered on their farm. It was one of two hundred farms estimated to have been destroyed or damaged by rioters. "The events of the weekend," opined the London *Times*, "lent grim support to the arguments of those who think the arrest last week of the five Algerian rebel leaders is likely to imperil France's relations with the two ex-protectorates of Tunisia and Morocco."[61] More than that, it was imperiling France's position in the entire Arab world. Britain had regretted letting France have Syria under the terms of the Sykes-Picot agreement and had attempted to snatch some or all of it out of French influence at the Versailles Conference after World War I. Now, Britain was finally in a position to get a leader friendly to itself and the Americans into power in Damascus—at the precise moment when it was also conspiring with France to invade Egypt.

In Paris that same day, Christian Pineau gave a strong speech at a lunch for foreign press. Not only was he unrepentant about the disorder France's kidnapping of the Algerians had caused, but he was angry that his nation was being accused of colonialism. "The present Government has the majority of the country and parliament behind it and it is determined to restore France's rightful place in the world," he said. "We shall fight for this whatever may be the decision of any international organisation."[62] With the French minister for external affairs now openly bragging that he was not going to be held back by the United Nations in the pursuit of French interests, Britain's hope that the invasion of Egypt could be made to look like a selfless peacekeeping mission seemed less likely than ever to be fulfilled.

0900 Washington DC // 1500 Budapest

A Russian voice crackled over a weak short-wave radio signal from an unofficial station in Budapest: "Their fight is our fight." The speaker claimed to be a Soviet colonel who had

defected to the Hungarian rebels and implored his fellow Soviet soldiers to join him.[63] In the streets, skirmishes continued.

Inside the Hungarian administration, Imre Nagy had been
trying to position himself as a moderate between the angry
rebels and the vengeful Stalinists. On October 27, his minister of defense (a staunch Communist) ordered Hungarian
troops to "annihilate the rebel groups." Nagy pointed to an
amnesty on rebels who laid down their weapons, which he had
declared days before, and vetoed the order. He also received a
delegation of rebels in parliament that day to discuss a possible
cease-fire. Under cover of that group, a few Hungarian opposition members—friends of Nagy's—managed to sneak into
the building. They told him that the rebels thought he was
responsible both for the Soviet intervention and for the imposition of martial law, and begged him to go into the streets himself to understand the mood of the population. Nagy seemed
shocked; one of the opposition members present reported that
he wept throughout their discussion.[64]

"Although he [Nagy] was always twenty-four hours late in
reacting to public demands, he was nevertheless twenty-four
hours ahead of the Party leaders," wrote the Hungarian historian Miklós Molnár.[65] In line with his long-held opinions on
the need for gradual, gentle change, Nagy had been trying to
manage a transition to something more like consensual government without getting countless more people killed on either
side. This strategy had not been convincingly communicated
to the population. After the meeting with opposition members,
Nagy realized that he must toughen up. He went with János
Kádár to meet Mikoyan and Suslov at the Soviet embassy, and
over the course of several hours managed to convince them
that any military attack by the Hungarian army or police or
by Soviet troops would guarantee that the government would
lose the support of the whole country. Though no minutes sur-

vive from this conversation, it was referred to afterward by its participants as a "turning point."[66]

At nine o'clock that morning, both Allen and Foster Dulles attended a meeting in Washington to discuss a speech the latter would make later in Dallas in support of Eisenhower's election campaign. It was largely about Hungary—but the Middle East had to be mentioned. As part of his comment on that region, Foster proposed to say: "We cannot guarantee a peaceful outcome. . . ."

Robert Amory, who had warned Allen Dulles about the possibility of the Israelis invading Egypt at the CIA Watch Committee meeting the day before, interrupted: "Mr. Secretary, if you say that and war breaks out twenty-four hours later, you will appear to all the world as *partie prise* [literally "captive party," or unwilling partner] to the Israeli aggression—and I'm positive the Israelis will attack the Sinai shortly after midnight tomorrow."

Allen Dulles appeared shocked. "That's much stronger than the Watch Committee's conclusion yesterday," he said.

"Okay," said Amory. "I'm sticking my neck out. I'm only a $16,000 a year CIA official, but I'm prepared to lay my job on the line that there's a war coming tomorrow or the day after."

Foster Dulles duly removed the line from his speech.[67]

The joint chiefs of staff discussed a possible Anglo-French invasion, and their memoranda were circulated to the White House as well as the State Department. By the end of October 27, both Eisenhower and Foster Dulles had documents on their desks that raised the possibility of Anglo-French collusion in an Israeli invasion of Egypt.[68]

Eisenhower, though, was not at his desk. He had been admitted to Walter Reed Army Medical Center for a checkup. His health was an issue in the election campaign: he had suffered a serious heart attack a year before and undergone an operation for ileitis in June. The checkup had been scheduled so that he could be publicly pronounced fit in time for the vote. He would remain in the hospital that night and into the next day.[69]

1400 Washington DC // 1900 London // 2100 Tel Aviv

That evening, the United Nations hosted a cocktail party for the diplomatic corps in Israel. The talk was all of the coming military action. It was widely expected that Israeli troops would enter Jordan in the next few hours. "An ambassador, leaving the cocktail party in evening dress on his way to an official dinner, was driving his own car," noted journalist Robert Henriques. "His chauffeur had been mobilised that morning. Another diplomat complained of a sore finger. He had spent the whole day typing a letter, since his secretary had been called up."[70]

Later, at the Dallas Council of World Affairs in Texas, Foster Dulles delivered his speech about Poland and Hungary. "The weakness of Soviet imperialism is being made manifest," he said.

Our Nation has from its beginning stimulated political independence and human liberty throughout the world. Lincoln said of our Declaration of Independence that it gave "liberty not alone to the people of this country, but hope to all the world, for all future time.". . .

Today our Nation continues its historic role. The captive peoples should never have reason to doubt that they have in us a sincere and dedicated friend who share[s] their aspirations. They must know that they can draw upon our abundance to tide themselves over the period of economic adjustment which is inevitable as they rededicate their productive efforts to the service of their own people, rather than of exploiting masters.

Yet, as Eisenhower had requested, Dulles also signaled to the Soviets that the United States would not interfere in Hungary. "The United States has no ulterior purpose in desiring the independence of the satellite countries," he said. "We do not look upon these nations as potential military allies."[71]

On the CIA's advice, nothing was said that could potentially suggest that Dulles knew about a coming Israeli invasion of Egypt, potentially in cahoots with the French or even with the French and the British. By the end of October 27, the three supposed NATO allies—Britain, France, and the United States—were playing a poker game. Everybody was bluffing about their intentions, and nobody was ready to show his hand.

7

SUNDAY, OCTOBER 28, 1956

NO PICNIC

0700 London // 0800 Algiers

American diplomat Chester Cooper woke to a cold, dank October morning that augured poorly for that afternoon's outing to the picturesque South Downs. The Coopers were supposed to be picnicking with their close friends, Patrick Dean and his family. In the event, neither the Coopers nor the Deans were obliged to endure the English weather. That morning, Dean placed what Cooper called a "disturbing" telephone call to explain that he had been summoned to an urgent meeting with Selwyn Lloyd.

Cooper went into the American embassy, where he learned that Israeli troops had been mobilized and that his president believed their target to be Jordan. After lunch, Dean telephoned again. His meeting had finished. The families drove together to Greenwich for tea instead. "It turned out to be a glum, silent afternoon," Cooper remembered. "I had never seen my friend so morose, so preoccupied." He asked why Dean was so tense. Was it Hungary, or the Middle East?

"You and I are in for much trouble," Dean replied, "and it won't be because of Hungary."

"He volunteered nothing further," Cooper recorded in a cable to Washington that evening. "Will check this worrisome matter again in morning."[1]

Anthony Nutting also spoke of his "feelings of impending doom" in the hours counting down to the attack, and of the enormous challenge not to reveal too much to the well-meaning family and friends who constantly engaged him in conversation about Suez. "'Why don't you do this? Why don't you try that?' friends would say," he remembered. "And all the time I longed to scream at them to shut up because we had decided what to do, and it was lunacy."[2]

Ahmed Ben Bella, the leader of the Algerian rebels, was still languishing in his cell in Algiers. A French colonel strode in.

"He told me they were going to settle Nasser's account," Ben Bella remembered. "They had already settled ours. Consequently, in Egypt and in Algeria, no more revolution, all would return to order. I looked at him, stupefied. Military men are sometimes so simplistic."

Ben Bella tried to explain that the revolution in Algeria had passed the stage where it depended on four or five men. It was not finished, he said. It was only just beginning. "But he shook his head; he kept returning to the same point. No more Nasser, no more Ben Bella, the problem was solved."[3] Remarkably, the entire French state appeared to have convinced itself of this line of thinking. "We must finish with Nasser," Maurice Bourgès-Maunoury, the minister of defense, often repeated to Christian Pineau and Guy Mollet. "Then we will have finished with the [Algerian] rebellion."[4]

Aside from the mobilization continuing in Israel, there was a great silence throughout North Africa and the Middle East that day. Arabs everywhere had gone on strike for twenty-four hours to protest the kidnapping of Ben Bella and other Algerian leaders. In Egypt, the streets of Cairo were deserted. Almost all of its three million people stayed home. Incidents of violence broke the quiet. Around a thousand protesters burned down the French consulate in Jerusalem. An estimated twenty-four thousand people demonstrated in Amman, Jordan, chanting anti-French slogans and attempting to torch the French consulate there, too. In Aleppo, Syria, a state of emergency was declared after mobs set fire to French buildings.[5]

An internal report at the CIA indicated that the rulers of Tunisia and Morocco were trying to restrain people from violence, with limited success. In Algeria and in Cairo, the CIA had detected that new command arrangements were already being made for Ben Bella's organization, the FLN. There was "no indication of any abatement of guerrilla activity." Furthermore, "the capture of the five leaders not only provided the Algerian nationalist movement with a set of martyrs, but promises to result in increased diplomatic and material assistance [to the Algerian rebels] from Morocco and Tunisia, where the moderate leaders probably will be forced to make substantial concessions to rising popular sentiment in favor of independence for Algeria."[6] The French remained unrepentant. After his conversation with the French colonel, Ben Bella and his compatriots were loaded onto a plane and flown to Paris. The streets of the French capital were closed, with police vans stationed along their route; the government was determined to avoid any risk of the city's sizable Algerian population attempting to liberate its prisoners as they were driven to the high-security La Santé Prison in Montparnasse. There they were to await trial.

1100 Budapest // 1400 Moscow

That morning, the Soviet and Hungarian militaries attacked the rebel strongholds in Corvin Alley and Széna Square. Hungarian Ministry of Defense loyalists and the Soviet authorities ordered this attack without Imre Nagy's agreement.

The rebels in Széna Square were temporarily driven out. The Corvin rebels, working loosely with the group commanded by Colonel Pál Maléter stationed at the nearby Kilián Barracks, managed to hold back Hungarian forces and the tanks of the Red Army.[7] Several tanks were destroyed. Nagy found out about this assault and called it off, but the rebels had already defeated it.

Belatedly, Nagy seemed to have found his guts. For the first time he took a strong stance in the Hungarian Politburo, calling for change. Anastas Mikoyan, attending as a "guest," was not convinced. "We respect Comrade Nagy, we consider him a sincere man, but at times he very easily gets under the influence of others," he said. "To be firm, one must take a decisive position."

Nagy was not intimidated. "Comrade Mikoyan turned to me and said that one must remain firm," he remarked to those assembled. "At the point where the interest of the party requires further movement, then I will not remain firm but go ahead." He continued, even more daringly in the light of the attack on the Corvin rebels that morning: "If we assess the broadly based movement as counter-revolution, as we did at first, then we have no choice but to suppress it with tanks and artillery. That would be a tragedy. We now see that this is not our way."[8]

The rebellion in Hungary was not helped by the only tool of American power that was in use: Radio Free Europe. The American-run station broadcast constant, violent criticism of Imre Nagy, advising ordinary citizens to join the fight for a complete revolution against his government as well as against the Soviets. "The programs did not advise prudence," wrote the Hungarian journalist and historian Charles Gati. "The

programs did not quote Western press reports explaining
Nagy's predicament. The programs did not speak of a possible
Titoist scenario, or of the Soviet Army's might and determination, or of the dilemmas of choice in the West."[9] Though it
is not true, as it has sometimes been claimed, that Radio Free
Europe repeatedly broadcast empty promises of American
military intervention at this point—it would do that only on
November 4—it did not tell its many Hungarian listeners that
Eisenhower and Dulles were publicly ruling out such an intervention. It is unclear whether or not overeager agents within
the CIA were responsible for Radio Free Europe's stance or
whether it came from managers or broadcasters at the station
itself. Whatever the truth, the broadcasts made it harder for
Imre Nagy to calm and unite the rebels, made it easier for the
Soviets to divide them, and encouraged thousands of ordinary
people to put themselves in danger.

In Moscow, hard-liners in the presidium criticized Suslov
and Mikoyan's mission in Budapest. Molotov sneered that they
were providing "calm reassurances" while Soviet policy "is
gradually moving toward capitulation." This was, in effect,
an attack on Khrushchev for failing to act more decisively.
"The American secret services are more active in Hungary
than C[omra]des Suslov and Mikoyan are," added Voroshilov.[10]
But Khrushchev held firm, conscious of the potential for disaster in Hungary if the Soviet Union were to impose its will by
force. "The English and French are in a real mess in Egypt,"
Khrushchev told the presidium. "We should not get caught in
the same company."[11]

1500 Jerusalem

David Ben-Gurion, still on his sickbed in Jerusalem, summoned the leaders of all parliamentary groups (except the
Communists) to his bedside. There, he told them of his plan

to attack Egypt by invading the Sinai. He received unanimous support.[12] A messenger was sent to Washington to deliver a top-secret document in a sealed envelope to Abba Eban, the ambassador to the United Nations. This document contained all the details of Israel's invasion plan, code-named Operation Kadesh.

Ben-Gurion made his own objectives clear. His interests were in the Eilat coastal strip and the Straits of Tiran, the entrance to the Gulf of Aqaba. He intended to reopen the straits, judging the permanent acquisition of this territory essential to the free movement of Israeli shipping. Israel would, during its campaign, attempt to conquer Sinai too—but he did not believe he would be able to hold it permanently in the face of the opposition he expected from the international community. Still, he hoped Operation Kadesh would damage Nasser politically and might even bring about his downfall. Finally, he told the assembled parliamentarians, "The Gaza strip is a hindrance; we've got to take it, but it's a burden to us. If I did believe in miracles I would like it to sink beneath the sea. . . ."[13]

1500 Washington DC // 2100 Budapest // 2200 Tel Aviv // 0000 Moscow

In Budapest that evening, Imre Nagy ordered several Stalinist former leaders—including Ernő Gerő—to leave for exile in Moscow. They boarded planes with their families and went. At the same time, from his bed at Walter Reed Army Medical Center, President Eisenhower sent off an appeal to Israel to stop mobilizing its troops. He returned to the White House in the afternoon and spoke to his speechwriter, Emmet Hughes, about the suggestion that he cancel a campaign trip to the Southern states. He dismissed the idea, fearing it would be misunderstood. "There'd be political yapping all around that the doctors yesterday *really* found I was terribly sick and ready to keel over dead." In fact, he felt fine, though the day in the hospital composing a letter to David Ben-Gurion in between medical examinations had not been cheerful. "Israel and barium make quite a combination," he remarked.

Hughes summed up the president's state of mind: "The whole Middle Eastern scene obviously leaves him dismayed, baffled, and fearful of great stupidity about to assert itself." This could probably be said of almost any world leader at any point in modern times, but it is less common for so many great stupidities to have been preparing to assert themselves all at once. "Maybe they're thinking they just *can't* survive without more land," Eisenhower mused of the Israelis. "But *I* don't see how they can survive without coming to some honorable and peaceful terms with the whole Arab world that surrounds them." France's action made him angry. "Damn it, the French, they're just egging the Israeli[s] on—hoping somehow to get out of their *own* North African troubles. Damn it, they sat right there in those chairs three years ago, and we tried to tell them that they would repeat Indochina all over again in North Africa. And they said, 'Oh no! That's part of metropolitan France!'—and all that damn nonsense."

The possible involvement of the British in this conspiracy still seemed inexplicable. "I just can't believe it," he said. "I can't believe they would be so stupid as to invite on *themselves* all the Arab hostility to Israel." He wondered if the British were daring him to defend the Tripartite Declaration of 1950: after all, the United States could be asked to step in on the side of Egypt.

He signaled the end of the meeting with a heavy sigh. "Well, I better get out of here," he said to Hughes, "or—despite all those doctors—these things will have my blood pressure up to 490."[14]

At the State Department, Foster Dulles was questioning the

Israeli ambassador, Abba Eban. Eban, who had not yet received the sealed envelope from Israel and did not know of the real invasion plan, said that his nation feared that the new joint command formed by Egypt, Jordan, and Syria was planning "the massive use of fedayeen activity," and aggression against Israel. This, he said, was the reason some reserve units had been called up.

Dulles interrupted to ask whether the statement "some reserve units had been called up" really covered what was happening. "The Secretary said that according to his information Israel was being totally mobilized." Though Dulles knew Ben-Gurion had been concerned about the possibility of Iraqi troops moving into Jordan under the British plan, this had not happened—and there was therefore no obvious provocation.

Eban replied that Iraqi troops still might threaten Israel. The mobilization, he insisted, was defensive.

Dulles retorted that "at no previous time had Israel been as safe as it was today." Jordan's government was weak and Egypt was distracted by the ongoing dispute with Britain and France over the Suez Canal. "For these reasons it was hard to see how Israel was endangered to such an extent as to require total mobilization. The Secretary thought, on the other hand, that Israelis might calculate that this was the best moment in which Israel could move."[15]

Eban repeated that Israel was acting defensively and its fears were well founded, but this only irritated Dulles. Afterward, the secretary of state checked Israeli government balances in New York banks, and was relieved to see that there had not been any unusually large withdrawals recently. If the Israelis had started pulling money out, it would have been a sign that they were up to something. They knew that the American government would freeze their balances in the event of aggression.

Eisenhower and Dulles had several frank and revealing telephone calls that evening. The most frank and revealing of them was placed by the secretary of state shortly after five thirty. They discussed evacuating American civilians and nonessential military personnel from Egypt, Syria, Jordan, and Israel. Eisenhower wondered if this made things worse. Dulles did not think so, though "it may lead to anti-American demonstrations and if the British strike it will lead to the inference we knew about it." Eisenhower reassured him that deniability was in place: "The Pres. said our statement today would almost certainly take care of that one—we don't know about the Br[itish]."

They went on to discuss the British and French military buildup on Cyprus—though Eisenhower still suspected there was some other plan brewing. "The Pres. said he can't believe the Br. would let themselves be dragged into it on this basis."

Eisenhower said he would wait out the night and see what the morning brought before warning Britain and France off aggression in the Middle East. Dulles argued that it would be too late then, if the invasion had already begun. The president was persuaded, and told him to go ahead. "The Pres. said it will be a world-shocking thing tomorrow."[16] On that point he was certainly right.

8

MONDAY, OCTOBER 29, 1956

"SANDSTORMS IN THE DESERT"

2200 (Oct. 28) Washington DC // 0500 Tel Aviv

Before dawn, a car with diplomatic plates drew up outside the Ministry of Defense in Tel Aviv. It contained the counselor from the American embassy, who explained to the sentries that his visit could not wait. He delivered Eisenhower's letter to David Ben-Gurion. Eisenhower had written that he had asked other Middle Eastern states to back off any aggression, and would discuss the situation with Britain and France, the other two parties in the Tripartite Declaration. "I feel compelled to emphasize the dangers inherent in the present situation and to urge your Government to do nothing which would endanger the peace."[1]

Eisenhower did not specify which country he expected to be Israel's target in the letter, but the Israelis knew the Americans still expected it to be Jordan. According to his biographer Michael Bar-Zohar, the Israeli leader noted that "there was something sad in seeing the head of a great Power with a completely erroneous idea of the situation, believing quite candidly that the seat of the fire was to the east of Israel and thinking of appealing to the very countries which, at that moment, were in collusion with Israel. The smoke-screen drawn over the operation had obviously been most effective."[2] It was. The Israelis even set up a fake fedayeen attack in the Negev desert and released news of it.[3]

"We all believed that we were going to attack Jordan, because the last attacks were against Jordan," remembered Uri Avnery, editor of the Israeli magazine *HaOlem HaZeh* at the time. "Our magazine came out on Tuesday and it took about twenty-four hours to print. We had prepared a cover of the forthcoming attack on Jordan. I had to rush to the printing press that day to change it at the last minute. It was a very well-organized distraction. We really believed it."[4] If even critical journalists like Avnery, who devoted himself to interrogating the Israeli government and armed forces, were convinced by the feint, it is not surprising that the president of the United States was drawn in.

In his diary, Moshe Dayan regretted the "not at all agreeable" situation of having to deceive the United States, but complained that Washington "has no specific solutions to the problems which face us so acutely." He was annoyed that Eisenhower encouraged "a peaceful and moderate approach," asking, "What content of reality is there to such well-worn phrases, and what is their practical impact on the terror attacks of the fedayun, or the blockade of Israeli shipping in Suez and the Gulf of Akaba, or the Egypt-Syria-Jordan military pact?"[5] Dayan felt, as did Ben-Gurion, that Israel again had no alternative.

0500 London // 0600 Budapest // 0700 Jerusalem // 0900 Moscow

At dawn, Soviet troops began to roll out of Budapest, leaving behind thousands of buildings ruined by tank and artillery fire. They were moving out of the city. People gathered in the streets to sweep away the shards of broken glass and cart off the blocks of fallen masonry.[6] The Hungarian government was determined to be gracious about the withdrawal. Radio broadcasts and newspaper articles exhorted people to behave civilly to the Soviets. For the most part, they did, except for a few incidents in which some Red Army soldiers who had run out of food indulged in some looting.[7]

Imre Nagy moved his office from Communist Party headquarters in Academy Street to the parliament building. It was not a break with Communism, which he still espoused, but it was a sign of independence from the old party ways. In parliament, he met a group of young rebels to discuss a possible cease-fire. He asked them to lay down their arms. They were unsure whether to do so without their demands being met.

"Boys," he said to them, "do you think that I'm not as good a Hungarian as you are?"[8]

The rebels were struck by this. They offered Nagy their support and agreed that they would give up their weapons once the Soviets had withdrawn. In practice, though, this agreement soon fell apart. The rebels still mistrusted the government, and instead demanded that they be incorporated by the Hungarian state into its army, police, and security forces.

For the first time in six days, Nagy had a chance to return to his home. The Western press was ecstatic. "The Hungarian people are winning," declared an editorial in the London *Times* that day. "They have broken the gates of their prison. They have seen the Government bow before their demands." The editors sounded a note of caution as well: "Certainly all eyes will have to be intent against trickery in the days ahead. But at the moment it seems that the people, rising against tyranny in the face of every odd, armed with little but their despair and courage and unity, have wrought a change that will transform far more than Hungary."[9]

This withdrawal was not what it seemed. The Soviets were consolidating their forces along a crescent line ninety miles east of Budapest and moving heavy armored units along the border between Hungary and the Soviet Union. This was a hedging of bets rather than a definite threat; Khrushchev was at this point unsure how to proceed. But Moscow had not given up.

0900 London // 1000 Paris; Algiers // 1100 Cairo // 1300 Moscow

In Paris, Ben Bella and his four fellow Algerian rebel leaders were charged by a military tribunal with attempted demoralization of the army and the nation. The penalty could be death. "The only fact alleged against them at present is the distribution of pamphlets in the Paris region," reported the London *Times*.[10] At the same time as it used the stick against the Algerian rebels, the French government proffered a carrot. Guy Mollet promised Algerians equal citizenship in the French Republic, free elections, and increased investment.

At noon in Cairo, an Egyptian diplomat who served as press attaché at the embassy in Paris was shown into Gamal Abdel Nasser's office. He had been sent by Tharwat Okasha—the Egyptian military attaché in Paris, who had been a Free Officer alongside Nasser. Okasha had an important message for Nasser, which he had learned from a mysterious but clearly well-connected French friend. Okasha and his friend had bonded over two things: a love of classical music, especially the works of Gustav Mahler and Richard Wagner, and a shared interest in communicating details of French plans for Algeria back to Cairo.

Two days before, Okasha's French friend had told him everything that had been decided in the secret Anglo-Franco-Israeli meetings at Sèvres. Okasha repeated all the details carefully to the press attaché, and sent him to Cairo.

This meeting was recorded only by a secondhand source—
Amin Howeidy, later Egyptian minister of defense and chief
of general intelligence. Howeidy claimed to have heard it from
the press attaché. According to him, Nasser was standing in
the office with one foot on a chair. The attaché told the full
story of the Protocol of Sèvres.

"This is very strange," said Nasser, and asked the man to
tell it again. He did. Nasser listened.

"Look here, my son," the president said. "Israel, France can
do it, but the British cannot at all co-operate with the Israelis. They have dignity, and they will hesitate 100 times to cooperate with the Israelis."[11]

Whether or not the precise details of this story are true,
Nasser had received several warnings of the forthcoming attack. The Egyptian military attaché in Istanbul had correctly
predicted on October 6 that Egypt would face an attack by
Israel, followed by an ultimatum from Britain and France,
followed by a joint attack by all three nations. This was particularly impressive and must have been guesswork, for he
made the prediction eight days before the crucial meeting at
Chequers in which the French informed Anthony Eden of the
potential for such a plan. A few other hints had floated by. One
report from Paris was written off as deliberate misinforma-
tion, and one man who turned up at the Egyptian embassy in
Paris offering details of the Sèvres meeting was turned away
as a crank.[12] Nasser's dismissal of Okasha's story, if accurately
reported, is not surprising: these rumors were not well sourced
and looked like blips amid a tide of information from much
more reliable sources indicating an Israeli attack on Jordan.
Nasser sent the press attaché away and felt relaxed enough to
attend a party that afternoon for his son Abdel Hamid's fifth
birthday.

0700 Washington DC // 1200 London // 1400 Jerusalem; Cairo

At lunchtime, Israeli forces moved from the Beersheba area in
the Negev desert toward the border with Egypt. Separate bri-
gades fanned out into the Sinai, toward Gaza in the north, toward Kuseima in the center, and toward Kuntilla in the south.
Four Israeli piston-engined fighter planes flew low over the
Sinai, descending to just twelve feet to cut the wires between
telegraph poles with dangling hooks and their wings and pro-
pellers. At two p.m., packed into requisitioned civilian buses,
the Southern Infantry Brigade, heading for Kuseima, reached
the point where the western Negev desert became Egyptian
territory.

Much of the Israeli Negev is rocky ridges, with a few streams
that appear in the cooler months and create gullies where desert plants and scrub can survive. It is not easy terrain, and in
1956 there was little infrastructure, but it was passable. Toward Egypt, the desert changes texture. When the Southern
Infantry Brigade vehicles reached Sabha an hour later, they
foundered in soft sand. The brigade continued on foot. Most
of its soldiers were mobilized civilians, unlikely to be at peak
military fitness, and their average age was over thirty. Trudging through deep, heavy sand under the beating sun would
have exhausted fitter men. They had eleven hours of this to
endure before they would reach Kuseima.[13]

At two p.m. Cairo time, reports came in to the Egyptian
army that Israeli troops had been spotted in Sinai. Nasser had
just watched his son blow out the candles on his birthday cake.
He received word and excused himself, telling his wife only
that he had been called into a meeting.[14]

Anthony Eden's press secretary, William Clark, returned
from a fortnight's vacation. When he arrived at 10 Downing
Street, he was told to stay in his end of the building and not to

go near the prime minister's private office. He went for lunch alone. When he was coming back through the garden gate, he saw military men milling about, waiting to go into the cabinet room. He was particularly surprised to see General Keightley, commander in chief of the Middle East Land Forces, who he had not even realized was in Britain.

Lord Mountbatten, the services' most incorrigible gossip, sidled up to Clark. "Well, I don't envy your job in the next few days," he said; "this will be the hardest war to justify ever."[15]

The Israeli border police guarding the central region near the Jordanian border had been told to take all measures necessary to keep order that evening. The local colonel, Issachar Shadmi, decided that this meant setting a curfew for Palestinian Arab villages, from five p.m. to six a.m. The news of the curfew was broadcast over the radio the same day it went into force. The border police unit commanders in the region were informed of the order by their commanding officer, Major Shmuel Malinki. Malinki implied that, in the event of anyone breaking the curfew, the police could shoot to kill.

Several platoons were charged with informing villagers in person. At the village of Kfar Kassem (or Kafr Qasim), close to the border with the Jordanian-controlled West Bank, a platoon arrived to announce the news—but too late in the day. They were told that many of the village's agricultural workers were already out at work, mostly picking olives.

After five p.m., the villagers returned as expected: a mixed crowd of men and women, boys and girls, riding on bicycles, wagons, and trucks. Even though he knew these civilians would not have heard about the curfew through no fault of their own, the unit commander Lieutenant Gabriel Dahan determined that they were in violation of it and therefore should be shot. Out of all the unit commanders given this order, Dahan was the only one to enforce it.[16]

As each small group of villagers arrived, the border police opened fire. Forty-three civilians were killed and thirteen injured. The dead were mostly children aged between eight and seventeen: twenty-three of them, plus fourteen men and six women. It was said that one nine-year-old girl was shot twenty-eight times. Another little girl watched as her eleven-year-old cousin was shot. He was dragged indoors and died in his grandfather's arms, blood pouring from the bullet wound in his chest. Laborers were ordered off their trucks in small groups, lined up, and executed. There were clashes between Arabs and border police that evening in which six more Arabs were killed.

The order to kill had not come from the top. It was traced back conclusively only as far as Major Malinki. When Ben-Gurion heard about the massacre, he was furious, telling his cabinet that the officers who had shot civilians should be hanged in Kfar Kassem's town square.[17] Yet the Israeli government covered the incident up with a press blackout lasting two months.

Despite the blackout, news of the deaths did spread. Israel's most famous poet of the time, Nathan Alterman, wanted to travel to Kfar Kassem and offer his condolences to the villagers. Though he was a close friend of Ben-Gurion's, the prime minister refused to let him go on the grounds that such a visit might publicize the incident.[18]

In 1958, eleven members of the border police stood trial in an Israeli military court, which judged the killings "blatantly illegal." Of the eleven defendants, eight were sentenced to between seven and seventeen years in prison, including Malinki and Dahan. The trial set a precedent in the Israeli Supreme Court that a soldier could be held responsible for obeying an illegal order. It was an explicit rejection of the "Nuremberg defense," so called following the trials of former Nazis—many of whom argued that they were only obeying orders.

The eight guilty men were all freed within three and a half years. Both Malinki and Dahan were pardoned and returned to official security work. Shimon Peres formally expressed regret for the Kfar Kassem massacre in 2007, when he was president of Israel. His successor, Reuven Rivlin, spoke at a memorial for the slain civilians in 2014. "A terrible crime was committed here," Rivlin said. "Illegal orders topped by a black flag were given here. We must look directly at what happened."[19]

In October 1956, though, the world knew nothing of these murders. The bodies of the Suez War's first forty-nine victims went unseen and unmourned, except by their own community.

1100 Washington DC // 1600 London // 1800 Cairo; Tel Aviv

Sixteen Israeli DC-3s, among them containing 395 paratroopers, flew over the Negev. Trudging through the desert below were the four Israeli forces, including Ariel Sharon's 202 Brigade heading for Kuntilla. They had thirteen French AMX light tanks. "Many of the trucks and half-tracks were also newly provided by the French," wrote Sharon. "We had pressed them into use despite the fact that they had arrived without any tools. There was no way to even change a tyre."[20] Almost sixty vehicles and most of the tanks had broken down in the sand by that evening. "With no road, there were places where the brigade's tractors had to tow every single truck and half-track," remembered Sharon.[21]

Above both Sharon's men and the DC-3s were high-altitude British reconnaissance planes ordered to survey the situation by Anthony Eden. Back in London, Eden was frantically telephoning the chief of the air staff every fifteen minutes to check whether Israel's paratroopers had landed so that he could begin his war.[22]

In Cairo, Mohammed Heikal arrived at the Mena House Hotel, near the pyramids, at six p.m. He was to dine with the new Greek ambassador. The hotel staff told Heikal he had an important call. He went to the telephone. It was Gamal Abdel Nasser.

"Something very strange is happening," Nasser said. "The Israelis are in Sinai and they seem to be fighting the sands, because they are occupying one empty position after another. We have been monitoring closely what's going on, and it looks to us as if all they want to do is start up sandstorms in the desert. We can't make out what's happening. I suggest you come over."[23]

The 395 Israeli paratroopers were dropped at Mitla Pass, thirty miles east of Suez.

At nightfall, the Israelis in the desert were resupplied by French planes, dropping everything from jeeps and guns to jerry cans of water and gasoline to cigarettes. These were brought from the British base on Cyprus, though the British affected ignorance of the flights.

Neither the CIA nor the British and French had a clear idea of how much resistance Israel might meet in Egypt, nor the extent to which its forces might now be armed with Soviet weaponry. "During the past year—right up to the outbreak of hostilities—the USSR poured planes, tanks, guns and a host of other equipment into Egypt, to a value of about a quarter of a billion dollars," Allen Dulles told a bipartisan White House meeting a few days later. "The first Soviet submarine for Egypt was en route from Poland when Israel launched its attack in Sinai."[24] Allen Dulles had picked up inside information about the Suez plot in France; it is possible that he may have picked up talk about submarine deliveries there, too. A French diplomatic document from October 15 alleged that gunboats and submarines were being sent from the Soviet Union to Egypt. The vessels in question were old German stock that the Red Army had seized from Koenigsberg, Danzig, and Elbing after

World War II. Their crews were said to be made up of Soviet sailors from East Germany and Central Asia. The report also suggested that seven former Nazi submarine officers in Egypt had returned to West Germany in disgust, refusing to serve in Nasser's navy because they believed he was cooperating with the Soviets.[25] It was hard to know who in this situation was considered the greater villain.

1128 Washington DC // 1628 London // 1828 Cairo

Foster Dulles telephoned Sherman Adams, Eisenhower's chief of staff, at 11:28 a.m. Adams brought up remarks by the Democratic presidential candidate, Adlai Stevenson, the previous summer, accusing the Eisenhower administration of being unprepared for anti-Soviet rebellions in the Soviet satellite states. These remarks had annoyed Dulles intensely at the time and annoyed him again now.[26] "The Sec. said he has been forecasting it for a year and a half," the minutes of the telephone call recorded. "Now they say we did not know about it."

Furthermore, said Dulles, "The situation in the ME [Middle East] is awful," adding that "there is a lot of evidence accumulating which indicates that the French with the British in [the] back of them are pushing into it."[27]

Dulles received a cable from C. Douglas Dillon, the American ambassador to France, stating firmly that "we are certain [the] French are not being frank with us and suspect they may be encouraging Israelis to take at least preparatory and possibly offensive military action." He suggested Dulles send a message to Pineau, strongly condemning any possibility of such military action and stating that the United States would not back French involvement. He suggested that the NATO council should discuss this matter immediately.[28]

It was too late. The Israelis were already a long way down the warpath. Mohammed Heikal arrived at his president's office

in Cairo. The Egyptian commander in chief, Abdel Hakim
Amer—one of Nasser's closest friends since his youth—was
also there, albeit somewhat shaken. He had just arrived back
from his trip to cement the Egypt-Syria-Jordan alliance. He
had been due to fly back from Damascus the previous evening,
but had delayed his return. This turned out to be fortunate.
An Israeli jet shot down the Ilyushin transport plane that he
would have been on as it flew over the Mediterranean. The
Israelis had tried to assassinate him. Everyone on board had
been killed: sixteen Egyptian officers and journalists, plus two
crew members.[29]

Heikal found both Nasser and Amer "in a state of bewilder-
ment." They knew Israeli paratroopers had landed at the Mitla
Pass, but there seemed to be no air attack. It seemed extraordinary that Israel would send troops a hundred miles into Egypt
without air cover. The Egyptians wondered whether the invasion of Sinai might be a feint, and the real target might be
either Jordan or the Gaza Strip. Still, Nasser did not believe
that Britain and France could be behind the attack. At that
moment, as far as the Egyptians were concerned, they were
near a deal to end the Suez Crisis at the United Nations. Heikal remembered the Egyptian command even wondering if
"a frustrated Israel was trying to settle its own private scores
with Egypt in a hurry," before the Suez question could be resolved amicably.[30]

1200 Washington DC // 1700 London // 1800 Budapest // 1900 Jerusalem; Cairo

Eisenhower was in Florida on the campaign trail. In his absence, Dulles sent a top-secret cable to the American embassies in London and Paris: "Bits of evidence are accumulating
which indicate that [the] French Government, perhaps with
British knowledge, is concerting closely with Israelis to pro-

voke action which would lead to Israeli war against Egypt with probably participation by French and British." He listed the facts as known: "conclusive but highly secret evidence" that the French had supplied the Israelis with more Mystère planes than they were permitted under the Tripartite Agreement, the Franco-British air buildup on Cyprus and naval units in the eastern Mediterranean, and the blackout of information from the French and British to Americans. "There are other items of information which cannot be reported here but which substantially round out the picture," he added.

There were two possibilities, he believed, and they might both happen at once. One would be "an alleged 'retaliatory' military movement [i.e., reprisal] by Israel which would quickly take over Jordan west of the river"—the West Bank. Egypt would undoubtedly come to Jordan's assistance, and that would provide a pretext for Britain and France to launch an attack on Egypt to avert war in the wider Middle East. The other possibility would be that Israel might attempt to sail a ship through the Suez Canal. It would be stopped by the Egyptian authorities—and that would create another excuse for Britain and France to attack Egypt under the terms of the 1888 Treaty and the Six Principles that Selwyn Lloyd had put forth at the United Nations.

Though he was wrong about both of these approaches, Dulles was right that a war was about to be started on a flimsy excuse. "As you know, it is [the] profound conviction of President and myself that if French and British allow themselves to be drawn into a general Arab war they will have started something they cannot finish and end result may very well be an intensive anti-Western sentiment throughout Middle East and Africa and intimacy with Soviet Union which will impair for [a] long time indispensable relations of Europe with Middle East and Africa," he wrote. "Furthermore, the process will greatly weaken economies of France, Britain and Western Europe, [and] under circumstances it is highly unlikely US will come to aid of Britain and France as in case of first and second World Wars where they were clearly victim of armed aggression."

He added, "We have no doubt that it may be calculated that Jewish influence here is such at [sic—as] to assure US sympathy with such operations as are outlined. However, if this is calculated we think it is a miscalculation."

The telegram was intended as background information so that the ambassadors could report back to Washington for immediate authorization if they could think of "any steps which might still avert what we believe to be [a] very dangerous course of action." It did acknowledge that it might be too late: "It is only [a] matter of hours rather than days before situation may become irrevocable."[31]

Dwight D. Eisenhower and John Foster Dulles were unusual in the twentieth century: an American president and secretary of state who were able and willing to say no to Israel. There were rumors at the time, which have been revived since, that Dulles's views on the matter may have stemmed from a particular dislike of Israel. It has even been suggested that he was an antisemite.

Dulles had admired German society from a young age. He had been a legal adviser to a member of the American delegation at the Versailles conference when he was thirty years old, negotiating the peace after World War I. Like his fellow American delegates, he argued strongly that Germans should not be subjected to a level of punitive reparations that would create permanent resentment or damage their nation's recovery. He came away from the conference convinced that Britain and France had demeaned themselves by punishing Germany so harshly. He began to believe that, for new, improved global powers—like the United States—to rise, the corrupt old empires must get out of the way.[32]

During the 1930s, Dulles's enthusiasm for Germany did not dissipate quite so swiftly as would have been politic. He was close friends with Hjalmar Schacht, the Weimar president of the Reichsbank, who became a strong supporter of the Nazi Party and was made Hitler's minister of economics in 1934. Together, Foster Dulles and Schacht worked to bring American finance to the Nazi state, rescuing Germany from economic disaster and helping build Adolf Hitler up into a strong leader. (Schacht fell from favor and was frozen out of Hitler's inner circle in 1937. He was tried at Nuremberg for his work in planning the war, but was acquitted.)

Sullivan and Cromwell, the New York law firm in which both Foster and Allen Dulles were partners before their political and intelligence careers took off, worked for a number of German firms in the 1930s whose operations at that time would later associate them with the German war effort and the Holocaust. These included arms manufacturer Krupp AG and chemicals company IG Farben. Many American firms worked for controversial German companies, and such links are easy enough to find—but the personal involvement of Foster Dulles and his sustained enthusiasm for the Nazi rebuilding of the German economy is noteworthy. During the 1930s, he wrote articles characterizing Britain and France as "static" societies—which had grown to their limit and were now merely defending their privileges—in contrast to the "dynamic" societies of Germany, Italy, and Japan, which he predicted would shape the future. Though he did not approve when these nations resorted to violence, he judged such violence unsurprising.[33]

The struggle within the Dulles family over Foster's involvement with Nazi Germany was shot through with tragedy.

Foster and Allen's sister, Eleanor, had fallen in love with David Blondheim, a divorced professor of medieval Jewish philology at Johns Hopkins University. Blondheim was from an Orthodox Jewish background, and the romance horrified both his family and the Presbyterian Dulleses. The couple waited to marry until after Foster, Allen, and Eleanor's father's death in 1931. David and Eleanor Blondheim grew increasingly alarmed at events in Germany; Blondheim became deeply depressed. When Eleanor found out she was pregnant in 1934, Blondheim was overwhelmed by guilt that he had abandoned his Jewish roots and would be starting a "mixed" family. On March 19, 1934, he poisoned himself with gas in the kitchen of their Baltimore apartment. Foster persuaded his widowed sister to drop her Jewish surname. The child, when he was born, was named David Dulles.

In 1935, Allen Dulles visited Berlin and formed what he described as a "sinister impression" of the way things were going. He decided Sullivan and Cromwell should close their office in Nazi Germany on political grounds.[34] Eleanor, too, visited Nazi Germany, and was appalled by what she saw. Foster resisted pressure from both his siblings, telling Eleanor she was "working herself up" over nothing. The Dulles brothers put it to a vote at the New York office of Sullivan and Cromwell in the summer of 1935, Foster passionately defending the firm's connection to Nazi Germany and Allen arguing that it must be severed. Allen won the vote unanimously. Reportedly, Foster was so disappointed by this decision that he burst into tears. He cheered himself up by continuing to visit Nazi Germany, making trips there with his wife, Janet, in 1936, 1937, and 1939. After the invasion of Czechoslovakia, he defended Germany's actions and argued publicly and frequently against the United States joining the war on the Allied side.[35]

"Until after the United States entered World War II, Foster

Dulles maintained his antipathy toward Britain and France and his pro-German sentiment," wrote CIA agent Wilbur Eveland. "When the Second World War ended, Dulles advocated strengthening Germany as the best means for the West to contain the Soviet Union." West Germany paid reparations to Israel from 1952, in recognition of the cost of resettling five hundred thousand Holocaust survivors and some compensation for looted property. Accepting this deal was controversial within Israel, where some felt it represented blood money; others felt it was practical and necessary. Eveland stated, "Reparations of any type were anathema to Dulles," and said that Israel's claim "received a cool audience from him."[36]

In 1949, Dulles ran for a New York Senate seat against Herbert Lehman. Lehman was Jewish, and there were suggestions at the time that Dulles's campaign was antisemitic. His past links with Nazi Germany were brought up. Some years later, Abba Eban, Israeli ambassador to the United Nations at the time of the Suez Crisis and later deputy prime minister of Israel, was asked if he thought Dulles was antisemitic. "I think that Dulles, like many Americans, distinguished in his mind between two concepts, between the State of Israel and between [sic] American Jews," said Eban; "with the American Jew there is a question of internal politics, and to an extent he entered into American politics. I presume there was a mutual action-reaction, and his attitude to them was governed by theirs to him, theirs to him by what they thought was his attitude to them. But having known him for a long time, I would repudiate an [sic] concept of anti-Semitism. On the contrary, I think he had a very large historic vision about the role of the Jewish people in history, and especially in religious history."[37]

Evelyn Shuckburgh, who was given to making disparaging comments about Jewish people himself in his memoir, was present at an unusually cordial meeting between Dulles and

Eden in Paris in 1954. The Arab-Israeli conflict was supposed to be discussed. "Dulles, however, gave us an enlightening account of the power and influence of the Jews in America," Shuckburgh wrote in his diary. "Subscriptions to Israel, alone of all non-local charities, are (quite illegally) exempt from tax. But he said we have just about twelve months to do something in, before another election looms up and makes all action impossible. A.E. for his part admitted the influence of the Jewish lobby in the House of Commons."[38]

Some suggested that Dulles's views were balanced, but that he could react badly to pressure—and pressure often came from the Israeli side. A few years after Suez, the American ambassador to Egypt and State Department official Raymond Hare was asked where he thought Dulles was on the spectrum of opinion regarding the Arab-Israeli conflict. "Mr. Dulles was right bang in the middle," said Hare. "But he was consciously in the middle. And anybody who tried to push him around either way—he resented it—because he sensed the significance of this thing and the importance of approaching it with complete even-handedness. And this was very conscious on his part. It wasn't just something that came that way."[39] This may have been a fair assessment, but Dulles's past affairs indicate that he had little natural sympathy for Jews or for the Jewish state. It does not appear he had much natural sympathy for Arabs either, aside from his strategic regard for Saudi Arabia.

By contrast, Eisenhower's relations with Jewish communities were positive. He saw Nazi concentration camps soon after their liberation and was sickened by the horror that had been wrought. He requested that congressmen and journalists visit to document them. His careful and considerate policy toward Jewish displaced persons in Europe after World War II—formed in conjunction with a specially appointed Jewish adviser—had earned him the approval of American rabbis, though his directives were subverted in practice by the far less compassionate General George Patton.[40] "Unfortunately for Israel, the Americans had for the first and last time a president who was not afraid of the American Jews," explains Uri Avnery. "He was so popular he could win elections without the American Jews."[41] In fact, Eisenhower was not sure of that, but he was not put off his stride. The United States was going to do what was right—whether it won him the election or lost it.

1500 Washington DC // 2000 London // 2100 Paris // 2200 Jerusalem; Cairo

Dulles's attempts to warn Israel off came to nothing. At around three p.m. in Washington, the White House press office ticker clicked out the news that Israeli troops had moved across the Egyptian border. Eisenhower was in the air at the time, just taking off from Jacksonville, Florida. On the way back to Washington, the plane made a scheduled stop in Richmond, Virginia, for Eisenhower to deliver an election speech on the danger to world peace.

"That danger is in various places, none more critical at this moment than at the ancient crossroads of the world, the Mid-East, where old civilizations meet and ancient animosities flash anew," he said. "Fears and hatreds deeply divide nations, with all of whom American would be, hopes to be, and seeks to be, a friend."

Mindful of what he had heard on the flight, he continued. "The news in this area is not good. But I do say this: In this specific case, as in all our efforts through the world for a just and lasting peace, here is my solemn pledge to you: by dedication and patience we will continue, as long as I remain your President, to work for this simple—this single—this exclusive goal."[42]

At the same time in London that evening, there was a

reception for the prime minister of Norway. William Clark saw the first lord of the Admiralty, Lord Hailsham, and dug for information about what was going on. "I know much less than you suppose," Hailsham replied, "and what I do know makes me profoundly unhappy."[43]

While minds in London, Paris, and Washington turned to the Middle East, the security of Budapest remained precarious. That evening, the American legation telegrammed Dulles to say that the nationalist rebels had risen spontaneously and were poorly led. "Leadership is weak, isolated, and represents different programs and degrees of willingness to compromise." It was not clear who among them should be negotiating with the Soviets or the Nagy government. This, the legation worried, could lead to "real danger" that the Soviets and the government "may finally decide that only solution is absolute suppression and real iron fist policy." The Soviets were "perfectly capable" of that, according to its assessment, and the only way to avoid it was for Western powers to give high-level political support and military material support.[44] If there had been even a small chance of that before the weekend, there was much less now. Israeli troops were already in Egypt and the United States' NATO partners were only thirty-six hours behind them.

At midnight Cairo time, General Abdel Hakim Amer sent out the first orders to Jordan and Syria through their new unified command. They were to mobilize for Operation Beisan, a plan to drive forces across the narrow midpoint of Israel from the West Bank to Nathanya, snapping the country in half and surrounding Jerusalem. King Hussein was thrilled to receive these orders: he wanted to invade Israel immediately. The Jordanian chief of staff, Ali Abu Nuwar, advised the king to wait until Syrian reinforcements arrived in a couple of days. The Jordanian army was not up to taking on the IDF on its own, and Abu Nuwar knew it. Hussein was persuaded to keep his powder dry. Yet the troops were mobilized. Already the Suez War was threatening to drag in more of the Arab nations.[45]

1900 (Oct. 29) Washington DC // 0200 (Oct. 30) Cairo

At around seven p.m., Eisenhower's car arrived back at the White House. He went directly to his residence, where both Dulles brothers were waiting to meet him, along with Herbert Hoover Jr., Andrew Goodpaster, Charles Wilson (the secretary of defense), Arthur Radford (chairman of the joint chiefs of staff), and others. Dulles mentioned that there had been a substantial increase in communications traffic between Paris and Israel the day before.

Admiral Radford said that he thought Israel simply wanted the Sinai Peninsula. Dulles said it went further than that. "The Canal is likely to be disrupted, and pipe lines are likely to be broken. In those circumstances British and French intervention must be foreseen. They appear to be ready for it, and may in fact have concerted their action with the Israelis."

Radford mentioned rumors that the British, French, and Israelis "have made a deal with Iraq to carve up Jordan." So effective had been the Jordan distraction that it was still possible to feel that that territory must be part of the operation.

Dulles continued, with reference to Egypt: "The French and British may think that—whatever we may think of what they have done—we have to go along with them."

Wilson agreed. "The Israelis must be figuring on French and British support, thinking that we are stymied at this pre-election period, and the USSR also because of difficulties in Eastern Europe."

The president was in no mood to be stymied. According to Goodpaster's minutes, he declared that "in this matter, he does not care in the slightest whether he is re-elected or not. He feels we must make good on our word [to defend Egypt]. He added that he did not really think the American people would throw him out in the midst of a situation like this, but if they did, so be it."

Dulles added that "one adverse result of this action may be a wave of anti-Semitism through the country," and there was a murmur of agreement.[46]

"All right, Foster," the president said to his secretary of state, "you tell 'em [the Israelis] that, goddamn it, we're going to apply sanctions, we're going to the United Nations, we're going to do everything that there is so we can stop this thing."[47] There is also a hint in the memoir of Jacques Baeyens, a diplomatic counsel to the French military, that the Americans warned the French and British off at this stage, too. "On 29 October, an official from the American embassy in Paris—perhaps he belonged to the CIA—let Colonel Saint-Hillier know that the allies would have less than twenty-four hours before an intervention by the White House," he wrote. "This information was also taken to General Ely who did not believe it: he was convinced that the United States would leave the issue alone on the eve of presidential elections planned for 6 November."[48]

Eisenhower and Dulles talked for two hours before producing a statement for the press. It did indeed talk tough—to the point of hinting at intervention. "At the meeting the President recalled that the United States, under this and prior Administrations, had pledged itself to assist the victim of any aggression in the Middle East. We shall honor our pledge."[49]

"A nice moralistic stand," commented Emmet Hughes, Eisenhower's speechwriter, in his diary for that day. "But what does it mean? And how does one back it up? Literally read, it would seem to admit of two choices. One: We shall 'assist' Egypt against Israel and against Britain and France if they move in. *Really?* Or two: We 'pledge' flowers for the funeral of Nasser."[50] Yet Eisenhower was committed to his moral stand.

Both Eisenhower and Dulles wanted to go straight to the United Nations. In a meeting at eight fifteen p.m., "the President said we plan to get there first thing in the morning—when the doors open—before the USSR gets there."[51] Eisenhower cared little for appeasement of his allies and believed they must abide by their word. Much of his appeal to American voters was based on the fact that he was not a professional politician. He had never even voted before the 1948 election, in which the Democrat Harry S. Truman had offered to retreat to the vice presidency if Eisenhower would lead the Democratic ticket. When he did finally stand as a Republican in 1952, he made his case on being a straight talker and cleanup man: pledging to end the war in Korea and to fight Communism and corruption. His personal popularity remained high in 1956 because he was seen as having delivered on these promises. And it flourished because—even with all the speechwriters and policy advisers and political grooming Washington could heap upon him—he still came across as an honest soldier from a farm in the Midwest who seemed like the kind of guy an ordinary voter might have a beer with.

Eisenhower's reaction to events in the Middle East was characteristically straightforward. Israel had broken the rules and Egypt was the victim. He was, therefore, going to defend Egypt. His first instincts were to apply sanctions to Israel and go to the United Nations. He stopped short of talking about force—but did not rule it out.

That night, at the Metropolitan Opera in New York, Maria Callas was singing the famously difficult title role in Vincenzo Bellini's *Norma*. Sitting in their respective boxes, dressed up in white tie and tails, were Sir Pierson Dixon, the British ambassador to the United Nations, and Henry Cabot Lodge, his

American equivalent. During the performance, as Callas sang out Norma's anguish at being betrayed by her lover, the two passed notes from box to box. Lodge told Foster Dulles afterward that the normally amiable Dixon "was ugly and not smiling" and "it was as though a mask had fallen off." Lodge mentioned to Dixon that Britain, France, and the United States must come to Egypt's aid against Israel. Dixon's response, as Lodge described it to Dulles the following morning, was "Don't be silly and moralistic. We have got to be practical." Dixon dismissed the draft American resolution proposed for the United Nations, saying he "simply could not understand what the United States was thinking of."[52]

As the men passed their notes at the opera, the exhausted soldiers of the Israeli Southern Infantry Brigade arrived at Kuseima close to three hours behind schedule. Over several hours of fighting that night, they would take the two hills they needed. The Israeli conquest of the Sinai was advancing. The die was cast.

9

TUESDAY, OCTOBER 30, 1956
ULTIMATUM

0600 London // 0800 Cairo; Damascus // 1000 Moscow

From Damascus, Shukri al-Kuwatly, the president of Syria, telephoned Nasser. Kuwatly was supposed to go to Moscow that day for a state visit but, with the Israelis invading Egypt, he was worried that he might be needed at home. Nasser told him to go: the Arabs might need an advocate in Moscow. Kuwatly went.

Meanwhile, agents from the Deuxième Bureau—Syria's military intelligence service—intercepted two Druze leaders with a huge cache of weapons, which they admitted had come from Iraq. The Deuxième Bureau quickly arrested several conspirators who had formed the British section of Operation Straggle. Though they did not crack the CIA's parallel conspiracy, Michail Bey Ilyan, the man picked by the CIA as Syria's new leader, fled that morning. He turned up on the doorstep of CIA agent Wilbur Eveland in Beirut, Lebanon.

"Last night, the Israelis invaded Egypt and are right now heading for the Suez Canal!" Ilyan exclaimed angrily. "How could you have asked us to overthrow our government at the exact moment when Israel started a war with an Arab state?"

He had tried to stop the coup but did not know if messages sent would reach people in time. He was certain they would think he had known about Israel's attack plan in advance and had betrayed them. "Your Secretary Dulles," he told Eveland, "is a cruel man. He surely knew what would happen when he encouraged us to go on."[1] Foster Dulles continued to hope the Syrian coup could be enacted anyway.[2] He telephoned Allen Dulles later that day, and asked if it would be possible to delay Operation Straggle rather than abandon it.

"The British are pressing us to go ahead," he said.

Allen replied that, much though he thought it would be "good to have an anti-Communist Government in" Syria, he "was suspicious of our cousins [the British] and if they want a thing, they [the CIA] should look at it hard. Not before Nov. 1."[3]

By eleven a.m., reports were reaching Cairo that Canberra reconnaissance aircraft had been seen over Sinai, Suez, and Port Said. "These were obviously British planes," said Mohammed Heikal. Nasser sent him to see the American ambassador, Raymond Hare, who suggested that the British might just be monitoring the safety of their civilians in the Canal Zone. Heikal reported this back to his president.

"It's not convincing," said Nasser.[4]

At the British and French embassies in Cairo, staff destroyed sensitive documents. The British stuffed eight large steel cage incinerators with papers and set fire to them, the *Manchester Guardian*'s correspondent observing that "the ashes floated out on the fresh breeze towards the Nile beyond the compound wall."[5]

"We had no time to separate the confidential from the rest," remembered the ambassador, Humphrey Trevelyan. "We burnt the lot, inside the chancery and outside on the lawn, until we were inches deep in ash and had showered the neighbourhood."[6]

1000 London // 1100 Paris; Budapest // 1200 Jerusalem; Cairo

In London, Selwyn Lloyd summoned the American ambassador, Winthrop Aldrich, to the Foreign Office. The night before at the opera, Pierson Dixon had learned that the Eisenhower administration was preparing to refer Israel's invasion of Egypt to the United Nations. If the United States declared Israel the aggressor in its document, Britain could be obliged under the terms of the Tripartite Declaration of 1950 to take military action on the side of Egypt. Lloyd begged Aldrich to ask his president not to do so.

Lloyd tried to argue to Aldrich that the Israelis were acting in "a clear case of self-defence," as their own cover story suggested. Though the Israelis, the Egyptians, and all the Western intelligence agencies knew there were no fedayeen bases in the Sinai, the *Jerusalem Post*'s piece about the Israeli invasion of the peninsula that day was obligingly headlined "Aim to Destroy Fedayeen Nests."[7] The military correspondent of the London *Times* was more suspicious: "The speed and depth of the Israeli penetration is not easily explicable in terms of a punitive raid—nor, perhaps, is the playing of martial music on the Israeli radio."[8] Aldrich was not impressed by Lloyd's argument, remarking that fedayeen attacks had "been largely negligible in recent months." He also observed that it did not look like a response to Egypt's refusal to allow Israeli traffic through the Suez Canal, for the canal had been blocked to them for several years already. (Furthermore, he might have added, Nasser had again allowed ships with Israeli cargo through the canal as recently as August—as long as they did not fly the Israeli flag.)[9]

Then Lloyd tried a different tack, pointing out that the British had £75 million worth of shipping in the canal at that moment and must defend it. Aldrich remained unmoved. Finally,

Lloyd told him that Guy Mollet and Christian Pineau were on their way to London from Paris for emergency talks. He told Aldrich they would be discussing what to do about the war in Sinai.

"I left him under no doubt that it would be a serious mistake to calculate that Jewish influence on us is such as to assure US sympathy with such Israeli operations," Aldrich reported to Washington after the meeting. "I was surprised to find him take [the] line that on contrary there is widespread anti-semitism in the US, which I also obviously rejected."[10]

After Aldrich left, the British cabinet met and were told Mollet and Pineau were on their way. There was squeamishness about the extent to which the Americans were being deceived. The chancellor, Harold Macmillan—who had been a cheer-leader for invading Egypt over the summer—was no longer cheering. "Our reserves of gold and dollars were still falling at a dangerously rapid rate," the cabinet minutes stated, "and, in view of the extent to which we might have to rely on American economic assistance, we could not afford to alienate the United States Government more than was absolutely necessary."[11]

The London talks with Mollet and Pineau were for show: a pretense of responding spontaneously to unexpected events. In reality, this entire plan had been agreed to five days earlier. The Conservative MP and junior Foreign Office minister Douglas Dodds-Parker accompanied Mollet during the lunch meeting. He got into his car at two p.m., and found in his red ministerial box a copy of the statement that was to be made later in the House of Commons. "I could not believe my eyes," he remembered. "Of all the alternatives put to the decision-makers, this seemed, and was to prove, the most disastrous combination of the unworkable and the unbelievable." He returned to the Foreign Office, where "officials began to call on me to protest and tell me of their intention to resign."[12]

High above the plains of Sinai, Soviet-built Egyptian MiGs and French-built Israeli Mystères were in the air. Nasser later said he had only thirty pilots to fly the 150 MiGs the Soviets had sent him.[13] Even so, four British reconnaissance planes were, to the British commanders' astonishment, intercepted by Egyptian aircraft. The Royal Air Force now feared that "the Egyptian radar control organisation is . . . considerably better than was anticipated."[14] The Israeli ground forces pressed on toward the canal. King Saud telephoned Nasser and assured him that Saudi Arabia, as well as Syria, was preparing to help him repel them. The armed forces of both nations were mobilized. Reports in Israel even suggested that Iraq had told Britain and France it might intervene if their attack on Egypt continued.[15]

King Saud was Foster Dulles's preferred Arab leader, and yet he had so far been consistent in supporting Nasser—signing a mutual defense treaty with Egypt in 1955, applauding the nationalization of the Suez Canal, and offering support to Nasser's new alliance with Jordan and Syria. Nasser had enjoyed a state visit to Saudi Arabia in September 1956, but Saud began to have his doubts during that visit, and Nasser had nurtured reservations for much longer.[16] Though Saud continued to back Nasser during the Suez Crisis, two major differences created friction between them. The first was Nasser's opposition to the Muslim Brotherhood, which had now found a second home for itself in Saudi Arabia. The second was Nasser's pan-Arab, anti-imperialist ambitions, which threatened Saud's own leadership and potentially his cozy relationship with the United States.

Saud's father, Ibn Saud, had been an ally of Britain. His interests had been promoted by St. John Philby—a British Arabist who had been a friend of Jawaharlal Nehru's at Trinity College, Cambridge, before becoming a British agent in Arabia. Philby promoted Saud in opposition to the efforts of

T. E. Lawrence, who saw the Hashemites as the best prospect
for British patronage. In 1924, Philby was obliged to resign
from his role as the British representative in Transjordan over
his alleged secret communications with Ibn Saud and the accusation that he had embezzled funds. He converted to Islam
in 1930, adopted the name Abdullah, and became an official
adviser to the Saudis. Philby helped Ibn Saud play off British
and American oil companies against each other. By a quirk of
fate, in October 1956, Philby and his favorite son, Kim—who
had recently been exonerated after he was suspected of spying
for the Soviets—were in Beirut, where Kim was working as a
journalist and simultaneously operating undercover for MI6.
(Sheikh Abdullah St. John Philby was summoned back to Ri-
yadh just before the Suez War by King Saud, on whose privy
council he still served. Kim Philby, who stayed in Beirut, eventually admitted he was a Soviet spy and defected to the Soviet
Union in 1963.)[17]

The private, American-owned Arabian American Oil Company (Aramco) convinced the United States government in
1943 that the Saudis were sitting on 20 billion barrels of oil—
equivalent to all the oil deposits that had been explored in the
United States at the time.[18] As a result, President Franklin D.
Roosevelt declared that year: "Saudi Arabia is vital to the defense of the United States."[19] In 1945, he agreed to meet Ibn
Saud on an American cruiser in the Suez Canal. Ibn Saud had
been disappointed at Britain's Middle East policy, which he
still believed favored his Hashemite rivals in Jordan and Iraq.
He was looking for a new friend—and found one in Washington. After World War II, American politicians believed
Saudi oil could help them maintain their nation's superpower
position—and hoped that the Saudis might stand as a bulwark
against encroaching Communism from the Soviet Union.

Saudi Arabia's oil revenues were huge—reaching $340 million in 1953 before dropping back to a still-impressive $290 million in 1956—yet Ibn Saud's son Saud faced financial and political problems. His father bequeathed him vast debts. Saudi Arabia was full of scheming princes with divergent ideas about how to run things. At the center of it all were Saud and his brother Faisal, who did not get on. Saud has generally been characterized by history as corrupt and decadent, squandering his oil revenues on fripperies and vice. Faisal has been seen as prudent, puritanical, and financially responsible.[20] The real picture was more mixed. There is a highly entertaining, gossipy account from 1955 in the American State Department archives of Prince Faisal partying in a hotel room guarded by a man with a machine gun. Faisal, it was said, opened a jeroboam of champagne for the informant, a senior Egyptian politician, and summoned what the politician described as "two of the cheapest women I have ever seen."[21] The State Department filed such reports away carefully in its archives and kept a straight face. The oil continued to flow.

Britain was frustrated by the United States' support of the Saudis. They were friendly with leaders Britain disliked, especially Nasser and Shukri al-Kuwatly, and unfriendly to the Hashemites. When the Saudis associated with Khalid Baqdash, a Kurd who was elected to the Syrian national assembly as a Communist Party member, politicians in London tried to convince the Americans that this meant Saudi Arabia was a tool of the Soviets. "The agents of King Saud, their pockets bulging with gold, are co-operating everywhere with the Communists against Western interests," Macmillan wrote to Eden after he visited Baghdad for a summit late in 1955. "The Saudis have no other outlet for their wealth than subversion; and it is no exaggeration to say that American (Aramco) money is being spent on a vast scale (about £100 millions a year) to promote communism in the Middle East."[22]

It was an exaggeration. The Americans were not taken in. Containing Communism was a priority, but the United States government had its own plans. Since 1951 or 1952, the idea had been floating around the CIA that they should promote what agent Miles Copeland described as a "Moslem Billy Graham" to spread Islamic fervor. Islamism—the political application of Islamic thought—was considered a possible cure for atheistic Communism. According to Copeland, the CIA "actually got as far as selecting a wild-eyed Iraqi holy man to send on a tour of Arab countries." He insisted that the project "did no harm." By the time of Eisenhower's first administration, though, some in the State Department considered that the House of Saud might fill this religious, anti-Communist role.[23] However flamboyantly the Saudi princes might carry on in private, they were publicly devout and served as the guardians of Islam's holiest sites in Mecca and Medina.

Eden admitted there were many differences between Britain and the United States in Middle Eastern policy. "The policies being pursued by King Saud were the most pernicious of these," he wrote. Eden believed Saud was bribing other Middle Eastern leaders to turn against Britain in an attempt to sabotage his Baghdad Pact. "As a result, an absolute monarch of a medieval State was playing the Soviet game," he wrote. "The fact that he was doing so with money paid [to] him by American oil companies did not ease the situation."[24] To Eisenhower, he wrote at the beginning of 1956: "It becomes increasingly clear that the Saudis, the Russians, the Egyptians and the Syrians are working together. If we don't want to see the whole Middle East fall into Communist hands we must first back the friends of the West in Jordan and Iraq."[25]

Relations between Britain and the United States in the Middle East had reached their prickliest over the Buraimi oasis—a tiny spot on the map about six miles in diameter, with a few thousand inhabitants. It was claimed by the British-backed sultanate of Muscat and Oman along with the sheikhdom of Abu Dhabi (who were prepared to share it with each other under joint administration), and at the same time by Saudi Arabia. It had been fought over for at least a century and a half, but since 1949 there had been a new urgency to the dispute: reports now suggested there were oil reserves in the territory. The Saudis occupied Buraimi in 1952, supported by Aramco. Initially, the British attempted to resolve this situation diplomatically. The American government approved of negotiations, hoping to stay out of the dispute itself.[26]

The Saudis violated the standstill agreement that had been fixed between the disputing states. Britain blockaded the food supply to the oasis. By 1953, the British Foreign Office was pushing for the Iraq Petroleum Company (IPC) and Anglo-Iranian Oil Company (AIOC) to begin operations in Buraimi, which would effectively assert British control. Foster Dulles was minded to side with the Saudis. The case dragged on at three levels: local competition among Saudi Arabia, Abu Dhabi, and Oman; corporate competition among Aramco, IPC, and AOIC; and a petulant if stifled disagreement between the British and American governments. Dulles traveled to the Middle East in May 1953 and concluded that Britain and France "are millstones around our neck" in the region. Winston Churchill, then British prime minister, complained to the American ambassador that "it was slightly irritating that Dulles in his globe trotting progress should be taking pains at every point to sympathise with those who were trying to kick out or do down the British."[27] Anthony Eden, then foreign secretary, told his private secretary of the Americans, "They want to replace us in Egypt too. They want to run the world."[28]

In October 1955, under Eden's premiership, British-led troops went into Buraimi and forced the Saudis out. Eden did

not inform the United States before the invasion went ahead.
The Americans were furious and demanded that Britain return to arbitration. The British would not. Selwyn Lloyd and
Anthony Nutting tried to convince Eden to accept a compromise suggested by one of King Saud's advisers, which would
have given the Saudis access to the eastern end of the Persian
gulf—a region then divided among various British-supported
monarchies—in exchange for Buraimi. Eden refused. Nutting remembered his attitude: "We had already surrendered
too much in the Middle East, he claimed. . . . The only thing
that the Arabs understood was force, and until recently we had
shown them too little of it."[29]

But the United States did not appreciate force being used
without their knowledge and against their interests. The Bu-
raimi affair put the Americans off joining Eden's Baghdad
Pact. In a telephone conversation in April 1956, Dulles told
Eisenhower, "There is a lot of trouble with the British on the
Saudi business."

Eisenhower asked, "What do they want to do?" He added
that he did not like the idea of the United States joining the
Baghdad Pact.

The minutes of the conversation imply that Dulles was not
keen on that prospect, either. "The Sec. said they [the British]
have some crazy ideas but he doesn't want to talk over the telephone."[30]

Eden's own analysis at the beginning of 1957 was that "it
may be that the United States['] attitude to us in the Middle
East dates from our refusal to give up Buraimi."[31] The issue
certainly informed Anglo-American relations over Suez. Herbert Hoover Jr. explicitly linked the issues in conversation
with the British ambassador as an example of Britain's perfidy:
"There had been Buraimi; then Jordan, and now Suez."[32] The
final fate of Buraimi would not be settled until 1974, when as

part of a wider deal the Saudis agreed to let it go to the United Arab Emirates. By then, explorations had confirmed that, despite all the international fuss over the place, there was no oil there anyway.

1000 Washington DC // 1500 London // 1600 Budapest // 1900 Moscow

Eisenhower's speechwriter, Emmet Hughes, spent half an hour with the president in Washington that morning and noticed "his face drawn, eyes heavy with fatigue, worry, or both." After the previous night's council with the president, it was generally agreed that "we couldn't go back on our word" and the Tripartite Declaration had to stand.[33] What this meant was that Britain, France, and the United States would have to inscribe an item at the United Nations Security Council naming Israel as the aggressor—exactly what Selwyn Lloyd had begged the Americans not to do a few hours before.

Foster Dulles, Herbert Hoover, and others met Eisenhower at the White House to discuss why the British and French seemed to be dragging their feet in the United Nations. Dulles remarked, "With reference to our NATO partners, we may have to decide whether to go along with our partners who are colonial powers."

Eisenhower read out a draft of a stern letter he planned to send to Eden and a report that British and French landings were expected in Egypt. The American delegate to the United Nations, Henry Cabot Lodge, telephoned from New York, and they settled the wording of the item they would inscribe at the Security Council. Dulles advised Lodge "to submit the item as revised, without British or French association." The secretary of state warned those present of "the danger of our being drawn into the hostilities as we were in World War I and II with the difference that this time it appears that the British and French might well be considered the aggressors in the eyes of the world, engaging in an anti-Arab, anti-Asian war."

Eisenhower replied that he did not think there was any justification for war. The nationalization of the Canal Company was "not enough." Dulles agreed, adding that the British had practically reached agreement with Egypt over the Suez dispute at the United Nations but had been delaying final resolution. This was not even about Suez, he said; it "is really a question of Algeria for the French and position in the Persian Gulf for the British." He predicted that oil pipelines would be blown up, and the British may find themselves ejected from Iraq. According to the minutes, "He suggested that it may be necessary for us to make major adjustments in our oil situation soon."

The thought of oil struck them all. Eisenhower thought that the British would soon find theirs drying up—"Unless they have reached some secret agreement with the Saudi-Arabians," which nobody thought likely while the Buraimi dispute was still unsettled.

British action seemed so deranged that all of them were searching for method in the madness. "The President wondered if the hand of Churchill might not be behind this—inasmuch as this action is in the mid-Victorian style." Following his stroke the previous week, Churchill was convalescing. Though Eden had tried to involve him, he was not involved. Eisenhower concluded that he "did not see much value in an unworthy and unreliable ally and that the necessity to support them [the British] might not be as great as they believed."[34]

At the same time that this meeting was going on in Washington, Imre Nagy's new cabinet took office in Budapest. Nagy announced formally that the one-party system was being abolished, and new elections would soon be held. New political voices sprang up immediately, some even distributing uncensored newspapers that day. According to an officer at the American legation, who had heard it from "what is regarded as [a] reliable source," the crowd caught a major from the AVH. They were planning to kill him, but were stopped by four partisan fighters. Though he deserved to die, the partisans said, if the crowd killed him, this fact would be used by the Hungarian government to damage the rebel cause. "Crowd agreed, stripped major of all his clothes and turned him loose."[35]

The mood had not settled after the Soviet withdrawal from the capital. "All day Budapest populace has been working itself up to stage of psychological frenzy," warned the American legation. Crowds marched on parliament to demand that Soviet troops withdraw from the country entirely by November 15 and that their preferred candidates, who were now the Catholic cardinal József Mindszenty and the rebel colonel Pál Maléter, be made prime minister and minister of defense respectively. "If demands not met, [they] are demanding Western intervention," the legation officer wrote.[36]

Nikita Khrushchev was, at this stage, making a genuine attempt at a political solution. He had been consulting with China's chairman, Mao Tse-tung. Mao was against military intervention. He had argued that the Soviets should allow the bloc more political and economic independence, and that "the working class of Hungary" should be allowed to "put down the uprising on its own."[37] In a meeting of the presidium that day, the Soviet leaders Zhukov, Shepilov, and even the normally hard-line Molotov and Voroshilov were united in their agreement that they must cooperate with Nagy.

"Don't soften the self-criticism," warned Nikolai Bulganin. "Mistakes were committed."

"There are two paths," Khrushchev said. "A military path— one of occupation. A peaceful path—the withdrawal of troops, negotiations." He summed up the presidium's opinion in favor of the peaceful path: "We are unanimous."[38] They agreed to publish a short declaration in *Pravda* the next day, extending de-Stalinization policies to the Soviet bloc. The declaration would proclaim equal rights, integrity, and sovereignty for all socialist states, and noninterference in each other's affairs. Apparently, they believed this would stop the fighting and have the virtue of "extracting us from an onerous position"— avoiding the need for intervention.[39]

"The content of the declaration is good—it could have been written by us Yugoslavs," wrote Veljko Mićunović, Tito's ambassador to Moscow. "But one fears that the declaration has come a lot too late. Most important is the fact that Soviet practice is in complete contradiction to this declaration." Furthermore, he noted, it was unlikely copies of *Pravda* would be read in Budapest, for the city was surrounded by Soviet troops and nothing could get through.[40]

"Politically, [the] Hungarian situation now seems to be in stalemate," wrote the officer at the American legation—albeit a "highly unstable stalemate which could very well result in application [of the] iron fist by Soviets." The officer detected little public confidence in Nagy, whose "chance of forming rallying point for Hungarians and bridge for Soviets seem to be decreasing daily." Hungary's only hope, the officer suggested, was an internationally secured guarantee for the removal of Soviet troops. "In absence [of] such agreement," it warned, "Legation foresees ruthless suppression of revolution, application [of] iron fist."[41]

"Our country has reached a crossroads," Nagy told Hungarians on official radio. "The government will continue to pursue democratization, abolish the single party system, and base its work on the cooperation of the coalition parties that emerged in 1945." He repeated that a request would be made to Moscow for the immediate departure of Soviet troops. He ended his speech with a call for a "free, democratic, and independent Hungary." Strikingly, he did not include the word *socialist*.[42]

1100 New York; Washington DC // 1600 London // 1800 Cairo

At eleven a.m. in New York, the United Nations Security Council convened. The British and French requested that it adjourn and reschedule to meet five hours later. Both nations were trying to delay any invocation of the Tripartite Declaration before they could issue their preplanned ultimatum.

At exactly the same moment in London—four p.m.—the sham talks between Eden, Lloyd, Mollet, and Pineau came to a close. At four fifteen p.m., Britain and France issued their ultimatum directly to the ambassador at the Egyptian embassy and the chargé d'affaires at the Israeli embassy in London. Both Israel and Egypt were ordered to stop fighting and withdraw ten miles from the canal. Egypt was told to accept a "temporary occupation of key positions on the Canal" by Anglo-French forces. If either government refused these terms, Britain and France "would intervene with the means necessary to ensure their demands are accepted"—within just twelve hours.

The pantomime nature of this performance was all too obvious. No forces were fighting near the canal on October 30, 1956, at four fifteen p.m. The front was between 75 and 125 miles east of the canal, where Egyptian troops were then engaging the Israelis in Sinai. "This meant that, at the moment of its issue, the powers who were pretending to put a stop to the fighting by separating the belligerents were ordering one of them—and the victim of aggression at that—to withdraw up to 135 miles, while the other, who happened to be the aggressor, was told to advance on all fronts between 65 and 115 miles!" wrote Anthony Nutting.[43] Listening to the radio, former civil servant Evelyn Shuckburgh was similarly dismayed.

"Staggered by this [ultimatum]," he wrote in his diary. "It seems to have *every* fault. It is clearly not genuinely impartial, since the Israelis are nowhere near the Canal; it puts us on the side of the Israelis; the Americans were not consulted; the UN is flouted; we are about to be at war without the nation or Parliament having been given a hint of it. We think A.E. has gone off his head."[44] One Foreign Office official asked another what was going on. "Don't ask me," replied the man, gesturing in the direction of 10 Downing Street; "ask that —ing madman over there."[45]

Undeterred, Eden announced the ultimatum to Parliament fifteen minutes later. "What we hoped for, what we asked for—what we prayed for—is that both parties to whom these appeals have been made [Israel and Egypt] will accept them, because if they do accept them then we truly believe that a new era can open in the Middle East," he said.[46] Labour MP Denis Healey asked if the American government had been consulted when the British and French issued their ultimatum, "and did they approve of that decision?" Eden replied evasively: "We have been in close communication not only with the United States Government, but also with the Security Council to whom we have sent these proposals."[47] Labour MP Tony Benn wrote in his diary, "It is impossible to see how this can now end without far graver disasters."[48]

The earthquake caused by the ultimatum was felt almost immediately on the other side of the Atlantic. According to the journalist James Reston, Eisenhower lost his cool completely: "The White House crackled with barracks room language the like of which had not been heard since the days of General Grant."[49] Chester Cooper, in the American embassy in London, heard a rumor that Eisenhower had telephoned Eden at this point "and had given him unshirted hell." The truth, Cooper thought, was more farcical. "Ike, it appears, did call Downing

Street, but mistook one of the prime minister's aides, who answered the call, for Eden himself. By the time Eden got to the phone, Ike had finished his tirade and hung up."[50]

A letter arrived in Washington from Anthony Eden, attempting to justify his action. "Egypt has to a large extent brought this attack on herself," he wrote, "by insisting that the state of war persists, by defying the Security Council and by declaring her intention to marshal the Arab States for the destruction of Israel." The prime minister said he would go to the United Nations Security Council, but added, "Experience shows that its procedure is unlikely to be either rapid or effective."[51]

Shortly afterward, Dulles telephoned Eisenhower. "The Pres. said his offhand judgment [on what to do about Britain and France] is hands off—he does not think we should help them and let them stew in their own juice for a while," said the minutes of the call. "He does not see how we can go before our people and say they are our friends and we have to rescue them etc. etc."

Eisenhower was determined to send a strong message to the British prime minister: "The Pres. wants to get over to him that we are a government of honor and stick by what we say."[52] His communication was short and cold. "It seems obvious that your Government and ours hold somewhat different attitudes toward the Tripartite Declaration of 1950," he wrote. "Since we have never publicly announced any modification of the Declaration or any limitations upon its interpretation, we find it difficult at this moment to see how we can violate our pledged word."[53]

In Moscow that evening, the Kremlin hosted a reception for the prime minister of Afghanistan. Molotov told everyone present that Britain and France were behind the Israeli invasion. The British ambassador, Sir William Hayter, assured

guests that this was not true and that Britain would undoubtedly condemn Israeli aggression at the United Nations, as it
always did. He returned afterward to the embassy and found
the text of the ultimatum. "As I read it I could not believe
my eyes," he remembered; "I even began to wonder if I had
drunk too much at the Kremlin."[54] The news of the Suez ultimatum provoked outrage in the Soviet Union but presented a
remarkable opportunity. For the past few days, the Soviets had
been the focus of international fury owing to their conduct
in Hungary. Now, thanks to Britain and France's ultimatum,
they were no longer the only villain on the international stage.

Khrushchev later tried to frame the situation as a conspiracy. "English and French diplomats in London and Paris met
with our embassy people over a cup of coffee or a glass of wine
and said, 'You seem to have some trouble on your hands in
Poland and Hungary,'" he claimed. "'We understand how it is
sometimes. We're having some troubles of our own in Egypt.
Let's have a tacit understanding between us that you'll liqui-
date your difficulties by whatever means you see fit, and you
won't interfere while we do the same.' In other words, the
imperialists tried to take advantage of the troubles we were
having in Poland and Hungary so that they could send their
troops into Egypt to reestablish colonial rule."[55]

Britain and France had planned to issue the ultimatum before the rebellion in Hungary became serious. Khrushchev's
conspiracy theory is an old raconteur's exaggeration, but it
does reveal something about his own motives. The Soviets had
made a mess in Hungary, and it was a great relief to them
that their NATO rivals were about to make an even bigger
mess in the Middle East. Better still, the Syrian prime minister, Shukri al-Kuwatly, arrived in Moscow at about the same
time that news of the Anglo-French ultimatum broke. Kuwatly's presence allowed the Soviets to look as though they were

consulting urgently with Arab leaders—even though, to Kuwatly's distress, they seemed to have no immediate intention of doing anything about the British and French action. By the time Kuwatly met Khrushchev, Bulganin, several presidium members, and Marshal Zhukov that evening, his emotions could no longer be contained. He demanded that the Soviets help Egypt.

"But what can we do?" Khrushchev asked him.

"Is it for me to tell you what to do?" Kuwatly shouted. "Egypt is being attacked, and Egypt believed you were going to come to her aid. If you do nothing, your position in the Arab world will be utterly destroyed."

"But what can we do?" asked Khrushchev, again.

Zhukov unrolled a map of the Middle East on the meeting table. "How can we go to the aid of Egypt?" he asked Kuwatly. "Tell me! Are we supposed to send our armies through Turkey, Iran, and then into Syria and Iraq and on into Israel and so eventually attack the British and French forces?"

"Marshal Zhukov, Marshal Zhukov," Kuwatly shouted in reply, "do you want me, a poor civilian, to tell you, the great marshal, the conqueror of Germany, what should be done?"

Soviet grandees were accustomed to hearing exotic combinations of flattery and fantasy, but this one seems to have stunned them into silence. "We'll see what we can do," Khrushchev concluded eventually, putting the map away. "At present we don't know how to help Egypt, but we are having continuous meetings to discuss the problem."[56]

The Soviets were inclined to prevaricate over action in Suez partly for the practical reasons Zhukov had outlined and partly because they had been hoping to improve relations with Israel. Khrushchev had recently welcomed Golda Meir to Moscow and apparently took to her. Yet he was aware of the heft of the Arab nations and their potential to upset his Cold

War rivals. Ahmed Ben Bella and the Algerian rebels had also visited Moscow in 1956, before their kidnapping. Khrushchev found he liked Ben Bella more than any other Arab leader, calling him "a highly intelligent man, a great son of the Algerian people."[57]

The Soviets had to make a choice. Britain and France had just made a move redolent of imperialism against a nonaligned Third World Arab nation. Members of the presidium were aware that their actions in Hungary had also looked somewhat redolent of imperialism. That evening, the American ambassador to the Soviet Union, Charles Bohlen, met Zhukov and attempted to press him on Hungary. Zhukov seemed relaxed. "Let them deal with it themselves," Zhukov said to him, echoing Mao's advice. The Soviet Union, he implied, would now leave Nagy alone. Bohlen reported: "Soviet Union [is] preparing [to] cut losses Hungary and accept high degree if not complete independence [in] satellites in general." He did warn, though, that "Soviet policy is reacting to fast developing events outside its borders and depending on these events can and indeed does shift accordingly." If Nagy's government lost control, he warned, Soviet troops might well stop withdrawing, and Moscow's whole policy of letting Hungary deal with things itself might change.[58]

Bohlen did not get far in his conversation with Zhukov before they were interrupted by Vyacheslav Molotov. Molotov changed the subject to Suez. He was convinced that the United States was in "cahoots" with Britain and France and could therefore have prevented the Israeli attack on Egypt.[59] This theory was all the Arab representatives in the Soviet capital were talking about, and it was believed by most, if not all, of the presidium. William Hayter telegraphed dryly to the Foreign Office in London, "No doubt you will be sending guidance soon on how to answer charges of this kind."[60]

Backing the Arabs was not only true to the Soviets' stated anti-imperialist principles, it also allowed them to trumpet those principles before the world at the exact moment they had begun to look badly tarnished. For Moscow, Suez was a gift. "It was with great reluctance that Father sanctioned the breach in Soviet-Israeli relations, which were only just beginning to develop," remembered Khrushchev's son Sergei. "But there really was no choice. He preferred to befriend the many millions of the Arab world."[61]

1400 Washington DC // 1900 London // 2100 Cairo

In Cairo, the Anglo-French ultimatum "was received with astonishment bordering on disbelief," remembered Mohammed Heikal. Though they were in little doubt that Eden wanted a war, it had been presumed that Britain would never risk alienating Iraq and its other Baghdad Pact allies by aligning with Israel to invade an Arab country. "Nasser found the whole situation made no sense at all." said Heikal. "It was, in fact, quite mad."[62] Collusion seemed so contrary to their interests—it was jeopardizing their commercial and political position throughout the Middle East, as well as risking their oil supply. Furthermore, though Nasser did not much care for Anthony Eden personally, he clung to a fundamental belief that the British would behave honorably. "This is all a lie," he said. "How can they lie? Is Eden a liar?"[63]

"Nasser did not in any way estimate that this ultimatum was serious," said one member of the government who met with him that evening.[64] The president thought it must be a bluff. At nine p.m., he sent for Sir Humphrey Trevelyan, the British ambassador, and rejected it. There was a blackout all over Egypt as night fell. "I was worried and asking myself what would be the reaction of the people," Nasser remembered. He drove to the Cabinet House. "All the way I listened to the people raising the slogan 'We will fight, we will fight.' And this was fresh hope to me, because my dependence by that time was on the people."[65]

Still fearing retaliatory air raids on Tel Aviv and Jerusalem, the Israeli government ordered blackouts too. Shopkeepers taped up their windows. Citizens dug trenches around their houses in accordance with precise instructions distributed by the civil defense service (they were to be six and a quarter feet deep). Drivers slopped dark blue paint over their cars' headlamps to dim them. "But nothing could ever disturb café life here," the *Jerusalem Post* reassured its readers. "At Kassit, dexterous waiters served their sidewalk tables as if nothing was going on and, although many of the servicemen and tourists were missing, the local artists made up for their absent colleagues by laughing a little louder and expounding in grander fashion." When the warning sirens wailed and distant ack-ack fire could be heard, the customers left their half-finished beers on the tables and scurried into shelters. The *Post* was pleased to note that, despite the interruption, everyone returned to their tables within the hour "and no one absconded with the bill [unpaid]."[66]

The mood was not so cheerful inside the Israeli government. Under the terms of the Protocol of Sèvres, the Anglo-French bombing campaign to knock out Egypt's air force, thus protecting Israel from retaliatory bombing, was supposed to start before dawn. That night, the British government belatedly realized that it would look bad to start bombing before its own ultimatum had expired. General Keightley was ordered to postpone the raid for a few hours. Keightley, who did not know that his government was colluding with Israel, resisted. He argued that a daylight raid would be more dangerous. Eden used this as an excuse to postpone the bombings even longer—for twelve hours in all.

None of this was communicated to the Israelis, apart from the decision to postpone. "Those bastards," wrote Moshe Dayan in his diary. "They make a political agreement in which one of the main clauses, one we insisted on, was an air strike on Wednesday morning, and here they casually postpone the operation by 12 [hours] with no warning, not even an apology, the bastards."[67]

In Washington, Dulles and Eisenhower were trying to decide how to respond to the ultimatum. Dulles remarked that it was "utterly unacceptable." He added that there was not much point in studying it; it was merely a pretext. "Of course by tomorrow they will be in." Eisenhower raised a concern that the Soviets would get involved: "Where is Egypt going to turn?"[68]

Eisenhower decided he must write back to Eden and Mollet warning them off their "drastic action." As he said to Dulles, "The whole purpose of that [reply] would be public—they are not going to pay the slightest attention to it." But it was essential to send anyway: "That establishes us before the Arab world as being no part of it."[69]

The Americans had already realized that the Soviets would exploit this situation—a possibility the British and French seem not to have fully considered. But circumstances were about to change again. Khrushchev's peaceable plan for Hungary might have gone ahead had it not been for an incident that day at the headquarters of the Budapest Party Committee on Republic Square. Public disquiet was triggered, according to some present, when a truck drove up bringing ample supplies of meat for the AVH officers inside the building; the butchers' shops nearby had almost run out. Somebody started a rumor that there were secret chambers under the building in which prisoners were being held and tortured. A crowd assembled and clashed with former members of the AVH. Shots were fired into the building and fire was returned from it.

The siege went on for hours before three tanks arrived from the Ministry of Defense—but the tank crews were soon converted by the crowd to the rebel side. Their guns swiveled round to point at the party headquarters. Jean-Pierre Pedrazzini, a twenty-nine-year-old star photographer from *Paris Match* (famous for having recorded the first meeting between Grace Kelly and Prince Rainier of Monaco), darted out from behind a tank to take a picture. There was a blast of gunfire and fourteen bullets ripped through Pedrazzini's abdomen, back, and legs. He died a week later.[70]

The rebels entered the building and tried to dig up the secret chambers. The chambers turned out not to exist, and no prisoners were found or liberated—but the rebels dragged out between twelve and twenty AVH men.[71] Some of these were just twenty-one or twenty-two years old, new recruits who had not been responsible for the years of torture and disappearances. They were beaten, spat upon, strung up from trees by their feet, doused with gasoline and set on fire. According to the British *Daily Worker* correspondent Peter Fryer, "Score upon score of secret police swung head downwards from the Budapest trees and lamp-posts, and the crowds spat on them and some, crazed and brutalised by years of suffering and hatred, stubbed out cigarette butts in the dead flesh."[72]

"To this day, I recall how this furious and frenzied crowd took pleasure at the mutilation of dead bodies," wrote the journalist and historian Charles Gati, who witnessed the scene. "I hasten to add that this was an exception to the rule; to my knowledge, such disgusting misbehavior did not happen elsewhere during the revolt."[73] Photographers and newsreel cameramen caught the images of these scenes on film for international news agencies. When the pictures got out, they seemed to confirm all the worst fears the Soviets had about the horror of a counterrevolution.

1500 New York; Washington DC // 2000 London // 2100 Budapest // 2200 Cairo

At eight p.m. in London, Eden returned to the House of Commons. Hugh Gaitskell, the leader of the opposition, came at him with a strong reply to his announcement earlier that day. Gaitskell pointed out that Britain and France were acting at the exact moment that the United Nations Security Council was meeting. "I cannot see any possible justification for that," he said. "There is nothing in the United Nations Charter which justifies any nation appointing itself as world policeman." He expressed dismay that the United States and other Commonwealth countries did not seem to have been properly consulted. "Is America supporting us? Is she giving us her full backing?" he asked. "If it comes to a vote in the Security Council on our action, if it is taken, can we be sure that the United States will vote with us, or are we doing this off our own bat without bothering whether the United States is going to support us or not?"[74]

Labour MP Alfred Robens also questioned Eden's attempts to imply that the United States had been informed: "It seems exceedingly strange, if that is the case, that there should be the statement from the United States State Department today that it had received no prior warning of the British and French intention to move troops into the Suez area if Egypt and Israel do not stop fighting." There were gasps of "Oh!" from the members in the chamber.[75]

"In this matter we have never claimed that we have acted in agreement with the United States," Selwyn Lloyd said, provoking more cries of "Oh!" from the chamber. "We have certainly been in close touch with the Government of the United States throughout this controversy, but we have never said that we have acted with their approval and authority."[76] A Foreign

Office official remarked dryly that evening, "It's rather fun to be at Number 10 the night we smashed the Anglo-American alliance."[77]

At three p.m. in Washington, exactly the same time as the Commons in London was having this discussion, and exactly the same time as Israel's 202 Brigade led by Ariel Sharon arrived at the Mitla Pass to meet up with their paratroopers,[78] Foster Dulles telephoned Lester Pearson, the Canadian secretary of state for external affairs. The Canadians, who belonged to the Commonwealth and had always been loyal to the British, were just as angry as the Americans that they had been deceived. Dulles started on a despondent note, admitting that his efforts had been "blown up," and the ultimatum was "as brutal as anything he has seen." Pearson replied even more bluntly, calling it "stupid." Dulles said the Americans had been "in complete ignorance," and Pearson added that the Canadians had too, and that it was "hard to believe they [the British] have not been doing something as it happened so suddenly." Dulles replied that "we have been blacked out re their activities for 10 days."[79]

Eden sent another telegram to Eisenhower, filled with untruths: "We would not wish to support or even condone the action of Israel," he wrote. He argued that the Canal Zone must be secured, and that—though Britain supported taking this issue to the Security Council—it had stepped in only because the United Nations could not act quickly enough. Eden attempted to assure Eisenhower that Britain's action "is not part of a harking back to the old Colonial and occupational concepts. We are most anxious to avoid this impression."[80]

"Here is something at last he is anxious for us to understand," Eisenhower remarked sarcastically to Dulles.

Dulles replied, "Now they have done it they are going to try to get us to go along with them."

Eisenhower was not inclined to do that. "The Pres. said if we let it go along etc. etc. where do we get along with them against Communism. The Pres. does not want to be associated with them in the Arab world."

Dulles read Eden's message again and then telephoned back to comment that he was "not impressed by its sincerity."[81]

Soon after this call, Eisenhower went into a meeting with the director of war mobilization. The president had already spotted one of the weakest links in Britain's plan: its dependence on oil. "They would be needing oil from Venezuela, and around the Cape, and before long they would be short of dollars to finance these operations and would be calling for help," the minutes of the meeting record him saying. "They may be planning to present us with a fait accompli, then expecting us to foot the bill." Describing himself as "extremely angry with both the British and French," Eisenhower said that he was inclined to let them "boil in their own oil, so to speak." Yet he did tell the director to look into the possibility of using fleet oilers to meet British shipping needs—noting that Britain could pay for these in sterling.[82] This was a big deal: Britain's dollar reserves had already been depleted to close to what many at the British Treasury considered a minimum sustainable level of $2 billion. The Treasury had further calculated that the dollar cost of losing oil supply through the Suez Canal would be an unsustainable $515 million a year. This included $303 million for additional oil from the Americas, $110 million from lost earnings on oil from the Middle East, $112 million on hiring tankers, minus a $10 million saving from reduced purchases of oil from the Middle East.[83]

When the United Nations Security Council reconvened that afternoon, something previously unimaginable happened. The United States publicly turned on its NATO allies. Eisenhower was unhappy about this, but was confident that he had domestic and global support. "And he was convinced that, however ironic the immediate circumstances, he was in an unassailable moral position," remembered Chester Cooper. "He was reacting to his deeply felt abhorrence of war."[84]

The resolution put to the Security Council by the United States indicated that Israel was the aggressor. It demanded an immediate cease-fire and the withdrawal of Israeli forces. It also urged all members to avoid the use or threat of force and to withhold any assistance from Israel until it withdrew its forces. This was a clear rebuke to Britain and France. The Security Council voted. With the United States were China, Cuba, Iran, Peru, Yugoslavia—and the Soviet Union. Australia and Belgium abstained.

Britain and France had little choice but to vote against this resolution. Because they were permanent members of the Security Council, their votes counted as a veto—and the resolution was not passed. Anthony Nutting was among those devastated by the use of the veto, to which Britain had never previously resorted. "We had done as the Russians had done, no less than seventy-eight times since the U.N. was started," he wrote bitterly.[85]

After the American resolution failed, the Soviets moved another. This offended the British slightly less—on the grounds, Eden explained, that it did not include "phrases explicitly directed against Anglo-French action." It removed the threat of sanctions and merely ordered the Israelis to withdraw. In the break between sessions, the British representative Pierson Dixon went to see his French opposite number, Bernard Cornut-Gentille, who was not only representing France but also presiding over the session. Cornut-Gentille collapsed during the break. It was said he had contracted malaria on a recent trip to West Africa; less discreetly, Christian Pineau wrote in his memoirs that Cornut-Gentille suffered a nervous breakdown. He lay on a sofa, shivering violently and insisting that he must soldier on for the honor of France. Nobody else thought this was a good idea. A doctor was brought in, and Cornut-Gentille was replaced by his deputy, Louis de Guiringaud. The French were going to use their veto again—and Dixon had been ordered to act with the French, whatever they did. "For the sake of solidarity, therefore, we acted together," Eden wrote, justifying why Britain deployed its veto a second time.[86]

Finally, a letter arrived from Egypt asking the Security Council to consider the Anglo-French ultimatum as an act of aggression. At this point, the representative from Yugoslavia suggested that since Britain and France were rendering the Security Council impotent by repeated use of their vetoes, the matter should go to an emergency session of the General Assembly. This procedure had been designed to get around Soviet intransigence. The Soviets had not yet caused it to be used. Britain and France just had.[87]

1700 Washington DC

A draft copy of a cable to be sent from Eisenhower to Eden is in the president's files from that day, written by himself. It is marked "not to be used."

"I must say that it is hard for me to see any good final result emerging from a scheme that seems certain to antagonize the entire Moslem world," Eisenhower wrote. "Indeed I have difficulty seeing any end whatsoever if all the Arabs should begin reacting somewhat as the North Africans have been operating against the French. Assuredly I hope, as I know you do, that we shall not witness any such spectacle as the Soviets have their hands on in Hungary. However, I assume that you have your plan all worked out and that you foresee no such dreary or unending prospect stretching out ahead."[88]

Emmet Hughes was with Eisenhower between 5:00 and 5:20 p.m. and found him anxious, though calmer than many in the White House or the State Department, "all of whom are whipping themselves into an anti-British frenzy."

"I've just finished writing an answer to an informative cable from Eden this morning, saying I understand and even sympathize with him on the problem he faces—but just hope he's figured out all the risks," Eisenhower said. "I'm not at all optimistic: I'm afraid the British'll come out of this with more loss of face. What are they going to do—fight the whole Moslem world?" If the Israelis just stopped fighting, he said, it would "be over within 24 hours."

But if it was not, said Hughes, "will we be joining Nasser against our Western allies?"

"Hell," said the president, "I don't know *where* we'll be at."

He explained that he still felt bound by the Tripartite Declaration and admitted, "If the Israeli[s] keep on fighting, we'll be in a hell of a fix. . . . I don't know . . . Maybe we'll just have to get off the hook by talking about Russian arms going to Cairo." He concluded, "I've just never seen great powers make such a complete *mess* and *botch* of things. . . . Of course, there's just nobody, in a war, I'd rather have fighting alongside me than the British. . . . But—*this* thing! My God!"[89]

Right after Hughes left, Dulles and Eisenhower discussed his letter over the telephone, Dulles advising that "the last part is a bit too much" and Eisenhower agreeing to hold off sending anything until the next day. But the minutes of other telephone conversations between the two men that afternoon show that their feelings mirrored those in the Kremlin. "The Sec. said what a great tragedy it is just when the whole Soviet policy is collapsing the Br and Fr are doing the same thing in the Arab world. The Pres. . . . certainly hopes we don't get into the position the Soviets are in over Hungary."[90]

August 1956: The Suez Canal, presided over by a colossal statue of its creator, Ferdinand de Lesseps. *(Gerard Gery/Paris Match/Getty Images)*

Happier Times: Gamal Abdel Nasser (*left*) meets Anthony Eden in Cairo on February 22, 1955. The smiles did not last. Two days later, Eden's Baghdad Pact was signed, creating a regional power bloc against Nasser. Four days after that, on February 28, the Israeli Defense Force staged a raid on the Gaza Strip. *(Popperfoto/ Getty Images)*

March 1, 1956: British foreign secretary Selwyn Lloyd (*left*) meets Nasser in Cairo. During their dinner, the British commander John Bagot Glubb was fired from his position at the head of the Jordanian army by King Hussein of Jordan. This event triggered Eden's desire to have Nasser "murdered." (*Bettmann Archive/Getty Images*)

April 1956: Soviet leaders visit London. *Left to right:* Nikolai Bulganin, Anthony Eden, Nikita Khrushchev, Selwyn Lloyd. "Bulganin can vote Labour if he likes," Khrushchev remarked, "but I'm going to vote Conservative." (*Keystone-France/Gamma-Rapho/ Getty Images*)

July 1956: Nasser (*left*) with his fellow leaders of the Non-Aligned Movement, Jawaharlal Nehru of India (*center*) and Josip Broz Tito of Yugoslavia (*right*). The three had been meeting at Tito's villa in the Brioni archipelago when Nasser received the news that the United States was canceling his Aswan Dam project. He would respond by nationalizing the Suez Canal Company. (*AFP/ Getty Images*)

Nasser is cheered by huge crowds after nationalizing the Suez Canal Company on July 26, 1956. *(Keystone-France/Gamma-Keystone/Getty Images)*

July 31, 1956: Though they were enraged by Nasser's nationalization, Lloyd (*left*) and Eden (*right*) could not go to war immediately. Their American allies pushed them into talks. *(Philippe Le Tellier/Paris Match/Getty Images)*

The widely loathed Stalinist leader of Hungary, Mátyás Rákosi (*seated, left*), listens as his more moderate opponent, Imre Nagy (*standing*), addresses parliament. *(Bettmann Archive/Getty Images)*

David Ben-Gurion, prime minister of Israel. *(ullstein bild/ullstein bild/ Getty Images)*

Allen Dulles, director of the CIA. The CIA and MI6 were planning a coup in Syria at the time the British and French governments would launch their invasion of Egypt. *(Bettmann Archive/Getty Images)*

Though CIA agents on the ground in Egypt admired and supported Nasser, Secretary of State John Foster Dulles preferred the Saudis as potential leaders of the Arab world. *Left to right:* President Dwight D. Eisenhower, King Saud of Saudi Arabia, and Vice President Richard Nixon. *(Bettmann Archive/Getty Images)*

The British and French governments realized they would have to plan their war against Nasser without American help. Eden *(left)* welcomes French prime minister Guy Mollet *(center)* and Minister for External Affairs Christian Pineau *(right)* to London, September 1956. *(Central Press/Hulton Archive/Getty Images)*

American-British relations were strained over Suez. John Foster Dulles (*left*) discusses the crisis at the United Nations with a defensive Selwyn Lloyd. (*Lisa Larsen/The LIFE Picture Collection/Getty Images*)

October 1956: The United Nations Security Council considers the dispute over control of the Suez Canal. (*Bettmann Archive/Getty Images*)

October 22, 1956: French forces kidnap and handcuff the leaders of Algeria's FLN rebel movement. *Left to right:* Mostefa Lacheraf, Mohammed Boudiaf, Hocine Aït Ahmed, Mohammed Khider, and Ahmed Ben Bella. *(GAMMA/Gamma-Keystone/ Getty Images)*

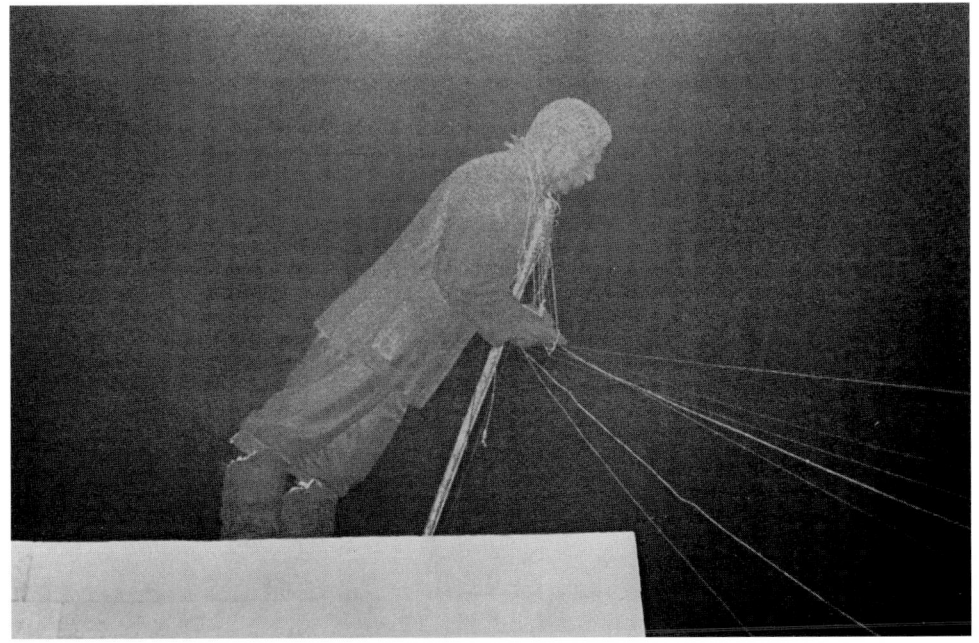

October 23, 1956: Anti-Soviet protesters in Budapest haul down a giant statue of Joseph Stalin in Heroes Square. *(Bettmann Archive/Getty Images)*

The Soviets initially allowed Imre Nagy (*center*) to become leader of Hungary. He had popular support but was a cautious reformer. *(ullstein bild/ ullstein bild/Getty Images)*

Pál Maléter, the charismatic Hungarian colonel who became a rebel leader at the Kilián barracks and then minister of defense. *(Keystone-France/Gamma-Keystone/ Getty Images)*

A Soviet officer, his body covered in slaked lime, lies dead near the rebel stronghold at the Kilián barracks in Budapest. *(Erich Lessing/ Magnum Photos)*

"Goddamn it, we're going to apply sanctions, we're going to the United Nations, we're going to do everything that there is so we can stop this thing": A tightlipped Eisenhower *(left)* walks through the north portico of the White House on October 29, 1956, after hearing of the Israeli invasion of Egypt. Charles Wilson, secretary of defense *(center)*; Foster Dulles *(right)*. *(AP/Press Association Images)*

October 30, 1956: The beaten and mangled corpses of AVH (State Security Police) men lie in the streets of Budapest. Their lynching would prompt both Khrushchev and Mao Tse-tung to think again about allowing change in Hungary. *(Photo by Jack Esten/Stringer/Getty Images)*

October 30, 1956: Ariel Sharon (*left, with map*) and his Israeli Defense Force men at the Mitla Pass in Sinai. Israel invaded Egypt to give Britain and France an excuse to intervene as "peacekeepers." *(Ministry of Defense/Getty Images)*

Moshe Dayan, the IDF's chief of general staff, with troops in Sinai. *(Francois Pages/Paris Match/Getty Images)*

November 1, 1956: An Israeli soldier writing a letter home during a break in the fighting in Rafah, Gaza Strip. The United Nations reported that hundreds of people were summarily executed by the IDF in Gaza during the Suez War. *(GPO/Getty Images)*

November 2, 1956: Rebel skirmishes continued in Budapest, though many believed at this point that they had won. Two days later, the Soviet army would crush the rebellion. *(AP/Press Association Images)*

November 4, 1956: Thousands gather in Trafalgar Square, London, to protest against the Suez War. Labour MP Aneurin Bevan told the crowd that Eden "is either a knave or a fool. In both capacities we do not want him." *(Mark Kauffman/ The LIFE Picture Collection/Getty Images)*

Soviet tanks roll through the streets of Budapest.
(Keystone-France/Gamma-Keystone/Getty Images)

An Egyptian boy near a British tank in Port Said. *(Bettmann/Getty Images)*

Nasser at his home after hearing of the Anglo-French invasion of Port Said. *(Howard Sochurek/ The LIFE Picture Collection/Getty Images)*

	EISENHOWER	STEVENSON
ALA.	149,329	209,569
ARIZ.	90,338	51,878
ARK	35,123	48991
CALIF.	475,226	389,007
COLO.	102,871	61,915
CONN.	710,059	406,56
DEL	92,328	75,16.
FLA.	512,308	361,09
	6,09	22,4
IDAHO	9,271	26,26

November 6, 1956: Dwight and Mamie Eisenhower and Patricia and Richard Nixon celebrate as the American people vote to give the president a second term. *(PhotoQuest/Getty Images)*

One of the blockships sunk by Egyptian forces in the Suez Canal to cut it off during the war. The British minister Anthony Nutting admitted, "In one case at least we had actually done Nasser's job for him by sinking a blockship after it had taken up its position." *(STAFF/AFP/Getty Images)*

November 1956: British soldiers sit on a captured Egyptian gun. Despite the jovial mood here, Britain's Suez adventure would end in disaster.

THE VICTORS

Eisenhower campaigns for re-election in New York City. *(Bert Hardy/ Getty Images)*

Nasser is hoisted aloft by cheering crowds in Port Said after Anglo-French forces withdraw from Egypt in December 1956. *(Rolls Press/Popperfoto/ Getty Images)*

In Philadelphia, Eisenhower's opponent, Adlai Stevenson, gave what the *New York Times* described as "one of [his] strongest addresses of the campaign." The crisis in the Middle East, he told his audience, revealed that the president was paying too little attention to United States interests. Eisenhower, he said, had been hunting quail in Georgia when Indochina fell to the Communists and was playing golf when they took Dien Bien Phu. "If a Democratic President rolled up a record like that," he said, "I'm afraid every newspaper in the country would call for his impeachment." Eisenhower, he alleged, was a "phoney"—a president elected as a front man "so that another man—or group of men—can run this country." As evidence of the president's alleged phoniness, he produced Eisenhower's mid-October broadcast to the American people expressing his hope that the Suez crisis was behind them: "Two weeks ago, the President appeared before you and told you he had good news about the Middle East."[91]

The electoral liability of Eisenhower's current position was far more serious than some quail and a few rounds of golf, as the president was aware. "It's looks as if we're in for trouble," he told his son John in a frank conversation that evening in the bedroom on the second floor of the White House. "If the Israelis keep going—and if the UN says so—I may have to use force to stop them; conceivably that could entail the use of all kinds of weapons." This was an incredibly broad hint, not even—in John's recollection—ruling out the use of nuclear weapons. He knew that war with Israel would cost him the Jewish vote. "Then I'd lose the election. There would go New York, New Jersey, Pennsylvania, and Connecticut at least."

"Wowie!" said John. "Couldn't you hold off taking action until the election is over?"

"That might be too late," his father said. "We'll just have to see."[92]

Dulles was due at an off-the-record dinner that night with a group of journalists. He used such dinners regularly to get his views out into the press without making official announcements. On Suez, he told them it was not so much from affection for Nasser that the United States was opposing Britain and France, but from a feeling that their methods were unacceptable. He characterized Suez and Hungary as colonial actions by Britain and France and by the Soviet Union, respectively. The United States had, he thought, been striking a difficult balance since World War II: maintaining its friendships with the imperial nations of Britain and France, while at the same time trying to befriend the newly independent countries escaping imperialism. He did not believe this balance could be held forever, and he was more inclined to move toward the new, dynamic states than stay bound to the old. Furthermore, he suggested, if the likes of Hungary and Poland might be about to liberate themselves from the Soviet embrace and become neutral, as Yugoslavia had, Europe would be less vulnerable; the United States might not feel so beholden to its NATO allies.[93]

Dulles based his opinion on the accurate information he had received that the Soviet Union was withdrawing from Hungary. Yet at the very hour he was speaking, Nikita Khrushchev was waking up after a sleepless night in Moscow. With the mutilated bodies of the AVH men still swinging from the trees and lampposts of Budapest, the position of the Soviets on Hungary was about to change dramatically.

10

WEDNESDAY, OCTOBER 31, 1956
PERFIDIOUS ALBION

**2300 (Oct. 30) Washington DC // 0400 London // 0500 Paris //
0600 Cairo**

At around three thirty that morning Cairo and Tel Aviv time, the Egyptian destroyer *Ibrahim el-Awal* (formerly, before Britain sold it to Egypt, HMS *Cottesmore*) began to shell the Israeli port of Haifa. It was fired on by a French ship and captured by the Israelis. "As the ship approached the harbor, most of her crew could be seen crowded at the rails smoking and staring glumly at Mount Carmel," reported the London *Times* correspondent in Tel Aviv.[1] The twelve hours of the Anglo-French ultimatum were not yet up—but the French had already engaged and put themselves visibly on Israel's side.

At six o'clock that morning, Cairo time, the ultimatum expired. It was four a.m. in London, and eleven p.m. on October 30 in Washington, DC. In Malta, British marine commandos were embarking. In Cyprus, British and French air transports were landing. A fleet of British and French battleships, including five aircraft carriers, was in the eastern Mediterranean. The order to attack was given at four thirty a.m. London time. "Thank God we're off!" the chief of the imperial general staff, General Sir Gerald Templer, told MI6 chief Dick White. "If anybody pulls us back now, I'll have his balls."[2]

In London, Chester Cooper received Washington's announcement that the American Sixth Fleet, also based in the Mediterranean, would be reinforced by what was called a "hunter-killer group": an aircraft carrier, two submarines, eight destroyers, and a tanker. "There was a rumor that the Sixth Fleet had orders to intercept British and French warships sailing toward Egypt," Cooper remembered. "At the Pentagon in Washington maps of the Middle East were in such demand that they had to be rationed."[3]

The Israelis at Mitla Pass struggled on without British air cover. Four Egyptian jets flew overhead. "We watched them for a horrified instant as they arranged themselves in attack formation and roared in toward us," remembered Ariel Sharon. "By that time the drivers were gunning their vehicles away from the convoy line and everyone else was digging in the sand like madmen, myself along with the rest."[4] Two Israeli Meteor planes swooped in to fight off the Egyptians.

Sharon was given permission to send a reconnaissance mission into the pass. "You can go as deep as possible," he was told by his commanding officer, "just don't get involved in a battle."[5] Though the Israelis were not expecting resistance inside the pass, they were shot at as soon as they went in—losing two half-tracks and a driver. They then proceeded to get involved in a battle. According to Sharon, who was always ready with an excuse when he stepped over the mark, this happened because he had told his men not to leave any dead or wounded in the field. Sharon remembered that one officer moved in. "And as he did he was drawn into battle with an entire Egyptian infantry battalion that had dug themselves into the ledges and caves of the cliff walls and had not been noticed by our planes."[6]

More planes arrived overhead, this time British-made Vampires. These were Egyptian planes, though Sharon pointed out that they had markings similar to the British: green, white, and red concentric circles as opposed to blue, white, and red. "I was so distrustful of British motives that even while we were shooting at these planes I was not convinced they were Egyptian," he wrote.[7]

"I would welcome direction at what stage or in what degree it is visualised we fight as the Allies of the Israelis," the commander of Operation Musketeer, General Keightley, telegrammed to the chiefs of staff that day. "The French are doing a lot covertly and are proposing to increase their effort."[8] But while the French were not especially concerned about being seen as allies of Israel, the whole British plan had rested on this fact remaining secret.

In Cairo, Nasser summoned the American ambassador, Raymond Hare, and asked him to pass on to Eisenhower a request for American support against Anglo-French aggression. If they attacked him militarily, he said, he would want military support. "He said his government had carefully considered the alternatives of turning to the USSR or the US and had decided on an appeal to the US," reported the State Department summary. Hare told Nasser that American military intervention was unlikely: Britain and France were still American allies. Nasser indicated that he understood this.

"In asking for our assistance, are you asking it in the hopes that there may be a favorable reaction, reciprocation," said Hare, "or are you doing it in anticipation that there will be an unfavorable answer and that you will be then at liberty to turn to the Soviet Union for assistance?"

"Nasser was at first somewhat taken aback at the directness of this approach," recorded the State Department notes.

"Please understand," said Hare. "This is really a very serious question, and it would be very helpful to me."

Nasser relaxed. "No," he said. "This is a serious thing, I mean it."

According to the notes, Nasser confirmed that the decision to ask for American intervention was "reached after careful consideration and with no discussion of turning to the USSR." He further added that he would neither surrender nor run away.

Nasser did not receive the military response he hoped for. The United States confirmed that it would pursue the issue through the United Nations. "Nasser thanked me very politely, but with a considerable lack of enthusiasm," remembered Hare.[9]

0900 London // 1000 Bonn; Budapest // 1100 Cairo // 1200 Moscow // 1330 New Delhi

That morning, American diplomatic staff drove around Budapest to survey the situation. "In dramatic overnight change, it became virtually certain in Budapest this morning that this Hungarian revolution [is] now [a] fact of history," the legation officer wrote delightedly. Soviet troops had gone. Two bridges across the river were clear. Rebels walked the streets freely. The Hungarian army appeared to be distributing food and running essential services. "Legation was doubtful that what has happened could be achieved without strong Western support," the officer went on. Yet it "appears logical premise that Soviets, having unilaterally decided to abandon military position in city without guarantee of ultimate nature of government that springs up behind must be seriously considering departure from Hungary within relatively short period."[10] The London *Times* reported that the withdrawal of Soviet troops appeared to have been completed without incident. "It was announced to-day that the big red star that has dominated the roof of the Parliament building will take some time to remove," it warned. "Meanwhile it is to be draped with the

Hungarian national colours—red, white, and green."[11] (The similarity to Egyptian colors was coincidental.)

This seemed too good to be true, and it was. "I could not sleep," said Nikita Khrushchev of the previous night. "Budapest was like a nail in my head."[12] Having issued the declaration in favor of a political solution in Hungary and more liberal and equal relations with the Soviet bloc—a declaration that appeared in millions of copies of *Pravda* that morning—he had been faced with two alarming pieces of news. First, Imre Nagy had brought up with Mikoyan and Suslov the question of Hungary leaving the Warsaw Pact. While Nagy had in the past frequently raised the possibility of Hungary following Yugoslavia to neutrality, the prospect of this happening at such a sensitive moment horrified the Soviet leaders in Moscow.[13] Second, Khrushchev heard the news that Hungarian rebels had the day before lynched a dozen or more AVH officers who were loyal to Soviet rule. The lynching stoked in Khrushchev's mind fears of what the Soviet leaders called another "White Terror," after the violence carried out against Russian rebels by the White Army of imperial Russia during the civil war of 1917–23. Suddenly, the Hungarian revolutionaries looked to him exactly like the "shock troops" of "fascists and imperialists" whom hard-liners like Ivan Serov had been warning about.

The massacre of the AVH men had made for a grotesque spectacle, and its images changed the minds both of Khrushchev and of Mao Tse-tung. The previous day, both of them had been inclined to let the Hungarians deal with the rebellion themselves. When Mao's agents reported to him that the atmosphere was turning anti-Communist, though, Mao sent word to Moscow that the Soviets must act.[14] After his sleepless night, Khrushchev was inclined to agree.

There was another significant factor in Khrushchev's

thinking: Suez. Khrushchev's response to the invasion of Egypt—which had so far been minimal, apart from offering some moral support—had been seen as too soft by some in the presidium. Inside the bubble of Soviet leadership, where comrades could move in or out of favor as abruptly and dramatically as schoolgirls in a clique, Khrushchev was by the morning of October 31 being perceived as weak. "As a result of the outbreak of armed conflict in Hungary the situation over Suez has suddenly worsened," wrote Yugoslav ambassador Veljko Mićunović. "Britain and France appear to think that the Russians are now busy with their very pressing worries in Hungary, are interested only in preserving the 'socialist camp,' and that they can't be bothered now to help Nasser over Suez."[15]

When the presidium met that day, Khrushchev took immediate action to forestall any mutiny. He asked his comrades straight off to reverse their decision to withdraw troops from Hungary.

"We should take the initiative by re-establishing order in Hungary," he told them. "If we leave Hungary, this will give a boost to the Americans, the English and the French—the imperialists. They will take this for weakness on our part, and they will launch a major offensive. In that way we would be laying bare the weakness of our positions. If we do that, our party won't accept it. The imperialists will then add Hungary to Egypt. We have no alternative."[16]

It is possible that Khrushchev would eventually have crushed the Hungarian rebellion anyway, but the situation in Suez pushed him. His mistaken belief that the United States was engaged in a major Western colonialist war in Egypt along with Britain and France informed his decision to act firmly and immediately. One member of the presidium, Maksim Saburov, raised the concern in the meeting that reversing the previous day's position might "vindicate NATO" and make the Soviets look bad.[17] But the emergency in Budapest, exacerbated by the attack on Egypt, won out. No matter what, Hungary had to be retaken. János Kádár and Ferenc Münnich, two reliable Hungarians, were considered for the leadership; Khrushchev thought Imre Nagy could be permitted to stay on as deputy if he cooperated. The committee asked Marshal Zhukov to plan a campaign to retake Hungary by force. It was code-named Operation Whirlwind.[18]

The United States was not collaborating with Britain and France as Khrushchev believed. By that morning, "diplomatic relations were virtually broken between Washington and London," wrote Chester Cooper. Officers at the embassy were told to stay away from Whitehall. Cooper, as a CIA link, was to stay and maintain contact with British intelligence: "Moreover, I would be the channel to Her Majesty's Government for whatever other business could not wait until the skies cleared."[19] From the embassy in London, American diplomats reported that "a number of [British] Foreign Office officials personally deplore the British action on Suez because the eyes of the world are being distracted from the brutality of Soviet imperialism."[20]

Foster Dulles spoke to Vice President Richard Nixon that day, and told him that the fact that Suez and Hungary were happening at the same time created a pivotal historical moment. Two things were important. The first: "It is the beginning of the collapse of the Soviet Empire—the second is, the idea is out that we can be dragged along at the heels of Britain and France in policies that are obsolete. This is a declaration of independence for the first time that they cannot count on us."[21]

As the rift running down the Atlantic deepened, another opened up between Britain and the Commonwealth. The Indian government issued a statement calling both the Israeli attack on Egypt and the Franco-British ultimatum "a flagrant violation of the United Nations Charter," and warned that it could lead to a much larger war.[22] The former Israeli prime minister Moshe Sharett was in Delhi that day, meeting Nehru on the way to a conference of Asian socialists in Bombay. Sharett stated that he was "absolutely certain" that what he called the "drastic retaliatory action" taken by Israel was an Israeli initiative alone, without British or French collusion. He blamed Egypt for Israel's invasion of its territory, claiming that the Arab states' prolongation of the Arab-Israeli conflict was "a standing invitation to outside intervention."[23]

In France, too, there was talk that this must have been collusion. "For weeks now, M. Mollet and M. Pineau have been defending themselves against criticisms of their failure to live up to their first promises to bring Colonel Nasser to heel, with assurances that the game is not played out," reported the London *Times* correspondent in Paris. "This has led to a crop of rumours about a secret diplomatic weapon." The minister of defense, Bourgès-Maunoury, had been telling anyone who would listen that Israel would be a "splendidly effective" weapon to use. The correspondent also noted that Mollet's speech in parliament that day had been given in praise of Israel and condemnation of Nasser—with little mention of the necessity to ensure freedom of navigation in the canal or the need to restore peace between Egypt and Israel. "These different factors, added together, have led many people, well outside the ranks of the Communists and their sympathizers, to suppose that the Israelis' aggression against Egypt was neither unwarranted nor discouraged by the French Government," wrote the correspondent.[24]

That morning, Anthony Nutting went into the Foreign Office to send his letter of resignation to Eden. Eden asked him to come to the House of Commons after lunch to talk.

Nutting went, and told Eden, "What we were doing now

seemed to me to be contrary to everything which he had always stood for—and hence taught me—during his political life."

Eden replied that he thought Nutting would be more worried about Israel's threat to Jordan than its attack on Egypt: "But when I pointed out that the threat to Jordan had been invented by us to cover our tracks, he did not pursue the argument." Nutting looked Eden in the eye. Eden looked away: "Already, I felt, he knew that he was beaten, having tried and failed to act out of character." Eden asked Nutting to keep his resignation secret for the time being. They agreed that the press would continue to be told the story that he was bedridden with asthma.

The two men shook hands. *"Tout casse sauf l'amitie,"* said Eden—everything breaks except friendship. "I hope, in spite of all this, that we shall see something of each other in the future."

"I have never seen him since that day," Nutting wrote, eleven years later.[25]

Even some of those in the Conservative Party who did believe Britain was morally justified in attacking Egypt were considering their positions. The junior Foreign Office minister Douglas Dodds-Parker—a right-winger who loathed Nasser—remembered that he thought about resigning that day, "not because the action was 'dishonourable,' whatever that meant in all the circumstances, but because it just could not work."[26]

Despairing at Britain's behavior in the United Nations overnight, the Labour leader Hugh Gaitskell considered a dedicated campaign of opposition to Eden's war. The parliamentary Labour Party met to discuss it. "Eden has broken every pillar of British foreign policy—the Charter, the Commonwealth, the Atlantic Alliance," said Denis Healey. He stated that the Israeli invasion of Egypt was "a put-up job" and a "tragic blunder by

Israel for Eden will use her and then destroy her." Another member, Fred Lee, suggested that British trades unions should take industrial action against the government.[27]

Since Nasser's nationalization of the Canal Company in July, Eden had always assumed that the opposition and the nation would unite behind him if he invaded Egypt. He had ignored countless signals to the contrary. Now the opposition was uniting against him—and it was by no means certain that he would be supported by everyone in his own party.

0730 Washington DC // 1230 London // 1430 Tel Aviv; Gaza City
In Washington, Eisenhower was up early for a breakfast meeting with his advisers. The air in the meeting, according to Emmet Hughes, "seems thick and heavy with the righteous wrath against Britain that is beginning to suffocate the White House. And the righteousness even seems petty—as if the *real* crime of London has been to contrive so thoughtlessly to complicate [the] President's re-election or at least whittle down his majority." Hughes remembered one adviser suggesting that an American plane fly over the Middle East with an atomic bomb, and threaten to drop it "if they *all* don't cut this nonsense out." The response from the rest of the meeting was a stony silence.

"I just don't know what got into those people," Eisenhower said, meaning the British and French. "It's the damnedest business I ever saw supposedly intelligent governments getting themselves into."[28]

Foster Dulles was now considering imposing "economic limitations" on Israel. He asked the Israeli ambassador to the United Nations, Abba Eban, to clarify Israel's intentions regarding withdrawal from Egyptian territory. Eban spoke to Ben-Gurion, and then reported back: "It is not the Prime Minister's intention to seize or hold Egyptian territory." Furthermore, he said, Ben-Gurion was ready to withdraw "if he receives certain reciprocal undertakings from Colonel Nasser from any source and commitments to refrain from hostile acts."[29] This was a bluff. The Israelis' operation specifically aimed to seize half the Sinai and open the Straits of Tiran. Moreover, from early afternoon on October 31, Israel's national radio station began broadcasting announcements in Arabic telling inhabitants of the Gaza Strip to keep their radios tuned for further instructions. The IDF was about to embark on a part of its operation aimed at ensuring Israel's longer-term security—but at the cost of the Palestinians as well as the Egyptians. It aimed to sever the tiny, refugee-packed enclave of the Gaza Strip from its protector, Egypt.[30]

1400 London // 1500 Budapest

In Budapest that afternoon, Imre Nagy stood to address a joyous mass demonstration in front of parliament. "My friends, the revolution has been victorious," he told them. "We have chased out the Rákosi-Gerő gang. We will tolerate no interference in our internal affairs."[31] Political prisoners started to be released in their hundreds, and soon thousands.

János Kádár, one of Nagy's fellow liberalizers, saw the Soviet observers Anastas Mikoyan and Mikhail Suslov to their armored vehicle. They were going back to Moscow. The goodbyes were not unfriendly. Afterward, Kádár went to Imre Nagy's office.

"Imre, have we done it?" he asked.

"We've done it, János," replied the prime minister, warmly.[32]

In London, Eden again addressed an angry House of Commons, posing as the guardian of Israeli security. "The Security Council resolution simply called upon the Israeli Government to withdraw within their frontiers," he said. "That seems to us in all the circumstances that have preceded these events to be a harsh demand, if it is to stand alone."[33] He told them that

Israel had accepted the ultimatum, but Egypt had rejected it. "What did you expect?" cried members from benches. The fighting, he alleged, was now nearing the canal.

"In the light of all these facts [*sic*], can anyone say that we and the French Government should have waited for a satisfactory resolution by the Security Council authorising definite action to stop the fighting?" he asked.

"Yes," roared the members in reply.

Hugh Gaitskell stood to describe the looming Suez invasion as "an act of disastrous folly whose tragic consequences we shall regret for years." He also raised the question of "an even worse story which is going around. . . . It is the story that the whole business was a matter of collusion between the British and French Governments and the Government of Israel."[34]

The speed with which Gaitskell had found out about the collusion demonstrates how foolhardy it was that Eden had believed he could keep something like this secret at all, let alone in perpetuity. A French senator had spent an indiscreet evening in a Paris nightclub showing off his inside knowledge in front of a Lebanese businessman. The Lebanese businessman had gone to William Yates, a young Conservative MP who was unusual in having sympathy for Nasser, and told him the whole story: Ben-Gurion had been to Paris, a plan had been agreed with the British and French governments to invade Egypt, and it was all about grabbing the Suez Canal. Yates took the Lebanese businessman to the Conservative chief whip, Edward Heath, but was rebuffed. So he took him to Gaitskell instead.[35] A week after the supposedly top-secret agreement was made, all the significant information had leaked out. It could just as easily reach Britain's enemies. Even more worryingly, bearing in mind Britain was deceiving most of them, it could just as easily reach Britain's allies.

The story spread on both sides of the House of Commons. The Conservative MP Nigel Nicolson had heard the evening before from Eden's press secretary "that it is all a deep-laid plot. The ultimatum was worked out beforehand. The Jews would accept, the Egyptians refuse, and then we would have the excuse to attack Egypt, depose Nasser, and sail away, leaving friendly governments in Cairo and Tel Aviv." He told this to his influential colleague Bob Boothby, who was shocked. "Eden would never try such a trick," Boothby said. "He'd be found out, and then he'd either have to resign, or lie."

"He chose to lie," said Nicolson. "We anti-Suez Conservatives could say nothing publicly about our suspicion, because in view of Eden's denial, it would simply not be believed, and we feared demoralising our servicemen as they were about to go into action."[36] The conspiracy limped on, making more and more people complicit in its deception.

1115 Washington DC // 1615 London // 1815 Tel Aviv; Jerusalem; Cairo

That afternoon, Ben-Gurion sent a desperate cable to Paris. "I am cast down and confused by the fact that at this hour we are still without news of an Anglo-French operation against the Egyptian airfields," he wrote. "We have parachuted battalions close to the Canal with the sole aim of serving your purposes, for this was not designed to serve ours."[37] Shortly afterward, British warplanes finally left the tarmac.

An American U-2 spy plane took off from the United States' base at Adana in Turkey. Its routine reconnaissance mission was to fly over specific points of interest and take photographs. This one flew over the eastern Mediterranean and down to Egypt. It was usual to fly over the targets twice. On its itinerary was Cairo's airport. The pilot flew over it, taking pictures.

Ten minutes later, he flew over it again, taking more pictures. The plane returned to Adana.[38]

At six fifteen p.m., Nasser was at home in Cairo, meeting the ambassador from Indonesia. A series of dramatic explosions outside signaled the arrival of British warplanes. Nasser rushed up to the roof to watch. "Their target was supposed to be Al-Maza, the military aerodrome," noted Heikal, "but in fact the bombs fell on the nearby international airport."[39] The original British plan had been to bomb Cairo West, the airfield where many of Nasser's Soviet Ilyushin bombers were kept. At the last minute, though, when planes were already in the air, word had been received in London that 1,300 American civilians were being evacuated along the road that ran alongside Cairo West. The prospect of accidentally killing hundreds of innocent Americans loomed. Eden hastily ordered that the planes change their target. Now, they were to aim for Al-Maza. Given only ten minutes to change their plans, though, the poorly briefed pilots mistook the nearby civilian airport for the military airfield.[40]

"We saw the lights of Cairo in the distance," one air gunner told a journalist from the *Daily Mirror* when he returned to base. "The airfield we attacked was beautifully lit up. There were many planes on it. We came in high, dropped our bombs and watched them explode."[41] According to the *New York Times*, Cairo was completely blacked out with all traffic stopped: "Flares from the attacking planes, however, lit up the big white and sand-colored buildings of this metropolis brighter than if there had been a full moon."[42]

"I still couldn't believe it," Nasser said later. "I quickly ran to the roof of my house. I had to see for myself. But it was true. British planes bombing Cairo's International Airport." The misdirected bombing raid was a useful warning: Egyptian Ilyushins were moved to Luxor and to Syrian and Saudi airfields, saving them from subsequent raids.[43] Nasser and his aides had doubted that the Anglo-French ultimatum was serious. Now they could see that it was.

"I felt that suddenly we were overcome by confusion and many of us were paralysed," remembered the Free Officer Abdel Latif al-Baghdadi. Fully aware that they had no real chance of winning a war against two of the world's most heavily militarized powers, many began to consider radical alternatives. The CIA had predicted they would fall back to guerrilla tactics, and this was discussed. As Baghdadi put it, they wondered whether "to save our country from ruin by surrendering and going underground in order to maintain the struggle against this conquest which would be thrust upon us."[44]

In Adana, the photographs taken by the American U-2 spy plane were developed. Most of them came out as expected. The only exceptions were the two photograph sets the pilot had taken of Cairo airport. The first set, as usual, showed aircraft on the ground. The second, from ten minutes later, was quite different. A field of fire engulfed the planes, the airport, and everything else around it. The U-2's flyover had been remarkably timed: the British Royal Air Force had bombed the site in the ten-minute gap between its two visits.[45]

The CIA used a wirephoto machine to transmit the U-2 pictures to the RAF in Britain for comment. According to a source inside the CIA, the RAF replied with a brief, blithe cable, perhaps not realizing the extent of their two governments' estrangement: "Warm thanks for pix [sic]. It's the quickest bomb damage assessment we've ever had."[46]

Late that afternoon, Ariel Sharon's Israeli forces had finally been able to withdraw from the Mitla Pass. After nightfall, two small groups were sent back in. "Moving slowly along the cliff face, they attacked one Egyptian cave and firing hole after another in hand-to-hand fighting," Sharon remembered.

For two hours the sounds of battle reverberated through the pass before finally giving way around eight o'clock to an ominous silence."[47] The Israelis had taken the pass—leaving, by Sharon's estimate, 260 Egyptians dead in addition to 38 of his own paratroopers.

1500 Washington DC // 2200 Cairo

News spread through Washington that British planes had been bombing Egyptian—but not Israeli—airfields. This, said Emmet Hughes, triggered "total crisis in White House."

"Bombs, by God," Eisenhower shouted. "What does Anthony think he's doing? Why is he doing this to me?"[48] There had been nothing in the Anglo-French ultimatum about air strikes; it had merely talked of a "temporary occupation of key positions on the Canal." According to the London *Times*, "The air in official Washington to-day is thick with cries of 'Perfidious Albion!'" Questions were being seriously asked in Washington as to whether Britain and France were still considered American allies. "Every official voice here, it seems, is raised to-day against a 'dangerous and desperate gamble' that is bound to fail, at the risk of provoking the Muslim world into a 'holy war' that will involve Britain and France from the Atlantic to the Persian Gulf," reported the paper. It added that American officials were predicting oil pipelines would be cut and the Canal would be blocked, "and the point that constantly recurs amid this dire speculation is that the United States will remain militarily aloof from it all."[49]

With the American presidential election campaign entering its final week, Eisenhower's political opponents tried to spin what was happening against him. Former president Harry S. Truman claimed that the American people "had been misled by the Eisenhower Administration." The Democratic candidate, Adlai Stevenson, claimed that the Republicans' policy in the Middle East had "plunged the world to the brink of war."[50]

"I have done my best [to stop the British]," Eisenhower wearily told the leader of the Republicans in the Senate. "I think it is the biggest error of our time, outside of losing China."[51]

A heavy atmosphere hung over the United Nations Security Council as it met to hear members condemn the British and French action as "aggression." Following Yugoslavia's suggestion that the Middle East crisis be referred to the General Assembly, there was a tense debate. Seven votes were cast in favor of Yugoslavia's proposal, including those of the Soviet Union and the United States, with two abstentions. Only Britain and France voted against—though they were, on this point, powerless to veto the decision. "It was at once apparent that a section of opinion in the council impugned the good faith of Britain and France in their present action and accused them of having been in collusion with Israel," noted the London *Times* correspondent. This was "an accusation which [British representative] Sir Pierson Dixon repudiated effectively, but without convincing the sceptics."[52]

Eisenhower was due to address the nation on television at seven p.m. Foster Dulles wrote him what Hughes called an "impossible" speech: "It recites and rambles, with no force of argument." Eisenhower sent Hughes off to rewrite it. Hughes sat in the cabinet room, from where he could see—to his considerable annoyance—the president relaxing outside, putting golf balls around on the White House lawn.

In London, the American ambassador Winthrop Aldrich spoke at a dinner celebrating British and American friendship. Amid the usual platitudes on the subject, his speech sounded a sharp note. "One of the little ironies of life is that I am here to propose this toast at a difficult moment of very grave anxiety, when our two Governments for the first time have just cast opposed votes in the Security Council. That is really a tragic thing," he said. "We now have a difference of opinion over a grave and difficult situation in the Middle East and how it should be approached, but I would certainly hope, and I feel perfectly confident, we shall reach an agreement on a position which we can both conscientiously support."[53]

Aldrich was trying to make the best of the situation, but many in London did not feel so confident. "There was need for speedy decision, certainly," said an editorial in the London *Times*. "It is also very true that Mr. Dulles's tactics have been both surprising and disappointing at many times; and agreement for action—especially on the eve of the Presidential elections—would not have been reached. Yet was the need for speed really so great that President Eisenhower had to hear about the Anglo-French ultimatum from Press reports?"[54]

At midnight Cairo and Tel Aviv time, French ships— escorted by Israeli destroyers—began to bombard army bases around Rafah at the extreme southern end of the Gaza Strip. Moshe Dayan and Mordechai Bar-On were there to watch. "The camps became an inferno," Bar-On wrote in his diary, though he complained that the difficulty of coordinating an international joint operation meant that some barrages were "rather unimpressive" and there were long gaps between them.[55] Dayan was even more disappointed. "We all expected that the pounding from the destroyers would be carried out on a European scale, and we conjured up familiar scenes from war-films of powerful shells exploding on the coast on the eve of a landing," he wrote in his diary. "But the leviathan gave forth a sprat."[56] The shelling of Rafah may not have been effective, but it was important to Israel for a different reason: the French armed forces had cooperated openly in a major preplanned operation with the IDF. It would be significant to the rest of the world for that reason, too.

1800 Washington DC

In Washington, Hughes continued to work on the president's speech, with Dulles at his side. "He is ashes-gray," wrote Hughes, "heavy-lidded, strained. His shoulders seem to sag."

"I'm just sick about the bombings," Dulles explained, "the idea of planes over Cairo right now!" He changed a sentence on Hungary from "There seems to appear the dawn of hope . . ." to "There *is* the dawning . . ."

Hughes took the final draft into Eisenhower's bedroom so the president could read it through as he dressed.

"I want to be sure we show clearly in here how vital we think our alliances are," Eisenhower said before he began. "Those British—they're still my right arm!"

He approved the text with minimal changes, and Hughes raced off to add the emphatic underlines to the large-text reading copy with a grease pencil. At 6:45 p.m., Eisenhower came into the Oval Office wearing a gray suit, and read through as Hughes pushed the pages over the desk to him. He finished the last at 6:56.

"Boy, this is taking it right off the stove, isn't it?" the president said.

The lights came up and the camera began to roll. Eisenhower sounded strong, assured and, above all, sensible. He avoided all of Britain and France's tidy euphemisms, like "police action" and "peacekeeping," and called what they had launched on Egypt an "armed attack."

"The United States was not consulted in any way about any phase of these actions," he said. "Nor were we informed of them in advance. As it is the manifest right of any of these nations to take such decisions and actions, it is likewise our right—if our judgment so dictates—to dissent. We believe these actions to have been taken in error. For we do not accept the use of force

as a wise or proper instrument for the settlement of international disputes."[57] He spoke of his belief in the United Nations
as the proper body to handle disagreements between nations.

Almost everyone in the room, from press and politicians to
camera technicians, seemed tense, Hughes remembered. "No
moment since Korea has seemed so charged with war peril."
The only man who seemed calm was the president himself.

He finished at precisely 7:14, and the broadcast ended on
schedule. As he left, he said to Hughes with a grin, "I had been
thinking maybe I'd have to have you hidden under the desk to
hand me page after page as I talked! Went fine, though."

Hughes had been skeptical of the president's leadership
during the crisis so far, but found himself alone in this opinion. The assembled reporters were profoundly impressed by
the president's speech: "So maybe, in all this fantastic frenzy,
we stumbled upon some way at least to articulate a United
States position that has *some* perspective, and dignity . . ."[58]

The relief and hope would not last. Half the world away,
on the borders of Hungary, Soviet forces were beginning to
gather for the next stage—and a desperate Soviet moderate,
Anastas Mikoyan, got back on a plane to Moscow to try to stop
them.

II

THURSDAY, NOVEMBER 1, 1956
"THERE IS SOMETHING THE MATTER WITH HIM"

0700 Moscow

Before dawn in Moscow, an emotional Anastas Mikoyan returned from Budapest and went in person to Khrushchev's house in the Lenin Hills. He hoped to make a last attempt to persuade the Soviet leader not to smash Hungary.

"Do you think it's any easier for me?" Khrushchev said. "We have to act. We have no other course."

"If blood is shed, I don't know what I'll do with myself," shouted Mikoyan.

"That would be the height of stupidity, Anastas," replied Khrushchev, who apparently thought his comrade had just threatened suicide (Mikoyan recalled later that he was merely threatening to resign). "You're a reasonable person. Think it over, take all the factors into account and you'll see we've made the right decision. Even if there is bloodshed, it will spare us bloodshed later on. Think it over and you'll understand."[1]

The Soviet leader got into his limousine and drove away.

0600 London // 0800 Cairo

"I woke up early to the sound of exploding bombs," wrote the Egyptian politician Abdel Latif al-Baghdadi.[2] Over the night of October 31 to November 1, British planes bombed four Egyptian airfields—belatedly fulfilling their agreement with the Israelis to knock out Nasser's air cover. Early on the morning of November 1, nine more airfields were hit. The British government claimed these hits were accurate and avoided any civil damage,[3] which was not true: they were wildly inaccurate. They did have a small positive effect from the point of view of the Anglo-French operation, for they helped demoralize the Egyptian air force.[4] "The affairs of Britain seem now to be in the hands of a madman," read the editorial in the *Egyptian Gazette* that morning.[5]

Nasser was in a better mood, "even lively," wrote Baghdadi.[6] He declared general mobilization and martial law. "We shall fight and we shall not surrender," he said in a broadcast. "We shall fight from village to village, from place to place."[7] That same morning, Nasser and Abdel Hakim Amer called off Operation Beisan—the planned attack on Israel by Jordan and Syria. The Syrian forces that had turned up in Jordan following the call for mobilization were poorly trained and equipped. The Jordanian chief of staff, Ali Abu Nawar, had not thought them up to slicing Israel in half. Most in the Jordanian government were intensely relieved not to have to invade Israel— apart from King Hussein himself, who had been raring to go. According to Nasser's friend Mohamed Heikal, King Hussein telephoned Nasser that day and told him that he would go ahead with Operation Beisan without Syrian help. "But Nasser begged him not to, saying that they were facing something much bigger than an Israeli attack and that it was essential for the Jordanian Army to be kept intact."[8]

Some years later, Abu Nuwar remembered "when Nasser said 'stop' and the King was urging me every minute to attack, I said 'no, Your Majesty, this would be suicide.'"[9] Nasser eventually managed to get the king to agree to an indefinite postponement of the operation. Abu Nuwar still feared Israel might attack Jordan. He told the British ambassador that Jordan's decision not to attack Israel must be kept secret: "If this became public he would be obliged to attack."[10]

Nasser had now heard snippets from his own intelligence contacts in the Syrian Deuxième Bureau about Operation Straggle/Wakeful, the British-American coup planned for Syria. With treason swirling around Damascus, he did not want to do anything that might destabilize Syria to threats from within or without. He feared Britain and France might rally to Israel's side there as they had in Egypt—and could perhaps even take the opportunity to invade and occupy Syria. The *New York Times* reported that Nasser "is said to be trying to persuade the Iraqis and Syrians to blow up foreign oil installations in their countries in retaliation for attacks on Egypt."[11] In fact, the opposite was true. On Kermit Roosevelt's urging, Nasser sent a message to the Syrians telling them "not to destroy oil pipelines as this is injurious to the interests of other countries not implicated"—meaning specifically the United States. This message arrived too late. The Syrians had already blown up three pumping stations, interrupting the flow from Kirkuk in Iraq to Tripoli in Lebanon—one of Europe's essential supply routes.[12]

0900 London // 1000 Budapest // 1300 Moscow // 1330 Delhi

The British ambassador to Moscow, William Hayter, telegraphed to London that the Soviet government "regard Suez as a heaven-sent distraction from Hungary." Things were even worse now that it was clear Britain and France were acting separately from the United States, though the Soviet press was still alleging that Washington was secretly involved in the collusion.

Hayter did not think the Soviets wanted to send troops to Egypt. They might consider doing so, though, if they were eventually convinced that the Americans were not involved. They might even "try to get together with the United States at our expense." A joint Soviet-American military action against Britain and France might have sounded far-fetched, but everything that was going on was far-fetched.

In any case, Hayter said, the Soviets would certainly give the Egyptians all possible aid: "Their prestige is heavily engaged with Nasser, and they will do all they safely can to avert another blow to it such as they have just suffered in Eastern Europe. . . . In either event, I fear we are in for a bad time in our relations with this country."[13]

The presidium met again to discuss Hungary. "We should enter into negotiations," said Anastas Mikoyan, still trying to press for a moderate course. "We should wait another 10–15 days and support this government." Yet he accepted that the Soviets would have to draw a line somewhere: "If the regime slips away, we'll need to decide what to do. We simply cannot allow Hungary to be removed from our camp."

"The danger of a bourgeois restoration has reached its peak," said Mikhail Suslov, who had returned from Budapest with Mikoyan but took a harder line. "Only by means of occupation can we have a government that supports us."[14] Mikoyan was now the only man arguing against immediate intervention. He lost. The order was given: Operation Whirlwind went into action.

That morning in London, American diplomat Chester Cooper's two young daughters complained of headaches and said they could not go to school. Gently, their parents extracted from them the real reason: "On the previous day their school-mates had berated Joan and Susan for being 'beastly' to England."[15] While in Washington the feeling was that the United States had been betrayed by Britain, in London it was the opposite. Nasser had not taken early reports of collusion or British action seriously because he could not imagine that the British would behave dishonorably. Many Britons felt the same as they started to hear rumors of collusion. It did not seem possible. They were accustomed to trusting their government.

The British government confirmed that Egypt had broken diplomatic relations but insisted that this did not mean Britain and Egypt were at war. The government in Cairo issued an order to seize all British and French property, including the Anglo-Egyptian oilfield, a subsidiary of Shell, and the French Société Egyptienne Pétrole.[16] Shocked by the news of the French openly fighting with Israel to shell Rafah the previous evening, as well as other incidents of French forces acting in close consort with the Israelis, Eden telegraphed to Mollet. "Actions of this sort, which cannot possibly remain secret, are extremely embarrassing," he wrote. "I hope you will agree that in our common interest they must be discontinued. Nothing could do more harm to our role as peacemakers than to be identified in this way with one of the two parties."[17] Mollet assured Eden that joint actions with the Israelis would be discontinued.

The British cabinet met at ten o'clock. A radical suggestion had been made by Lester Pearson, the Canadian minister for external affairs. When he flew in the Royal Flying Corps in World War I, Pearson became known as Mike; his instructor did not consider Lester a manly enough name for a fighter pilot. He had headed the United Nations committee that had drawn up the plan for the partition of Mandatory Palestine into Israel and a Palestinian state and had been the Canadian representative at the founding of NATO, serving as its chairman in 1951.

Pearson's suggestion was that the United Nations itself could compose a fighting force, which could be sent to police Israel's borders in place of Britain and France. Sending international peacekeeping forces to a conflict zone was a new idea. The United Nations had sent military observers to Israel and the Palestinian territories in 1948, and to Kashmir in 1949. It had never before established a force under its own command to separate warring states. The League of Nations, the predecessor organization to the United Nations between the wars, was widely considered to have failed on account of having no "teeth": it commanded no army and could not enforce its decisions against strong countries.[18] If Britain and France were able to ignore the United Nations now, this would mean the world's second attempt at an international parliament might founder just as the first had.

Many in the British Conservative Party were strongly in favor of the United Nations. Eden had been its public champion, though he frequently expressed irritation with it in his private notes. If Eden was already beginning to regret attacking Egypt, the possibility of a United Nations force might have offered a way out. Had it been true that Britain and France had intervened for peacekeeping purposes, it would have made sense to give way to an internationally sanctioned alternative.

But there was pressure on Eden from the right of his party to go on with Operation Musketeer. William Clark, Eden's press secretary, remembered that "[Antony] Head kept reminding us that the first objective of this whole operation was to get rid of Nasser, and that would never be done by the UN."[19] The prime minister was persuaded by this, and may have been influenced by opinion polls that day—53 percent of British voters surveyed said they supported the November 1 invasion. Dr. Henry Durant of the pollsters Gallup explained to the BBC that there was a significant right-left divide. Of Conservatives, 89 percent supported Eden, while 63 percent of Labour supporters opposed him: "You see, that is a very sharp split indeed."[20] There was pressure from the French, too. Eden "was embittered by what he called Eisenhower's 'betrayal,'" remembered Christian Pineau—using the French word *trahison*. Pineau told Mollet he was worried about Eden's health: "It is not yet a 'breakdown' but we're not far off."[21]

Following their meeting the previous day, Hugh Gaitskell and some Labour Party leaders went to see the American ambassador, Winthrop Aldrich. They praised the United States' action at the United Nations and "strongly urged that we not relax our firm opposition to the 'Eden-Mollet folly,'" according to the report sent back to Washington. Calling Eden's policy "monstrous," Gaitskell told Aldrich that "continued strong US action in the UN was the only way to heal the injury being inflicted on the Anglo-American alliance by Eden."[22]

There was even a suggestion that opposition to Eden existed at the highest level. Queen Elizabeth II kept her political opinions to herself but, according to some members of her staff, she doubted her prime minister. Unusually, she requested top-secret daily reports on the progress of military operations and intelligence to be delivered to her from November 1. These would continue to be delivered until November 22.[23] She also received messages from Commonwealth governments—which Eden himself did not always see. As a result, according to Martin Charteris, one of the queen's private secretaries, the monarch "in some ways was better informed than many members of the cabinet." Another adviser added, "Nothing was kept from her. She knew about the secret deals beforehand."[24]

Lord Louis ("Dickie") Mountbatten, admiral of the Fleet and an opponent of the Suez offensive he was supposed to be helping to lead, was a cousin to the queen. He had brokered the marriage between his nephew, Prince Philip of Greece and Denmark, and the then Princess Elizabeth in 1947. Their son Prince Charles, just coming up to his eighth birthday, would refer to Mountbatten as his "honorary grandfather." During the Suez crisis, "Dickie was talking to her [the queen]," said Charteris. "He wanted her to know what he thought about it—he was saying something like 'I think they are being absolutely lunatic.' He was typically devious. He didn't mean it as a message to be conveyed directly to Eden, but he hoped she would pass it on to him as her own thoughts."

There is a tradition of confidentiality between monarch and prime minister. It is, therefore, impossible to say whether the queen did pass these thoughts on to Eden or not. Charteris thought she may have said something gently doubting; he imagined it along the lines of "Are you sure you are being wise?"[25] In 1976, the London *Sunday Times Magazine* published an article by Robert Lacey, suggesting that the queen had been passionately against the Suez intervention but could not stop it. Anthony Eden, who was then seventy-nine years old and still vainly attempting to defend his reputation, suspected that Mountbatten was one of the two sources Lacey claimed.

"I did not attempt to deny it," wrote Mountbatten in his diary. "I said I had been asked officially . . . to see this man to help him, and had answered all his questions."[26] Charteris also remembered the queen's impression of Eden during the crisis. "I think the Queen believed Eden was mad," he told a biographer. When the prime minister came for his weekly meetings with the queen, he "ranged up and down and wouldn't sit still. He was edgy, jumpy."[27]

The world was still learning of the bombing of Cairo, but international reactions—including those from Commonwealth leaders and from Baghdad Pact allies—were damning. Frosty reports arrived at the Foreign Office from India, Pakistan, and South Africa.[28] Jordan severed political relations with France and recalled its ambassador from Paris. "The present battle is not Egypt's battle alone but the battle of all Arab nations," said King Hussein. "The aggression on Egypt is being carried out by world Zionism, enemy of peace, and world Judaism, supported and incited by Britain and France." The only messages of support for Britain and France that the London *Times* could find to print were from the prime ministers of Australia and New Zealand, though New Zealand's prime minister expressed concern that Eisenhower had not been informed.[29]

The problem with efforts to convince Britain's allies of British innocence was all the evidence to the contrary. Britain was attacking Egypt and leaving Israel alone. William Clark went on to a government public relations meeting that day. There was much concern about the effect of any collaboration with Israel on relations with Iraq. "It was agreed that anything we could do to play down Israeli collaboration with Britain was to be done," Clark remembered, "but the more extreme suggestions, e.g. that we should drop just one bomb on Tel Aviv, were agreed to be impracticable."[30] This idea appears to have been toyed with only by the public relations department.

That same morning, the leader of the Hungarian Catholic Church, Cardinal József Mindszenty, was released from eight years of imprisonment and returned to Budapest. He went to his old chapel to pray and then talk to the press. "Thank God I am in good health," he said, "both physically and mentally, though I was very seriously ill when I was in prison." One of the reporters told him that he, too, had been in prison, to which Mindszenty replied, "It seems that everyone who is honest has been in prison at one time or another." Tanks were posted at either side of his palace and soldiers patrolled the courtyard, armed with grenades and tommy guns.[31]

Inside Budapest, the possibility that the Soviets might back off was now beginning to be believed by the general population. Some shops, offices, and factories reopened. Imre Nagy was aware that new Red Army units were crossing the border into Hungary from Ukraine. Two Soviet divisions would soon surround Budapest, with another five stationed elsewhere in Hungarian territory. This was a violation of the Warsaw Pact, the treaty that held the Soviet bloc together. If the Soviets did not withdraw the troops, he told the Soviet ambassador, Yuri Andropov, he would denounce the pact.

Andropov was unflusterable. The new units, he said, were only being sent to relieve those that had been fighting before, to protect their retreat and to protect the Russian population in Hungary. This was not, he insisted, a new aggression. Indeed, the Soviets were ready to negotiate a "partial" withdrawal.

Unconvinced, Nagy awaited further information.[32] Some of his cabinet were clearly unnerved: one of János Kádár's aides observed Kádár looking "white as a sheet, his lips were trembling and he fell into some sort of hysterical fit."[33]

Remarkably, Nagy managed to keep news of the Soviet troops arriving in Hungary secret from the people in Budapest. He hoped to resolve the situation diplomatically without causing panic. As a result, the mood in Budapest was cheerful. "The rebels, having just achieved a victory over the former régime, despite Soviet intervention, were scarcely worried by the clouds on the horizon," wrote the Hungarian historian Miklós Molnár, who was there at the time. "For them the sky was blue. . . . Neither the shadow of events in the Near East nor the perplexing nuances of American statements influenced the attitude of the Hungarians."[34]

Meanwhile, Nikita Khrushchev and Georgy Malenkov had

embarked on a grueling schedule of flights to meet Warsaw Pact leaders and inform them of Operation Whirlwind. They had already been that day to Brest, on the border with Poland, to meet Władysław Gomułka and other representatives of the new Polish administration. Gomułka objected vociferously to the idea of military intervention. They were unable to talk him around. Now they had moved on to Bucharest, where they found a more positive reception from the leaders of Romania, Czechoslovakia, and Bulgaria—all of whom were Communist hard-liners, worried that the spirit of rebellion might infect their countries next. Todor Zhivkov, the leader of Bulgaria, encouraged the Soviets "to adopt every appropriate measure, including military intervention, as soon as possible" to defeat "imperialist intrigues" and "preserve the system of people's democracy in Hungary."[35] The Soviets appreciated his enthusiasm, but they needed little encouragement.

0800 New York // 1300 London // 1400 Budapest // 1500 Cairo

By two p.m., Nagy was receiving definite reports that more and more Red Army troops were streaming across his border. He telephoned Yuri Andropov back and formally withdrew Hungary from the Warsaw Pact. His ministers unanimously approved his action. Hungary was now a neutral nation. The rebels and their supporters were thrilled. They did not realize that Nagy had done this because Soviet troops were heading straight for them. They believed the prime minister was finally aligning himself with the rebellion's first demand: to get Soviet troops out of the country.

At that same moment, the British government's Egypt Committee assembled in Rab Butler's office in the House of Commons to address the drying up of Britain's oil supply. It agreed to a 10 percent cut in oil consumption throughout Britain, to be put in place on November 7, with tighter restrictions and formal rationing to follow as soon as possible. The situation was worse than the Egypt Committee had anticipated before the invasion. It had been foreseen that some rationing might be necessary, but the committee had assumed that the government would have recourse to additional supplies from the Americas. It had also not anticipated that the oil pipeline from Iraq to Lebanon would stop functioning. "In present circumstances, there must inevitably be doubts about these assumptions and the reduction in oil imports might well be more serious," the minutes admitted.[36]

Later that afternoon, William Clark saw Macmillan. He told him he was worried about the deep divisions in public opinion and how all this would affect the economy. "Macmillan said that the trouble was that the people thought oil just came out of taps," he remembered.[37]

As the Egypt Committee was meeting in London and Nagy was withdrawing from the Warsaw Pact, a correspondent for the London *Times* in the Gaza Strip watched thousands of people—some lifelong residents of the Strip, and some refugees from the 1948 war—escape into Egypt. The route "was choked with fleeing Arab refugees, bare-footed or riding distracted donkeys," he reported. "Many of the refugees had taken to the sea in frail little boats." The IDF had dropped leaflets from planes calling for Egyptians to surrender. Trapped in a battleground between two nations, many Gazans fled.[38]

An hour and forty minutes later—8:40 a.m. in New York—Foster Dulles telephoned Eisenhower in Washington. Neither knew what was happening in the Gaza Strip. The United Nations General Assembly would be meeting at five p.m. Eastern time, and the American delegation was wrestling with the question of whether they should put sanctions on sales of arms to Israel. According to the telephone minutes, Eisenhower said that the United States "should not do anything that makes us look as if we are trying to get an excuse to pick on Israel. If we do anything against them, then we have to do something against Fr and Br." Dulles replied, referring to Eisenhower's statement about adhering to the Tripartite Declaration, "If we give aid to Israel when she is an aggressor it makes a mockery of everything."[39]

1000 Washington DC // 1600 Budapest

Imre Nagy informed all the foreign diplomats in Budapest of Hungary's new neutral status and appealed to the United Nations to defend that status against the oncoming Soviet invasion. He spoke on national radio, attempting to inspire fortitude among the people without scaring them.

"We appeal to our neighbours, countries near and far, to respect the unalterable decision of our people," he said. "It is indeed true that our people are united in this decision as perhaps never before in their history. Working millions of Hungary! Protect and strengthen with revolutionary determination, sacrificial work and the consolidation of order, our country, the free, independent, democratic and neutral Hungary."[40]

1100 Washington DC // 1700 Paris; Budapest // 1800 Gaza City

As the sun sank low toward the horizon of the Mediterranean Sea, the mosques, minarets, white houses, and date palms of Gaza City presented a sedate picture to the *Times* correspondent watching from a viewpoint on a nearby hillside. There was no sound except for the tweeting of sparrows. "Here and there, in the dry grasses, a slight movement could be detected, perhaps of a steel helmet, perhaps of the muzzle of some weapon," he wrote. The IDF was preparing to strike.

"Then, just as the red sun brushed the surface of the sea, the pretty scene exploded," he reported. "Aircraft had come out of the sky and smoke and dust spouted out of the earth round Gaza like huge, spreading shrubs. There was the sound of bursting bombs, of anti-aircraft fire, of light artillery and mortars."

A long procession of armored vehicles and half-tracks "appeared from nowhere" and moved toward the city. The Israeli soldiers sang songs, and one addressed the journalist in English. "They were equipped, not as the scrappily armed militia of the 1948 war, but as a modern fighting force able to move into war with all the precision and steady confidence of men trained to perfection and at least as well armed as their enemies," he wrote.[41] The aerial bombardment raged on. The IDF was breaking Gaza's defenses and cutting off its access to Egypt.

Addressing the National Security Council in Washington, Foster Dulles remarked that "recent events are close to marking the death knell for Great Britain and France." He argued that the United States must break with its allies or risk losing the whole Cold War. "For many years now the United States has been walking a tightrope between the effort to maintain our old and valued relations with our British and French allies on the one hand, and on the other trying to assure ourselves of the friendship and understanding of the newly independent countries who have just escaped colonialism," he said. But the United States could not balance on the tightrope forever. "Unless we now assert and maintain" American leadership, he argued, "all of these newly independent countries will turn from us to the USSR. We will be looked upon as forever tied to British and French colonialist policies." He warned that "the United States would survive or go down" depending on what it decided to do now.[42]

Eisenhower telephoned Dulles at 12:25 p.m. and said he had drafted another letter to Eden. "It might do some good and it might not but it told of what we are trying to do today in the

UN and what they might do to minimize resentment and save face."[43]

Foster Dulles telephoned Eisenhower back soon afterward, discussing again the position in the United Nations. Dulles indicated that "substantially the program [of arms sales] he had indicated would be suspended. All this had been done in the case of Egypt already. It would suspend military shipments to Israel."

Eisenhower asked him whether the rest of the American delegation there agreed with him on this point. Dulles replied, "Yes but they would like to go stronger."[44]

The American military was going stronger, at least in terms of sending out warning signals to its supposed allies in the Mediterranean. "That day, American planes were sighted over the [British and French] convoys," wrote Chester Cooper, "and that night, American warships, lights blazing, passed through the French fleet."[45] One British admiral warned that there was "constant danger of an incident" with American aircraft flying close to British ships, and noted that day: "Have been continually menaced during past eight hours by US aircraft approaching low down as close as 4000 yards and on two occasions flying over ships."[46] General Keightley, the commander of Operation Musketeer, later remarked that the movements of the United States Sixth Fleet "endangered the whole of our relations with that country."[47]

Meanwhile, the French were trying an old trick on the Americans: a Red Scare. That evening, Christian Pineau met American ambassador Douglas Dillon in Paris and told him that France had heard from its sources in Syria that the Soviet Union was planning military intervention in the Middle East using Syrian bases. To forestall a wider war, he suggested that the United Nations General Assembly summon the foreign ministers of France, Britain, Israel, and Egypt to appear before it immediately. This would delay Soviet action by two to three days, "by which time he had good reason to hope the whole affair would be finished."

The Americans were not convinced by Pineau's scaremongering, for the information coming from their own ambassador in Moscow, Charles Bohlen, contradicted it. Though Bohlen admitted that the Soviets did "not in any way rule out clandestine assistance to Egypt," he did not believe there was any plan for full intervention. He noted, though, "If the hostilities spread to other parts of the area [i.e., the Middle East] the present declaration is no guide whatsoever to Soviet action."

To Dillon, Pineau "emphatically denied any intention of extending the Franco-British occupation farther into Egypt." He hinted at how France and Britain really felt: "He said the position of Nasser was a matter to be left up to the Egyptian people; he hoped that, after seeing the catastrophe which Nasser had prepared for them, they would themselves in due course get rid of him."[48]

In the House of Commons in London that evening, an extraordinary spectacle took place when the minister of defense, Antony Head, announced the British raids on Egyptian airfields. Labour members booed and jeered at Eden, who refused to answer the question of whether Britain was at war.

"We knew something very dirty was going on," one opposition member told Anthony Nutting. "But in the face of the Government's denials we couldn't prove it; and so in our frustration we just saw red and all of us completely lost our tempers."

"A storm of booing would break out as soon as Anthony entered the Chamber, and would rise to a crescendo of hysteria when he actually rose to speak," remembered Lord Kilmuir. "At one point the chances of fighting actually breaking out between Members was very real, so intense were the passions on each side."

"It was a deplorable scene, totally unworthy of the Mother of Parliaments," wrote Nutting. A journalist watching from the press gallery called it "quite the most shattering experience I've ever sat through."[49]

The Speaker was obliged to adjourn the House for half an hour to let members simmer down. On the Commons record, it is recorded as "Grave Disorder."[50]

"Can you stand it?" the prime minister's horrified wife, Lady Eden, asked the leader of the opposition's wife.

"The boys must express themselves," replied Mrs. Gaitskell sharply.[51]

"I am not in the least attempting to dodge these questions," insisted Eden when he returned.[52] A Labour member moved a motion of censure: "That this House deplores the action of Her Majesty's Government in resorting to armed force against Egypt in clear violation of the United Nations Charter, thereby affronting the convictions of a large section of the British people, dividing the Commonwealth, straining the Atlantic Alliance, and gravely damaging the foundations of international order." It was voted down by the Conservative majority, who replaced it with the statement "That this House approves of the prompt action taken by Her Majesty's Government designed to bring hostilities between Israel and Egypt to an end and to safeguard vital international and national interests, and pledges its full support for all steps necessary to secure these ends." Yet according to Robert Rhodes James, who was then a clerk in the Commons and later became a Conservative MP, "Even those ministers who remained committed supporters of the operation were becoming severely rattled." He added, "One felt that the House of Commons was close to a collective nervous collapse, so fraught was the temper of the time."[53]

The attacks became personal. "I have not seen from the Prime Minister in the course of the last four or five months, or even longer, any evidence of that sagacity and skill that he should have acquired in so many years in the Foreign Office," the Labour politician Aneurin Bevan told the House. "Indeed, I have been astonished at the amateurishness of his performance. There is something the matter with him."[54]

That night, a conservatively estimated two thousand students marched through the West End to the Houses of Parliament, chanting, "We don't want war." They blocked traffic on Charing Cross Road. Outside the House of Commons, a demonstration estimated even more conservatively at two hundred people gathered, shouting, "We want peace," and "Eden must go." Inside Parliament, a Labour MP complained that mounted police had charged into the crowd and said he had spoken to two people who had been beaten up: a young lady who was nearly crushed by a horse and a young man who had been thrown over a wall and set upon by several policemen. A Conservative member replied that the protesters were "clearly, both from the banners they carried and from the things they said, organized Communist groups."[55]

Another five hundred students marched in Manchester, carrying placards saying "Hands off the Middle East." There were clashes in Oxford, with two undergraduates arrested. Conservative student protesters pelted antiwar protesters with tomatoes, water bombs, and intriguingly, a red fez.[56] A group of dons sent a telegram to Eden, stating, "This meeting of 73 Oxford dons of differing political opinions condemns the Government's military aggression as foolish and wrong and demands that it should stop now."[57] These people were not all Communists. The public mood was beginning to shift.

1700 New York

Lester Pearson arrived at the United Nations building on Forty-Second Street in New York at five p.m. He found it in turmoil. The secretary-general, Dag Hammarskjöld, was on the brink of resignation over Britain and France breaking the United Nations Charter. Pearson reminded him that the Soviets had done so many times and he had not resigned then.[58] In the General Assembly, the United States pushed for a resolution demanding an immediate cease-fire and the withdrawal of all foreign troops.

Pearson wanted to go further. His proposal, as the British cabinet had heard that morning, was for an international force under United Nations command to be sent to the Sinai. He also wanted to have a conference to discuss the future of the Middle East and seek a path to lasting peace.

"If the United Nations were willing to take over the physical task of maintaining peace in that area, no one would be better pleased than the British Government," said the British representative, Pierson Dixon. This was not true, but the British government had decided to keep saying it because ministers believed the risk of the United Nations getting its force together before they had taken the canal was low. Even if it did, this might not be a problem—for a reason Britain and France did not yet reveal to the United Nations. The two European powers were still arguing that their invading forces were performing a selfless "police action." Therefore, they hoped to persuade the United Nations that their soldiers already in the field could continue to do their jobs as planned—under a United Nations flag. There would be no need for any withdrawal. The United Nations would merely take a role in commanding the existing Anglo-French operation, giving victory over Nasser an impermeable veneer of legitimacy.[59]

0100 (Nov. 2) New York

Foster Dulles arrived at the United Nations late after a rough flight from Washington through terrible storms. He was to give the most important speech of the crisis to the General Assembly.

"I doubt that any delegate ever spoke from this forum with as heavy a heart as I have brought here tonight," Dulles began. "We speak on a matter of vital importance, where the United States finds itself unable to agree with three nations with whom it has ties, deep friendship, admiration, and respect, and two of whom constitute our oldest, most trusted and reliable allies."

He described the invasion, the ultimatum, the British and French use of the veto in the Security Council. He acknowledged faults: "The United Nations may have been somewhat laggard, somewhat impotent in dealing with many injustices which are inherent in this Middle East situation." Yet he insisted that Britain and France's action was unacceptable. "If we were to agree that the existence of injustices in the world, which this organization has so far been unable to cure, means that the principle of the renunciation of force is no longer respected and that there still exists the right wherever a nation feels itself subject to injustice to resort to force to try to correct that injustice, then, Mr. President, we would have, I fear, torn this charter into shreds and the world would again be a world of anarchy."

Dulles mentioned his own attempts to push Britain and France into the diplomatic route, not missing the opportunity to praise himself: "I doubt if in all history so sincere, so sustained an effort has been made to find a just and a peaceful solution." He described the long summer of negotiations, conferences, and SCUA—and reminded everyone that peaceful options had not yet been exhausted. He declined to talk in any mincing terms about peacekeeping by Britain or France. Instead, he insisted, "the violent armed attack by three of our members upon a fourth, cannot be treated as other than a grave error, inconsistent with the principles and purposes of the charter and one which if persisted in would gravely undermine our charter and undermine this organization."

In his peroration, he issued a stark warning about maintaining world peace: "There is great danger that what is started and what has been called a police action may develop into something which is far more grave." With one eye on Hungary, he warned that even if it did not, "the apparent impotence of this organization to deal with this situation may set a precedent which will lead other nations to attempt to take into their own hands the remedying of what they believe to be their injustices. If that happens, the future is dark indeed." He concluded with a hint that the Suez crisis could spiral into a nuclear World War III. "We thought when we wrote the charter in San Francisco in 1945 that we had seen perhaps the worst in war, that our task was to prevent a recurrence of what had been, and indeed what then had been was tragic enough," he said. "But now we know that what can be will be infinitely more tragic than what we saw in World War II."

He proposed a draft resolution calling for an immediate cease-fire on all sides and withdrawal of invading forces, for the embargo of all military goods into the zone of conflict, and for free navigation of the Suez Canal to be restored.[60]

The speech was precisely expressed, powerful in tone, and explosive in content. Dulles and Eisenhower had just chosen the United Nations over NATO. Many in the First World, let alone the Second and Third Worlds, had never believed such a thing could happen. Yet the United States had just turned on its own allies in front of all of them, with unmistakable ferocity.

"If that had been my very last act on earth, it would have been exactly as I would have wished it," Dulles told an aide of his performance. "I would have liked it for my epitaph."[61]

An epitaph was not yet required though, after Dulles's speech, his colleague Herman Phleger thought he looked unusually exhausted. Phleger encouraged the secretary of state to return to the Waldorf-Astoria Hotel. But Dulles's colleagues were worried that if Dulles left, other delegates might also bail out before the vote. Dulles stayed.

The vote finally took place at one o'clock in the morning. Dulles had his resolution passed by sixty-four votes to five, with six abstentions. Only Australia and New Zealand could be prevailed upon to vote with Britain, France, and Israel.

To Dulles's surprise, Canada was among the abstentions. Lester Pearson explained that the cease-fire and withdrawal were not enough without the extra measures of a United Nations force and a peace conference. If Israel and Egypt simply retreated, he pointed out, nothing would change. "What then?" he asked. "What then in six months from now? Are we to go through all this again? . . . [It] would be a return to terror, bloodshed, strife, incidents, charges and counter-charges, and ultimately another explosion."[62]

After the vote on Suez, the Italian delegate drew the assembly's attention to a cable that had just come in from Imre Nagy in Budapest. Soviet troops were returning to Hungary. Nagy reported that he had asked Yuri Andropov to withdraw them and had reminded Moscow that Hungary no longer belonged to the Warsaw Pact. Under the circumstances, Dulles felt he must stay on through another long trawl of speeches. It was five a.m. by the time he arrived back at his hotel. According to Phleger, the secretary of state was tired and out of sorts. He drank a large glass of Overholt whisky and insisted that his colleagues wake him in time for the ten thirty flight back to Washington that morning.[63]

Late that same night, Hungarian cabinet ministers János Kádár and Ferenc Münnich went in secret to the Soviet embassy in Budapest. They were escorted by the Soviets to the military base at Tököl on Csepel Island, From there, they were flown to Mukachevo in the Ukraine. In Mukachevo, they were greeted by Leonid Brezhnev. The Hungarians boarded separate planes and continued to Moscow. While much of the world slept, Dulles's fear that other nations might take into their own hands the remedying of their perceived injustices was being fulfilled. The Soviets were already secretly ensuring that a successor government to Imre Nagy's administration was ready to take over.

12

FRIDAY, NOVEMBER 2, 1956
"LOVE TO NASTY"

0900 London // 1000 Paris // 1100 Gaza City; Suez

On the morning of November 2, representatives of the United Nations Relief and Works Agency for Palestine Refugees in the Near East (UNRWA) in Gaza persuaded the Egyptian commanders to surrender to avert further bloodshed among the civilians, refugees, and United Nations staff. One Egyptian platoon refused to surrender and held out until midday; a Palestinian brigade continued to hold out for another day in Khan Yunis, to the south. Journalist Robert Henriques, who was traveling with the Israeli forces, claimed that few Egyptian soldiers were taken prisoner: "Many of them buried their weapons and uniforms in the sand and wandered back in their underclothes, 150 miles, to Egypt."[1] In fact, an estimated four thousand Egyptian and Palestinian soldiers were rounded up by the IDF and police after being trapped in Gaza when it was severed from Egypt. From Baghdad, Nuri es-Said "begged" the British government to make Israel release its Egyptian prisoners. Otherwise, he feared, Britain would be blamed throughout the Arab world for their capture, too.[2]

The shell and bomb damage from the previous night's

offensive could be seen on military emplacements around the outskirts of Gaza City. The central market square filled up with Israeli soldiers. "They danced, sang, laughed, shouted, patted the backs of passing Arabs, and gave bars of chocolate to urchins who seemed to be getting over their shyness rapidly," reported the London *Times* correspondent. But most of the Arabs he saw outside this cheerful scene looked poor and shabby, especially the refugees living in patched, dirty tents. One Israeli soldier told him that some refugees had clapped their hands when they saw Israeli troops. "They thought," he said, "that our coming meant their return to the homes they left in 1948."[3] It did not.

The outlook from London was bleak. Key to the British and French case for intervention had been the principle of keeping the Suez Canal open. Nasser had prepared blockships filled with heavy cement, scrap iron, and empty beer bottles in the Great Bitter Lake. They could be sunk deliberately in the canal to obstruct any traffic.[4] The Anglo-French force had meant to destroy the blockships before they could be moved into position. Despite their efforts, at least four ships had been sunk at the northern end of the canal. Anglo-French airstrikes had again gone off target. As Anthony Nutting noted with despair, "In one case at least we had actually done Nasser's job for him by sinking a blockship after it had taken up its position."[5] Forty-seven ships eventually were sunk in the canal. The Egyptians also blew up the supports of El Firdan Bridge, collapsing it across the waterway. By November 2, the canal was unusable, cutting off Europe's main oil supply route and global shipping.[6] "Instead of keeping the Suez Canal open, the [Anglo-French] action closed it," wrote CIA agent Miles Copeland, "as the dumbest intelligence analyst, either British or American, could have predicted."[7]

At the highest levels of the British government, there was

still dithering over when or even whether to begin the landing. "I was reminded of the scene from *The Pirates of Penzance* in which the policemen are on the wharf and presumably about to embark to do battle with the pirates," wrote American diplomat Chester Cooper. In the Gilbert and Sullivan comic opera, the ladies on the wharf encourage the policemen to go forward to glory; the policemen keep singing about how they will go, without actually moving—to the increasing frustration of the ladies. "As of that Friday, the 'policemen' were still on the wharves and airfields of Cyprus, and I among others was not at all sure that they would, in fact, ever really 'go.'"[8] Many Britons, as well as Americans, did not believe they could go ahead at the price of further enraging the United States. That morning, Selwyn Lloyd asked Anthony Nutting to help him draw up a formal plan for the United Nations to step into Britain and France's place. Lloyd thought he might be able to get Lester Pearson to move his plan in the General Assembly after the weekend, on Monday November 5. "He had thrown us a straw and we were clutching at it in a desperate attempt to extricate ourselves from our predicament," Nutting wrote.[9]

While Eisenhower was exerting maximum pressure to pull Eden back, Mollet was exerting maximum pressure to pull him further in. "In the [French] ministry of defence," Pineau wrote, "nervous tension peaked. The British 'delay' was spoken of as a real sabotage of the operation."[10] Mollet and Pineau now wanted the joint invasion to go ahead on Monday, at the same time as the General Assembly session during which Lloyd was hoping they could get out of it. This was a day in advance of the original schedule, and meant that paratroopers would have to be dropped in just forty-eight hours, on Sunday morning. But naval support could not be moved. The seaborne forces would arrive on Tuesday morning regardless of any speedup of the parachute drop—so British and French paratroopers would have to hold their own for two whole days without heavy backup. The French suggested that the Israelis could take Kantara, on the east side of the canal, to protect the paratroops. This, of course, would confirm to the world the true extent of the conspiracy with Israel, which Eden still believed he could hide. It had, for instance, still not been fully revealed to the commander of Operation Musketeer, General Keightley—though he was beginning to have his suspicions. As he wrote to the chiefs of staff that day, "The situation regarding Franco-Israeli cooperation is getting increasingly disturbing."[11]

The admiral of the Fleet, Lord Mountbatten, gave Eden's private secretary a letter to pass on to the prime minister unopened. "I know that you have been fully aware over these past few weeks of my great unhappiness at the prospect of our launching military operations against Egypt," he wrote. He had carried out the prime minister's orders, he said, "although I did not believe that a just and lasting settlement of any dispute could be worked out under a threat of military action," but now that the bombing had started he could remain silent no longer. He was writing, he said, "to beg you to turn back the assault convoy before it is too late, as I feel that the actual landing of troops can only spread the war with untold misery and world-wide repercussions." He concluded forcefully: "You can imagine how hard it is for me to break with all service custom and write directly to you in this way, but I feel so desperate about what is happening that my conscience would not allow me to do otherwise."[12] Eden telephoned Mountbatten back, claiming that no civilians had been killed. The prime minister would not turn back the convoy.

"Only one hope remains, that the United States will use its power to stop the fighting and so save us from the worst consequences of our government's insanity," wrote the philosopher

Bertrand Russell to the *Manchester Guardian* that day.[13] Following the United States Sixth Fleet's maneuvers threatening the British in the Mediterranean, some thought the United States Navy might use its military power to stop the war. There is some evidence that this was considered. The American admiral Arleigh Burke, speaking characteristically plainly in 1966, remembered that he had discussed with Foster Dulles what the American Sixth Fleet should do.

"The British can't do it," Burke said, referring to the invasion of Egypt. "And the reason why the British can't do this is, because they are totally unprepared." Burke had talked to Mountbatten, who had told him that the British navy and the Royal Air Force had been sitting around in Malta and Cyprus for months over the summer while politicians prevaricated. Then, all of a sudden, the order had come to move—and they were not ready. (Gerald Templer, chief of the Imperial General Staff, disputed this: he argued that "we were certainly ready with our available resources," but "wishful political thinking could not alter the facts of geography"—the ships could not be sped up.)[14]

"For God's sake, let's give them [the British] the craft—give them ours," Burke said to Dulles. "They're over there. They've got to make this thing successful."

Dulles told Burke that he did not think the British should succeed.

"Well, we've got to support them, I think," said Burke.

"No, we can't," Dulles replied.

Dulles asked where the Sixth Fleet was. Burke told him it was probably northwest of Cairo. The fleet was keeping a close eye on the British, and pilots were flying over them. "And then he had the idea that, maybe we could stop them," Burke remembered.

"Mr. Secretary, there is only one way to stop them," Burke

said. "We can stop them. But we will blast the hell out of them."

"Well, can't you stop them some other way?" asked Dulles.

"No," said Burke. "If we're going to threaten, if we're going to turn on them, then you've got to be ready to shoot. . . . We can defeat them—the British and the French and the Egyptians and the Israelis—the whole goddam [*sic*] works of them we can knock off, if you want. But that's the only way to do it."

Burke did not describe Dulles's reply. He did say that he felt it necessary to leave the situation open for the commander of the Sixth Fleet, Vice Admiral Charles R. Brown. "I gave him orders to go to sea, to be prepared for anything, to have his bombs up, to be checked out, so that we would be ready to fight either another naval force or against land targets."

"Who's the enemy?" Brown asked.

Burke replied, "Don't take any guff from anybody."

"I didn't know who the damned enemy was," he remembered ten years later, "because we were having this discussion."[15]

Among some in the State Department and CIA in Washington, there was a feeling that Foster Dulles was taking the wrong line. "I confess I have continued to feel that we went too far," said Richard M. Bissell of the CIA a decade later. "If we had found ways to drag our feet for two or three days, the British and the French could have consolidated their hold of the Canal." Bissell was overstating the case—the British and French did not have the canal and were at least four days away from being in position to take it, so there was no question of consolidating their hold within two or three days. "And I think we probably could have preserved at least a reasonably righteous posture, at the same time doing less damage to our European alliance."

Bissell had several arguments with Allen Dulles. "Allen was

quite touchy about it," he remembered. "He was very defensive of his brother's stated attitudes and position."

After the crisis, though, Allen Dulles and Bissell discussed it again, and Allen revealed more. "Don't you realize that the individual who was really furious with the British and French and absolutely insistent on the action we took was Eisenhower not Foster?" Allen asked. "Foster probably would have played this quite differently."[16] James Hagerty, Eisenhower's press secretary, agreed. The line on Suez, he said, "was Eisenhower's decision, and no one could make that decision, but himself, in that campaign. It was his decision to do exactly what we did."[17]

1200 London; Edinburgh // 1300 Paris // 1400 Cairo // 1600 Moscow

In Moscow, the Hungarian politicians János Kádár and Ferenc Münnich—the men the Soviets had secretly flown in from Budapest the previous night—had been given a makeover. A week of political turmoil had not done their personal grooming any favors, and their Soviet handlers judged them too scruffy to appear in front of the presidium. They were taken shopping in Moscow and fitted out with new wardrobes. Kádár was scandalized when they tried to force him into Italian shoes: "What would the comrades say back home if I showed up in flashy shoes?"[18]

Once they had been smartened up, Kádár and Münnich met with the Central Committee of the Communist Party. Kádár proposed a political solution to the rebellion; Münnich called for military intervention by the Soviets.[19] Radio stations in Moscow began to broadcast warnings to Budapest not to make "a wrong step" and alleged that "reactionary counterrevolutionaries" were being strengthened by reinforcements from Austria, who they alleged were encouraged by the United States.[20]

In London, opposition members in the House of Commons tried to force Eden to say whether he would accept the decision of the United Nations General Assembly that there should be a cease-fire in the Middle East. Eden refused to answer, saying that he needed to study the resolution and the speeches made for and against it before making a statement to the House. Labour MP Arthur Henderson asked him if he could at least halt any further attacks on Egypt until he had read the resolution. "No, Sir; I can give no such undertaking," Eden replied.[21]

Hundreds rioted in Edinburgh as antigovernment protesters clashed with supporters. Fireworks, bags of flour, tomatoes, and eggs were thrown. One student attempted to set fire to a Union flag in the university's Old Quadrangle. The student was "severely handled," reported the London *Times*, though it did not say whether by police or counterdemonstrators. There were further scuffles at Leeds and Oxford universities.[22] The Labour MP Tony Benn bought up yards of blue and white ribbon to make badges to distribute among British supporters of the United Nations.[23]

Meanwhile, Britain and France tried to work out how to respond to Dulles's United Nations resolution and his intimation that, were they to press ahead, they would be responsible for World War III. "The resolution put peace in a strait-jacket," Eden wrote mournfully later.[24] Christian Pineau arrived in London that afternoon. "It was a most unhappy encounter," remembered Nutting. Eden and Lloyd now felt they must reply to the United Nations in meek terms, stating that the Anglo-French "police action" would graciously defer to the command of the United Nations if Israel and Egypt agreed to a United Nations force remaining in place. Until then, only limited numbers of British and French troops would be stationed between the forces of Israel and Egypt. The original plan for Britain and France to hold the Suez Canal and its ports until

Nasser fell from power or caved to their demands was struck out. So, too, was the determination of Britain and France to restore canal transit rights to Israeli ships. "This was a somewhat miserable mouse to emerge from the mountain of great hopes on which Eden and Mollet had jointly set their hearts less than three weeks earlier," Nutting wrote.[25]

The United Nations General Assembly met that morning in New York. It was, according to Eden, "in an emotional mood. There was talk of collective measures against the French and ourselves."[26] He would later insist that Britain and France had always been acting selflessly in defense of "world trade" and that their actions had been misunderstood by the Americans. "The old spoor of colonialism confused the trail," he wrote.[27]

"The mood of the United Nations is grim, and there are enough extremists around to inflame opinion further against the two western Powers and Israel, however much the United States and several others may counsel moderation," wrote a *Times* of London correspondent. "Especially among the Arab countries is there talk about the use of sanctions against the parties concerned. Such talk may be mere bombast, but if the fighting goes on much longer they may try to translate it into action."[28]

Lester Pearson met with Dag Hammarskjöld and Foster Dulles to try to bolster support for his own resolution. Pearson's plan called for a cease-fire to be followed by the arrival of a United Nations force and broader Middle East peace negotiations. Hammarskjöld was initially dubious about the prospects for a United Nations force. He could not imagine which countries would send troops or where they would send them. He was concerned about whether it would look as if the United Nations were setting up a force just to get Britain and France out of trouble. He knew that would enrage the Soviets. If the force could in any way be seen as threatening Egypt's sovereignty, it would enrage the Arab world, too.

In the United States, right-wingers were relishing the opportunity to speak the language of postcolonial liberation. "For the first time in history we have shown independence of Anglo-French policies towards Asia and Africa which seemed to us to reflect the colonial tradition," said the vice president, Richard Nixon, in a speech that day. "This declaration of independence has had an electrifying effect throughout the world."[29]

Eisenhower was worn down by it. "Life gets more difficult by the minute," he wrote to his friend Alfred Gruenther. "I really could use a good bridge game." He continued: "I believe that Eden and his associates have become convinced that this is the last straw and Britain simply *had* to react in the manner of the Victorian period. . . . But I don't see the point in getting into a fight to which there can be no satisfactory end; and in which the whole world believes you are playing the part of the bully, and you do not even have the firm backing of your entire people."[30]

In Cairo that afternoon, Nasser's cabinet was debating a possible surrender. Salah Salem, one of the original Free Officers, argued that Nasser should address the nation, explaining that Egypt was going to surrender to prevent further disaster. "Let us rise and give ourselves up to [Humphrey] Trevelyan, the English Ambassador," he concluded.

"My opinion, Salah, is that it is more honorable for me to commit suicide, before doing such a thing," replied Abdel Latif al-Baghdadi.

"Far better for us all to commit suicide here, before taking such a step," said Nasser. He ordered vials containing phosphate-cyanide—enough for all of them. "I am serious about what I've said," he added.[31] Salem backed down.

If Egypt's army were defeated and the invaders occupied Cairo, Nasser planned to "organize and lead a guerrilla resistance movement." He readied an underground press and communications network. Fedayeen cells were activated, safe houses were set up, and arms were stashed in secret locations. He sent a team to organize a secret emergency headquarters between Cairo and Alexandria in the Nile delta, near Tanta.[32] He also made a tactical decision to pull his Fourth Armored Division out of Sinai and back over the Suez Canal. This pulled them out of the probable trap that had been laid for them in the desert and put them in place to defend the mainland. At this suggestion, Abdel Hakim Amer was horrified. The Egyptian army, he averred, would never retreat.

"It's not a matter of dying heroically," Nasser told him. "It's a matter of fighting heroically."

Amer had to admit that he had visited the military academy a few months before and witnessed a lesson in which the trainee officers were being instructed in the mechanics of withdrawal. So outrageous had he found this that he had stood up and declared that the entire subject of withdrawal was being taken off the Egyptian military curriculum from that moment.

Patiently, Nasser sat down with Amer and tried to run through a war-gaming exercise. "I am going to be [Moshe] Dayan and you Amer," he said. "Let us try to work out what each of us is likely to do."

Still Amer resisted. "Nobody is going to surrender or escape and everybody is going to fight," Nasser told him. "Pull yourself together, Hakim. The whole army will be converted into a guerrilla force and pulled deep into Egypt, and let them fight us there. Your behavior is unmanly; the first shots have hardly been fired."

As Amer squirmed, he continued. "I don't want you people

issuing any orders. There is no countermanding my orders. Don't you understand they are trying to destroy the army, that it is a three-way conspiracy? If you can't do any better than mope like old women then you will be arrested and tried."[33]

According to Heikal, "Nasser was sorely tempted to dismiss him [Amer] on the spot."[34] He did not, but instead telephoned all the senior officers in the Fourth Armored Division himself and ordered them directly to get out of Sinai. Nasser was now in charge of the civilian and military response of his country, and that response was going to be delivered with all possible force. The Egyptians knew they were outgunned—but they had resisted British military occupation before, and they would resist it again.

1100 Washington DC // 1600 London // 1800 Cairo // 2000 Moscow

A group of British and French airmen in Cyprus prepared two bombs for that evening's raid. Slogans were written on them in chalk. One said, "Nasser's Rock and Roll"; the other began as "Love to Nasser" but the last three letters of his name were crossed out and replaced with "ty" so that the message read "Love to Nasty." The *New York Times* correspondent noted that these "were not spontaneous: both were lettered on bombs for the benefit of a group of visiting photographers."[35] The British and French military public relations officers may have misjudged the international mood. The reaction to their operation throughout the Arab world was grim. In Amman, the Jordanian government delivered a note to the British ambassador stating, "Ministry also see in this action a form of united Anglo-French-Israel plan begun with Israel aggression which aimed at justifying armed Anglo/French intervention against Egypt and her sovereignty to realize illegal Anglo/French objects in the Suez Canal." The British ambassador was

so outraged at the suggestion that he refused to accept the note
and handed it back to the Jordanian prime minister in person. "He took it without comment," the ambassador noted.[36]
An internal CIA memorandum on French actions in Algeria
and Suez noted, "France has taken action in both areas which
does much to insure [*sic*] that the transition from French to
Moslem rule in North Africa will continue to be accompanied
by violence and which may preclude the future economic
development of Morocco and Tunisia in concert with France."
The kidnapping of Ahmed Ben Bella and the Algerian leaders
had been bad enough. Now, with the Suez intervention, the
CIA confidently expected "an extension of general hostilities
throughout North Africa."[37]

"Why, if Britain intends to resist Israel[i] aggression, have
no attacks been made on military installations in Israel instead of confining the bombardment to Egyptian targets?" the
Saudi Arabian deputy foreign minister, Yousef Yassin, asked
the correspondent from the London *Times*. If the journalist
had an answer, he did not report it. Instead he noted that Ri-
yadh was being expensively rebuilt. It was now "ablaze at night
with fairy lights, luminous mosaics, and Arabic texts in Neon
lighting, giving the impression of a Disney land." Yet even
in this otherwordly place, opinion was united: "There is no
doubt of the widespread popularity of Colonel Nasser or of the
bitterness, resentment, and mistrust felt towards Britain. . . .
As in the surrounding Arab States, he is welcomed here as the
unifier of the Arab world and the defender of the Muslim faith
against Israel[i] aggression."[38] Iskander Mirza, the president
of Pakistan, requested a meeting of Muslim members of the
Baghdad Pact—everyone except Britain—in Tehran. Britain's
most reliable ally, Iraq, agreed to attend. Exactly as so many
of Eden's advisers had predicted over the summer, the specter
of British cooperation with Israel had made it impossible for

Britain's Arab friends to remain loyal. According to an American diplomatic report, "Nuri appeared quite ill and shaken, and high-level Iraqi officials in general are deeply despondent over the difficult situation which the current situation presents to Iraq."[39]

Israel had now taken east and central Sinai. The Egyptian army was obeying Nasser's order to withdraw to the mainland, but the troops fought fiercely around El Arish—holding the Israelis off until the morning of November 2. According to journalist Robert Henriques, traveling with Israeli troops, when the IDF soldiers took El Arish, they found radios left playing and abandoned tables already set for meals. Amid the confusion, "a couple of Egyptian jeeps pulled up at a petrol station in the town and asked to be refuelled. An Israeli soldier started to serve his customers before he realised that they were all Egyptian officers."[40]

Neither side was immune to mix-ups. One Israeli tank squadron opened fire on what it believed to be an Egyptian tank squadron, taking out an impressive eight tanks in five minutes. When the clouds of dust churned up by the firing and the treads settled, it turned out that they had in fact just shot to pieces a fellow Israeli squadron. "Our capacity for misadventure is limitless," wrote Moshe Dayan in his diary.[41]

British air raids over Cairo took out the radio transmitters. A propaganda station called Voice of Britain, based in Cyprus, occupied the frequency usually used by Nasser's Voice of the Arabs. Voice of Britain began to broadcast Operation Musketeer's psychological operations material. "You have taken to hiding in little villages," the announcer said. "Do you realise what that means? We shall have to come and bomb you there. Imagine your own village being bombed. Imagine your own wife and children, your mother and your father, your grandparents having to run away from home. . . . We shall find you and bomb you, however much you hide. . . . You made only one mistake. You trusted Nasser."[42] Voice of Britain was broadcast from a requisitioned BBC Arabic Service station. The Arab staff made four attempts to sabotage it and one to make an unauthorized broadcast. As a result, three of them were placed under house arrest.[43]

With his own radio station off air, Nasser could no longer communicate directly with ordinary Egyptians. "The only way for me was to go to El Azhar [mosque] and give a speech," he remembered. "And I went to El Azhar in an open car and there were aeroplanes over Cairo attacking the military targets. But the people were in the roads by that time, and all of the time I was in the open car they were raising the slogan 'We will fight, we will fight.'"[44]

Nasser attended Friday prayers at El Azhar. Afterward, he spoke to the enormous crowd that had gathered. He explained why Egyptian forces had retreated from the Sinai, saying they had done so to avoid a trap: Britain and France had planned to draw them into the sands so they could snatch out the heart of Egypt. When he told them the Egyptian army had ransacked British stores along the Suez Canal on its way back to the mainland (tens of thousands of tons of British ammunition, military equipment, and vehicles were still stored there under the terms of the 1954 Canal Zone evacuation agreement), the applause was so loud that his speech could no longer be heard.

"In Cairo I shall fight with you against any invasion," he said. "We shall fight to the last drop of our blood. We shall never surrender."[45] He told them that Egypt had always been a graveyard of invaders. This became the theme for one of many popular songs at the time, "The Nile, Graveyard of All Invaders," often sung along with "O Gamal, Opener of the Door of Freedom."[46]

Though there were rumblings in the Egyptian military and

government against Nasser's leadership, the great majority of the Egyptian people united behind him. This revealed how unrealistic the British psychological operations plan was. A scattering of leaflets dropped from foreign aircraft and some poisonous radio broadcasts from Cyprus were not, in a matter of days, likely to turn the Egyptian public against their popular leader while the country was being attacked by all of its worst enemies at once. If anything, Anglo-French propaganda may have backfired to shore up Nasser's support.

According to his friend Mohammed Heikal, Nasser "had been encouraged by the demonstrations in Trafalgar Square and elsewhere. So, though he would be grateful for any aid the Russians could give, he did not want to coordinate action with them." The Soviets did not want to coordinate action with Egypt either, while they were preparing to invade Hungary. There was a diplomatic reception in Moscow that night attended by the Egyptian ambassador, Mohamed el-Kouni, and Nikita Khrushchev. When the two spoke, everyone in the room craned their necks to see if they could read what was going on from their faces.

"We are full of admiration for the way in which you are resisting aggression," Khrushchev told Kouni, "but unfortunately there is no way in which we can help you militarily. But we are going to mobilize world public opinion." Kouni reported this lukewarm endorsement in a telegram to Cairo.[47]

Foster Dulles arrived back in Washington. At the airport, he was asked by a journalist whether he would resign. Instead of replying, he "laughed heartily." The United Nations, he said, had done a great thing by passing his resolution. "Never before has there been an example of such solidarity before all the world, dealing with such a grave matter."[48]

When he got back to his office, Dulles telephoned Henry Cabot Lodge, the American ambassador to the United Nations, in New York, to discuss the progress of the separate resolution on Hungary. Lodge told him the British and French were "in a very emotional condition—they say there will be a bad impression at home if we are in a hurry to get them on the dock and drag in Russia." According to the transcript of the conversation, Dulles replied that he thought the British and French wanted to hide behind their association with the United States. "The Sec. thinks it is a mockery for them to come in with bombs falling over Egypt and denounce the SU [Soviet Union] for perhaps doing something that is not quite as bad [in Hungary]. L.[odge] agrees. The Sec. wants no part of it."[49]

Throughout its existence, the Eisenhower administration's attitude to the Soviet bloc had been to talk tough while acting little. Eisenhower did not want a direct confrontation with the Soviet Union, especially from the mid-1950s, when the nuclear threat became more serious. The Soviets felt the same. American policy on the Soviet satellite states was openly to encourage "passive resistance" to Soviet-controlled regimes. The feasibility of mounting American special-forces operations in satellite states was explored, but only from behind desks in Washington. "Viewed as a potential theater of Special Forces operations, Hungary is singularly unpromising," noted a report prepared for army intelligence in January 1956 by researchers at Georgetown University. Geographical conditions in the country were considered to provide poor cover for special forces, and the level of active resistance to Soviet domination was not clear. Even so, the report noted, "It may be argued that in no other European satellite is passive resistance so widespread, intense, and current . . . what is now dissidence may be converted into active resistance with the proper leadership." Special forces would have a favorable prospect of rallying dissidents against the regime in some areas. "Furthermore, hot war conditions may radically change the resistance picture and other actors related to the feasibility of Special Forces operations."[50]

Violent intervention in the Soviet bloc was not in the cards, but violence itself—as long as it was undertaken by residents of the satellites rather than Americans—did not seem unpalatable to the Eisenhower administration during the summer of 1956. "Avoid incitements to violence or to action when the probable reprisals or other results would yield a net loss in terms of U.S. objectives," said a National Security Council policy statement approved by the president on July 18, 1956. "In general, however, do not discourage, by public utterances or otherwise, spontaneous manifestations of discontent and opposition to the Communist regime, despite risks to individuals, when their net results will exert pressures for release from Soviet domination."[51]

Richard Nixon had gone further in a National Security Council meeting in July 1956: "The Vice President commented that it wouldn't be an unmixed evil, from the point of view of U.S. interest, if the Soviet iron fist were to come down again on the Soviet bloc, though on balance it would be more desirable, of course, if the present liberalizing trend in relations between the Soviet Union and its satellites continued." If the Soviet Union was not going to get nicer, it would help justify the American cause if it got much, much nastier.

Though Dulles and Nixon shared a strong antipathy to Communism, Dulles did not seem so exhilarated by the prospect of Soviet brutality. In the same meeting, he advocated a realist view. Movements termed *national Communist*—meaning non-Stalinist and non–Soviet controlled, like Tito's government in Hungary—would be tacitly supported by the United States, in the hope they might "loosen the ties" with the Soviet Union. "Once these ties were loosened by the development of a national Communist government, it might ultimately be possible to go much further and to change the character of the Communist government in the satellites."

While expressing his "emphatic agreement" with this policy, Nixon warned that it must not, under any circumstances, become public that the United States was supporting any form of Communist government—even a liberalizing one. "Accordingly, he hoped that everybody, from those present all the way down the line, would keep their mouths shut on this subject." The Treasury secretary, George Humphrey, worried about the policy statement leaking out: "Imagine what would happen if portions of this paper were ever published in the newspapers. The effect on the Administration would be murderous."[52]

On November 2, the American legation in Budapest was still attempting to encourage some form of intervention by Washington, however soft. A diplomat there noted that "the attitude of the people on the streets has been touchingly pro-American and that the potentiality of US influence in this period is tremendous."[53] At the very least, he hoped for further statements and talks on economic assistance. But the Eisenhower administration was in a bind: clear on the need to position itself internationally as different from and more appealing than the Soviets, while being effectively on the same side as them on the Suez question. If the United States were to capitalize on this moment to promote its opposition to imperialism in the postcolonial world, this was no time to stoke the fire in Hungary. With Khrushchev's administration blaming foreign and especially American agents for the rebellion, it did not take a great deal of imagination to see how any form of American intervention there might be spun by the Soviets to look like hypocrisy.

1830 Brioni

A storm raged in the night over the Adriatic Sea. At his villa in the Brioni Islands, President Josip Broz Tito of Yugoslavia made his way down through the squall to the landing stage next to the villa with his ambassador to Moscow, Veljko Mićunović, and the second and third most powerful Communist politicians in Yugoslavia after Tito himself, Edvard Kardelj and Aleksandar Rancović. The wind whipped the sea into gigantic peaks and troughs, but eventually a small boat appeared and was roped to the dock. From it emerged Nikita Khrushchev and Georgy Malenkov, both looking sick as parrots—the latter barely able to stand. "Malenkov was pale as a corpse," remembered Khrushchev. "He gets carsick on a good road."[54] The boat trip had been bad; the plane before it, worse. Malenkov had spent most of the flight lying down, unable even to sit. "Khrushchev said it had been worse than in the war," wrote Mićunović.[55]

"The Russians kissed us on both cheeks," remembered Mićunović. "It was a very strange scene on that little empty quayside." He was shocked: the Soviets and the Yugoslavs had been at odds for nearly seven years, and now there were kisses. "I still seem to feel Malenkov's fat round face, into which my nose sank as if into a half-inflated balloon as I was drawn into a cold and quite unexpected embrace," he wrote later.

Just half an hour later, a meeting began in the villa. The only people present were those six: no note takers, no interpreters, no secretaries. In his diary, Mićunović recorded the content of the talks, which went on from seven p.m. that evening until five a.m. the next morning. Though his account differs from Khrushchev's own, it was set down much nearer to the event when it was fresh in his memory. Both versions are revealing of Khrushchev's reasoning and state of mind.

Khrushchev opened the talks in an emotional fashion, "saying that Communists in Hungary were being murdered, butchered, and hanged." He said he did not know whether Imre Nagy was merely a tool for the West or had always been an agent of imperialism. But the restoration of capitalism now looked alarmingly likely. "What is there left for us to do?" asked Khrushchev. "If we let things take their course the West would say we are either stupid or weak, and that's one and the same thing. We cannot possibly permit it, either as Communists and internationalists or as the Soviet state. We would have capitalists on the frontiers of the Soviet Union." Soviet troops were mostly in place, he told them, but it would take "a couple of days" before they were ready to stop the counterrevolution.

Khrushchev was worried that this had happened at a moment when the presidium had been distancing itself from Stalin: "There were people in the Soviet Union who would say that as long as Stalin was in command everybody obeyed and there were no big shocks, but that now, ever since *they* had come to power (and here Khrushchev used a coarse word to describe the present Soviet leaders), Russia had suffered the defeat and loss of Hungary."

The crisis in Suez, Khrushchev said, presented an opportunity. Of course there would be a fuss made in the West and at the United Nations about what he would do in Hungary, but with Britain, France, and Israel waging a war with Egypt, he expected that to be "less" than could normally be expected. "They are bogged down there, and we are stuck in Hungary," he explained.

Malenkov outlined the Soviets' military plan. "It is clear that the Russians are going to intervene frontally and with great force, because they are completely isolated from the Hungarian people," wrote Mićunović; "in fact, the population is opposed to the Russians."

Mićunović's version of events was loyal to Tito, portraying him as a bold critic of Soviet policy. Conversely, Khrushchev claimed Tito supported him wholeheartedly. "I expected even more strenuous objections from Tito than the ones we had encountered during our discussions with the Polish comrades," said Khrushchev. "But we were pleasantly surprised. Tito said we were absolutely right and that we should send our soldiers into action as quickly as possible. . . . I would even say he went further than we did in urging a speedy and decisive resolution of the problem."[56]

Mićunović instead asserted that the Yugoslavs advocated for "some political preparation, an effort to save what could be saved." They suggested setting up a new government composed of Hungarians. Khrushchev and Malenkov vaguely agreed, though they were disillusioned with the leaders they had installed in the past, Rákosi and Gerő. "Khrushchev used coarse language about Rákosi and then even worse language about Geroe," Mićunović remembered. Khrushchev told them that Rákosi had offered to go to Budapest to help the Soviet cause, but he had told him frankly, "Go down there and the people will hang you."

"That idiot doesn't understand the most elementary things," remarked Malenkov.

For the next couple of hours, they discussed possible Hungarian leaders. Tito suggested that the Soviets favor the more liberal János Kádár (who had once been accused of being a Titoist) over the hard-line Ferenc Münnich.[57] Then Khrushchev told them he had also been talking with the Chinese. He said that Chou En-lai, the Chinese premier, and Liu Shao-chi, the chairman of the Standing Committee of the People's Congress—Mao's number two and number three—had come to Moscow. "The Chinese had apparently agreed to everything and had been in contact with Mao Tse-tung by telephone. He had agreed completely with the decision to intervene in Hungary." Khrushchev went on to complain about the perfidy of the Poles for a while. "As usual when he is talking to Yugoslavs and wants to put them in a good mood, as though he were making some concessions to them, Khrushchev told some un-flattering stories about Stalin," Mićunović added.

Mićunović believed that night that he and his fellow Yu-goslavs might have encouraged Khrushchev to rethink Imre Nagy's fate. "Whenever the question of Imre Nagy came up, Khrushchev would generally repeat, 'They are slaughtering Communists in Hungary,' as though it was all being done on decisions taken by Nagy's government and carried out by its services," he noted. But he thought Tito had managed to soften him on this and said Khrushchev ultimately agreed that Nagy "could do much to help and to preserve his reputation as a communist."[58] Maybe, the Yugoslavs hoped, they might have talked the Soviets down from all-out war.

1600 Washington DC // 2100 London // 2200 Budapest

Yet the Soviet war plan was already well advanced. According to a later United Nations report, Hungary had by this time "to all intents and purposes been reinvaded." There were around 2,500 trucks, 1,000 supporting vehicles, and somewhere be-tween 75,000 and 200,000 men and women of the Red Army in Hungarian territory. Imre Nagy was still trying to negotiate with Moscow, hoping desperately that the enormous military presence in his country was merely "a show of strength."[59] The government in Moscow continued to deny that anything was happening.

Charles Bohlen, the American ambassador to Moscow, was at a reception that evening hosted by the Syrian embassy. He spoke to Nikolai Bulganin. "He denied that there had been any reinforcements from outside Hungary," Bohlen reported, "but said there had been much movement [of] Soviet troops inside country which might have created impression [of] re-inforcements." The reception ended before Bohlen could press

Bulganin on further points, but Bohlen did note that other Soviet leaders—Shepilov, Zhukov, and Sokolovsky—left early, and Khrushchev was nowhere to be seen. "I asked Voroshilov and Mikoyan whether he was ill and they said no he was at home, and in explanation said it was impossible for all of them to attend all receptions."[60] Khrushchev's visit to Tito was a closely guarded secret.

In London, the minister of transport and civil aviation appeared on television that night to warn the public that there was now a "gap in this great pipeline of oil. As soon as the gap arrives, there will have to be some restriction on oil consumption in this country." In Chester, the chancellor of the exchequer, Harold Macmillan, was giving a speech in support of a Conservative candidate at a by-election. He was unable to avoid questions about Suez. Macmillan expressed a desire to see the United Nations intervene, and he sounded shaken: "The quicker it gets going the better I shall be pleased," he said. "Then we shall be only an advance guard. The strain is greater than the economy of the country can bear."

He attempted to justify the government's action. "I hope when history judges this matter it will be said: 'These men have made mistakes, but they have had the courage to act instead of slinking into the easy way of passing the buck to someone else.'"[61]

At the United Nations in New York that evening, Britain, France, and the United States reunited to ask the Security Council to consider the situation in Hungary following Imre Nagy's appeal. The discussion was held up because it could not be decided whether the Hungarian representative was loyal to the previous Stalinist regime or could be considered to represent Nagy's government. The indications were that, once the representative's credentials could be established and the Western powers could be certain of a strong pro-Nagy Hungarian voice, a resolution condemning Soviet aggression could be brought up in the Security Council. "Should Soviet Russia veto this resolution, as it is expected to do, then the matter could be referred to an extraordinary meeting of the General Assembly (just as was the complaint against Britain and France over the Suez affair yesterday)," explained the *Times* of London, "and there is little doubt that Russia would then find herself almost as unpopular in the eyes of member States as Britain and France now are."[62]

If this was a move by Britain and France to take the heat off themselves, the president of the United States would not go along with it. Eisenhower gave a speech in Philadelphia that night. He also linked Suez and Hungary, though not to Britain's or France's benefit. He expressed pride that the United States had declared itself against the use of force in either conflict. "We cannot and will not condone aggression," he said, "no matter who the attacker, no matter who the victim."[63]

2200 Washington DC

After his triumph at the United Nations the day before, Dulles had flown back to Washington that morning and put in a full day's work. He went home afterward for dinner and backgammon with his wife, Janet, then retired to bed at around ten p.m. As he slept, a telegram clicked through at the office from Henry Cabot Lodge, the American ambassador at the United Nations. Lodge reported a "strained and difficult" discussion with his British and French counterparts. Pierson Dixon, the Briton, "charge[s] US has lost interest in Hungary and now only wants [to] increase pressure on UK and France under GA [General Assembly] Suez resolution." Dixon thought the Americans believed that Britain was advocating action on Hungary only in order to distract the world from Suez. "I explained US has not lost interest in Hungary but considers situation there too confused to permit our pressing substantive resolution to final vote," Lodge wrote. He recommended that the United States back off introducing resolutions with France and Britain at all—but from now on bring them on a solo basis. This was a major move and would be a further visible break with the United States' tripartite allies. "Please instruct urgently," the message ended.[64]

According to the time stamp on the telegram, this arrived seven minutes after midnight. At almost exactly the same time, Dulles was woken up by searing abdominal pain. It ebbed, and he went back to sleep. A few hours later, it happened again.

He telephoned his special assistant, William Macomber. "I've been taken ill, Bill," he said, "and I want you to come over here. The doctors are coming and the ambulance is coming. And I want you to be with me and sort of take charge of this until the Department opens. You can get in touch with Mr. Hoover. I don't know how ill I am. But please come over. In the meantime, I want you to call [Eisenhower's press secretary] Jim Hagerty and explain to him what's happening and get his advice as to how we should play this from the public relations angle."

Even in acute pain, Dulles never lost his focus on running the State Department. He was also conscious of the need not to damage Eisenhower's electoral chances. "Mr. Dulles thought that his going into hospital at this key moment would remind an awful lot of people of the President's earlier heart attack and could possibly have an adverse effect on their willingness to vote for him," Macomber remembered. When Macomber arrived, the paramedics were trying and failing to carry the tall and now unexpectedly fragile Secretary of State down the spiral stairs from his bedroom. At last, Dulles sat and inched his way down in a crouched position, step by step.

Dulles was taken to Walter Reed Army Medical Center,

where he was soon given a stark diagnosis. It was cancer. He would have to have an operation without delay. He would be out of action completely until Monday.

Dulles told Macomber to find Hoover. "I want you to say to him that for everything but Suez, he's Secretary of State," said Dulles. "No non Suez problems can be brought to me. He'll have to run those things."

"In other words, on the key issue of the time, which was Suez, . . . he kept control of [*sic*] all through his illness," said Macomber later. "It was an enormously impressive example of self-discipline."[65] Even though he stayed on top of developments, the fact that Dulles was pulled off the political front line in the State Department and the United Nations did lessen his influence over events. Suez and Hungary had just been overtaken by a personal crisis he could not ignore.

13

"HELP THE BURGLAR, SHOOT THE HOUSEHOLDER"

0500 Brioni

Talks between Khrushchev and Tito ended abruptly before dawn. "For some moments there was a general silence," Veljko Mićunović remembered. "It was a rather awkward pause, with no one inclined to attract the attention of others for further conversation, since there was nothing more to be said on the political questions." He added (usefully for posterity, for it was a break with usual Soviet convention): "Practically no alcohol had been drunk at dinner and none was served during the talks."

Khrushchev and Malenkov returned via their boat and plane to Moscow. "Flying conditions were exceptionally bad," wrote Mićunović.[1] The storm that had been raging the day before had abated neither metaphorically nor literally.

0600 London // 0700 Budapest // 0800 Khan Yunis

Chester Cooper was summoned to his embassy before the sun was up in London for a call on the secure telephone line. The voice on the other end was that of Robert Amory, deputy director of the CIA. "He shouted so loudly that I could have heard him across the Atlantic without a telephone," Cooper remembered.

"Tell your [British] friends," Amory yelled, "to comply with the goddamn ceasefire or go ahead with the goddamn invasion. Either way, we'll back 'em up if they do it fast. What we can't stand is their goddamn hesitation waltz while Hungary is burning!"

Cooper was shocked at this new offer to "back up" a British invasion, and felt he should discuss it further with his fellow diplomats. He went home after the call, returning to the embassy at nine a.m. By then, news of Foster Dulles's sudden illness had reached London. "And so, at the most critical moment of crisis in both Hungary and the Middle East, John Foster Dulles was taken out of action," Cooper wrote. "Responsibility now rested with a well-meaning, but basically uninterested President and with an unimaginative, relatively inexperienced, reportedly anti-British acting secretary, Herbert Hoover, Jr."[2]

Cooper was wrong in saying that Eisenhower was uninterested. If anything, he was too interested, according to the Israeli ambassador to the United Nations, Abba Eban, who had worked well with Dulles. "The next thing was that he [Dulles] was in hospital," Eban remembered, "and we had to deal with Eisenhower in his full righteous fury, and an extremely unprepossessing gentleman called Herbert Hoover, and [Henry Cabot] Lodge who was more concerned with the twelve Arabs than with the solitary Israeli in the United Nations."[3]

Amory's instruction to the British to go ahead was based on Allen Dulles's assessment of the situation—that Nasser might be on the verge of falling. A letter was drafted for Eisenhower to send to Eden, suggesting that Britain could cooperate with the cease-fire after achieving its objectives. It was not sent.[4]

There were two problems with this policy initiative, which came from the headquarters of the CIA in Washington, not from the better-informed CIA agents on the ground in the Middle East. First, Nasser was not on the verge of falling. Second, Britain was not able to achieve its objectives with any speed.

According to Cooper's recollection, he met with the Joint Intelligence Committee that morning and passed on to his British contacts the advice that they should either cease firing or invade—adding that he was "not speaking without instructions."[5] But if this was a sign of a possible change in direction from Washington, it arrived at a moment when the campaign directed from London was in chaos: the French were still pressing for landings to be sped up and the British were still dithering. After the meeting, Cooper spoke to a British acquaintance—a liaison officer working between intelligence and military staff.

"What's going on? Cooper asked. "Is there going to be a landing or not?"

The officer took him upstairs to a temporary operations center. A harried-looking colonel sat behind a desk heaped with papers.

"Cooper wants to know where the hell our troops are," the officer said to the colonel.

"Our troops?" replied the colonel. He pulled back a curtain covering a map of the Mediterranean and pointed to a flotilla of colored pins in the blue between Malta and Egypt. "There they are. In the middle of the bleeding Med!"[6]

According to CIA agent Wilbur Eveland, "It seemed obvious that Britain and France were either so ill prepared or so inept that they'd never reach their presumed objective, Cairo."[7] The slow progress of the British and French was deeply irritating to the Israelis. The Israeli ambassador in London saw Sir Ivone

Kirkpatrick of the Foreign Office and told him it was "absolutely essential" that the British and French troops should now arrive without delay. "He had seen no very recent reports, but according to reports three days old, there was considerable dissension amongst the Rulers of Egypt," Kirkpatrick wrote in a minute to the Africa Department. "The Israel Government would not be much surprised if the Egyptian Rulers did not begin murdering each other fairly soon. I got the impression that he was telling me this in order to reinforce his argument that it would be a fatal error to relax the pressure."[8]

The French were amenable to speeding the operation up. Eden discussed the French and Israeli call for a swifter landing of troops with his cabinet and military advisers that morning, but seemed unable to come to a decision. Antony Head, minister of defense, was put on a plane to Cyprus to meet with the commanders there to assess if this would be feasible.[9] There was another consideration, too: the need to make the whole operation look like a peacekeeping intervention rather than a straightforward invasion. To this end, the British also considered the possibility of slowing the operation down—and ditching the element of surprise. The commanders in London sent a message to General Keightley in the Mediterranean: "For very strong political reasons we may wish to make an announcement that the landing will be at Port Said in order to save the lives of civilians, thus sacrificing tactical surprise." They added: "We assume you still have flexibility to postpone landing for up to 48 hours as before?"[10]

"Since we were launched on this operation the whole emphasis has been on speed," Keightley replied in an exasperated tone. He was not sure whether a postponement would be possible. "Incidentally it will cause a complete break with the French on [sic—to] whom we have given a solemn undertaking we will not postpone except for bad weather," he added.

"What is behind this suggestion?"[11] The suggestion, came the reply, was that this might allow for an extended period of aerial and psychological warfare to make the landing in Port Said easier—"though it is realised that this is a slender hope."[12]

A few days before, when he had first begun to feel the pressure, Eden had requested a message of support from Winston Churchill. Churchill was still recovering from his minor stroke and was too tired to write one, but authorized his private secretary Anthony Montague Browne to draft it for him. "World peace, the Middle East and our national interest will surely benefit in the long run from the Government's resolute action," it concluded. "They deserve our support." It was published on November 3, to Eden's delight. "My dear Winston, I cannot thank you enough for your wonderful message," he wrote, expressing his hope that it would influence American opinion. "These are tough days—but the alternative was a slow bleeding to death."

"Thereafter everything came to pieces," remembered Montague Browne. "I find it painful to recall the details of our decline. . . . WSC [Churchill] sank into a mood of deep melancholy."[13]

In Budapest, Imre Nagy made the rebel colonel Pál Maléter his minister of defense in response to public demand. At ten a.m., he recommenced what he hoped were good-faith negotiations with the Soviets about their military presence in Hungary. His hope was misplaced. The Soviets were already acting: closing Hungary's border with Austria to the west and occupying railway stations, highways, and border stations in the east.[14] The CIA learned that "at least 600 Soviet tanks" had now entered Hungary from the Soviet Union and Romania.[15] Owing to the press and radio blackout, the people of Budapest did not have this information.

The last Egyptian and Palestinian fighters in the Gaza Strip were still holding out against the IDF in Khan Yunis, a former caravanserai and British fortress town in the south of the strip. But their comrades in Egypt had withdrawn from the Sinai, and they were cut off from any relief or resupply. It was only a matter of time before the IDF would take Khan Yunis, and it did so that morning.

Early in the afternoon, the governor of the Gaza Strip formally surrendered to the IDF's Southern Command. "The surrender act was written by a young Israel army officer on a sheet of paper torn out of a copy book and placed on a map folder," reported the *Jerusalem Post*. It was written in Hebrew and Arabic. After he had signed it, the governor was taken prisoner. Other military defenders were taken prisoner, too, and marched away in columns. "There is something theatrical in all this but the square is littered with empty cartridges," wrote the *Post* correspondent. "From near and far come the intermittent stutter of a machine-gun or boom of a mine exploding. No[t] all the soldiers received the surrender order, or perhaps they do not feel like abiding by it."[16]

Or perhaps those shots were something else. There were conflicting stories about what triggered the events in Khan Yunis that day. According to the Israeli authorities, they met with resistance to their occupation, and the resisters included some Palestinian refugees. According to the Palestinian refugees, Israeli troops went through the town and the refugee camp, rounding up any men in possession of arms and allegedly some without.

What happened after that, though, was independently documented. A large number of civilian men and boys, aged approximately between fifteen and fifty-five, were escorted roughly into open squares and lined up against walls, including those of the Ottoman caravanserai. They were shot and killed where they stood by IDF troops. The director of UN-RWA reported some weeks later that he had compiled a list "from sources he considers trustworthy" of 275 people who had been summarily executed. This included 140 refugees and 135 local residents of Khan Yunis. There was another such spate of executions a few days later at Rafah, in which a further 111 people were estimated to have been killed. The United Nations report also mentioned "the many serious surgical cases caused by the fighting and the subsequent incidents at Khan Yunis and Rafah, where a number of refugees were severely wounded." How many were wounded is not known.[17]

"I still remember the wailing and tears of my father over his brother," said the Palestinian refugee Abdel Aziz al-Rantissi, who was nine years old in 1956 when he watched the IDF kill his uncle in Khan Yunis. "It left a wound in my heart that can never heal. I'm telling you a story, and I am almost crying. . . . They planted hatred in our hearts."[18] When Rantissi grew up, he became one of the founders of Hamas, the militant Palestinian Islamic organization that grew out of the Palestinian branch of the Muslim Brotherhood. Hamas refused to renounce violence against Israel; Rantissi was one of the strongest voices against compromise. He served as leader of Hamas briefly in 2004 until he was assassinated by the Israeli air force, which blew up his car with a missile launched from a helicopter.

Eisenhower and Dulles had worked for years to bring the two sides of the Arab-Israeli conflict together. Eden claimed by his Suez action to be separating combatants and ensuring peace. Yet the violence that was done in the Suez War had the opposite effect. Members of Eden's administration did not know of these murders. But they could have foreseen that stoking the Arab-Israeli conflict would produce uncontrollable violence, and in fact they had: this was one reason so many

British advisers, civilian and military, warned Eden off involving Israel in any attack on Egypt. Rantissi's case illustrates how the Suez War scattered dragon's teeth on all-too-fertile soil. Across the whole of the Middle East, not just in Israel and Palestine, these would for decades bear gruesome fruit.

1200 London

In the House of Commons—convened unusually on a Saturday—the Labour leader Hugh Gaitskell pointed out that the rapid advances made by Israel across the Sinai meant that the fighting was all but over. Consequently, there were now no grounds for an Anglo-French intervention.

Eden insisted that the British and French must be allowed to finish their "police action" to protect the canal and "to pave the way for a definite settlement of the Arab-Israeli war." He said the British and French would "most willingly" stop if three conditions were met. First, the Egyptians and Israelis must accept a United Nations peacekeeping force. Second, the United Nations must put that force in and maintain it until an Arab-Israeli peace settlement was reached. Third, until a United Nations force could be put in, Egypt and Israel must both agree to accept "limited detachments of Anglo-French troops to be stationed between combatants."[19] It was not a climbdown—but Eden had, for the first time, publicly hinted that he might be amenable to a United Nations force taking over his "peacekeeping" mission. From the back benches, a voice called out, "Burglars."

"We are not burglars," Eden replied testily. "The right hon. Gentleman the Leader of the Opposition has himself told us that we brought some fighting prematurely to an end."

"The Prime Minister is perfectly right," Gaitskell said. "What we did was to go in and help the burglar and shoot the householder."[20]

0925 Washington DC // 1425 London // 1625 Cairo // 1725 Moscow

"At this moment thousands of young English men are sitting on landing craft moving from one destination in the Mediterranean towards the shores of Egypt," Labour MP Denis Healey told the House of Commons. "I spent some time in the last war in exactly that situation." Healey claimed he had known what he was fighting for, and had been confident that the cause was just. "I know that there are many hon. and right hon. Members opposite who sincerely believe that our cause is just," he said. "I respect their convictions, but they must know also that there are many men in those landing craft who do not believe that our cause is just."[21]

The Egyptians claimed to have shot down fourteen British, French, and Israeli planes, including nine over Cairo. "At least one was seen falling near the centre of the city, and two explosions were heard," reported the London *Times*. "Excitement followed, and crowds were seen running in streets, pursued by police."[22] Twisted wreckage was displayed in Tahrir Square. A British frigate in the Gulf of Suez was attacked by four aircraft and shot one down. The downed plane had been thought to be an Egyptian MiG, but the crew on the frigate thought it might have been an Israeli Mystère or Sabre. This caused excitement in the Admiralty and Foreign Office. Shooting down an Israeli plane made the British attack look even-handed; they did not have to tell anyone it had been an accident. The Foreign Office ordered the Allied Forces Headquarters to put out a statement, reading: "British frigate operating in Gulf of Suez has shot down an Israeli aircraft which interfered with her patrol."

"You will realize value of such a release, if facts can be confirmed," read the secret instructions from the Foreign Office. "Meanwhile can you arrange non-attributable publicity for this report."[23] The story duly appeared in the London *Times* the following Monday, repeating verbatim the government statement.[24] The British government did not intentionally comply with the request of some of its allies in Iraq reported by the British ambassador in Baghdad that day: "Our friends are saying that even a single bomb on an Israel air field or a single action to stop Israel detachments advancing would restore their confidence in us."[25]

Nasser was cheered by crowds as he drove through Cairo, but the mood in Egypt was one of "incredulous sorrow," according to the London *Times*. There had been a notable shift in the tone of Arab press coverage over the previous week. On October 28, the day of the Arab general strike against the kidnapping of the Algerian rebels, France was the greatest villain in the Arab world. After Israel's invasion of Egypt on October 29, Israel took over that role. By November 3, though, much of the Arab press blamed Britain, with Iraq's *al-Hurria* newspaper joining many deploring "the traditional enmity of Britain" toward Egypt. The *Times* correspondent in Cairo reported that "one is constantly approached by Egyptians, as bewildered as they are angry, for an interpretation of British motives and an assessment of Sir Anthony Eden's personal character, almost as if they were hoping that they could be persuaded by some explanation other than the familiar one of 'imperialist conspiracy' which nothing will now eradicate."[26] Yet while the anger against Britain and France was real, Egypt was offering an olive branch as well as resistance. In the United Nations, Dag Hammarskjöld announced that Egypt had said it would cease fire if Israel also stopped fighting and the British and French called their war fleet off.[27]

Nasser was becoming desperate and depressed. According to Abdel Latif al-Baghdadi, who spent time with him that day, "He did not know a thing of what the Army was doing" and felt cut out of events by the military commanders. So worked up did he get over this that "he almost lost his self-control." He was thrilled, though, when Baghdadi told him that he had seen an enemy plane shot down near the Misr al-Jadida air base. "When Gamal heard these words he took my face between his two hands and kissed me," remembered Baghdadi. "In truth, I lied to him for what had fallen by this air-base were none other than the reserve fuel tanks of one of the planes."[28]

Anthony Nutting called together three ministerial colleagues—his co-minister of state, Lord Reading, and the joint parliamentary undersecretaries of state, Douglas Dodds-Parker and John Hope—in Reading's room at the Foreign Office. He told them his resignation was going to take effect that night, and he told them why. They were, Nutting remembered, "deeply shocked and angry at having been kept in the dark about actions and decisions which, as Ministers, they could be called upon to defend in Parliament. For a moment, they seemed to be on the point of walking out with me." They discussed it and decided they must not: if all four went at once, the consequences for the Conservative government could be fatal. Reluctantly, they stayed.

Nutting returned to his own office to find the atmosphere among senior civil servants even more mutinous. They had worked out what was really going on, he wrote, and "felt deeply in their hearts that they could no longer serve a Government which had so debased our name and fame in the eyes of the world. In all my five years as a Foreign Office Minister I had never seen such a demonstration of real indignation from officials normally the epitome of unruffled calm." They were not, he reminded them, responsible for political policy: civil servants were there to advise and facilitate. Eventually, he persuaded them, too, not to resign.[29]

At 11:10 a.m. that morning, Eisenhower met Herbert Hoover

Jr., the acting secretary of state, and legal adviser Herman Phleger to discuss the Hungarian question at the United Nations Security Council. According to the minutes of the meeting, Hoover noted that "Secretary Dulles did not want to join the British and the French, and the President said that such a thought was almost absurd."[30]

In Moscow, American ambassador Charles Bohlen was at a reception for the Syrian president Shukri al-Kuwatly in the Kremlin. Khrushchev appeared with Malenkov, back from their secret trip to Yugoslavia, and was immediately surrounded by other members of the presidium. Later, though, he came up to Bohlen. The Soviet leader opened the conversation by saying he assumed NATO was pleased at the possibility of what he called "dislocation" in the Warsaw Pact. Bohlen asked him about Soviet intentions in Hungary. Khrushchev said negotiations were going on between the Soviet and Hungarian governments and matters "would be straightened out."

Bohlen protested that the Soviets were still putting more troops into Hungary. Khrushchev replied that they had enough troops there already, but said, "We will add more and more if necessary." He added that this was "not a joke."

Khrushchev then raised the subject of Egypt and accused the United States of failing to prevent the Suez invasion. The Americans could, he thought, have stopped it if they had wished. Bohlen replied that the "president and US government had done everything they could to restrain Israel" and that the United States had raised the matter in the United Nations. Khrushchev repeated that the "voice" of the United States would have been strong enough to stop the war, implying that he still believed the United States had been privy to Britain and France's plot. If this was his drift, Bohlen did not catch it—and the conversation was interrupted by the departure of Kuwatly. "The only discernible virtue in Khrushchev that I can see is his brutal frankness," Bohlen wrote. "He is first Soviet official who has admitted Soviets intend [to] send amount of troops necessary [to] achieve their projectives [*sic*] in Hungary."[31]

That evening, at nine p.m. Moscow time, many in the presidium supported the hard-line Ferenc Münnich for leader of Hungary. Khrushchev, perhaps influenced by Tito, disagreed. He preferred the slightly softer János Kádár, and sold him to his comrades as the candidate it would be easier to control.[32] In Hungary itself, the Soviets were negotiating with Nagy's government—but in Moscow they had already chosen his successor.

1400 Ottawa; New York; Washington DC // 1900 London

Eden made a formal broadcast to the nation on television that evening. "If you see a fire the first question is not how it started, but how to put it out," he said, claiming that the British and French intervention had been a spontaneous response to Israel's action. "What we did do was to take police action at once. . . . Our friends inside the Commonwealth and outside could not, in the very nature of things, be consulted in time. You just cannot have immediate action and extensive consultation as well. But our friends are coming, as Australia and New Zealand have already done—and I believe that Canada and the United States will soon come—to see that we acted with courage and speed to deal with a situation which would just not wait."

In fact, Canada and the United States were coming closer to seeing that Britain had planned the whole thing. As the Canadian prime minister said after Eden's speech, the Suez crisis had "strained both the western alliance and the bonds of the Commonwealth more than any event since the second world war."

"All my life I've been a man of peace, working for peace, striving for peace, and negotiating for peace," Eden went on. "I've been a League of Nations man and a United Nations man. And I am still the same man, with the same convictions, and the same devotion to peace. I could not be other, even if I wished, but I am utterly convinced that the action we have taken is right."

The prime minister spoke clearly, without stuttering, reading from a script with a clipped, rhythmic tone like a vicar delivering an overrehearsed sermon. The political historian Peter Hennessy remarked that every time he rewatched the footage of Eden's broadcast, he was "struck by the sincerity of Eden's exhausted self-belief."[33] Eden had convinced himself that his actions were in pursuit of righteousness, even if the actions themselves were not righteous. It was this belief that he was clinging to that day. He would be unable to pry himself away from it for the rest of his life.

1745 Washington DC // 2245 London // 2345 Budapest // 0245 (Nov. 4) Moscow

At Tököl, on Csepel Island just outside Budapest, a delegation of senior Hungarians had gone to meet their adversaries at Soviet military command. They were hoping to negotiate the Red Army's withdrawal. The Hungarians were led by Colonel Pál Maléter, now minister of defense. Maléter was accompanied by a minister of state, the chief of staff, and another colonel.

The Soviets played nice. They had invited the Hungarians to a lavish banquet with three Red Army generals. As the time neared midnight, toasts were being drunk. Suddenly, armed Soviet security police burst into the dining hall. They were led by Ivan Serov, head of the KGB, his Mauser pistol drawn.[34]

General Mikhail Malinin, the most senior of the Red Army

generals present, appeared genuinely shocked by Serov's interruption and protested vociferously. Serov strode over and whispered something to him, which nobody else could hear. Malinin took it in, shrugged, and told his fellow Soviets to leave the room. They stood and walked out.

Serov took the Hungarians prisoner. He had already ensured that Budapest was surrounded by Soviet forces. Now he had efficiently beheaded the Hungarian military command. Imre Nagy, with increasing concern, repeatedly tried to telephone Maléter for updates. There was no reply.

1900 New York // 0000 London // 0100 (Nov. 4) Budapest

In New York, the United Nations Security Council met to discuss the Soviet troops advancing on Budapest. The Soviets, as usual, vetoed a resolution. In the General Assembly, Lester Pearson pushed through a resolution formally requesting that Dag Hammarskjöld submit a plan for a United Nations Expeditionary Force for Egypt.[35]

At around midnight, Abba Eban, Israel's ambassador, pulled a completely unexpected move. "Israel agrees to an immediate cease-fire," he said, "provided a similar answer is forthcoming from Egypt."

Israel had, by this point, achieved all its objectives aside from the capture of Sharm el-Sheikh. There seems no evidence that it was prepared to give up on capturing Sharm: the calculation made was, perhaps, that in the twenty-four hours or so after the announcement of a cease-fire, it could still do so.[36] Egypt had already accepted the General Assembly's call for a cease-fire, so Israel's formal condition had already been fulfilled. Only two nations were now holding out against peace. The whole world's thoughts were expressed by the ambassador from Ceylon, who asked, "What further reason is there for the UK and France to intervene?"[37]

Pierson Dixon, the British representative, sent an urgent message back to London. In just a few hours, the General Assembly would reopen. If Britain continued with its assault on Egypt, it could face international sanctions. "It is hard to be sure whether Soviet action in Hungary will deflect the impact of further military operations in Egypt," he wrote. "I fear that it will contribute to a mounting indignation against the use of force by large Powers, which will make our own actions seem all the more heinous." Even if Britain could take the most scrupulous care to avoid civilian casualties in Egypt and contrast this with the behavior of the Soviets in Hungary, he did not think the United Nations would be convinced. There was only one option: "If we could swiftly announce that we were now in a position to suspend military action and were awaiting the arrival of an international force the position would of course change at once."[38]

The official justification for Anglo-French intervention had evaporated. The combatants had agreed to stop fighting. Yet the supposed peacekeepers' joint assault force was still sailing steadily across the Mediterranean—into a profoundly uncertain engagement.

14

SUNDAY, NOVEMBER 4, 1956
REAPING THE WHIRLWIND

2320 (Nov. 3) Washington DC // 0520 Budapest // 0620 Cairo
In the early hours of that morning a series of shots rang out,
echoing in the separate cells where Pál Maléter and the other
Hungarians who had been arrested by Ivan Serov the night
before were kept. Each man assumed his fellows had been executed. In fact, these were mock executions—staged by Serov
to break his prisoners' spirits before the KGB started its questioning.[1]

During his own interrogation some months later, Imre Nagy
would tell of how he had slept the night in parliament and was
woken early with the news that Soviet troops had begun to
occupy Budapest. "While the telephone rang constantly, I was
informed of the latest news from the whole country," he told
his interrogators. "The calls came in from everywhere, asking
what should happen now, what was to be done. Since I could
not answer every call, even when the caller insisted on talking
to me, I instructed those taking the calls that there should be
no resistance, that provocation must be avoided, and that it was
forbidden to shoot at Soviet soldiers."[2]

At the behest of his remaining allies, Nagy addressed the

nation while it was still possible. Against an audible backdrop of gunfire, his voice crackled over the radio in the dark before dawn. "In the early hours of the morning Soviet troops have started an attack against the Hungarian capital with the apparent purpose of overthrowing the lawful democratic government of the country," he said. "Our troops are engaged in battle. The government is in its place. This is my message to the Hungarian people and to the whole world."[3]

Fifteen minutes earlier, Soviet radio had announced János Kádár as Hungary's new prime minister. Kádár declared that he had left Nagy's administration, saying that "reactionary forces" were threatening to bring landowners and capitalists back into power in Hungary. He was therefore forming a new government. He appealed publicly to Soviet forces to oust Nagy and help him.

Later, Kádár said he had pursued this course because it was impossible to stand by while the "White Terror slaughtered, first in Budapest, then in the provinces, intelligentsia and Communists, then all those who sympathized with the Communists and then all patriotic democrats." Though some members of the previous regime and the AVH had been killed, there was no evidence for a "White Terror." Yet Kádár insisted that the rebels had planned to hand Hungary over to the "imperialist colonizers." He had therefore used "every possible force, including the assistance of Soviet units, to prevent the counter-revolutionary war. . . . The interests of the State and the people compelled us to choose this way as the only possible way out of the grave situation. And so we chose it."[4]

In the small hours, Cardinal József Mindszenty was driven to parliament. He found what remained of Nagy's government in chaos. No one could work out what order to give the army: in the end, they were dismissed. "I could no longer bear to see everybody losing his head," remembered Mindszenty.

He left the room and met a friend, who told him his car had been taken and all the bridges across the Danube had been sealed off by Soviet troops. "We concealed our cassocks under our coats and made our way between rows of Russian tanks safely to the embassy of the United States of America," Mindszenty remembered. Just half an hour after he walked through its doors, a cable arrived from Eisenhower granting him asylum.[5]

At six a.m., Nagy too left parliament and sought asylum in the Yugoslav embassy. By the end of the day, a few dozen other leading politicians and their families would be in there with him. Only one cabinet member remained in parliament: the political philosopher István Bibó. He issued a statement defending the Hungarian rebellion against all charges of counterrevolution and fascism. He called for "passive resistance" against the invading Soviet army and whatever puppet government it might install.

"I am not in a position to command armed resistance," he admitted. "I joined the cabinet a day ago, I have not received any information on the military situation, and it would be irresponsible of me to dispose of the dear blood of Hungarian youths. Hungary has paid with enough lives to show its insistence on freedom and justice to the world. It is now the turn of the great powers of the world to show the authority of the principles laid down in the UN Charter and the power of the freedom-loving people of the world."[6] Bibó declared Anna Kéthly, a social democrat minister from Nagy's administration, Hungary's representative abroad. On Nagy's urging, Kéthly had attended the Socialist International in Vienna on November 1. Unable to return to Hungary that day, she had flown to New York to petition the United Nations.

In the Yugoslav embassy, Imre Nagy was listening to the radio. He heard János Kádár's voice summoning help from

Moscow. One of his fellow refugees remembered Nagy's only comment: "They will execute me."[7]

It had been Gamal Abdel Nasser's turn for a sleepless night. "He admitted that he had wept and that he had apparently lost the state," remembered Abdel Latif al-Baghdadi, who had breakfast with him in Cairo.[8] Egypt accepted Canada's plan for resolution of hostilities and repeated the offer it had made the day before of a cease-fire. Meanwhile, the British minister Antony Head and the chief of the Imperial General Staff, Gerald Templer, had arrived in Cyprus to reassess the war plan.

Everything was to be reined in so that the operation looked as much as possible like the peacekeeping initiative Eden was trying to pretend it was—and to differentiate it from what Khrushchev was doing in Hungary. Keightley was persuaded to abandon the element of surprise and warn Port Said inhabitants to leave their homes twenty-four hours ahead of the planned assault there. Both British and French battleships would avoid using their big guns: nothing above 4.5 inches would be fired. Following Nasser's order for Egyptian forces to retreat from Sinai to the mainland, Port Said was sparsely defended. It might be possible for paratroops to be dropped ahead of schedule the next morning, meaning that they might take the town by the evening without a naval bombardment. If so, the bombardment planned for November 6 would be canceled too. Keightley estimated they could take Ismailia by November 8, and Suez itself by November 12.[9] Most important, the visitors relieved Keightley of any political objective. There would be no strike against Cairo. Nasser would not be toppled. Operations would now be strictly confined to the Canal Zone.[10]

Jacques Baeyens, a diplomatic counsel to the French armed forces, recorded a conversation with his military chief in Cyprus after the meeting with Head. "It is clear that Eden's government faces growing parliamentary opposition . . . while on the international stage Paris and London are the object of general reprobation directed and orchestrated by the Kremlin and the White House," he wrote. "Conclusion: it is necessary to go as fast and as far as possible, to take our dues."[11]

0700 London // 0800 Budapest

For the last few hours, the telephones in Hungary's parliament had been ringing constantly. The calls came in from regional revolutionary councils and from the industrial districts around Budapest. The Soviets were coming. The Soviets could not be stopped. Valiant rebels put up barricades on the roads and tried to push the Red Army back. For the most part, they were lightly armed and could barely slow the advance. This was not the guerrilla battle of Budapest of the previous week. Operation Whirlwind was a war of conquest.

The Associated Press in Vienna received telex messages from a newspaper office in Hungary, though they were sent by a combatant rather than a journalist. He could hear shells exploding nearby and jet planes roaring overhead. There were, he estimated, about 200 to 250 people in the building, aged from fifteen to forty, around 50 of whom were women. They had rifles, carbines, and machine guns and were making Molotov cocktails and hand grenades as the tanks approached. "People are jumping up at the tanks, throwing hand grenades inside and then slamming the drivers' windows," he reported. "The Hungarian people are not afraid of death. It is only a pity that we can't stand this for long." Later, he added, "It can't be allowed that people attack tanks with their bare hands. What is the United Nations doing?"

The United Nations was waiting for the question of Hungary to go to the General Assembly after the Soviet veto in the Security Council. This bureaucracy could not be bypassed. It had no army. It was still trying to work out if it could create one for Egypt. "We will hold out to the last drop of blood," the man telexed to Vienna. "Downstairs there are men who have only one hand grenade. I am running over to the window in the next room to shoot. But I will be back if there is anything new." He repeated, "Where is the UN? . . . The Parliament and its vicinity is crowded with tanks. . . . Planes are flying overhead but can't be counted there are so many. The tanks are coming in long lines."

He went to shoot, then returned to the telex machine. "They just brought us a rumor that the American troops will be here within one or two hours. . . . Don't worry about us. We are strong even if we are a small nation. When the fighting is over we will rebuild our unhappy country."[12]

American troops were not on the way. By eight a.m., the Soviets had the airfields and roads, the Danube bridges, the central telephone exchange, and parliament. The last words heard on free Budapest radio were spoken by the writer Gyula (Julius) Háy, appealing to the intellectuals of the world to come to Hungary's aid. "You know all the facts," he said. "It is useless to comment on them. Help Hungary! . . . Help! Help! Help!" Then, with a snap, the air went dead.[13]

*   *   *

The people of Britain were agitated that morning, both for and against their government. An excoriating editorial appeared in London's liberal, middle-class *Observer* newspaper, written by the former Liberal MP and chairman of the *Observer*'s board of trustees Dingle Foot, and by the paper's editor, David Astor. "We had not realised that our Government was capable of such folly and such crookedness," it said. "Never since 1783 has Great Britain made herself so universally disliked. That was the year in which the Government of Lord North, faced with the antagonism of almost the whole civilised world, was compelled to recognise the independence of the American Colonies. . . .

"In the eyes of the whole world, the British and French Governments have acted, not as policemen, but as gangsters," it continued. "It is no longer possible to bomb countries because you fear that your trading interests will be harmed." It called for Eden to go.[14] Many readers felt this editorial was disloyal; some canceled their subscriptions. But more yet seemed to agree with it.

Twenty thousand members of the public crammed into Trafalgar Square and Whitehall in a protest organized by the National Council of Labour. The Labour MP Anthony Greenwood—"wearing a strident red tie," according to the London *Times*—spoke to the crowd, claiming the British government had imperiled the United Nations "merely to satisfy the conceit and vanity of that foolish man Sir Anthony Eden." The most prominent politician of the socialist left, Aneurin Bevan, also spoke. "If Eden's sincere in what he is saying—and he may be—then he is too stupid to be prime minister," the ebullient Welshman said. "He is either a knave or a fool. In both capacities we do not want him."[15]

Chester Cooper was among those in the square. "What I saw that day was a depth of feeling on the part of young university students, of old manual workers, and of many ages and classes in between that I had not realized existed in Britain," he wrote. "The vast majority was loudly and passionately opposed to Eden and his Middle East policy." Some of those present were pro-Eden, "but the police removed them from the square when they appeared to be in danger of being drawn and quartered by the angry crowd. The march toward Number 10 had ugly overtones; large scale violence seemed likely if the demonstrators broke through the cordon of police."[16]

When he heard about the demonstration, Winston Churchill was horrified—especially when he was told that some
in the crowd were foreigners. "I would never have believed
that we would allow that gutter-muck to come to insult us and
dictate our national policies in Trafalgar Square," he told his
private secretary.[17]

The semblance of unity behind Eden in the British military
and government was falling apart. Lord Mountbatten had not
been reassured by the prime minister's claims that his targets
in Egypt were military. He wrote to the first lord of the Admiralty, Lord Hailsham, in sharp terms. The situation in Egypt,
he said, was extremely bad, and civilian casualties could not
be avoided. "However repugnant the task the Navy will carry
out its orders," he wrote. "Nevertheless as its professional head
I must register the strongest possible protest at this use of my
service; and would ask you as the responsible Minister to con-
vey that protest to the Prime Minister." There was an explosive final paragraph: "I recognise that a serving officer cannot
back his protest by resignation at a time like this, so I must ask
you to handle this whole matter on behalf of the Navy. Bearing in mind all the implications I must ask you, after consulting the Prime Minister, to give me an order to stay or to go."

Hailsham passed this on to Eden, pointing out that it would
be "disastrous" to relieve Mountbatten of his duties at this
point. He wrote to Mountbatten ordering him to stay at his
post. "If anything happens to impair the honour of the Navy I
must resign," he noted. "In the meantime you are entitled to
be protected by a direct order from me."[18]

Following Eden's broadcast to the nation the night before,
Hugh Gaitskell requested the right to reply. Eden let it be
known through his chief whip, Edward Heath, that forces
were now committed and therefore it was inappropriate for the
opposition to oppose the government. Gaitskell took it up with

the BBC: granting a right to reply to any ministerial broadcast considered "controversial" was within its power. The BBC
dithered. Gaitskell threatened to accuse it publicly of suppress-
ing the opposition. The BBC permitted him to go ahead.[19]

Gaitskell used his response to destroy Eden's case. The invasion could not be about protecting British lives and property,
he said, for there was no rescue operation in place; British civilians in Egypt had been put in far greater danger by military
action. It could not be about keeping the canal open, for the
canal had been blocked. And it was evidently not about separating two armies, for airfields had been bombed and troops
landed only on one side, Egypt—and then a hundred miles
behind the front.

"I cannot but feel hearing today's heart-breaking news from
Hungary, how tragic it is that at the very moment when the
whole world should be united in denouncing this flagrant,
ruthless, savage aggression by Russia, against a liberty-loving
people, I can't help feeling how tragic it is that we, by our
criminal folly, should have lost the moral leadership of which
we were once so proud," he said. He called for Britain to accept
the United Nations resolution for an immediate cease-fire.

Finally, he talked of Eden. "I bear him no ill will," he said.
"We have been personally quite friendly. But his policy this
last week has been disastrous. And he is utterly, utterly dis-
credited in the world.

"Only one thing can save the reputation and the honour of
our country—Parliament must repudiate the Government's
policy. The Prime Minister must resign."[20]

"The week just past has been the worst by far in my life,"
wrote Eden's press secretary, William Clark, in his diary. "The
knowledge of collusion, the deception, the hypocrisy . . . I am
really getting a bit hysterical myself. It seems to me that the
PM is mad, literally mad, and that he went so that day [Octo-

ber 5] his temperature rose to 105°." Clark felt compassionate toward Eden when he was in his presence, but whenever he left the prime minister, "my violent bitter contempt and hatred for a man who has destroyed my world and so much of my faith burns up again. Then I long to be free as a journalist to drive this government from power and keep the cowards and crooks out of power for all time."[21]

1530 London

There was a bleak meeting of Eden's Egypt Committee at three thirty p.m. Selwyn Lloyd read out a letter from Baghdad. "Today our contacts with Iraqis through the Administration, who were previously our convinced friends, have been closing down," wrote the British ambassador there. "We shall soon be cut off from sources of contact and co-operation, apart from the risk any moment of violent demonstrations. Almost all we have built up here over many years and with such pains has been shaken nearly beyond repair."[22] A telephone call came through from Pierson Dixon in New York, warning again that a resolution was about to be passed in the United Nations putting sanctions on Britain and France, probably withholding oil.

"Oil sanctions!" exclaimed Harold Macmillan. "That finishes it."[23]

A letter from Dag Hammarskjöld at the United Nations demanded that Eden call off the war immediately, in time for Hammarskjöld to announce it to the other parties at eight p.m. London time. Hammarskjöld wrote that he believed the General Assembly would reject outright the prospect of any British and French forces forming part of the United Nations force in Egypt. Until this point, Eden had convinced himself (and apparently many in his cabinet) that British and French forces could be transferred nominally to United Nations control—

but would effectively be able to finish their mission and take the canal.

Following the resolution passed overnight, the United Nations would now send troops to Egypt—and Israel had indicated that it might accept a cease-fire. This would have allowed Eden to cancel the British land invasion. Yet at the same time, Head reported from Cyprus that paratroops could be dropped ahead of schedule the following day.

There were three choices. The first was to proceed with the parachute drop at Port Said the next morning as Head suggested, repeating the offer to hand over to the United Nations as soon as the canal was secure. As part of this option, Eden would also insist that the United Nations accept British and French troops as part of its peacekeeping force.

The second was to delay the parachute drop for twenty-four hours until the morning of November 6. This would allow time for Egypt and Israel to accept the principle of a peacekeeping force and for the General Assembly to consider whether to authorize Anglo-French forces as peacekeepers. This second option was a gamble; it risked the military operation's success but had the potential to look more legitimate.

The third was to call off the war altogether, as Eden put it, "on the grounds that we had in fact put an end to the Israeli-Egyptian conflict."[24] Eden did not admit that he had also started it.

Eden spoke with Lloyd. On the grounds that they did not yet have the canal, both agreed that the show must go on. They prepared themselves to take the case for the first option to the full cabinet that evening.[25]

1200 Washington DC // 1700 London // 1800 Budapest

Using the discreet series of interconnecting corridors between the Whitehall buildings, which kept him safely out of public view, Eden crept from his office in Downing Street to the Cabinet Office Building. From a corner window, he peeked down at where the protest against his policy was still going on. "I could see a large and angry crowd, in which tempers were evidently running extremely high," he wrote later. "Opposite Downing Street, near the Cenotaph, the marching stopped. As the crowd grew larger, the shouting grew louder. Some of the most militant demonstrators had clearly resolved to get into Downing Street. The police were equally determined to prevent them, and those on horseback charged the crowd when they began to break down the temporary barriers that had been erected to keep them out. It was a terrifying scene."

Fireworks and a smoke bomb were thrown among the horses. Mounted police beat demonstrators with batons. "One middle-aged woman, in respectable Sunday navy blue, screamed in terror, 'Don't kill me,'" reported the *Manchester Guardian*, "and her husband took up a defensive posture." Eight policemen were injured, including one who was dragged from his horse. Casualties among the protesters were not recorded, though the *Guardian* mentioned that two or three people were taken away in ambulances. Twenty-seven were arrested.[26]

The police regained control, and the crowd was diverted toward Parliament Square. With hindsight, at least, Eden would be struck by what was happening. "This was not a demonstration organised by a few left-wing extremists," he admitted in his autobiography. "It was supported by thousands of people who genuinely believed that what was happening was politically, militarily and morally wrong."[27]

At five p.m., Clarissa Eden remembered, her husband came into the drawing room at 10 Downing Street with the cabinet secretary. He had dramatic news. Building on their offer of a cease-fire the previous night, the Israelis were now saying that they would negotiate with Egypt and other Arab states immediately—bringing the war, and potentially the Arab-Israeli conflict, to a close. Eden called the cabinet to another meeting, during which he spoke privately to Lord Salisbury, Harold Macmillan, and Rab Butler.

There are conflicting versions of what happened at that meeting from Lady Eden, Butler, the official minutes, and others present, though the differences may merely be due to the fact that this was a long meeting where lots of conditional variants on the three possibilities Eden set forth were discussed. Broadly, it appears that three or four cabinet members were inclined to call off the war altogether: Walter Monckton, Lord Salisbury, Patrick Buchan-Hepburn, and possibly Butler. "I took the line that were the news [about Israel] correct, we could not possibly continue our expedition," Butler wrote in his memoirs. "It had not been my idea that we were going in to stop hostilities, but if they had already stopped we had no justification for invasion." Yet other witnesses suggest Butler opted for the compromise position of the twenty-four-hour postponement, along with Lord Kilmuir, Derick Heathcoat-Amory, and possibly Iain Macleod. The rest of the cabinet agreed with Eden and Lloyd that the paratroop drop should go ahead the following morning. According to the official records, everybody agreed ultimately to support whatever majority view emerged—with the exception of Monckton. Lady Eden claimed that both Monckton and Nigel Birch dissented and wanted to resign; she also claimed Lord Selkirk dissented but "was unintelligible."

Eden was driven to "consider his position," according to Butler. Lady Eden records that her husband "told them if they wouldn't go on he would have to resign. Rab said if he did resign no one else could form a government."[28] Then a message came through from the Israeli minister Golda Meir contradicting the news. The Israelis were not about to start negotiating with

Egypt or other Arab countries. "Everyone laughed and banged the table with relief, except Birch and Walter Monckton who looked glum," reported Lady Eden.[29] The war was back on.

The demonstration in Trafalgar Square could be heard through the window. "There was a steady hum of noise," remembered Selwyn Lloyd, "and then every few minutes a crescendo and an outburst of howling or booing."[30] The cabinet was not put off its stride, and agreed with Eden and Lloyd to pursue the first option: to press on.

By this time, thought Chester Cooper, following the animated telephone call he had received from Robert Amory the previous day and Dulles's hospitalization, "a reconsideration of policy [was] taking place throughout Washington. By the weekend, the Administration was softening its recriminatory approach towards London, Paris, and Tel Aviv and seemed anxious to close the breach in the Western alliance."[31] In fact, the picture was more complicated. Eisenhower was still angry—but the question of Hungary was now acute, and the United States needed the backing of its allies at the United Nations. The president wrote a strong letter to Bulganin that day, describing himself as "inexpressibly shocked" at Soviet policy. "I urge in the name of humanity and in the cause of peace that the Soviet Union take action to withdraw Soviet forces from Hungary immediately," he went on, "and to permit the Hungarian people to enjoy and exercise the human rights and fundamental freedoms affirmed for all peoples in the United Nations Charter."[32]

Christian Pineau sensed the reconsideration of policy in Washington and attempted to capitalize on it. He made a broadcast declaring that the whole of France would "bow before the courage and martyrdom of a [Hungarian] people ready to die for their independence." He added sniffily that the United Nations "and certain Governments" should not have bothered to "devote precious hours to saving the face of an Egyptian dictator" instead of focusing on Hungary.[33]

"For months or years to come it will be a matter of debate whether Britain's attack on Egypt sparked Russia's attack on Hungary," opined the *Manchester Guardian*.[34] Many suspected the timing was opportunistic. At the United Nations, "the Soviet Union was promoting this controversy [in Suez] in order to provide a cover for their own bloody repression in Hungary," remembered Eisenhower's adviser Herman Phleger, "and they were constantly using this to test the United States' determination to stand by the [United Nations] Charter in order to show that, if we didn't stand up to the Charter with respect to Suez, that then it was no crime for them to violate the Charter in Hungary. There isn't any doubt that the Hungary situation played a part in this."[35]

Hungary "greatly complicated the Suez problem," continued Phleger. "The revolt was met by the most blood-thirsty Communist repression which immediately called for action by the UN. But it accented the fact that if the UN were to deal lightly with what might turn out to be an Israeli-British-French invasion, it couldn't condemn as severely as it ought, the action by the Soviet Union in Hungary."[36]

From Austria, American diplomats were reporting that Hungarian refugees were streaming over the border—"2000 so far today is latest guess"—in every place the Soviets had not yet set up surveillance. The Austrian government appealed to the UN High Commissioner for Refugees for emergency support.[37] An American diplomat in Zagreb reported: "Hunted in area around Cakovec near Hungarian border November 4. Plenty rabbits. No (repeat no) Hungarians. However, radio Zagreb reported border crossings without saying where."[38]

Clare Booth Luce, the American ambassador to Italy, sent a private note to Eisenhower. "Mr. President, Franco British action on Suez is a small wound to their prestige but American inaction about Hungary could be a fatal wound to ours," she wrote. "Let us not (rpt not) ask for whom the bell tolls in Hungary today. It tolls for us if freedom's holy light is extinguished in blood and iron there. . . . And while we wait for the next light to break which surely will then be very ugly and very atomic, we will hear a growing torrent of tongues in many lands turning the deathless glory of Hungary into America's everlasting shame." She begged the president to appear in person before the United Nations General Assembly, to call NATO into session, to assist Austria in case of aggression spreading there, to "confine" Soviet diplomats in the United States until American equivalents in Hungary were released, and to break diplomatic relations with Moscow if the Soviet army continued to fire on civilians.[39]

The United States did nothing. According to the diplomat Robert Murphy, everybody in the State Department "was terribly distressed, considered every possible avenue of the solution, what could be done, and really none of us had whatever imagination it took to discover another solution. We were just boxed." He went on: "Even some of the Swiss at that point, who have not been noted for their great bravery for entering into risks, said, 'For God's sake, let's show some courage'—well now, what did that mean? How do you show that courage? Because I don't have the slightest doubt that any intervention on our part would have meant confrontation militarily with the Soviet Union."[40]

Inside the CIA in Washington, Frank Wisner was the agent most closely connected to Hungary. Wisner believed passionately in helping the rebels. Yet as the twin crises of Suez and Hungary unfolded, the Dulles brothers had both begun to feel that giving any form of help beyond moral support would be impossible. If they aided Hungarians under threat of invasion by a much stronger power in the form of the Soviet Union, why not aid Egyptians when they were menaced by Britain and France? According to the British writer and historian Leonard Mosley, this was too much for Wisner to take. He lost his temper in one meeting, shouting that everybody present was "a bunch of goddamned Commies," and was obliged to take several days off. "Soon Polly Wisner was calling up anxiously to say that Frank kept taking out his revolver and talking to it," wrote Mosley.[41]

"The hollowness of American political rhetoric suddenly struck me," remembered CIA agent Wilbur Eveland, then in Beirut. "[O]n October 29, the White House had recommitted the United States to aiding any victims of aggression, but what were we doing to help the Egyptians and the Hungarians? Nothing: trapped now by the perfidy of our own allies, we could do little but make speeches designed to encourage peoples who had taken the United States at its word."[42]

Back in 1952, during Eisenhower's first presidential campaign, Foster Dulles had a series of debates with the Democratic politician Averell Harriman on how best to approach the Soviet bloc. Dulles argued for actively pursuing liberation, though by encouraging rebellion rather than sending American troops. "I violently disagreed with his liberation policy," said Harriman. "I thought that was a very ill-advised form of playing domestic politics with international problems. I was gravely concerned that the Eastern Europeans would misinterpret it, that they'd consider that we could do something to go in and help them free themselves."

So it came to pass in Hungary. "I recall quite vividly that I said, 'Foster, if you follow this policy you're going to have the death of some brave people on your conscience,'" said Harriman. "That was the way I felt about it. I wasn't playing politics."[43]

"Poor fellows, poor fellows," said Eisenhower of the Hungarians during the revolution. "I think about them all the time. I wish there were some way of helping them."[44] But the Americans did not help them. The United States government remained wary of gradual change in the Soviet bloc, despite the example of Tito. While the Hungarian rebels opposed the straitened form of Communism that had been imposed on Hungary, as well as Soviet occupation, they were not explicitly antisocialist or pro-American: Imre Nagy remained a Marxist-Leninist and continued to call for incremental reform until it was too late. The Hungarian journalist and historian Charles Gati explained the situation using that most American of all analogies, baseball: "Americans wanted to believe that they did not have to settle for a single because a home run was possible. They wanted to believe that the appeal of freedom was so strong that they would not have to use force and yet the oppressed people would rise—and somehow prevail."[45]

0200 (Nov. 5) New York

As news of the crushing of Hungary came through, discussion at the United Nations alternated between the Soviet bloc and the Middle East. Lester Pearson had been lobbying hard from seven p.m., both in the assembly and through intense negotiations with the key players, for his plan to establish a United Nations Expeditionary Force for Suez. Dag Hammarskjöld presented his preliminary proposals on this force. He suggested it be drawn from countries that were not members of the Security Council. He nominated the Canadian General E.L.M. Burns, chief of staff at the United Nations Truce Supervision Organization (UNTSO) in the Palestinian territories, to head the force. At the same time, Israel declared that it no longer recognized existing armistice agreements and demanded the withdrawal of UNTSO from the Gaza Strip. It seemed that Israel might now be planning to occupy Gaza permanently.[46]

Hammarskjöld's plan was supported by fifty-seven countries and opposed by none, with nineteen abstaining. The abstentions included Britain, France, Israel, Egypt, and all the Soviet bloc nations (Yugoslavia supported the plan). Pearson's resolution was passed as United Nations General Assembly Resolution 1000. At last, the world council had teeth.

The Soviet representative spoke to condemn Britain and France for their "hypocrisy" and "barbarous bombing" of Suez, and for what he called their "rape" of the Egyptian people. Henry Cabot Lodge, for the United States, replied: "God knows, I want to see bloodshed in Egypt stopped. There is cynicism in the Soviet representative's words while his army is spilling blood in Budapest." At 3:13 a.m., news arrived of the full Soviet assault on Hungary. The council reconvened, with every member apart from the Soviet Union and Yugoslavia condemning the action.[47]

"It was a night of suspense for all who listened through the small hours to direct broadcasts of the United Nations debate, which were sometimes switched to Vienna for the latest word of the tragedy closing on Budapest," reported the London *Times* correspondent in Washington, "and it is this that fires the American mind with horror and distress far surpassing the mixed emotions of resentment and dismay over the Anglo-French intervention in Egypt."[48]

Though he had stood strong in public, Gamal Abdel Nasser was now close to cracking under the stress. He was prone to bouts of weeping over the impending loss of Egypt's freedom. He felt Abdel Hakim Amer had kept him out of military planning, and had weakened too far the defenses in the Canal Zone. He had been listening to a popular song by the singer

Abdel Halim Hafiz. The lyrics went: "We have left Egypt a trust in your hands."

"I have been questioning myself," Nasser said to Mohamed Heikal. "Have I behaved well towards this trust or not?"

Nasser insisted that Amer strengthen the defenses around Port Said, adding a third battalion of infantry to the two already there, six hundred national guards, several companies dedicated to organizing guerrilla war, and four Soviet SU-100 tank destroyers, which had arrived only on the evening of November 4. He also sent a train loaded with small arms to be distributed among the people. These would arrive just before dawn the next morning.[49]

Nasser wanted to go to the front himself. "We told him the area was being strafed and bombed and that his car would be seen," remembered Heikal. "But he refused to listen to us."[50] That night, under cover of darkness and without telling Amer, he traveled to Port Said with his close colleague Abdel Latif al-Baghdadi. They drove past the wrecks of scores of military vehicles, shot to pieces by British, French, and Israeli planes. Nasser's morale sank lower and lower.

"These are the remnants of a destroyed army," he observed miserably. In English, he added, "I was defeated by my own army."

"Don't give up," Baghdadi replied.

"You know I never despair," said Nasser.

Yet Baghdadi feared for his friend. "I felt," he remembered, "that a broken man was in front of me."[51]

They arrived in the small hours to the news that Anglo-French forces were landing. Nasser's mood was lifted by the high morale of defenders at the front—and there was no time for a private breakdown. The president turned his car around and headed back to Cairo.

15

"HIT 'EM WITH *EVERYTHING* IN THE BUCKET"

0000 New York // 0500 London // 0700 Port Said

Midnight New York time was the deadline Dag Hammarskjöld had set for Britain, France, Israel, and Egypt to cease all hostilities if they were to comply with the General Assembly's resolutions. Precisely fifteen minutes after that deadline, British and French warplanes zoomed low over the twin towns of Port Said and Port Fuad. Incendiary bombs scattered explosions throughout the towns, setting factories, shops, schools, and houses aflame. The bombardment of Port Said was followed by 668 white, black, green, and khaki parachutes floating down to land, each bearing a British soldier; and 500 parachutes bearing the men of the French 2 Régiment Parachutistes Coloniaux. "And then the Egyptian anti-aircraft guns, machine-guns, tanks and rifles opened up," wrote the *Daily Mirror* correspondent, who parachuted with the British forces. "As I dropped towards an airfield runway strewn with barrels to keep us from landing, I saw Egyptian troops in slit trenches point their rifles towards me and start shooting. Everywhere they were waiting for us."[1]

The French paratrooper Pierre Leulliette, a veteran of the conflict in Algeria, jumped just after a fellow paratrooper he referred to only as "Sergent B." Leulliette remembered bullets whistling past him as he landed on the sludgy sand. He scrambled out of the way of field-gun fire. "Yet, in a flash, I took in an image which I shall never forget: hanging from the top of a palm tree by the straps of his parachute, Sergent B.'s body was slowly dripping blood into the sand. He had, apparently, been . . . shot in full flight. His large body was swaying in the palm fronds, sharp as spears."[2]

The paratroopers arrived on a flaming plain strewn with rubble that had, till half an hour before, been neat, terra-cotta-brick residential streets. Part of Port Said was destroyed. In other areas, houses and offices still stood. Troops searched what was left. Douglas Clark, a British artillery observer who had been called up from reserves to serve at Port Said, saw shots coming from one large house. The soldiers blew the door open with a bazooka.

Inside, the assistant adjutant found a piano on a dais. He called Clark over. The piano bore an inscription saying that it had belonged to the long-departed King Farouk, and had been bought by the owner at a sale of his property. "My companion opened the lid, and standing there, fully caparisoned for war, he played and sang the song which, set to the tune of the Egyptian National Anthem, is known to every soldier who has ever served in Egypt," Clark remembered. "Farouk was asked to perform an extremely painful gymnastic feat, and [Queen] Farida was told that about which, if it was true, she herself must have been increasingly aware." This elliptical description hardly does justice to the doggerel lyrics, of which there were several versions. A sample verse went:

"Oh we're all black bastards,
And we all love our king,

Stanna shwya, kwise kateer,
Mungariya, bardin."

These approximately transliterated Arabic words were phrases known to British troops: "wait a moment, very good, something to eat, later." In some versions, Farouk's sympathies for the Nazis were detailed; others focused on the queen's charms ("Queen Farida, Queen Farida, all the boys want to ride her") and requested that she *"shufti kush"* ("show cunt").[3]

Civilians who survived the bombing fled along the docks clutching their screaming children. Hundreds leaped into dhows and feluccas, overloading and in some cases sinking the tiny boats. Many fell into the water as they struggled to escape. The Reuters correspondent saw "three plumes of smoke rising 1,500 feet into a sunny sky, a grim corona of fire twinkling at their heart"—the Shell Oil refinery, hit by British bombs and spewing out dense black clouds that billowed back across the desert. Paratroopers grappled hand to hand with lightly armed Egyptian defenders, moving from the ruins of one house to the wreckage of another as they swept through the remains of the town. "The smell of blood and smoke pervaded everything," added the Reuters correspondent, "a sinister undertone to the waft of salt from the near-by sea."

In Gaza, an Israeli loudspeaker truck drove through the mud-walled alleys. "Now is your last chance to surrender," it broadcast, addressing the fedayeen. The IDF claimed that three hundred fedayeen had already given themselves up and said it was "screening" the rest of the men in Gaza. "Hundreds of white-and-black robed Arabs squat in courtyards facing the wall, prior to screening, or are being marched away to prison," reported the *Jerusalem Post.* "The same goes on in El Arish and Khan Yunis."[4] Unsurprisingly, the newspaper did not mention that dozens or perhaps a few hundred of these men were shot without trial. The Israelis stated that two months' worth of supplies had been looted from UNRWA stores by desperate Gaza residents. A military government was installed and set about rebuilding the infrastructure to link the Gaza Strip to Israel.

0230 New York // 0730 London // 0930 Cairo; Sharm el-Sheikh

It was two thirty a.m. in New York. Dag Hammarskjöld was angry with the Israelis. Under private pressure from France, they had now added conditions to Abba Eban's offer of a ceasefire. These were effectively impossible to fulfill. Israel now required that Egypt declare it was no longer in a state of war with Israel, that Egypt attend peace negotiations, that all blockades and boycotts of Israel must end, and that all fedayeen in countries neighboring Israel be recalled.[5] Hammarskjöld thought these conditions represented "an open insult to the United Nations and it was impossible to do diplomatic business with such people."[6]

At that unsociable hour, Hammarskjöld was meeting the British and French representatives at the United Nations, Pierson Dixon and Louis de Guiringaud. In contrast to his fury at the Israelis, he was relatively open to the British and French replies supporting the principle of an international force, though he was suspicious about Eden's insistence that the Anglo-French invasion force could transition into United Nations peacekeepers. This was a moment of opportunity: Hammarskjöld seemed inclined to assume Britain was acting in good faith. Dixon felt there was some chance Britain and France might retrieve their dignity and even some form of victory from Operation Musketeer.

Shortly after Dixon left, Hammarskjöld received news that British planes were again bombing Cairo. These bombs were aimed at military targets—a railway line, a military airfield, and a barracks—but the targets were situated in or near populated areas, and it was likely civilians would be killed. As far as Hammarskjöld was concerned, these bombings destroyed any good faith he may have had in Britain's motives. Now, he believed, it would be impossible for a United Nations force to go in until "those who had disturbed the Peace and refused the United Nations demand for cessation of hostilities should have first been declared morally in the wrong."

He telephoned Dixon. Dixon reported to London that Britain would be in a difficult position when the United Nations reconvened later that day: "They [Britain's critics] will be in a very ugly mood and out for our blood. . . . Between them they might well cook up an appeal by the Arabs to the Soviet Union to come in and help them." By continuing to attack, he wrote, Britain was at risk of "alienating the whole world." He added: "I do not see how we can carry much conviction in our protests against the Russian bombing of Budapest if we are ourselves bombing Cairo."[7]

At the same moment, the Israelis were taking their final target, Sharm el-Sheikh. The Nine Brigade of the IDF had already made two attacks on the town, one the previous evening and another overnight. Egyptian forces resisted, and the Israelis were twice beaten back. Early in the morning of November 5, Nine Brigade had begun an all-out assault in concert with Ariel Sharon's troops, who made a fast advance from the other side, building on two days of exhaustive bombardment with artillery and napalm. They took Sharm at nine thirty that morning. Nasser's forces retreated to the west bank of the Nile. Two hundred Israeli troops had been killed and eight hundred wounded, but they had achieved their objectives.[8] Britain and France were still a long way short of theirs.

1000 London // 1100 Paris // 1200 Cairo; Port Said

Douglas Clark was smoking a cigarette on the wharf at Port Said, watching British troops herd Egyptians onto the beach. Those in military uniform were prisoners. Others were in civilian clothes.

"Are you taking the civilians to the beach for safety?" Clark asked a soldier.

"Not bloody likely, sir," he replied. "They're no more civilians than I am. Every one of them had a rifle. Caught us out proper, they did. We started to treat 'em like civilians until they began to whip weapons from under their galabiyas. D'you know, sir, even the kids have got rifles; and they're firing 'em, too. And you can't fire back at 'em, not at kids, can you, sir? But the Troop Commander had the answer. He whipped their rifles away and then booted their arses to help 'em on their way to the beach. You should have heard some of 'em yelp!"

Egyptian civilians would afterward claim mistreatment by British forces at Port Said. In his memoirs, Clark denied this, arguing, "It was only to be expected that the Egyptians should make such allegations." He claimed that the Egyptians "swarmed" the beach demanding British food handouts and medical care, an assertion that does not quite sit with his previous implication that soldiers had to shepherd people onto the beach. British soldiers had helped old ladies and babies to safety, he wrote, and even tended to enemies who "had been yelling and firing [at them] with all the abandon of drunks at a shooting gallery." He complained that "the Egyptians knew no code of war. It was immaterial to them whether a Commando was helping one of their own people or not. Just as long as he wore a green beret, he was fair game." According to the code of war, specifically the Geneva Convention of 1949, uniformed members of an armed force who had not laid down their arms or been placed hors de combat by injury were still considered legal combatants.[9]

Back in London, the junior Foreign Office minister Douglas Dodds-Parker was walking through Speaker's Court to the Commons when he was waylaid by Harold Macmillan "in an anything but unflappable state."

"We must stop, we must stop," Macmillan told him, "or we will have no dollars left by the end of the week."

"I restrained myself from saying that surely in the circumstances as Chancellor he should have arranged to have sufficient dollars, or do without them, before he agreed to the launching of the operation," wrote Dodds-Parker in his memoir.[10]

Macmillan was facing what he believed to be a catastrophic situation: Britain's dollar reserves were running out. Those reserves might be vital for the functioning of the nation if Britain's oil link to the Middle East could not swiftly be restored. The Treasury now calculated that replacement oil would have to be bought from the Americas at a cost of $800 million a year—an impossible sum.[11]

Several drains on Britain's dollar reserves had come at once. India chose to pull its deposits in Britain out at this precise point, ostensibly to fund a new five-year plan; China withdrew its deposits in Britain to give to Egypt; speculators from several Middle Eastern oil-producing nations transferred their funds from British to Swiss banks. (British banks were then paying around 7 percent interest and Swiss banks only around 2 percent; many Swiss bankers simply redeposited the money in London, but the transfer of funds from sterling to Swiss francs nonetheless had an impact.) The speculators of Wall Street and the United States Federal Reserve began to dispose of their sterling. "Secretary of the Treasury George Humphrey, with Eisenhower's encouragement, was applying

the bluntest weapon in America's nonmilitary arsenal," wrote
Chester Cooper, "a financial squeeze."[12]

The Treasury had debated in October whether to borrow
from the International Monetary Fund (IMF) to shore up
Britain's reserves. The governor of the Bank of England and
many Treasury officials argued that it should not. The governor warned Macmillan that going to the IMF at that point
might be "regarded on a second view as a sign of weakness,"
and the officials agreed: they believed there was more danger
to sterling from a further loss of confidence, especially in European markets, than from a potential clash with Egypt. This
turned out to be bad advice. France did borrow from the IMF
in mid-October, and therefore was better prepared for a run on
the franc than Britain was for a run on the pound.[13]

Macmillan's advisers might have offered different advice
if they had been aware of the plan for the Suez operation. It
seems likely that they would have felt very differently had
they foreseen the possibility of Britain's oil supply being cut
off. The cabinet might well have viewed military action less
enthusiastically if it had been informed of how dire the risks
to Britain's financial stability were.

Macmillan was the only person who knew both sides of this
story—who heard all the fiscal advice and who knew what
Eden had planned. It appears he did not work out how they
would collide with each other. Historians and politicians afterward accused him of incompetence. It is hard to vindicate
him. It has even been hinted that he may have caused the sterling crisis deliberately to push Eden out of the prime minister's office, so that he could step in himself.[14] Though it is true
that the two men disliked each other, this seems like a conspiracy theory too far: Macmillan's behavior during the crisis
speaks of panic, not design.[15] He was out of his depth; Britain
was out of its depth, too. The only hope now was to appeal to

the mercy of Washington. "Without credits from the United States, we should therefore be unable to buy the oil we needed; and the Americans were violently opposed to us," wrote Anthony Nutting.[16]

Yet Eden wrote again to Eisenhower that day justifying his continuation of the war. He had to invade, he insisted, or else "Nasser would have become a kind of Moslem Mussolini" and would soon have brought down the governments of Iraq, Jordan, Saudi Arabia, Iran, Libya, and the whole of North Africa—a rather more lavish assessment of the Egyptian president's powers than even Nasser's supporters might have made. He pleaded that Britain had undertaken its "police action" only as a last resort on the basis of "a genuine sense of responsibility . . . to all the world." He assured the president that the British would be delighted to hand over to a United Nations force: "As you can imagine, no one feels more strongly about this than Harold[,] who has to provide the money. We do not want occupation of Egypt, we could not afford it, and that is one of many other reasons why we got out of Suez two years ago." And he was petulant about the difference between Suez and Hungary: "It is indeed ironical that at this very moment, when we are being pilloried as aggressors, Russia is brutally re-occupying Hungary and threatening the whole of Eastern Europe, and no voice is raised in the United Nations in favour of intervention there."[17]

0830 New York // 1330 London // 1430 Budapest // 1530 Cairo // 1730 Moscow

"Dark reaction prevails in Hungary," announced the commander of the Soviet troops in that unhappy country on its national radio. "Counter-revolutionary gangs are looting and murdering. The Government of Imre Nagy has collapsed. Hungary addressed herself to the Soviet troops to re-establish order in the country. . . . We address ourselves to the soldiers and officers of the Hungarian army to fight for sacred victory." The Red Army soldiers, he declared, were merely Hungary's "selfless friends."[18]

Those in Budapest reported tanks crunching through the streets and soldiers shooting civilians indiscriminately. "Bread queues were fired on by Soviet tanks," wrote Peter Fryer of London's *Daily Worker.* "I myself saw a man of about seventy lying dead outside a bread shop, the loaf he had just bought still in his hand."[19] The Soviets had reportedly overrun the Egyptian embassy (an intriguing choice under the circumstances) and the Astoria Hotel. They had taken everything, even the clothes from the porters' restroom. Many of these troops were not Russian; it is unclear how much they knew about who or why they were fighting. The story was repeatedly told in Hungary and in the Soviet Union that Soviet troops from far-flung regions—generally Tartars or Mongols—had not been informed by their commanders that they were in Budapest to quell a Hungarian rebellion. Instead, they had been told that they were in Egypt fighting "Anglo-French imperialists." The story inevitably added that these troops "mistook the Danube for the Suez Canal." Though this tale made it into the United Nations report on the rebellion, it has the ring of an urban myth.[20] Conversely, it was true that some Hungarian rebels were frustrated to find they were not fighting Russians at all. "I found myself shooting at bewildered Ukrainian peasant boys who had as much reason to hate what we fought as we had," remembered one young rebel. "It was an embittering shock to find that one can't confront the real enemy even in a revolution."[21]

American observers in Budapest reported "steady fighting sporadic all over city . . . artillery, tank and mortar fire predominate[;] systematic searching of buildings in city, probably for insurgent[s]. Resistance continuing."[22] But that resistance had no help from outside and was being crushed. From Bonn, an American diplomat observed, "There is widespread belief that UK and French aggression in Egypt made it easier for Soviets to launch attack in Hungary and concomitantly made it doubly difficult for West to condemn Russian action. Best typifying this reaction is lead editorial in 'Die Welt' stating both sides have equally 'dirty hands.'"[23] From Budapest, and from Cardinal József Mindszenty, now settled in the American embassy, came an alarming report considered "reliable" by the American legation that the Soviets were going to attempt to retake the Kilián Barracks by advancing through the Second University Clinic of Children. "If this step taken which seems most probably [sic] 200 to 300 additional children will be slaughtered." Mindszenty conveyed his "earnest request for [American] intervention [with] Moscow."[24]

"I am one of the millions who watching the martyrdom of Hungary and listening yesterday to the transmission of her agonized appeals for help (immediately followed by the describing of our 'successful bombing' of Egyptian 'targets') have felt a humiliation, shame, and anger which are beyond expression," wrote Lady Violet Bonham Carter, the former president of the British Liberal Party, close friend of Winston Churchill, and daughter of former prime minister H. H. Asquith, in a letter to the *Times*. "We cannot order Soviet Russia to obey the edict of the United Nations which we ourselves have defied, nor to withdraw her tanks and guns from Hungary while we are bombing and invading Egypt. To-day we are standing in the dock with Russia. Like us she claims to be conducting a 'police action.'" With dismay, she concluded: "We have coined a phrase which has already become part of the currency of aggression."[25]

1000 Washington DC // 1500 London // 1600 Paris

In Washington, the president and his advisers were discussing the unforeseen consequences of the Anglo-French invasion. Staff secretary Andrew Goodpaster worried that "the French might be trying to widen and worsen the conflict for their own ends, which may . . . begin to depart from those of the British." Everyone was worried that a landing in Alexandria, if it was attempted, would result in a long war. Herbert Hoover Jr. was worried about Syria, believing the Soviet Union might consider sending forces there. Eisenhower assured him that Syrian airfields were in a poor state of repair, though he did ask Allen Dulles to keep a watch on them just in case. Richard Nixon worried that the United States was on the same side as the British socialists, saying that it was "too bad that [Aneurin] Bevan is allowed to make political capital out of supporting the same position that we hold, since any swing to that school of thought would be tragic for us."

Nixon also worried that in the United Nations, India was abstaining from condemning the Soviet Union over its action in Hungary. Eisenhower replied, "Nehru thinks of only one thing, which is colonialism, by which he means the white over colored people." The president suggested that he could write to Nehru, "bringing out that we are witnessing colonialism by the bayonet in Hungary."

But the biggest thing worrying all of them was oil. Owing to the Syrian sabotage operations over the weekend, supplies from the Middle East to Europe were now dwindling. Only one pipeline remained functional: the Tapline, the American-maintained pipe running from the Saudi oilfields to pop out on the Mediterranean coast at Sidon in Lebanon. The Saudis vehemently opposed the British and French action. As Hoover pointed out, "The oil supply of NATO military forces in Western Europe may soon be endangered." With the world on the brink of war, this was no time to risk that.

Eisenhower suggested that any American heavy tankers and all fleet oilers currently assigned to nonmilitary purposes should be put to immediate use. While mobilizing American oil ships, though, he moved away from the idea he had mooted on October 31 of letting the British pay for their oil in sterling. As the minutes of the meeting (written by Goodpaster) recorded: "With regard to the oil problem faced by the French and the British, the President felt that the purposes of peace and stability would be served by not being too quick in attempting to render extraordinary assistance, and the Vice President reinforced this view."[26]

Eden had complained that Nasser's control of the Suez Canal was a "thumb on our windpipe" because the Egyptian leader could cut off Britain's oil supply. Now that thumb belonged to the president of the United States.

1100 Washington DC // 1600 London // 1700 Paris

In Paris, Christian Pineau was distributing a new crop of imaginative tales. He told the British ambassador that Nasser would have resigned on Saturday but decided to stay in his post only after the American embassy in Cairo told him the United States government insisted he must stay in office. The British ambassador told the American ambassador in Paris, Douglas Dillon. "Pineau apparently is spreading this story in French government circles here," Dillon telegraphed wearily back to Washington.[27]

When this claim was put by the State Department to the embassy in Cairo, ambassador Raymond Hare replied stoutly that he had last seen Nasser on Friday: "There was no discussion at that time, nor had there been previously, of any question of Nasser's resignation. Only comment in Friday's discussion which might be considered as having indirect bearing on subject reference[d] [in State Department's] telegram was expression [of] Nasser's intention not even [to] evacuate his family." A line of the cable is still redacted in the State Department's record, but it goes on to say that though there have been "varying degrees of despondency" following the destruction of the Egyptian air force, the people of Cairo were not giving up. "On contrary attitude has been 'if they want us, let them come and get us.'"[28]

Anti-American feeling was widespread in Paris, where many felt that the United States' focus on Suez was obscuring the plight of Hungary. The reaction of the French, Dillon reported, was "extremely violent." One prominent journalist, a Hungarian-born French correspondent for *Paris Match* who had been one of the last people out of the country, had written provocative reports. "He [is] very emotional over slaughter and lays large share of blame on US because of Radio Free Europe broadcasts inciting population to revolt, followed by refusal of concrete help from US," Dillon wrote. "This line can be very damaging to US therefore prompt action required to show our continued interest, our refusal to give up hope in face of Soviet atrocities and our solidarity with Western allies regarding future course of action."[29]

The mood was different in London, where Eden's government was now caught off balance. In the House of Commons, Selwyn Lloyd argued valiantly but unconvincingly that he could not "ensure that the Israelis withdraw from Egyptian territory until we are physically in the area to keep the peace."[30] Anthony Nutting was watching. "Amid a crescendo of angry protests from the Opposition, he was subjected to one of the toughest cross-examinations ever endured by a Minister of the Crown," he remembered. "If our purpose was to keep the peace and police the area, then why, he was asked, were we dropping leaflets threatening to bomb Egyptian villages and telling the Egyptian populace that they had 'committed a sin' by placing their 'confidence in Abdel Nasser and believing his lies'?"[31] This particular leaflet was read out by the Labour MP Aneurin Bevan, who added, "In my respectful submission we have here not a military action to separate Israeli and Egyptian troops; we have a declaration of war against the Egyptian Government, in the most brutal terms." He asked Lloyd, "Will the Government stop lying to the House of Commons?"[32]

The Labour MP Victor Collins read out part of the text of another Anglo-French leaflet dropped over Egypt the previous day: "We have the might and we shall use it to the limit if you do not give in." He asked Selwyn Lloyd, "Can the Foreign Secretary say whether, in principle, there is any difference between that and the Russian threat to the Hungarians, except that they gave four hours' notice and we gave twelve hours' notice? . . . Can he say whether the Egyptians were guilty of the same crime as the Hungarians—wanting to run their own country in their own way?" Lloyd said he would need to see a copy of the leaflet before he could answer.[33]

While Eden's government was on the ropes in the House of Commons, though, the commanders of Musketeer had reason to believe their operation might be on the verge of salvation. At five p.m. Cairo time, the local Egyptian commander in Port Said met British and French officers. The Egyptians asked that the British and French reconnect the water supply to Port Said and stop "killing civilians." The British commander on the ground asked for a surrender, which the Egyptians refused to provide on grounds that it would have to be approved in Cairo. A temporary cease-fire was agreed until nine thirty p.m. that night, then extended to ten thirty p.m.

As the message about this cease-fire was relayed from the ground commander to General Keightley in Cyprus and from

Cyprus to London, it grew in the telling. In Cyprus, it was understood to mean the British and French would the next morning face no opposition to their landing. In London, it was taken to mean the surrender was already complete. Britain and France had won.

"Our most sincere congratulations to you all," read London's delighted response. The invaders were ordered to occupy Ismailia and Suez immediately "with minimum loss of life," perhaps by arrangement with the local Egyptian governors. Further air bombings were canceled. The United Nations was informed right away.

The news was passed to Eden in the Commons. Thrilled, he leaped up and interrupted Lloyd to announce that General Keightley had ordered a cease-fire. There was happy uproar from the government benches and confusion among the opposition. Conservative members called for Gaitskell's resignation.

Eden rushed back to Downing Street and summoned the chiefs of staff, embracing them joyously. "Oh my dear Chiefs, how grateful I am to you!" he exclaimed. "You have been magnificent! It's all worked out perfectly!"[34]

1500 Washington DC // 2000 London // 2100 Paris // 2200 Port Said // 0000 Moscow

At midnight in Moscow, the Soviet foreign minister, Dmitri Shepilov, sent for the British ambassador, William Hayter. He gave him a message from Bulganin for Eden, and said similar messages were going to Mollet and Ben-Gurion.

Hayter read the text. "I said that a message of this kind called for no comment by me, especially in the present international situation," he reported to London. "Shepilov replied that he did not expect comment; he only asked me to pass it on."

Hayter returned to his embassy and began the time-consuming process of communicating the long, rambling note.

Bulganin condemned the collusion between Britain, France, and Israel—not only as unjustified violence against Egypt and its people, but as a threat to world peace and freedom. "The Suez Canal question has been merely the pretext for Anglo-French aggression, which has other and more far-reaching aims," he wrote. "It cannot be concealed that, in fact, there is now being launched an aggressive brigandly war against the Arab peoples with the object of liquidating the national independence of the Middle Eastern countries and the restoration of the régime of colonial slavery which the people had overthrown."

The most controversial and, for the Western powers, most terrifying paragraph of Bulganin's letter—which had actually been drafted by Khrushchev himself[35]—implied that the Soviets might be about to play their trump card.

"What would have been the position of Britain, if she had been attacked by stronger Powers, with all kinds of modern offensive weapons at their disposal?" the letter asked. "And remember that such countries at the present time need not even send their naval and air forces to British shores, but could use other means, such as rocket techniques. If rocket weapons were used against Britain and France, you would no doubt call this a barbarous act. But how is this different from the inhuman attack carried out by the armed forces of Britain and France on an almost unarmed Egypt?"[36]

This message would widely be read as a threat by the Soviet Union to launch a nuclear attack on London and Paris. Bulganin had made no clear demands or threats. He had not described the possible scale or target of such an attack, nor when it might be launched, nor the circumstances that would provoke it; nor had he actually said that nuclear, rather than conventional, weapons would be mounted on any rockets fired. But he had alluded to the Soviets' medium-range arsenal and equated an act of war against a Third World power with an act of war against a First World power.

The British government had not completely failed to anticipate the possibility of a Soviet attack on its own territory. "If we should be destroyed by Russian bombs now, that would be better than to be reduced to impotence by the disintegration of our entire position abroad," Harold Macmillan had said while grandstanding to Foster Dulles in London on August 1. The loss of Britain's position in the Middle East would reduce Britain "to a status similar to that of Holland," which was implicitly the worst thing the British chancellor could imagine and explicitly worse than a nuclear holocaust.[37]

On September 11, Bulganin had written to Eden noting British and French military concentrations in Cyprus, "in the neighborhood of the Suez Canal area." Bulganin judged that this was designed to threaten action against Egypt, should Egypt refuse to place the canal under international administration. He warned Eden then: "Small wars can turn into big wars. . . . I must tell you, Mr. Prime Minister, that the Soviet Union, as a great power interested in the maintenance of peace, cannot hold aloof from this question."[38]

Bulganin's ominous tone of November 5 built on this earlier threat. "Though there is an element of bullying bluff in this intolerable message I am afraid there is no doubt that the Soviet Government are working themselves up into a very ugly mood," Hayter wrote. He did not comment on the likelihood of an attack on Britain or France, but considered it possible the Soviets might "take independent violent action against our forces in the Middle East." It was essential, he advised, that Britain must "get in step" with its American allies again without delay: "Only clear and early proof of this will stop these people from committing dangerous acts of folly."[39]

Bulganin's letter to Guy Mollet was phrased in similar

terms. His letter to David Ben-Gurion included an extra sting. For the first time in the Soviet Union's relationship with Israel, he cast doubt on its future existence—a point of extreme sensitivity for the Israeli government. "The whole of peace-loving humanity condemns with indignation the criminal action of the aggressors who have tried to undermine the territorial integrity, sovereignty and independence of the Egyptian state," Bulganin wrote. "Entirely ignoring this fact, the Israeli government, acting as a tool of imperialist external forces, is continuing its crazed adventure, challenging all the people of the East who are fighting against colonialism and for their freedom and independence." Israel's behavior, Bulganin said, "is sowing among the peoples of the East a hatred for the State of Israel—a hatred which will inevitably impact on Israel's future and will call into question Israel's very existence as a state."[40]

So shocked was Ben-Gurion at this that he confessed in his diary, "If his [Bulganin's] name hadn't been signed on it I could have thought that it had been written by Hitler."[41] Soviet arms, he believed, were then flowing into Syria. If they now came with Soviet soldiers attached, Israel could face a much greater threat—one that might drag the whole region into war.

1530 New York // 2030 London // 2230 Port Said

The Egyptian authorities in Port Said unloaded new Czech rifles and machine guns that had arrived a few hours before, put them on trucks, and gave them out to any civilians who would take them.[42] That afternoon, they had been broadcasting around the town that World War III had begun. The Soviets, they said, had already bombed London and Paris and were on their way to help Egypt.

Though the timing of these broadcasts, beginning just a few hours before the official issuing of Bulganin's threat, was remarkable, there is no evidence that the script in Port Said was dictated to the Egyptians by the Soviets, as the British and French would later claim, nor even that it was inspired by their move. Communications between Port Said and the outside world had been deliberately targeted by the Anglo-French assault. There was only one underwater cable remaining with a telephone line, which they had neglected to cut.

General Moguy, the Egyptian commander in Port Said, had used it to telephone Nasser earlier in the evening. Finally, he rejected the British and French conditions for cease-fire. He claimed he did so on his own authority. Other sources say Nasser ordered him to fight on.

At ten thirty p.m., gunfire rang out again in Port Said. Anthony Eden's perfect victory was being shot to pieces.

1600 Washington DC // 2100 London // 2200 Paris // 0100 (Nov. 6) Moscow

Nikolai Bulganin continued to press the strong new Soviet line on Suez in a cable to Eisenhower, which arrived in Washington at four p.m. that afternoon. He proposed something extraordinary: a joint Soviet-American task force to liberate Egypt. "The United States have a strong fleet in the Mediterranean," he told the president. "The Soviet Union also has a strong fleet and strong air units. The joint and immediate use of these means on the part of the United States and the Soviet Union, if the United Nations so decides, would be a competent guarantee of stopping aggression against the Egyptian people and against the Arab countries." If Britain and France's invasion were not stopped, he warned, "it could develop into a third world war."[43]

The Soviet offer of a joint force had been Khrushchev's idea. He telephoned Vyacheslav Molotov: "Vyacheslav Mikhailovich, I think that we should address ourselves to the President of the

United States with a proposal to take joint action against the aggressors who have attacked Egypt."

"Eisenhower will never agree to join forces with us against England, France, and Israel," replied Molotov.

"Of course he won't," agreed Khrushchev, "but by putting him in the position of having to refuse, we'll expose the hypocrisy of his public statement condemning the attack against Egypt."[44]

Eisenhower declined the joint venture, stating publicly that it was "an obvious attempt to divert world attention from the Hungarian tragedy." He could hardly do otherwise. Americans were due to cast their votes for or against his reelection the very next day: this was no time to sign up with the Soviets. When Khrushchev received his rejection, though, he was jubilant, believing that it revealed all the American claims of standing for fine principles of liberty and justice to be lies. "We had unmasked them!" he crowed.[45]

At five p.m., Eisenhower met his advisers. They all agreed that the Soviet suggestion of joint military action was "unthinkable." Herbert Hoover, citing CIA information, opined that Nasser's position was "wobbly." He thought the British and French may now be in a position "from which they cannot pull back until Nasser is out."

This was new, Eisenhower said. The British had been saying their aim was to "deflate" Nasser, not topple him.

Hoover suggested that Dag Hammarskjöld might have asked Nasser to resign, though it is not clear he had any evidence to back this up. It may have been speculation, or a result of listening to Christian Pineau's far-fetched stories. He added, "The British may still have a coup in mind, as Nasser's position deteriorates."

Eisenhower responded dryly, "Tell Nasser we'll be glad to put him on St. Helena and give him a million dollars."

But the threat of Soviet intervention had them worried. "Those boys are both furious and scared," said Eisenhower. "Just as with Hitler, that makes for the most dangerous possible state of mind. And we better be damn sure that every Intelligence point and every outpost of our Armed Forces is absolutely right on their toes." According to Emmet Hughes, whose notes on the meeting are livelier than the official minutes but are corroborated by them, Eisenhower added darkly: "You know, we may be dealing here with the opening gambit of an ultimatum. We have to be positive and clear in our every word, every step. And if those fellows [the Soviets] start something, we may have to hit 'em—and, if necessary, with *everything* in the bucket."

It was not only the Soviets, then, who were threatening to turn this conflict into a nuclear war.

Somebody (the official minutes do not say whom) suggested that Eisenhower could get in touch with India's prime minister, Jawaharlal Nehru. The president leaped on this suggestion, saying he would "like to send a message to Nehru to bring Nehru's weight to bear on the side of peace and a limitation of the hostilities."

A messenger brought in an urgent telegram from Charles Bohlen, the ambassador in Moscow, advising that they should push for an immediate cease-fire in the Middle East to avoid Soviet military action. "There has to be some way out of this impasse," Eisenhower said with a sigh.

The president's aide, Herman Phleger, said that the standoff in the Middle East was now so tense, and the stakes so high, that the crisis had become a zero-sum game: "Either Nasser must fall—or Eden must fall."

"All I can say is—it's one hell of a way to conduct a *world* election," said Eisenhower, and closed the meeting.[46]

16

BACK DOWN

0200 London // 0300 Paris // 0400 Cairo

In the middle of the night, Nikolai Bulganin's letters arrived in London and Paris. According to Peter Wright's memoir *Spycatcher*—a book notoriously unreliable in places, but illuminating in others—MI5 had bugged the Egyptian embassy in London, and were intercepting messages between it and the Egyptian embassy in Moscow. Information from this source, Wright alleged, raised the eyebrows of the Joint Intelligence Committee (JIC). One message from Moscow apparently recounted a conversation between the Soviet foreign minister and Egyptian ambassador in which the Soviets said they were preparing aircraft for a confrontation with Britain.

"The panic provoked by this cable, which was handed straight to the JIC, did as much as anything to prompt Eden into withdrawal," Wright wrote. He admitted that the Soviets had swept the Egyptian embassy for bugs and found a Special Facilities washer he had fitted to a telephone in the code room while disguised as a Post Office engineer. He wondered whether the messages sent were therefore deliberate: "They did not want us to assume they were bluffing. The best way of ensuring we took their posture seriously would be if we obtained information from an unimpeachable source, for instance from a secret cable."[1]

As the arms race sped up over the course of the 1950s, Nikita Khrushchev knew that the Soviets were behind the Americans. For several years, while Soviet nuclear scientists—including his own son, Sergei—toiled to catch up, he resorted to bluff. He bragged often about how many missiles the Soviets had and what an enormous range they could cover. It was mostly nonsense. On one occasion, he claimed the Soviets were popping out missiles like sausages from a machine.

"How can you say that, since we only have two or three?" asked Sergei in private.

"The important thing is to make the Americans believe that," his father replied. "And that way we prevent an attack."[2]

In November 1956, the Soviet arsenal consisted of two models. The T-1 (M101) was a single-stage, liquid-fueled tactical attack missile, which could carry an 800-pound nuclear warhead. Its maximum range was around 450 miles, which fell well short of London or Paris. The T-2 (M103) was a two-stage, liquid-fueled intermediate range ballistic missile, which could carry a 700-pound nuclear warhead and could possibly reach up to 1,100 miles, though it had not yet been range-tested that far. This gave it a chance of hitting something important and Western, but it had been produced on a small scale and was not yet deployed in significant numbers. Full production would begin in 1957. The Soviets made no obvious move to deploy any of their missiles to locations that might have allowed them to attack the Operation Musketeer launch bases in Cyprus, nor cities in Western Europe. The Red Army was still focused on Hungary.[3]

"Some accounts well after the event imply that officials in London discounted the Soviet threat," wrote Chester Cooper.

"But that is not the way I remember it at the time. . . . Some British intelligence officers, to be sure, were skeptical that Moscow could throw nuclear missiles from Soviet territory into Britain—but they were not *certain*. And they knew the consequences of their being wrong were grave indeed."[4]

Neither the United States nor the Soviet Union wanted a war, nuclear or conventional. Both administrations believed it necessary to act as if they were prepared to launch nuclear weapons, as much or more for domestic political reasons as to hold each other at bay. The theory of mutual assured destruction would not be articulated publicly in American policy until the 1960s, but the principle that a nuclear state ought appear too dangerous to hit was understood by both Eisenhower and Khrushchev.

Among the many problems with mutual assured destruction was that it assumed everyone would act rationally. Both Eisenhower and William Hayter had indicated the previous evening that they did not feel the Soviets could be relied on to act rationally. With nuclear weapons in play, any fleeting moment of irrationality—or miscalculation, or misunderstanding—had the potential to trigger global disaster.

At three o'clock in the morning Paris time, Guy Mollet summoned Douglas Dillon, the American ambassador. Dillon dragged himself out of bed, dressed for the cold, and drove in the dark to the Hôtel Matignon.

Several French cabinet members were already assembled at Mollet's official residence. Mollet handed him some yellow sheets, which had come off a news machine. They contained the statement from the Soviets as reported by the TASS news agency, threatening nuclear war. (The Soviets soon published an official government statement, which was more carefully phrased than the TASS statement. "But that Tass statement really did scare these people," Dillon said.)

According to Dillon's recollection, "Everybody was scared to death." Mollet asked him how the American government would respond if the Soviets attacked France.

"Well, there's no doubt that it would be a violation of the NATO Treaty," Dillon said. "I'm sure we'd be at your side."

"Well, *you* say that, but what about Washington?" Mollet asked. "They've been saying these terrible things about us. Would they do this?"

Dillon reassured him that Eisenhower would respond to a direct attack. Mollet asked him to contact Washington for confirmation, but Dillon pointed out that night had already fallen on the other side of the Atlantic: he would not be able to get a reply for hours. At that exact moment, a telephone call came through. It was Anthony Eden in London, telling Mollet he could at most keep the attack going only until the next morning, November 7.

"All right," said Mollet.

"It's clear that the French, that night, did not want to stop, and they would not have stopped if the British hadn't stopped," said Dillon.

Mollet pointed to a spot on a map of the Suez Canal, about two thirds of the way up, indicating where he believed French forces were currently fighting. "By ten o'clock tomorrow we might even have the whole thing," he told Dillon mournfully.

Mollet was mistaken as to the French position, believing that his nation's forces were already surrounding Ismailia and might therefore be only twelve hours away from taking the entire canal, down to the southern port of Suez itself. "Well, of course," Dillon said, "it turned out the next day, when the smoke cleared, that they weren't anywhere near the city they were supposed to have been in."[5]

0400 London // 0500 Paris // 0600 Cairo

As Dillon later realized, British and French forces were at that point still at the northern end of the canal. Confusion about the operation continued. "We are completely in the dark about the situation in Egypt," telegraphed Ralph Murray at the Allied Forces Headquarters to the Foreign Office in London. "I can not [*sic*] even see newspaper reports. The four papers which do arrive are three days old and I should have no time to scour them in any case." He requested a daily telegram of collated information covering internal security, government measures, public feeling, the positions of foreign communities and religious minorities in Egypt, and the locations within Egypt of diplomatic personnel and base contractors.[6]

Commando units landed at Port Said, aiming to meet up with the paratroop forces dropped the previous day. French paratrooper Pierre Leulliette remembered clearing the canal area for the landings. He and his fellow soldiers came across a dozen or so fishermen, who put their hands up and shouted in Arabic—declaring, he thought, that they were not soldiers.

"No unnecessary prisoners! They're a nuisance and a waste of food!" barked one French paratrooper.

"A voice in the hearts of some of my comrades was whispering 'Kill! Kill!'" remembered Leulliette. "They had hardly slept and hadn't had time to drink their coffee, so they were in a foul temper that morning."

The French opened fire. One by one, the fishermen slumped and fell into the waters of the canal—except two, who dived in to hide among the boats. One soldier, whom Leulliette called "Première Classe L"—equivalent in rank to lance-corporal— stood on the boats and waited for the men to surface.

"Première Classe L. had obviously never had such fun,"

Leulliette wrote. "After a few minutes, a face emerged. 'Rat-a-tat-tat!' went Première Classe L.'s automatic rifle. The head disappeared, riddled and shot to pieces at point-blank range. Three minutes went by and the head again appeared, streaming with blood and water, a horrible sight. Another burst. The water covered it for good. A large, pink bloodstain slowly spread on the surface and then dispersed."[7] The last fisherman met the same end.

In the wake of the commandos came a motor launch bearing the three splendidly uniformed task force commanders, General Stockwell, Admiral Durnford-Slater, and Air Marshal Barnett, along with the French General Beaufre. The launch proceeded toward the grand headquarters of the Suez Canal Company. Shots peppered out from Egyptian guerrillas stationed in the building. One bullet whizzed past Stockwell's thigh. "I don't think they are quite ready to receive us yet," remarked Durnford-Slater.[8]

When they managed to land, the commanders found chaos. The Egyptian guerrilla resistance was scrappy but well armed and effective. They soon gave up trying to broker a cease-fire with anyone there. Musketeer headquarters in Cyprus telegraphed London with the news that the Egyptians had refused the surrender they thought they had secured the previous evening. "General Stockwell reports that it is abundantly clear that this was the result of intervention by Cairo," the telegram noted, though it was not actually as clear as all that. "Operations were therefore resumed."

Eden could see what he had left of the moral high ground crumbling away under his feet. "Prime Minister is concerned at the renewal of fighting with no certain explanation," the Ministry of Defence telegraphed back.[9] At the same time, emergency messages were being sent from Anglo-French headquarters to their task forces warning: "Russia may intervene in the Middle East with force. Action will be taken forthwith so that all airfields are at the maximum state of preparedness for an attack against them. In particular the greatest possible dispersion of aircraft will be achieved and maintained. Naval and army force will also take appropriate action to meet this threat."[10] British and French forces were now actively preparing for an attack on the Soviet Union or its bases.

0400 Washington DC // 0900 London // 1300 Moscow

In response to Bulganin's letter, the CIA in Washington lifted the embargo it had put on sharing intelligence with the British authorities. Chester Cooper went into a meeting with the Joint Intelligence Committee in London, able to talk freely for the first time. "I had recently become used to seeing these men, my friends, gray with exhaustion," he remembered. "Today they were ashen. They were worried. Really worried. For the past many hours they had been grappling with Moscow's unexpected, hideous threat." He told them the United States thought Bulganin's letter was a bluff. As a result, "The room seemed brighter."[11]

The American diplomat Robert Murphy noted that not everyone in Washington was so sure. "We must stop this before we are all burned to a crisp!" he remembered one "high ranking official of the State Department" exclaiming.

"I am inclined to suspect that fear of the bomb motivated Sir Anthony Eden during this period more than he ever admitted," Murphy wrote, "more perhaps than he himself realized."[12]

Most of the Middle Eastern diplomats in Moscow did not believe the Soviets would bomb Britain or France. They did believe the Soviets might hit British and French ships in the Mediterranean, attack invasion forces in Port Said and Malta, or even create a diversionary incident somewhere else in the

Middle East. "What was generally agreed was that if the Russians were bluffing and did nothing, their reputation in the Third World would be destroyed for at least ten years," wrote Mohamed Heikal.

There is a hint from Egyptian sources that the Soviet Union may not have been bluffing entirely. The Egyptian ambassador in Moscow, Mohamed el-Kouni, was summoned to see Nikita Khrushchev.

"This will make them stop," said Khrushchev, speaking of Bulganin's letter.

"You know, Mr. Chairman," said Kouni, "you nearly broke my heart when you spoke to me at the reception four days ago." Khrushchev had told him the Soviets could not help.

"I meant to give you a misleading message," Khrushchev replied, "because I knew you would report it back to Cairo in cipher. We think the Americans and British have broken your ciphers and we wanted them to think we were not going to intervene. So we had to use you as a tool in this deception. Please forgive me."[13]

This story chimes with Peter Wright's claim that the Soviets used lines of communication they knew would be intercepted to disinform Western powers. Of course, Khrushchev may merely have been flattering the Egyptians: the presidium had been far more occupied with Hungary than with Suez until November 4. Yet with the world as tense as it was at the beginning of November 1956 and British and French forces already preparing to hit Soviet targets, it need not have taken a nuclear bomb to escalate this situation. A conventional attack on the Anglo-French force in Egypt might have been enough.

London was facing up to the prospect of nuclear annihilation from the east and financial annihilation from the west. A run on the British pound was now in effect. The British chancellor, Harold Macmillan, had spent much of the night on the telephone to Washington, including a call to Walter Reed Army Medical Center. From his sickbed, Foster Dulles made the position of the United States stark. If Britain called a cease-fire, the United States would help rescue sterling. If Britain did not, it would not.

"It's ruin either way but it's better the quick way," admitted Macmillan.[14] Having been a great supporter of the Suez operation, he now committed fully and forcefully to stopping it. Previously, as the former Conservative politician Brendan Bracken put it, Macmillan's "bellicosity was beyond description," and he seemed to want "to tear Nasser's scalp out with his own finger nails." From this point on, though, "he might be described as the leader of the bolters."[15]

Macmillan went to Lloyd to explain to him how grim the country's financial position was. The immediate problem was oil. Britain was no longer able to buy oil from the Arab nations. Its alternative was to buy oil from the United States, but Eisenhower was now going to force it to spend dollars—which it could not afford. The only way to keep the lights on was to ask the Americans for credit, and the Americans would not give credit until the advance south of Port Said stopped.

0945 London // 1045 Paris

At nine forty-five a.m., the British cabinet met. "The Chancellor of the Exchequer had rightly been to see the Foreign Secretary about our financial position earlier that day and I knew that it was grim," Eden remembered.[16] Macmillan told the cabinet it was much grimmer than they thought. Britain's gold reserves had lost $280 million in a week thanks to Operation Musketeer, he claimed. He was wrong about this: they had lost $50 million in the first two days of November, going up to $85 million by the end of the first week. The reason for his extraordinary overestimate is unknown. It has been suggested that he might have mistaken dollars for pounds: £100 million was then worth $280 million. The economic historian Diane Kunz argued that Macmillan cannot possibly have been so incompetent, and instead must have ramped up the figure intentionally to stop the war: he "used the most effective device at hand to convince any reluctant colleagues of the danger facing Britain."[17] Macmillan's private diary of the crisis might have answered questions about his reasoning and motivation definitively, had he not destroyed it.

There was resistance to stopping the operation, for the objectives had not been achieved. Only Port Said was occupied, not Ismailia nor the port of Suez itself; the canal was not secured, and Anglo-French forces were not yet in position to unblock it. If the world had to wait for a United Nations force to be constituted and travel to Egypt, the canal might remain blocked for months.

Yet the arguments in favor of stopping immediately were now overwhelming. Israel and Egypt had stopped fighting, so the Anglo-French justification for war had evaporated. There was the Soviet threat; even if the rocket attacks were discounted, the cabinet considered the possibility of Soviet forces intervening in Egypt or Syria feasible. According to Anthony Nutting, it was the prospect of devaluing sterling again and perhaps losing its status as a reserve currency that prompted the cabinet to call a complete halt that day—though Eden (and several others) did so with much reluctance.[18] Butler, Salisbury, and Macmillan were all now ready to accept Dag Hammarskjöld's plan. Though Lloyd still supported Eden's inclination to fight on, the prime minister could not carry the cabinet.

In 1987, Lord Home, who was Commonwealth secretary during the Suez crisis, was asked why Eden ignored several warnings from the Treasury dating back to August 1956 that, without American support, sterling would be put under intense strain.

"A warning is a different thing from it happening, isn't it?"

Home replied. "You often get warnings of this sort and then the results are different." He conceded that the cabinet only really took the prospect of a sterling crisis seriously on November 6, when the Americans effectively issued their own ultimatum. "I think what really turned the scale and made the Chancellor of the Exchequer that day so terribly anxious was the American action in really putting the Sixth Fleet alongside us in the Mediterranean, for all the world to see, and therefore announcing in effect that America was totally against us. And the effect on sterling as a result of that was catastrophic. It was the actual effect on sterling rather than the warnings, I think. Perhaps we ought to have taken the warnings more seriously."[19]

The cabinet voted to stop the war. Ministers had to take their decision as swiftly as possible before eleven a.m., for at that hour they all had to proceed to Westminster. Tuesday, November 6, was the official state opening of the British Parliament. The Queen, clad in white fur and long white gloves, proceeded from Buckingham Palace to Westminster in the Irish state coach, drawn by four white horses. Tradition commanded that she speak in the House of Lords. The political lines in her speech were written for her by her government, and so she too was now obliged to say things that were not true while bedecked in all the glorious regalia of British monarchy. "My Government have been gravely concerned at the outbreak of hostilities between Israel and Egypt," she said. "They resolved, in conjunction with the French Government, to make a quick and decisive intervention to protect the lives of our nationals and to safeguard the Suez Canal by separating the combatants and restoring peace. My Government have proposed that the United Nations should take over responsibility for policing the area, as a prelude to a satisfactory settlement in the Middle East."[20]

Immediately after the state opening, Eden rushed to a telephone and called Christian Pineau and Guy Mollet in Paris.

"I don't think we can go on," said Eden to Mollet, according to Pineau's memory of the conversation. "The English can take a lot of things, but I do not think they would be willing to accept the failure of sterling which would have considerable consequences for the Commonwealth. And the pressure is getting worse from day to day." He said the British cabinet had voted in favor of a cease-fire to take effect in a few hours.

"That's very quick," Mollet replied. "Could we not wait two or three days? In those two or three days we could gain some advantages. We could occupy more of the Canal which would put us in a better negotiating position when the final say of settlement comes."

"No," said Eden. "I cannot hold out any longer."

"Try to," Mollet pleaded.[21]

But Eden would not. He said he would soon be informing Eisenhower of his move.

Mollet was not the only one who thought a few more hours might have made a difference to the outcome of the Suez crisis. "After we prevailed upon the invaders to withdraw, senior people in the Foreign Office and the British Defence Ministry were insisting that if we had delayed our outcry for just twenty-four hours Nasser would have fallen," wrote CIA agent Miles Copeland. "We were amazed at such nonsense, inasmuch as there was no intelligence whatever to support it. . . . Moreover, not one of our British friends could give us a rational estimate of what would have happened to our benefit if he *had* fallen."[22]

By coincidence, Mollet and Pineau were with the chancellor of West Germany, Konrad Adenauer, when they spoke to Eden. The negotiations to form the European Economic Community were almost complete. "France and England will never be powers comparable with the United States and the Soviet

Union," Adenauer remarked to Mollet. "Nor will Germany. There remains to them only one way of playing a decisive role in the world, which is to unite to make Europe. England is not ripe for it but the Suez affair will help to prepare her spirits. As for us, we have no time to lose: Europe will be your revenge."[23]

In London, Eden's press secretary, William Clark, was on his way to the prime minister's private office at the House of Commons when he ran into Lord Mountbatten.

"You not resigned yet?" Mountbatten asked.

"Of course I have," Clark replied, "and you?"

"I can't think why they haven't sacked me," admitted Mountbatten. "I've said such outrageous things."

The two of them continued to the Commons.[24]

1300 Sharm el-Sheikh

A platform had been constructed from two command cars. Atop it stood Moshe Dayan and two other senior officers of the IDF. They faced an audience of hundreds of Israeli soldiers, watching with pride as the blue and white Israeli flag was hoisted on an Egyptian mast on the golden-sanded shores of the Red Sea. Sharm el-Sheikh had "one of the most spectacular views I have ever seen," wrote Dayan. "Its waters are deep blue (Egyptian prisoners warned us against swimming there for they are teeming with sharks) and they are framed by hills of crimson rock."[25]

Dayan read out a letter from Ben-Gurion. A review of the troops was held, and that was it; the Sinai campaign was over. Israel held the territory. Before the campaign, Dayan asked Ben-Gurion if he thought they would keep it. "I hope so, but I'm not sure," the old man had said. "We shan't hang on to it with the same tenacity as we did over Jerusalem." Yet now, in victory, he was thrilled with his spoils. "After all, Sinai never has been part of Egypt," he claimed.[26]

0837 Washington DC // 1337 London // 1437 Paris // 2237 Peking

Eisenhower met Allen Dulles, Herbert Hoover Jr., and others at 8:37 a.m. in Washington. "If the Soviets attack the French and British directly, we would be in war," he told them, "and we would be justified in taking military action even if Congress were not in session." He also added that if current American reconnaissance missions found any Soviet air force presence in Syrian bases, he thought "there would be reason for the British and French to destroy them."[27] Eisenhower may have been furious still with Britain and France for their perfidy, but he would not tolerate an attack by the Soviet Union on NATO allies.

Somewhat late to the party, China announced that the Egyptian embassy in Peking had received two million telegrams of support from the Chinese people and that 250,000 Chinese had volunteered to travel to Egypt and take up arms against the imperialists.[28] While these numbers were doubtless impressionistic, they underlined again the potential for the Suez crisis to spiral into a far greater war. "In the rest of Africa and Asia, from Japan to Casablanca, the reaction to the British-French-Israeli attack on Egypt has been one of virtually unanimous revulsion," remarked Allen Dulles. "Earlier doubts as to Nasr's ambitions, and outrage over the tragic events in Hungary, have been drowned out by a wave of revived age-old hatred of Western imperialism and colonialism."[29]

With the threat of nuclear war and global conflagration looming, Eisenhower maintained his cool. He went to Gettysburg to cast his vote in the American presidential election. Owing to the global crisis, he was forced to cancel his plan for an immediate postelection golfing holiday. According to his secretary, this was the real blow: "He's as disappointed as a kid who had counted out all the days to Christmas."[30]

1230 Washington DC // 1730 London // 1830 Budapest

William Clark returned to Eden's private office at the House of Commons at five thirty p.m., about thirty minutes before the cease-fire was due to be announced. The British ambassador to Paris was on the telephone, saying that Mollet was begging Eden to delay the announcement by another half an hour at least. "I don't think the PM was even told," remembered Clark.

Another telephone call came through at 5:55 p.m., this time from Eisenhower on the brand-new transatlantic connection. Eden took it. There is a transcript of the call in the American archives. Eden spoke with dignity but tightly; Eisenhower was more relaxed and conveyed an easy, almost unconscious sense of authority.

"We cease firing tonight at midnight provided we are not attacked," said Eden.

"I see," Eisenhower replied.

"What you may call the long cease-fire, the cessation of hostilities, that is more complicated," Eden said.

Eisenhower understood that this was about the "technical troops"—the men who were supposed to secure and clear the canal. "The point I want you to have in your mind is that the cease-fire tonight has nothing to do with technical troops," he said. "You cease anyway."

"Unless attacked," rejoined Eden. The prime minister then added that he had to go to Parliament. "Would you authorize me to say that you think this is helpful outside . . ."

The president interrupted. "You can say that I called to say how delighted I was you found it possible to cease fire tonight so that negotiations could start."

He had to repeat this a couple of times so Eden could write it down. Eisenhower told him that he did not want any quibbles with the cease-fire: United Nations troops would arrive quickly so that Britain and France could withdraw quickly. Eden, who still hoped British and French troops would stay in Egypt, expressed his hope that American troops would join them: "Are we all going to go out?"

"I would like to see none of the great nations in it," Eisenhower replied. "I am afraid the Red boy [the Soviet Union] is going to demand the lion's share. I would rather make it no troops from the big five."

Eden was clearly flustered by this refusal and asked for time to think it over. "If I survive here tonight," he said, referring to what he was about to face in the House of Commons, "I will call you tomorrow." He asked how Eisenhower was doing.

"We have given our whole thought to Hungary and the Middle East," admitted the president. "I don't give a damn how the election goes. I guess it will be all right."[31]

"I gathered that Ike was very stern indeed," wrote Clark, "insisted on the ceasefire (but agreed to congratulate Eden on it publicly) and insisted absolutely on Anglo-French withdrawal from Suez." In his memoirs, Eden remembered Eisenhower's tone differently. "He was vigorous and in good spirits," Eden claimed. "He was delighted by our order to cease fire and commented that we had got what we had set out to do; the fighting was over and had not spread." According to the minutes of the call, Eisenhower made no comment about the fighting not spreading. "There seemed no doubt at that moment that friendship between our two countries could be quickly reanimated," Eden concluded.

Clark returned to Downing Street to write his formal resignation letter. Before he could finish, he was summoned back to the House of Commons to see Eden again. "All he wanted was that I should put out the message of congratulation from Ike and make it clear that it came after the announcement of the ceasefire 'or it will look as if he was influencing me,'" Clark wrote. "I gladly told this last lie for the PM."[32]

Eden entered the House of Commons to a "profound silence," reported the *Times*. But the silence "was shattered with a great cheer at the announcement of the British cease-fire [pending] at midnight." Most of the cheering came from the Labour benches, but some on the Conservative side too waved their order papers.

Eden summoned all the dignity he could to make a case for his own victory. Though this case was based in significant portions on untruths and obfuscations, he expressed himself eloquently and attempted to turn the debate back to the subject of peace in the Middle East and beyond. If the British and French invasion had encouraged the United Nations to intervene, he told the house, "the better it will be for the peace and future of the world." Though this appeared to be a claim that he had promoted peace by starting a war, it was the cue for government supporters—excepting a few dissenters—to cheer again. Eden phrased the defeat to allow his fellow Conservatives to feel it as a victory. Even the convalescing Sir Winston Churchill was seen to rise to his feet to join the applause.

Eden went on to defend his campaign from Bulganin's accusation about "barbarous bombing," claiming that the British had gone to great lengths to minimize civilian casualties in Egypt. "They will in any event be in no way comparable with the casualties that have been and are still being inflicted by the Soviet forces in Hungary," he said. "The world knows that in the past three days Soviet forces in Hungary have been ruthlessly crushing the heroic resistance of a truly national movement for independence."[33]

"The adrenalin that accompanies high drama is dangerous when the drama ends, as this one had, so suddenly and so harshly," wrote Robert Rhodes James, later Eden's biographer, who was watching from the gallery. "Suddenly, he looked aged and ill, defeated and broken."[34]

Eden made it through his parliamentary performance, but his health failed soon afterward. "I will never forget the last act of the Grecian tragedy," wrote Gerald Templer, the chief of the Imperial General Staff. "The Prime Minister in his bed at 10 Downing Street, his wife sitting on the bed and holding his hand. Who else was there? The four Chiefs of Staff. Not a Minister. A broken man."[35]

At the United Nations in New York, Dag Hammarskjöld announced that Britain and France had agreed to the cease-fire. "There were emotional scenes as delegates, who had feared the worst after yesterday's menacing move by Moscow, realized that the threat of another world war had been lifted, and hastened to congratulate the Secretary-General and one another," reported the London *Times* correspondent in New York.[36]

"It was the BBC news bulletin, it might have been six or it might have been seven p.m., I can't remember when it was exactly," said General Sir Kenneth Darling, chief of staff to the army task force commander, General Stockwell, "when suddenly we heard on the tannoy [loudspeaker] echoing round the ship the news that there would be a ceasefire at midnight GMT, which was 0200 hours on the 7th, local time. We were just astounded. It came straight out of the clear blue sky. The whole thing was brought to a halt and it had hardly started."[37]

The French paratrooper Pierre Leulliette was about a mile outside El Kantara by his recollection when the order—"so incredible that we thought at first that it was some huge joke"— came to halt. "We even withdrew a bit in astonishment," he remembered. "We dug fresh holes in the sand for the night. But we no longer knew which way to face. Even in Indo-China, said the veterans, where you were betrayed daily by everyone, they wouldn't have dared do anything like that."[38]

The cease-fire order was delivered to General Keightley, the operation's commander. His reply did not sound happy. "Egyptian armed children from 12 years upwards are being nuisances," Keightley complained, and warned that the main problem would be "irregulars[,] civilians and children continuing to fire on our men and probable accusations of our having broken the cease fire."[39] There was disquiet among the fighting men, too. Douglas Clark, in Suez, felt that the United Nations had it all wrong. When the Soviets retook Hungary, he thought, "the United Nations did not even consider sending an international force to stop the retaliatory slaughter; but in Port Said, where we were merely recovering our own property, U.N.O. immediately decided to send a force to stop a war which had already come to an end." Historians might quibble with several assertions in that sentence, but Clark insisted in his memoirs: "Everybody in the bridgehead had the feeling of being let down." The Soviet bomb threat, he said, was "empty"—and the real man to blame was "the President of the United States, who at the moment of our landing was seeking re-election on a 'peace ticket,' [and] had taken up an uncompromisingly hostile attitude towards us by denying us the oil he could so easily have supplied."[40]

On a bright and clear autumn day for most of the United States, American voters headed for the polls. "No other American election can, like this one, have been overtaken in the home stretch by the onrush of world events, the anguishing omens of the future, which have virtually swept it from the headlines," wrote the *Times* correspondent in Washington; "and the irony is that for purposes of the Republican campaign the world had been depicted as such a comfortable and safe place to live in." The central issue of the election, wrote the American journalist James Reston, had become "how America is to be governed for four long years in a world of crumbling empires, suspicious alliances, rising nationalism, and social, political, economic, and military revolution."[41]

In some northern industrial states, as well as California and Texas, pollsters commented on an increased turnout, above 1952's figures—"in response, it seemed, to the gravity of the hour and the President's exhortation last night that citizens should use their 'priceless privilege' for which people in Hungary were dying."[42]

In Budapest, the fighting continued. "Heaviest continuous shelling yet," reported the American legation. "One defender [of the] Kilian barracks reported [it was] bombed first time early Monday morning. Said defenders 700–800 strong when fighting restarted but men no problem because 'when one [is] killed there [is] always someone, maybe a woman, to pick up his rifle.'"[43] The Soviets had now cut all escape routes out of the country, and the resurgent AVH was mounting what a Reuters report called "a wild fury of revenge." Soviet troops were said to be hanging rebels and displaying their bodies on bridges over the Danube River. Those rebels who surrendered were given a concession: they would be shot instead of hanged.[44]

Béla Lucza was twenty years old and fought with the rebels at Corvin Alley. He was one of the last holding out—but now found himself surrounded by a ring of Soviet soldiers. One of them punched him. Another kicked him and raised his gun. Lucza put his hands in the air. "What the hell do you want here?" he shouted. "I am a Hungarian, this is my home and this is no Suez for you." The Soviet officer shot him twice: one bullet hit him in the head and the other glanced off the side of his mouth. Lucza fell to the floor and pretended to be dead. The officer shot a third time at his heart. The shot missed, but ripped a bone out of his shoulder. Though he was blinded, Lucza survived by playing dead. "I knew they thought I was a capitalist and all," he remembered. "I wanted to face him, to give him a piece of my mind when the blast came."[45]

The British journalist Peter Fryer was a Communist himself and believed that what he saw in Hungary was a travesty of every principle of that philosophy. He accused the Communist government under Rákosi and Gerő of "the most abominable methods, including censorship, thought control, imprisonment, torture and murder."[46] His dispatches attesting to the reality of the revolution and of Soviet persecution horrified the loyal Stalinist staff of the *Daily Worker*, who refused to publish some of them. He resigned and was expelled from the Communist Party.

The Yugoslavs were disgusted by Soviet behavior. "They are already describing them [the Hungarian rebels] officially as a counterrevolution," Veljko Mićunović wrote angrily in his diary. "So to 'defend the revolution' in Hungary they have sent Soviet troops against Budapest in revolt and are seeking the causes of the revolt from here all the way to America: In their view everyone else is to blame, they alone are in the right!" To Mićunović, it seemed any prospect of liberalization within the Soviet bloc was slipping away. "It is now simply impossible to talk about the policy of the Twentieth Congress and de-Stalinization when the Soviet Union is restoring order in Hungary by means of armed force and is threatening to do the same for other countries of Eastern Europe," he wrote.[47]

Mićunović saw Khrushchev that evening. It was Soviet National Day, the anniversary of the October Revolution, and Khrushchev was wearing a dark suit with two gold stars— decorations reserved for special occasions. He met Mićunović near St. George's Hall in the Kremlin, where that night's grand reception was being set up.

Though Khrushchev was cross with the Yugoslavs for giving Imre Nagy asylum in their embassy in Budapest, he was

triumphant about Suez. He believed that the United States' refusal to join a Soviet-American force had struck a propaganda
blow against it: "The United States was exposed as an accom-
plice in the Western plan to attack Egypt."

His conclusion made a certain stark sense from a Soviet in-
ternationalist point of view. "The defeat of the West was complete," Mićunović wrote, characterizing what Khrushchev had
said. "Nasser remained, and the Arabs would be even stronger
after this idiotic war-making by the French and British."[48]

"Father was extraordinarily proud of his victory," said
Khrushchev's son Sergei.

"I've been told that when Guy Mollet received our note, he
ran to the telephone in his pyjamas and called Eden," Khrushchev remembered later. "I don't know if this story is true, but
whether or not he had his trousers on doesn't change the fact
that twenty-four hours after the delivery of our note the aggression was halted." Khrushchev's biographer William Taubman added: "The lesson he learned and applied in later crises
was both that nuclear weapons were all-powerful and that he
didn't need many of them."[49]

Nasser's closest chroniclers, his wife Tahia and his friends
Mohamed Heikal and Abdel Latif al-Baghdadi, do not record
his reaction to the cease-fire. There was little immediate cause
for celebration. The armed forces of three foreign powers were
still in Egyptian territory; the Egyptian armed forces had so
far failed to evict them; and there was no guarantee that the
untried United Nations Expeditionary Force would retrieve
Egypt's sovereignty or dignity from this situation. Over the
following couple of days, the few testimonies that exist seem
to hint that Nasser still felt out of sorts. Baghdadi recorded
his continuing gripes with colleagues, especially Abdel Hakim
Amer, and his complaints about the army's "spirit of surrender" and "paralysis" following the British and French attack.[50]

When the Canadian General Burns met him on November 9, he was wearing "an ancient grey cardigan and looked rather tired, but still vigorous and confident."[51] According to press reports, the reaction in Cairo was subdued. News from the Canal Zone was confusing. Some Egyptians had rejoiced at the prospect of Soviet intervention, while others had feared it. Few now welcomed Ben-Gurion's announcement that Israel had won.[52] While Israel had won a military victory over Egypt, though, Nasser had won a diplomatic victory against Britain and France. British and French forces had not taken and could not take the whole canal. They were nowhere near toppling his government.

At 9:21 p.m. London time, Eden cabled Mollet. "The President of the United States telephoned me on his own account. There is no doubt at all that the friendship between us all is restored and even strengthened," he asserted. "I feel that as a result of all our efforts we have laid bare the reality of Soviet plans in the Middle East and are physically holding a position which can be decisive for the future." He offered his thanks to Mollet for his loyalty and understanding: "I am sure history will justify us."[53]

1900 Washington DC // 0000 London // 0100 (Nov. 7) Paris // 0200 Cairo; Tel Aviv // 0400 Moscow

At midnight, Britain's imperial adventure in Suez ended. Ten years after the event, the British historian Hugh Thomas wrote that "the spectacle of over one hundred thousand men setting off for a war which lasted barely a day and then returning has few parallels in the long gallery of military imbecility. The 'grand old Duke of York' at least got to the top of the hill."[54] (In an old English nursery rhyme, the duke pointlessly marches ten thousand men up to the top of a hill and then down again.)

In Washington, Eisenhower's campaign team had holed up in the presidential suite at the Sheraton Park Hotel to watch the election results come in. "The air is stale with smoke from hundreds of cigarettes nervously puffed and snuffed out," wrote Emmet Hughes, the president's speechwriter, "with scores of whisky glasses half-gulped and left to stand and turn to water, with simple sweat from all the brows and bodies waiting, waiting, waiting . . ."

Eisenhower was in an ebullient mood, perking up still more as the news came in that he was leading strongly in some Southern states. "Louisiana? That's as probable as leading in Ethiopia!" he exclaimed. But he stopped around midnight and sat down, telling Hughes he needed to rest. "*Emotions* are the things you got to watch out for. So all the doctors say. The worst is anger. . . . And after anger, any great emotional strain or worry is bad. . . . But these *are* the things that do affect the heart. . . . Haven't had a twinge since the first one [heart attack], but . . . just got to be careful, I guess. . . ."

Then came the news that they had won Alabama—the first time since 1876 that that state had voted for a Republican. There was joy, and then impatience as Eisenhower waited for Adlai Stevenson to concede. "What in the name of God is the monkey waiting for?" he growled. "Polishing his prose?" Then, as Stevenson appeared on the television screens, he stalked quickly out of the room, saying, "I'm just looking for a drink."

A few minutes later he reappeared, having changed into a blue suit and regained his presidential composure. He gathered up his family and went downstairs to appear before the cameras. His speech, according to Hughes, was unrehearsed.

"With whatever talents the good God has given me," Eisenhower said, "with whatever strength there is within me, I will continue . . . to do just one thing: to work for 168 million Americans here at home—and for peace in the world."[55]

Though it had been brief, the Suez War had been messy. Its cost could not merely be estimated in the thousands of lives lost, the soldiers and civilians injured, the infrastructure, homes, and property destroyed, or the expense of mounting the failed operations. The cost also included the follow-on effects of the stoppage of oil through the pipelines and international trade traffic through the Suez Canal, the sterling crisis, and the economic damage to all the countries involved.

There were even greater costs, which could not be calculated in figures: the cost to British prestige, the cost to Britain's, France's, and the West's relations with the Arab world in the short and long term, the cost to the already distant prospect of Arab-Israeli peace, the cost to trust within NATO, the cost to the reputation of the United Nations, the cost to the liberty of Hungary.

For all that expenditure of money, power, prestige, and lives, Britain and France had failed to meet their objectives. The Suez Canal was closed and still held under Egyptian national control; the Algerian rebellion would not quiet down but would grow; and Gamal Abdel Nasser was still president of Egypt.

"THE CURSE OF THE PHARAOHS"

Dwight D. Eisenhower was reelected president of the United States by a landslide. He carried forty-one states with 457 electoral college votes, while his Democratic opponent, Adlai Stevenson, carried seven with 73 votes. Eisenhower won 57.4 percent of the popular vote, an increase of 2.5 percent on his majority in 1952.

On the morning of November 7, twenty-two thousand Anglo-French troops in Egypt were in command of Port Said. They had advanced south down the Suez Canal to El Cap. That day, members of the Baghdad Pact—Iraq, Turkey, Iran, and Pakistan—met and passed a resolution demanding the immediate withdrawal of British and French troops. The pact had been an attempt to reassert British influence in the Muslim world. Even the nations acquiescent in that now turned on Britain. Britain's other important regional ally, Jordan, severed its bond by renouncing the Anglo-Jordanian defense treaty a few weeks later.

"You have cut off the British lion's tail and we have drawn his teeth!" Nikita Khrushchev exclaimed to the Egyptian ambassador, Mohamed el-Kouni. "Now he can neither roar or bite!" According to Mohamed Heikal, the Soviets promised Nasser that all the arms and armaments he had lost during the war would be replaced: "the aeroplanes free of charge and the rest at half their cost price."[1]

Immediately after the crisis, Allen Dulles worried that "the precipitous military action by Britain, France and Israel have [*sic*] provided the Soviet Union with new opportunities which it has begun to exploit."[2] But the warmth between the Soviets and the Egyptians did not last. Nasser arrested some Egyptian Communists soon after the Suez War and attempted to mend his relations with the United States. The Soviets tried a soft-power approach by organizing a film festival in Cairo, but annoyed the Egyptians by sending what Heikal called "a supply of films which were nothing but blatant communist propaganda." The Egyptians canceled several screenings, and the event ended in acrimony.[3] Fears about the Soviets attacking British and French troops still in the Canal Zone continued through November but came to nothing—though the British drew up a third Musketeer plan, code-named Musketeer Renewed, in case of emergency.[4]

In the inner circles of the British government, the mood was morose. "Anthony very depressed," wrote Lady Eden in her diary. "It looks as if the Dulles regime is going to continue."[5] Eden telephoned Eisenhower and invited himself and Mollet to Washington, hoping to patch up the special relationship—at least for the sake of public appearances. In a boisterous mood after his election victory, Eisenhower casually agreed that Eden could visit. The White House chief of staff, Sherman Adams, who was with the president when he received the call, thought that the president "was too anxious to restore the traditional friendship between the Americans and the British to let pride or the nursing of hurt feelings keep him from eagerly accepting Eden's offer to get together again."[6]

According to Chester Cooper, though, "neither Eden nor

Eisenhower had reckoned with the mood in Foggy Bottom. In the view of Acting Secretary Hoover and other officials, a visit by the prime minister and the premier to Washington before Britain and France had complied with the United Nations' resolution was bound to be regarded by the Third World as American connivance with the ex-imperial powers; any credit the United States had accumulated in the Middle East, Africa, and Asia during the previous ten days would be dissipated."[7] Hoover telephoned Foster Dulles in his bed at Walter Reed Army Medical Center. Dulles telephoned Eisenhower and insisted that he disinvite Eden and Mollet until Britain and France had withdrawn fully from Egypt.

Eisenhower did so. Afterward, he went to the hospital to talk to Dulles in person. Dulles's aide William Macomber remembered the secretary of state propped up with pillows in his big, high bed; Eisenhower sitting in a little chair beside: "Mr. Dulles kind of peered over the bed and sort of down at him a little bit, and the President was sitting there looking up at Mr. Dulles."

"Foster, I understand why you thought it was a bad idea and why it should have been called off, and as you know we called it off. I quite agree. But I want to explain to you what I had in my mind when I did it," Eisenhower said. Dulles listened as the president spoke.

"I'll always remember Mr. Dulles looking down at him," said Macomber. "All he said was, 'Well, Mr. President, I think it was right that we called it off.' And the President, after having asked, 'You understand why I did it?'—I think he expected: 'I see.'"

Macomber was shocked. "I told Mr. Dulles later I thought it was kind of mean, on the morning that he'd been elected President of the United States, to be so stern," he said. "But the President just let it drop and went on to other things. But it was an interesting episode in their relationship."[8]

Israel emerged from the crisis with a sense of victory. "The Sinai campaign was the greatest and most glorious in the annals of our people," claimed Ben-Gurion on November 7. It had, he said, restored "King Solomon's patrimony from the island of Yotvat (Tiran) in the south to the foothills of Lebanon in the north." He announced that Sharm el-Sheikh was now an Israeli town named Mifratz Shlomo, and hinted that Israel planned to keep Sinai, too: "Our army did not infringe on Egyptian territory. . . . Our operations were restricted to the Sinai Peninsula alone."[9]

Eisenhower sent a message to Ben-Gurion telling him that if he kept Sinai, he would "bring about the condemnation of Israel as a violator of the principles as well as the directives of the United Nations."[10] Herbert Hoover informed the Israeli embassy that all aid from the United States would be terminated. Sanctions might be taken up against Israel at the United Nations, and it could even be booted out of that organization. According to the journalist Robert Henriques, Hoover's personal message to Ben-Gurion was particularly abrupt: "If you do not withdraw your troops from Sinai, you personally will be responsible for the outbreak of the Third World War."[11]

Ben-Gurion tried to arrange a private meeting with Eisenhower to discuss it, but the president refused to meet him until the Israelis had relinquished Egyptian territory. And so, on November 8, Ben-Gurion wrote to Eisenhower: "We have never planned to annex the Sinai Desert . . . [We will] willingly withdraw our forces."[12]

Though the principle of withdrawal had been accepted, Israeli troops stayed in Sinai and the Gaza Strip; their complete withdrawal would be announced by Dag Hammarskjöld on March 8, 1957. During the intervening four months, they mapped and photographed every part of the Sinai and hid caches of food and water in anticipation of future wars. "When we were finally forced to leave, I took it very hard," Ariel Sharon remembered. "Most of all I could not understand why we withdrew from Gaza and from the settlement Ben-Gurion had established there. The relentless terror from the strip was one of the main problems we had tried to solve with this war. Our overriding goal had been to find a way of forcing Egypt to accept responsibility [for fedayeen activity] and put an end to it. And now the Egyptians would be coming back. It was as if we had not solved anything at all."[13]

Though there was already much animus toward Israel across the Arab world, the Suez crisis made it worse. "The readiness with which Israel collaborated in this shameful grand conspiracy bore out the Arabs' fears that Israel was a spear-head and instrument of colonialism in the Middle East," wrote the Sudanese foreign minister Muhammad Ahmed Mahgoub. "Israel had, therefore, more than ever before become a serious and immediate threat to the security and well-being of the fifty million Arabs in the Middle East."[14] After Suez, Nasser's public speeches became more militantly anti-Israel and stressed a more urgent desire for the liberation of Palestine.[15] Owing to the deal it sealed with France at Sèvres for a nuclear reactor at Dimona, Israel would ultimately become a nuclear power as a result of the Suez crisis. While this may have made some Israelis feel safer, it would fuel ambitions toward nuclear arms in the hostile surrounding states. The specter of nuclear escalation in the Middle East would rise to haunt the region in the twenty-first century.

*   *   *

Operation Musketeer failed. Many claimed this was because it went too slowly. "Had it been possible to compress the operation into two or three days," the then permanent secretary at the British Ministry of Defence, Richard Powell, said later, "the world would have been faced with a fait accompli and could have settled down to accept it."[16] Speaking in 1966, American admiral Arleigh Burke thought that Dulles might have supported the British if they had pulled the operation off more rapidly. "There's certainly no doubt that he was solidified in his position because of the failure of the British to really pick the rose," he said. "They fumbled it, and they made a mess of their operation."[17] White House staff secretary Andrew Goodpaster agreed: "Whatever their purpose was, they chose the world's worst method of carrying it out and as the days went on and we read all about this parachute attack that was going to occur and it didn't occur and it didn't occur, and the pressure was building up, really any chance of it being carried through was lost in the way that this was done."[18]

Musketeer was hamstrung by political considerations from the beginning. It was hastily and carelessly repackaged to fit the fake peacekeeping scenario dreamed up at Sèvres, and was repeatedly reimprovised as it went on to fit rapidly changing political objectives. Even if it had been put into action as originally conceived, though, it would have been impossible to compress the operation into two or three days. As the chief of the Imperial General Staff had repeatedly advised, the nearest usable harbor was Malta, 1,100 miles from Port Said. This crossing would take warships six to seven days at full tilt. The psychological warfare component in Phase 2 was intended to turn the majority of the Egyptian people and army against Nasser. Even with Musketeer spread over a couple of weeks, this phase was too brief to have any chance of success, and over two to three days it could barely have been started. Logistically, as the joint chiefs of staff had been pointing out since the summer, the fight from the canal to Cairo was not likely to be as quick and easy as Eden hoped and might take weeks. Operation Musketeer was not fit for purpose, and no amount of wishful thinking from politicians would change this. "It was not a well done military operation at all," remarked Eisenhower. "It looked clumsy. I don't know what happened."[19]

In London, Eden's government attempted to argue that the intervention was positive, for it had stiffened the resolve of the United Nations to deal with the issue of the Suez Canal. This convinced few: it was, as the Labour MP Denis Healey described it, "like Al Capone taking credit for improving the efficiency of the Chicago police."[20] There was a vote of confidence in Eden in the House of Commons on November 8. The Conservative MP Nigel Nicolson went to see the chief whip, Edward Heath, beforehand. "I said that I would support the government only if he could assure me that we were not attempting to topple Nasser by a subterfuge," remembered Nicolson. "He held my gaze steadily, and said nothing. I thanked him for his honesty, and left."

The Conservatives still had a majority, so Eden survived the vote—though Nicolson and six other Tory MPs abstained. Even so, "Nothing I have done in my life affords me greater pleasure in recollection than the moment at 10pm on November 8, 1956," wrote Nicolson forty years later, "when I sat in the library of the House of Commons, deaf to the appeal of the division bells."[21] Nicolson was deemed a "traitor" by the extreme right-wing League of Empire Loyalists. His constituency party held a ballot of confidence in him. He narrowly lost and was obliged to resign his seat at the next election.

In the House of Commons, the loyal Conservative MP Peter Thorneycroft argued that Soviet plans had included "the takeover of the Middle East, using Nasser as her instrument." British troops, he said, discovered on the ground that Egypt "had been armed to the teeth by Russia," though since Nasser had been public about his arms deals with Czechoslovakia for over a year, this was not a revelation. Moreover, after news broke of Nasser's Czech arms deal in late 1955, Britain had ramped up its own sales of weapons to Egypt in an attempt to forestall further Soviet deals. In the first half of 1956, Britain sold four times as many arms and explosives to Egypt as it did to Israel, and fifty times as many aircraft and aircraft parts. (Over the previous five years, those ratios had been two and a half times and three times, respectively.) When British forces assessed the war matériel they had captured from Egypt, there were four times more British-made weapons than Soviet or Czech weapons.[22] Thorneycroft omitted to mention this. "We intervened to stop the war, and we perhaps stopped it in the nick of time, before the Egyptian air force, organised by Russia, ran amok in the Middle East," he claimed.[23]

Operation Musketeer had damaged what credibility Britain had in the Middle East. "Popular sentiment against Nuri [es-Said, Britain's ally] is rising in Iraq," noted Allen Dulles, "and he may become 'ill' and retire, at least for the time being, leaving the country to more nationalistic elements. At present strong anti-British sentiment in Iraq has resulted in a desire to reconsider the Baghdad pact structure in order to exclude the British and obtain United States' membership."[24]

General Burns, the Canadian chief of the United Nations Expeditionary Force, arrived in Cairo on November 8. Nasser suspected that this force would be a proxy to enforce the same "international" control of the canal that the British and French had wanted. He refused to accept troops from nations he saw as British stooges—Australia, New Zealand, Canada, and Pakistan. Lester Pearson was exasperated: Canada had, after all, brokered the deal, and had gone against its ally Britain to do so. He himself was under attack from conservative politicians and press in Canada and Britain for supposedly taking Nasser's side. Dag Hammarskjöld persuaded Nasser to accept a compromise. Though there would be no Canadian infantry soldiers, Canadian administrative and logistical staff could be attached. The force itself was made up of troops from Norway, Sweden, Finland, Denmark, India, Indonesia, Colombia, Brazil, and Yugoslavia, under Burns's command. Their first job was clearing the canal of the ships Nasser had used to block it. With his consent, they began on November 14.

One of the problems for the United Nations Expeditionary Force was that its members had no uniform apart from those of their own countries—yet they had to be distinguishable from the fighting men of Britain, France, Israel, or Egypt. Somebody at the United Nations came up with the idea that they should wear berets in the organization's distinctive blue. There was no time to have them made, so the Expeditionary Force borrowed thousands of American plastic helmet liners, which were spray-painted blue.[25] The blue berets or blue helmets of the United Nations would become an international symbol of peacekeeping for the rest of the century and beyond.

*   *   *

The "special relationship" between Britain and the United States took a hit from the Suez crisis. For the Americans the problem was deceit, according to their ambassador in Paris, Douglas Dillon. "This led to further disenchantment with the British, and particularly with Eden personally." By contrast, the relationship between the United States and France did not suffer too seriously, though there was bad feeling. "The Americans were hoping, in North Africa, to substitute their presence for ours," wrote Christian Pineau twenty years later, rather overestimating their ambition. "They reckoned the same in Vietnam and we know what disasters and what horrors they accomplished."[26]

"The French felt that they were being a little bad, I think," Dillon said. "There was a little guilty conscience. But once they decided to do it, they were really going to do it and see it through . . . the French were more frank all through it. I think that was the reason. The British consistently misled us, misinformed us and the French did not."[27]

Eden and his supporters felt the Americans had been disloyal. In the absence of full disclosure about the Suez plot, many British politicians and soldiers, as well as ordinary citizens, blamed the United States for thwarting what they believed to be a nobly intentioned, if incompetent, peacekeeping operation. Anthony Montague Browne, Churchill's private secretary, admitted that he did not realize the British government "could be politically so inept, militarily so dilatory and indecisive and nationally so disunited, even gutless," but added that even so he could not believe "that the Americans would turn on us with such joyful malevolence."[28] The joyful malevolence was blamed on Foster Dulles by the British press—"but their bitter comments did not bother Dulles," wrote the American diplomat Robert Murphy. "In fact, he seemed to enjoy their attitude. If they wanted to assign to him, rather than to Eisenhower, the dominant role in our Suez policy, that did not displease Dulles."[29]

Speaking a few years later, Eisenhower expressed his frustration that some Britons felt betrayed by the Americans. "And you know, strangely enough, later when things didn't go the way they thought they should in Britain, some of their press began to charge us with pulling the rug from under them and letting the British down," he said. "Nothing could have been further from the truth. We'd told them from the very beginning that would be our attitude. . . . I just couldn't think of anything worse than to have Britain and the United States completely on the outs on anything. This was a place where we differed possibly because of differences of background and all the rest of it, and I don't mean to say that I think we were perfect in our solutions. But we thought we were following principle and that's a pretty good place to stay."[30]

Eisenhower's anger with Eden grew over the final months of 1956. Winthrop Aldrich, the American ambassador to London, was surprised by Eisenhower's vitriol. "The President just went off the deep end. He wouldn't have anything further to do with Eden at all. He wouldn't even communicate with him."[31] Aldrich claimed that for the rest of Eden's prime ministership he was obliged to conduct all important Anglo-American business with Rab Butler, Lord Salisbury, and Harold Macmillan, with whom the president was still on speaking terms.

By November 9, Britain was plummeting headfirst into an economic crisis. The United States refused to support the pound with credits and would not let the International Monetary Fund (IMF) do so, either.[32] Saudi Arabia embargoed oil exports to Britain and France that day; Lebanon embargoed tankers that were loading oil for Britain and France.[33] The British government introduced its national reduction of 10 percent in oil consumption. Motorists were asked to abandon their cars. By the end of November, Britain's total gold and dollar reserves stood at $1,965 million—less than the $2,000 million that the Bank of England and the British Treasury considered was a minimum to keep the sterling area afloat. To make matters worse, from that sum the Treasury still owed $175.5 million to service its loans from the United States, another $5 million to the United States for a Marshall aid loan, $70 million to the European Payments Union and $7.5 million to Canada for its wartime loans, which altogether would debit another $258 million.[34] "And the interesting thing about the whole affair, which is often forgotten in Britain, is that the only successful use of sanctions in history was the Americans over Suez," remarked the Labour MP Denis Healey.[35]

CIA agent Miles Copeland had little sympathy for the British. "They blamed their losses on American pressures, arguing that had they been allowed to follow through to final success the outcome would have been favourable," he wrote. "But, here again, *all* the intelligence we had indicated the opposite." By 1956 the British intelligence services had neglected Egypt for several years, staffing their operation with low-caliber people and preferring to rely on self-serving fantasy rather than uncomfortable fact. The CIA had worked closely with Nasser and understood more clearly what was going on.

The British government had done every one of the worst possible things it could do with regard to its reputation in the Arab world. It had colluded with Israel; it had invaded a sovereign state on spurious grounds; it had prioritized oil and trade over honor and justice; it had raised the specter of imperialism, which it had been trying for years to bury; and, perhaps worst of all, the military operation it had done all these things to facilitate had failed. There was no point blaming the Americans for any of this. "Maybe we had there a 'historical folly,' as Barbara Tuchman was later to describe acts of leaders based on preconceived fixed notions while ignoring all contrary signs," Miles Copeland wrote. "But I thought then, as I think now, that the British thrive on folly, so they'll always soldier through somehow."[36]

In November, Selwyn Lloyd went to Washington. From his bed in Walter Reed Army Medical Center, the secretary of state asked the British foreign secretary, "Selwyn, why did you stop? Why didn't you go through with it and get Nasser down?"

"Well, Foster, if you had so much as winked at us we might have gone on," Lloyd replied.

Dulles, according to Lloyd's recollection, "replied that he could not have done that."

Lloyd was astonished by Dulles's line. "If ever there was an occasion when one could have been knocked down by the proverbial feather, this was it," he wrote.[37]

On November 20, the diplomat Douglas MacArthur II (nephew of the World War II general of the same name) had a meeting with Eisenhower at the White House. According to MacArthur, "the President brought up the question of the great undependability and unreliability of Nasser and the fact that it would be most desirable if he were eventually gotten rid of."[38] The expression of this sentiment at this point would have exasperated the British. Chester Cooper agreed that the administration in Washington "deplored" Nasser. "In the back of their minds (and perhaps locked in the vault of the National Security Council) may have been some more graceful and gradual approach toward Nasser's disposal or subvention," he wrote. "Eden and Mollet chose a blunter instrument, direct military attack. Eisenhower and Dulles refused to condone, let alone participate in, the carnal act. Instead, they chose a posture of high virtue and then paraded their chastity before the world. But this did not mean that the Administration was . . . above enjoying the rewards of sin, if they just happened to fall its way."[39]

Yet Allen Dulles, among many others, appeared to doubt the potential for getting Nasser down. "Politically, there is no organized opposition to Nasr," he told a congressional meeting at the White House on November 9. "As yet no one aspires to take his place."[40] The CIA agents in Egypt still tended to back Nasser. If there was a lesson for the United States government to take from Suez regarding its own practice, it was that the CIA in Washington often made substantial misjudgments, which it could have avoided had it paid closer attention to the reports provided by its own field agents.

Even Eden himself ultimately accepted that it would not have helped to see Musketeer through. In his memoirs, he wrote, "In the months after these events I repeatedly read and heard the comment, especially from the United States, even from those in high authority: 'If only you had gone on.'" But the United States government, he now realized, would never have changed its attitude—though he attributed this to the enmity he believed the Americans had against the British. "The United States Government had engaged their authority in the lead against us and would not have been appeased had Anglo-French forces occupied more of the canal or even the whole of it. In all probability they would only have been more indignant."[41]

Eisenhower proposed building up another leader of the Arabs to challenge Nasser—but not the British loyalist Nuri es-Said. According to MacArthur, "The President said he thought the person to build up was King Saud, who was a great spiritual leader and keeper of the holy places, etc."[42] After Suez, Eisenhower overcame his instinctive distaste for Middle Eastern monarchies to strengthen American ties with countries like Saudi Arabia and Jordan, which he hoped would contain Nasser's Egypt.[43]

In December, the British Labour MP Richard Crossman visited Israel and admitted to David Ben-Gurion that Britain "was now totally dependent on the will of the U.S." Ben-Gurion warned that this was dangerous. "It is imperative to establish a United States of Europe," said the Israeli prime minister, using Winston Churchill's phrase. "The existence of two free forces in the world, independent of each other but friendly and allied, will ensure world peace."[44] Yet over the following decades Britain would prove resistant to uniting Europe or taking a strong leadership role within it, allowing the United States greater and greater global sway.

Though they continued to be allies and would cooperate again within a year, the bad blood between Britain and the United States did not entirely ebb.[45] A decade later, Chester Cooper was on the White House staff. Lyndon Johnson, then president, wanted the British to join his war in Vietnam against Ho Chi Minh, "whom he regarded, just as Eden had once regarded Nasser, as the devil incarnate." Cooper was asked to persuade the British to back the Americans up. He approached his contacts in Whitehall, and suggested that at the very least the British might send medical teams. "The answer from Downing Street was 'Sorry. The Prime Minister would have great difficulty in the Commons. Most Members of Parliament think Washington is morally in the wrong. And many remember the American reaction to Suez.'"[46] At last, then, Suez may have done Britain an unexpected favor, by keeping it out of one of the twentieth century's messiest wars.

*   *   *

János Kádár returned to Budapest in a convoy of Soviet tanks and armored vehicles on November 7 to take up his position as leader of Hungary. When they reached parliament, he went inside and found his wife, Mária.

"You should have left this shit to Rákosi's lot," she said. "It shouldn't be you doing this."

Kádár's colleagues were shocked by his transformation. He had acquired more in Moscow than just a natty suit: his whole personality seemed to have changed from that of an amiable relative liberal to an imperious ruler.[47] Around November 10 or 11, the last of the armed rebels in Hungary were defeated by Soviet troops. Several thousand of the fifteen thousand or so Hungarians who had taken up arms were killed; more than half of the dead were under the age of twenty-five. The new regime issued an order to round up anyone connected to the revolution. More than a hundred thousand were arrested; thirty-five thousand faced trial; twenty-six thousand were jailed. It is thought that around six hundred were executed.[48] Nineteen-year-old rebel Csaba Varró was among those marked for death, though his sentence was commuted to life imprisonment. He remembered that the prisoners—many of whom, like him, were still in their teens—communicated by tapping in Morse code on the pipes of the heating system. His cell was next to the door through which people were dragged to the gallows. "The most harrowing scene was when they cried out: 'Please, don't avenge our deaths!'" he remembered. "Even those who were really innocent and still had to die, often cried out, 'Don't avenge our deaths!'"[49] It was a remarkable plea to cease all further bloodshed.

In Moscow, the mood was upbeat. Some students and staff at Moscow State University tried to spoil it by holding rallies denouncing the Soviet intervention in Hungary and shouting anti-Soviet slogans. KGB forces were dispatched to arrest them. A thorough purge of higher education was carried out to avert any further trouble.[50]

"The whole thing had been crushed in a single day," was how Veljko Mićunović characterized Khrushchev's view of Operation Whirlwind. "There had been practically no resistance. Kádár was a very good Communist and he would now extend and strengthen the government."[51] The Soviets left checkpoints to the west and south of Hungary unguarded for some weeks, perhaps hoping the rebel element would leave; two hundred thousand people made it to Austria or Yugoslavia before the borders were sealed again.

Despite his bullishness to Mićunović, Khrushchev had been badly shaken by the rebellion. At a New Year's party a few weeks later, he declared that he and his comrades were all Stalinists: a reversal of the Secret Speech. He made more statements in favor of Stalinism during the weeks after that. He felt he had tried to change too fast and lost control. In hindsight, 1956–57 would mark the high point of cooperation between China and the Soviet Union. The upsets in Poland

and Hungary confirmed Mao Tse-tung's view that Khrushchev was not mature or sophisticated enough to lead the Soviet Union. Mao began to make speeches implying that Khrushchev and his like were weak-spined and incapable of analysis: they were not good Marxist-Leninists, and "lack revolutionary morality."[52] Though the two men would theoretically continue to cooperate until 1960, fissures in the Moscow-Peking relationship were visible.

Khrushchev's remarks to the presidium on October 31 had linked Suez and Hungary. That day, he had thought Egypt was in danger of falling to imperialists. He could not allow a similar victory for Western interests—as he saw them—on his own periphery. Britain and France's action in Suez was a factor in Khrushchev moving his policy in Hungary away from tolerance and toward violence, both because he had to look tough and because he could. As a CIA report judged afterward, "the military conflict in the Middle East offered them [the Soviets] both the desired diversion of world politics and international public attention and an opportunity for new political interventions."[53]

Yet if Suez condemned Hungary, Hungary may have spared the world a greater conflict. The fact that the Soviet leaders' attention was taken up by Hungary for the crucial days of the crisis meant they had little time to consider the requests of Shukri al-Kuwatly and others to send troops to Egypt.[54] If the Soviets had intervened militarily in Egypt against Britain, France, and Israel at an early stage, the potential for the Suez crisis to explode into World War III might all too easily have been realized. As it was, Khrushchev could not give Suez his full attention until troops had been dispatched to Hungary on November 4. Bulganin's inflammatory letters were sent overnight on November 5–6. By November 6, Britain was facing a major economic crisis, violent protests in the streets, and international sanctions. Though Khrushchev believed his rocket threat was decisive, and it probably did have a psychological effect in London and Paris, Eisenhower had already taken the steps that would force Britain and France into retreat.

Had the Suez invasion not interrupted the Hungarian rebellion, paralyzing NATO and the United Nations, the Hungarian rebels might have received outside help. The rebels themselves hoped and pleaded for it; they had advocates in the American legation in Budapest and in Washington. Eisenhower was determined to avoid a direct confrontation with the Soviets. It is unlikely he would have sent American armed forces unilaterally. Yet something could have been done through international organizations, especially if nonaligned nations like India could have been brought on board. In the event, nothing was done. The message to other "captive peoples" was clear: if you rebel, the United States will not help you, and the Soviets will crush you with overwhelming force. There was discontent in other satellite states at the time. If things had gone better in Hungary, more rebellions might have been inspired. The whole history of Europe and the Cold War might have developed differently.

*   *   *

On November 21, it was announced that Anthony Eden was leaving London for three weeks on the orders of his doctor. Rab Butler would fill in for him temporarily. Two days later, Eden and his wife departed for Jamaica and Goldeneye, the beachside villa owned by James Bond creator Ian Fleming. This was a public relations disaster. The austerity-bound British public generally felt that a serving prime minister ought not reward himself for orchestrating the biggest foreign policy disaster of the postwar era with an extended holiday in the Caribbean. "Torquay and a sun-ray lamp would have been more

peaceful and patriotic," admitted Fleming's wife, Ann.[55] Lady
Eden attempted to defend the choice: "A spell in Berkshire or
somewhere would not have been any good, as Anthony would
simply have gone on working." He did anyway, issuing dozens
of cables from Goldeneye about the United Nations force, the
clearance of the Suez Canal, and the machinations of politics
in London.[56]

"Jamaica is a beautiful island, but sinister," wrote Lady
Eden. "There were strange tom-toms beating in the night—
but when I asked Violet, the cook, what was going on she said,
'Sal-va-tion Army.' I was not wholly convinced."[57] Though every James Bond novel had been written at Goldeneye, none of
007's cool rubbed off on the prime minister. Fleming was not
impressed with his guest, writing to a neighbor about Britain's performance in the Suez crisis: "In the whole of modern
history I can't think of a comparable shambles created by any
single country."[58]

Eden returned to London on December 14, still valiantly
arguing that he had meant all along for the United Nations
to come in to stop a Soviet advance. Few believed him, not
least since Guy Mollet had already blurted out the truth. On
December 9, the French prime minister told a press conference that there had been collusion with Israel and that Britain
and France had hidden it from the United States because they
knew Eisenhower would try to stop it.

On December 20, Denis Healey asked Eden in the House of
Commons whether Britain had had any foreknowledge of the
Israeli attack. "There were no plans got together [with Israel]
to attack Egypt," he replied. Commenting in 1994, Healey remembered: "He told a straight lie."[59] Cabinet members continued to insist that there had been no conspiracy. "The wild
accusations of collusion between the British, French, and Israeli Governments which were hurled by the Labour Party

had absolutely no foundation in fact," lied Lord Kilmuir in his 1964 memoirs.[60] That afternoon, Eden told the cabinet secretary Sir Norman Brook to destroy all records of Britain's collusion with Israel. Brook apparently did so the same day.[61] The attempt to cleanse the historical record did not work: far too many people knew the truth. As with most cases of the destruction of documents, all it did was make the perpetrators look even more guilty.

Guy Mollet continued as prime minister of France without any sense of shame. "I have only one regret: not to have been able to go all the way—but this was not determined by France," he said. "As far as I am concerned, I accept the entire responsibility of the Suez Operation, and I am convinced that I did my international duty."[62] Christian Pineau was frank about the Protocol of Sèvres negotiations and the extent of collusion in a 1965 interview with the John Foster Dulles Oral History Project at Princeton, then expanded this into a full account in his 1976 book on the subject of the Suez War.[63] In the longer term, though, Suez fueled discontent with the government inside the French army—discontent that eventually led to a greater crisis over Algeria in 1958 and the collapse of the French Fourth Republic.[64]

On December 22, British and French forces finally withdrew from the Suez Canal Zone, taking with them all their furniture, rugs, and chandeliers. The French also took a clock given to Ferdinand de Lesseps by the Empress Eugénie. The British took a marble bust of Napoleon.[65] The final few British and French troops embarked at Port Said the day before Christmas Eve alongside the colossal bronze statue of de Lesseps.

With the invading troops leaving Egyptian territory, cheering throngs hoisted Nasser's picture aloft. The next day, a large crowd assembled along the quayside in Port Said. A ring of explosives was set around de Lesseps's statue. With tremendous

force, the memorial to the Frenchman who had started it all
was blown up, its torso toppling forth into the water through a
great cloud of smoke and dust. All that remained of de Lesseps
were his boots and the stone pedestal. As a fitting memorial to
the whole affair, that was allowed to remain: a pair of boots
on a pedestal, to match the similar pair of boots on a pedestal
that had been a Stalin statue before the rebellion in Budapest.
Unfortunately, only one of these imperial influences had been
permanently vanquished.

*   *   *

The winner of the Suez War was Gamal Abdel Nasser. His
army had lost every battle. As it turned out, that did not matter.
Britain and France had to back down—as did Israel, eventually. Nasser secured the Suez Canal for Egypt. "The prestige of
Colonel Nasser in the Arab countries has never been greater,"
declared a headline in *Le Monde* on November 8.[66] It was not
just the Arab countries. Throughout the nonaligned and Communist world, Nasser was acclaimed as the Third World hero
who had defeated two great Western empires.

"In the end, the Suez affair became a personal business, a
duel between two men," wrote Mohamed Heikal. "It was a
situation that could only end in total victory for one and total
defeat for the other. Nasser won and he never felt one speck of
pity for Eden." When he saw Eden fall from power and lose his
health, Nasser remarked, "It was the Curse of the Pharaohs."[67]

Dwight D. Eisenhower emerged from the Suez and Hungarian crises with his international and domestic reputation
enhanced. He had publicly taken a stand in favor of what was
right, though that meant opposing two major NATO allies,
Britain and France, as well as the United States' best friend
and protégé in the Middle East, Israel. He was able to do this
without causing permanent damage to NATO. He refused to

be intimidated just before his own election by the threat of losing the Jewish vote if he took a stand against Israel, or of losing the conservative vote by siding with left-wing elements internationally. With the Hungary drama playing out along-side Suez, he drew a moral distinction between American and Soviet behavior—even if he did not intervene. Though the United States found itself on the same side as the Soviet Union over Suez, he avoided consorting with the Soviets to any extent that might have damaged his government's aims or endorsed their government's excesses. He had proven his credentials as a peacemaker on the world stage—not for the first time, but against the greatest odds, living up to his own declaration that the only way to win World War III was to prevent it. He also won his second presidential election. Eight years later, an American journalist asked Nasser what had saved him at Suez: was it the Soviets, the opposition in Britain, the United Nations, India, the Arabs? Nasser replied with one word: "Eisenhower."[68]

"I find it difficult to believe, but I have been told by sources in whom I have confidence that, at the UN, delegates from Third World countries were actually smiling at our delegates as they passed them in the halls," wrote CIA agent Miles Copeland. "But it didn't last, because . . . [of] something called the 'Eisenhower Doctrine.'"[69]

The Eisenhower Doctrine of 1957 would commit American troops to defend any Middle Eastern government "endangered by armed aggression from any nation controlled by international Communism." CIA agent Wilbur Eveland, listening to the draft speech, despaired: "Thinking perhaps of his boyhood in the Midwest, Eisenhower liked the term Mideast, and I sighed as it popped up all over the speech." More serious, though, was the worry he shared with the other CIA men who had known and supported Nasser all along: that the suits in Washington failed to understand Arab concerns, framing them all as being about "the danger that stems from international communism."

"Who, I wondered, had reached this determination of what the Arabs considered a danger?" Eveland wrote. "Israel's army had just invaded Egypt and still occupied all of the Sinai Peninsula and the Gaza Strip. And, had it not been for Russia's threat to intervene on behalf of the Egyptians, the British, French, and Israeli forces might now be sitting in Cairo, celebrating Nasser's ignominious fall from power."[70] According to Miles Copeland, "The Eisenhower Doctrine infuriated those Arab states which our political action campaigns were trying to bring into line, and only stimulated the prevailing inclinations to venality among our political mercenaries."[71]

As far as many Arabs were concerned, this was all part of the Americans' long-term plan to replace Britain and France as the biggest foreign player on the oil-rich sands of Middle East. "We thanked them," remembered Nasser's ally Amin Howeidy, later minister of defense and chief of general intelligence. "But everybody thought the Americans wanted to kill us by seizing our throats."[72] This may have been vividly expressed but was not far off the mark. "We must fill the vacuum of power which the British filled for a century" in the Middle East, Dulles said, "not merely the ability to act in an emergency but day in day out presence there."[73] The Eisenhower Doctrine declared that the United States would now assert its primacy as an international player in the Middle East. Britain's sterling crisis showed how weak its grip on that region really was, and how easily it could be lost if the oil dried up. The Suez crisis did not itself trigger political changes such as Britain's decolonization of Africa and Asia, but it exposed the existing trend of British decline and American ascendancy—and once that trend was exposed, it was unstoppable.[74]

"The genius of you Americans," Nasser told Copeland, "is that you never make clearcut stupid moves, only complicated stupid moves that make us wonder at the possibility that there may be something we are missing." He added that the Eisenhower Doctrine was "one of the shrewdest mistakes ever made by a Great Power diplomat." Copeland added that he realized later in life that "many of our 'stupid moves,' if that is what they were, were made for very good reasons and not by stupid people."[75]

The scheming of Britain, France, and the United States over oil, politics, and power helped create and fuel the problems of the Middle East for decades afterward. Nations and peoples were used as assets or weapons. The enemies of enemies were falsely considered to be friends. Lines were drawn in the sand, blown away, drawn again. All of this was done with precious little foresight about where it might lead.

There were plenty of well-informed, reasonable, and not at all stupid people within the British, French, and American administrative and intelligence systems that made these decisions. Many of them did warn their governments of the likely consequences of giving succor to extreme religious organizations, dividing territories, building up tyrants, and creating wars. Their advice was too often discarded. Men like Eden and Mollet—and frequently men like Foster and Allen Dulles—had their eyes on greater prizes and did not always want to hear the arguments against seizing them. But, for a signal moment in October and November 1956, the president of the United States of America did exactly the right thing for the right reasons. Britain and France's invasion was wrong. Even aside from its threat to Egypt's sovereignty and to the balance of power in the Middle East, and even aside from the catastrophic effect it had on their own foreign policy objectives, it seriously undermined the United Nations. It could have damaged it fatally, had it not been for the efforts of Lester Pearson. Many feared at the time that it might even trigger World War III—especially once the Soviets were involved. Eisenhower did not flinch. He just made it stop.

Eisenhower's refusal to let Britain and France win at Suez shifted the balance of power globally. Britain did not have to go along with everything the Americans wanted, as it would demonstrate during the Vietnam War—but if it tried to act outside the Commonwealth against the interests of the United States, Washington could and might slap it down. The whole world saw that some former colonial subjects could overtake their former colonial masters. During the Second World War, when the term *superpower* was coined to describe states that could exert extraordinary power on a global scale, there were considered to be three of them: the United States, the Soviet Union, and the British Empire. Now there were two.

FATES

During 1957, **Guy Mollet**'s government faced a worsening situation in Algeria as the rebellion grew. Though there were four hundred thousand French troops on the ground, the rebels would not be defeated—and after Suez, the Arab world was more united than ever against French rule. His government fell in June 1957. The French Fourth Republic collapsed entirely the following year. France reconstituted itself in 1958 as the Fifth Republic under the leadership of General **Charles de Gaulle**. Both Mollet and **Christian Pineau** continued their political careers, though neither again achieved such high office. Mollet lives on in the French language as *molletisme*, which means, in politics, pretending to be a left-winger to win an election, but then allying with right-wing forces or becoming an arch-conservative oneself on achieving power.

Ahmed Ben Bella, the Algerian rebel leader kidnapped by French forces on October 22, 1956, was imprisoned in France until 1962. When Algeria won its independence, he was released and became the country's first president. He was deposed in a coup in 1965 and was kept under house arrest for many years before eventually going into exile. He was finally allowed to return to Algeria in the 1990s, and witnessed the beginning of the Arab Spring before his death in 2012 at the age of ninety-three.

Maurice Challe, the French general who delivered the news of the Franco-Israeli plot to Eden, became disillusioned with the French government when it looked likely to give independence to Algeria in 1961. With three other retired generals, he attempted to stage a coup aimed at toppling President Charles de Gaulle and installing military rule in France and Algeria. It failed. Challe was sentenced to fifteen years in prison. He served five and was given an amnesty by de Gaulle in 1968.

On July 14, 1958, a group calling themselves the Free Officers, modeling themselves on Nasser and his associates, overthrew the government of Iraq. **King Feisal, Crown Prince Abdulillah,** and members of their family were taken into the palace courtyard and shot. Anthony Eden's friend **Nuri es-Said** attempted to flee the next day disguised as a woman. He was captured and killed. The naked corpses of Abdulillah and Nuri were "dragged through the streets of Baghdad amid scenes of unmentionable beastliness," Eden wrote.[1] The British embassy in Baghdad was ransacked and burned.[2]

John Bagot Glubb, "Glubb Pasha," moved back to Britain with his four children: Godfrey, who converted to Islam and became known as Faris; an adopted Bedouin daughter, Naomi; and two Palestinian refugees, John and Mary. Glubb Pasha wrote twenty books in retirement. He died in 1986. A service of thanksgiving for his life was held at Westminster Abbey, at which King Hussein of Jordan gave a speech praising his integrity and devotion to the Arab world.

Though he was widely seen as an impetuous and insecure young ruler at the time of the Suez crisis, **King Hussein of Jordan** ultimately became an assured monarch and a force for peace in the Middle East. Jordan became only the second Arab nation to make peace with Israel when he negotiated it in

1994; Egypt was the first, in 1979. When Hussein died in 1999, he was lauded by the leaders of the United States and Britain, as well as those of Israel and the Palestinian territories.

King Saud of Saudi Arabia subscribed to the Eisenhower Doctrine in 1957, which brought him into conflict with Egypt. Saud attempted to have his former ally Nasser assassinated in 1958, paying a Syrian intelligence officer £1.9 million to do the job. The hit failed and was exposed. Nasser's popularity was boosted by his survival; Saudi Arabia was deeply embarrassed. There was a lengthy power struggle between Saud and his brother Faisal, which Faisal won. Saud was deposed in 1964. He went into exile and was offered asylum by a forgiving Nasser. Yet he fell out with Nasser again in 1967 and lived his remaining two years in Greece. The United States has continued its close alliance with Saudi Arabia under successive monarchs.

The **CIA** made another attempt to stage a coup in Syria in April 1957, but it came to nothing. The agency tried once again over the summer of that year, but in August the Syrian authorities discovered the plot and kicked out the conspirators—including the United States military attaché. The Soviets benefited from these failed attempts to undermine Syria's government.[3] **Allen Dulles** resigned as director of the CIA after the disastrous Bay of Pigs invasion of Cuba in 1961. He destroyed most of his papers, excepting a few thin and magnificently uninformative files, which remain at Princeton University.

Following his battle with cancer in November 1956, **John Foster Dulles** convalesced in Key West, Florida. He recovered and returned to his position as secretary of state. In April 1959, though, his health finally forced him to resign. He died the following month.

Imre Nagy was given a guarantee of safe conduct from the Yugoslav embassy by the new leader of Hungary, **János Kádár**. This was not honored. When he left on November 23 with his fellow refugees and climbed onto a bus provided, he found it full of Soviet officers—who took them straight to Soviet headquarters. Tito was furious. Khrushchev was unrepentant. "As soon as Nagy was delivered to his apartment, he was put under arrest—as well he should have been!" he remembered.[4] In a secret trial, Nagy was found guilty of treason and of organizing the overthrow of the Hungarian state. He was hanged in July 1958, along with **Pál Maléter** and others. They were buried in a prison yard and later moved to unmarked graves, into which they were dumped facedown. The KGB realized afterward that this had been terrible for the image of Communism. Nagy and his colleagues would be the last people in the Soviet bloc to be sentenced to death after a political trial.[5] They were disinterred and reburied with full honors in 1989. It was estimated that two hundred thousand Hungarians attended Nagy's belated funeral.

Cardinal József Mindszenty, the Catholic leader who had been imprisoned for eight years under Communist rule in Hungary, enjoyed his freedom for just four days in 1956. He remained in the American legation in Budapest for the following fifteen years. Eventually, in 1971, the Hungarian government allowed him to leave the country. He spent his remaining years in exile in Vienna, dying in 1975.

Frank Wisner, the CIA agent who had most wanted the United States to aid the rebellion in Hungary, suffered a mental breakdown and was hospitalized in 1957. He killed himself with a shotgun in 1965.

Nikita Khrushchev remained leader of the Soviet Union for a few more turbulent years, involving himself in the Cuban

Revolution and the Cuban Missile Crisis, authorizing the building of the Berlin Wall, and falling out with Mao Tse-tung's China. In 1964, he was ousted by a consortium led by the chairman of the presidium, Leonid Brezhnev. When Brezhnev died in 1982, he was succeeded by **Yuri Andropov**, who had been Soviet ambassador to Hungary at the time of the 1956 rebellion.

Josip Broz Tito continued liberalizing as president of Yugoslavia, relaxing travel restrictions and allowing the Catholic church to operate. He reduced his active role in government from the mid-1970s, and died in 1980.

By the early 1960s, the Soviets began to realize that they needed to allow Hungary more leeway. Kádár softened the most egregious aspects of Communist rule. There was an echo of the Hungarian rebellion in the Prague Spring of 1968 in Czechoslovakia, which was crushed by five invading armies: those of the Soviet Union, Poland, East Germany, Bulgaria—and Hungary. The **Eastern Bloc** endured until the 1980s, when the Soviet Union began to weaken and its leader, Mikhail Gorbachev, began a process of *glasnost* (openness). From 1989, Communist governments fell mostly peacefully in Poland, Hungary, East Germany, Bulgaria, and Czechoslovakia, and violently in Romania. These, and the final collapse of the Soviet Union in 1991, ended Communism as a system in Eastern Europe and Soviet-controlled Asia.

Lester B. Pearson, the Canadian secretary of state for external affairs, was credited with creating the United Nations Expeditionary Force on November 4, 1956, ending Britain and France's claim to be peacekeepers in Suez. In recognition, he was awarded the Nobel Prize for Peace in 1957. John Foster Dulles, who was closely aligned with Pearson but was incapacitated during those crucial days, never received the Nobel Prize he was said to have coveted. Pearson served as prime minister of Canada from 1963 to 1968.

David Ben-Gurion stepped down from the Israeli prime ministership in 1963 for "personal reasons," partly to do with continuing political fallout from the Lavon affair. He continued to be involved in politics, notably during the Six-Day War, until he finally retired in 1970 to his kibbutz in the Negev desert. He died in 1973, immediately after the Yom Kippur War.

Ariel Sharon faced an inquiry as to whether he had overstepped his orders during the Suez War by sending a large force into the Mitla Pass on October 31 instead of a reconnaissance group, and whether he had disobeyed orders by engaging in a battle. This further exacerbated his feud with **Moshe Dayan**, who believed him to have been guilty.[6] Such was Sharon's intimacy with Ben-Gurion that he was soon forgiven and was sent to study military science at the British Army's Staff College in Camberley, England, in 1957. He returned to Israel and played a commanding role in the Six-Day War, the Yom Kippur War, and the Lebanon War. He served as Israel's prime minister from 2001 to 2006, when he was incapacitated by a stroke. Under his leadership, Israel controversially disengaged from the Gaza Strip, withdrawing the IDF and bulldozing Jewish settlements. Sharon died in 2014. **Shimon Peres**, the key negotiator between France and Israel, served twice as Israel's prime minister and as its president from 2007 to 2014.

Sir Anthony Eden resigned from the British prime ministership on January 9, 1957. On January 18, he left for another holiday, as far away as possible: the prime minister of New Zealand invited him to spend the rest of Britain's winter in the Southern Hemisphere's summer. To the surprise of some who doubted his health, he lived for another twenty years—and never gave up protesting his righteousness over Suez. Despite the disaster of Suez, Britain did retain some influence in the Middle East. On four further occasions, it considered military action against Nasser again: the 1957 Syrian crisis, the aftermath of the Iraq revolution in 1958, the 1964 Yemen crisis, and in 1967 during the blockade of the Straits of Tiran.[7]

After Eden's resignation, **Queen Elizabeth II** was presented with a choice between **Harold Macmillan** and **Rab Butler** as her next prime minister. Macmillan had been a Suez hawk; Butler had been more cautious. Even so, the pressure of right-wing forces within the Conservative party ensured that it was recommended to the queen that she choose Macmillan. "In the myopic eyes of the Tory die-hards, Butler had helped to give India away and had revamped Conservative policy after 1945 so that it was indistinguishable from pale pink Socialism," wrote **Anthony Nutting**; "and now he was accused of having given in to blackmail from America and the United Nations and surrendered the last position of strength from which we might have negotiated a settlement of the Suez Canal question on our terms."[8] The queen accepted the party's recommendation and chose Macmillan. At Eden's request, the new prime minister destroyed his apparently candid diaries of the Suez crisis, dating between October 4, 1956, and February 3, 1957.[9]

When his second term as president of the United States ended in 1961, **Dwight D. Eisenhower** retired to his farm in Gettysburg, Pennsylvania. His vice president, **Richard Nixon**, lost the election to the Democrat John F. Kennedy. Eisenhower died in 1969. Nixon served as president from 1969 to 1974, his second term ending in resignation and humiliation following the Watergate scandal.

Gamal Abdel Nasser remained a towering figure in Arab and African politics. He led the United Arab Republic of Egypt and Syria for its brief existence. He resigned as leader of Egypt after his defeat at the hands of Israel in the Six-Day War, but withdrew his resignation the next day. In 1968, he began the War of Attrition against Israel. He died of a heart attack just after an Arab League summit in 1970, prompting mass mourning throughout the Arab world.

The **Suez Canal** reopened to shipping, except for Israeli vessels, on April 9, 1957. Thereafter, it was managed by the Egyptian Suez Canal Authority, the nationalized successor to the Suez Canal Company. British and French claims that Egyptians would be unable to run the canal themselves proved unfounded. Its revenues now provide the government of Egypt with around $450 million a month. A second Suez Canal was opened in 2015.

ACKNOWLEDGMENTS

I would like to thank my exceptionally wise and insightful editors, Iain MacGregor at Simon & Schuster in London and Jennifer Barth at HarperCollins in New York, for everything they have done for this book. Thanks also to the excellent teams at both publishers, including Harriet Dobson, Jo Edgecombe, Mathew Johnson, Martin Lubikowski, Humphrey Price, and Sue Stephens at Simon & Schuster, and Nikki Baldauf, Leah Carlson-Stanisic, Gregg Kulick, Renata Marchione, Erin Wicks, and Martin Wilson at HarperCollins. I would also like to thank my brilliant agents, Natasha Fairweather and Yasmin McDonald, and everyone at United Agents, for all their help.

Thanks to the excellent staff at a number of archives and libraries, many of whom have been of immense help in identifying and tracking down material. These include, in the United States, the National Archives at Archives II in College Park, Maryland, especially Connie Beach who retrieved a file for me in record time which I would otherwise have missed; the Seeley G. Mudd Manuscript Library at Princeton, New Jersey; the Library of Congress. In Britain, the National Archives, Kew; the British Library; the London Library. In France, the Archives Diplomatiques in Paris. I would also like to thank Gladstone's Library in Hawarden for being the best possible place to write.

This book owes a debt to the work of the late Keith Kyle, whose book *Suez* (originally published in 1991) was a landmark archival history on the subject. Sadly, I did not have the privilege of meeting Mr Kyle, but I was lucky enough to meet his widow, Susan, in 2013. I would like to thank her for our interesting conversation. I would also like to thank Uri Avnery for a fascinating discussion at his home in Tel Aviv in March 2015, which I have quoted from several times in this book. Warm thanks to Professor Avi Shlaim of St Anthony's College, Oxford, who very kindly read through a version of the manuscript before publication. Any mistakes that remain are of course my responsibility.

I would like to thank all those who helped me to understand this book's historical locations in Hungary, Israel, and the Palestinian Territories, especially Haim Berger for showing me Sde Boker and the Negev, and Yamen Elabed of Green Olive Tours for a fascinating tour around the West Bank; also Aysha Raja for her improbable enthusiasm for visiting Port Said and the Suez Canal with me. Thanks also to my generous and wonderful hosts on my research trips: Nesrine Malik and Declan Walsh in Cairo, Huma Imtiaz and Timothy Homan in Washington, DC, and Dora Napolitano, Federico Fernándes, Julia, Damian, Elsa, and Tomi in Paris.

Thank you to everyone who has given advice, offered me leads, discussed the subject, or contributed in other ways. These include Jad Adams, Rafay Alam, Anthony Bale, Adi Bloom, Faisal Devji, Kareem Fahim, Nicky Goldberg, Maya Jasanoff, Vedica Kant, David Kirkpatrick, Wm. Roger Louis, Henry Lovat, Amira el Nemr, Matthew Parker, Timothy Phillips, Sasha Polakow-Suransky, Imogen Robertson, Rachel Shabi, Catherine Shoard, Thomas Small, Nicole Taylor, Eugénie von Tunzelmann, David Wearing, Andrew Whitehurst, Maor Wolf,

Robyn Young, and dozens more to whom I must apologize for not naming individually.

Finally, I would like to thank my parents, Carol Dyhouse and Nick von Tunzelmann, for their love and support, which I am delighted to return; and to Mike Witcombe: *köszönöm, ani ohevet otcha, habibi.*

NOTES

Abbreviations in notes

AWD—Allen Welsh Dulles

DBG—David Ben-Gurion

DDE—Dwight David Eisenhower

GAN—Gamal Abdel Nasser

JFD—John Foster Dulles

NSK—Nikita Sergeyevich Khrushchev

RAE—(Robert) Anthony Eden

ADLC—Archives Diplomatiques, La Courneuve, Paris, France

AWDP—Allen Welsh Dulles Papers, Seeley G. Mudd Manuscript Library, Princeton University

DDEP—Dwight D. Eisenhower Library Papers relating to John Foster Dulles, Public Policy Papers, Seeley G. Mudd Manuscript Library, Princeton University

FRUS—Foreign Relations of the United States; published as a series in hard copy or available online at http://uwdc.library.wisc.edu/collections/FRUS

JFDP—John Foster Dulles Papers, Public Policy Papers, Seeley G. Mudd Manuscript Library, Princeton University

JFDOHP—John Foster Dulles Oral History Project, Seeley G. Mudd Manuscript Library, Princeton University

USNA—United States National Archives, Archives II, College Park, Maryland

UKNA—United Kingdom National Archives, Kew

Prologue: "I Want Him Murdered"

1. In his 1967 memoir, *No End of a Lesson*, Nutting said Eden's words were "I want him destroyed, can't you understand?" The proofs for the book said "removed" rather than "destroyed"; see Philip Murphy, "Telling Tales Out of School: Nutting, Eden and the Attempted Suppression of *No End of a Lesson*," in Smith, *Reassessing Suez 1956*, 208. In 1984, though, Nutting admitted that he had toned down Eden's language. He told the makers of the Channel 4 documentary *End of Empire* that Eden had said "Can't you understand that I want Nasser murdered?" "He actually used that word," Nutting added, emphatically. Lapping, *End of Empire*, 262.

2. Anthony Nutting, *No End of a Lesson* (London: Constable, 1967), 33–35.

3. GAN, Mar. 10, 1953, BBC Summary of World Broadcasts, 1952–1970; in James, *Nasser at War*, 1.

4. Eveland, *Ropes of Sand*, 100–1.

5. Lapping, *End of Empire*, 263–64.

6. Steve Morewood, "Prelude to the Suez Crisis: The Rise and Fall of British Dominance over the Suez Canal, 1869–1956," in Smith, *Reassessing Suez 1956*, 14.

7. Ferdinand de Lesseps in Kyle, *Suez*, 15.

8. Lord Palmerston to Lord Cowley, quoted in Evelyn Baring, *Modern Egypt* (1910; Cambridge, UK: Cambridge University Press, 2010), 72n.

9. Yergin, *Prize*, 19–39.

10. Georges Clemenceau to Woodrow Wilson, Dec. 15, 1917, in Yergin, *Prize*, 161.

11. Admiral Sir Edmond Slade in Barr, *Line in the Sand*, 65.

12. RAE, House of Commons Debates, vol. 318, Nov. 24, 1936, col. 256.

13. Recommending the Anglo-Egyptian treaty to the House of Commons, RAE stated that "the United Kingdom is entitled under the Treaty to be assured that the Canal will be adequately protected by the alliance for all time." RAE in Parliamentary Debates (Hansard), 5th series, vol. 318 (House of Commons), Nov. 24, 1936, col. 259.

14. Eden, *Full Circle*, 224.

15. Carlton, *Eden*, 129–30.

16. WSC in McNamara, *Britain, Nasser and the Balance of Power in the Middle East*, 15; original in *British Documents on the End of Empire*, series A, vol. 1, doc. 25.

17. WSC in McNamara, *Britain, Nasser and the Balance of Power in the Middle East*, 17–18.

18. See Carlton, *Eden*, 258.

19. Frank Pakenham, Earl of Longford, *Eleven at No. 10: A Personal View of Prime Ministers 1931–1984* (London: Harrap, 1984), 83–84.

20. See Carlton, *Eden*, 11–12. The "uncontrolled rages" quote comes from Lord Moran, Winston Churchill's doctor.

21. Kyle, *Suez*, 40; Neguib, *Egypt's Destiny*, 94.

22. RAE in Kyle, *Suez*, 44.

23. Khrushchev, *Khrushchev Remembers*, 431.

24. Copeland, *Game of Nations*, 68.

25. Conversation in Winn, *Nasser*, 51.

26. Chester Cooper and ex-king Farouk in Cooper, *Lion's Last Roar*, 53. On Farouk's luggage, see Fullick and Powell, *Suez: The Double War*, 2.

27. Mahgoub, *Democracy on Trial*, 73.

28. Khrushchev, *Khrushchev Remembers*, 433.

29. Copeland, *Game of Nations*, 90.

30. "I think Jock Colville was deeply mistaken in suggesting that towards the end of his tenure WSC had felt 'a cold hatred' for his successor. It was more irritation at being under pressure to depart and grave doubts about the consequences." Montague Browne, *Long Sunset*, 213.

31. Ibid., 132.

32. Carlton, *Eden*, 296.

33. Shuckburgh, *Descent to Suez*, 76.

34. See John S. D. Eisenhower, *Soldiers and Statesmen: Reflections on Leadership* (Columbia: University of Missouri Press, 2012), 17–19.

35. Dwight D. Eisenhower, *Crusade in Europe* (1948; Baltimore: Johns Hopkins University Press, 1997), 61–62.

36. Eden, *Full Circle*, 253.

37. Ibid., 256.

38. Cecil B. DeMille, *The Autobiography of Cecil B. DeMille*, ed. Donald Hayne (London: W. H. Allen, 1960), 386.

39. It would perhaps have been slightly less appropriate to note GAN's resemblance to Wilcoxon when he appeared as Richard the Lionheart, enemy of the great Muslim hero Saladin, in DeMille's *The Crusades* (1936)—though that film is surprisingly generous to Saladin.

40. For full details of this agreement, see Charles B. Selak Jr., "The Suez Canal Base Agreement of 1954: Its Background and Implications," *American Journal of International Law* 49, no. 4 (Oct. 1955): 487–505.

41. GAN, 1953, in James, *Nasser at War*, 5.

42. See James, *Nasser at War*, 5–6.

43. Steve Morewood, "Prelude to the Suez Crisis: The Rise and Fall of British Dominance over the Suez Canal, 1869–1956," in Smith, *Reassessing Suez 1956*, 30.

44. Galpern, *Money, Oil, and Empire*, 144.

45. David Cannadine, *Ornamentalism*, 190.

46. Eden, *Full Circle*, 500.

47. Mahgoub, *Democracy on Trial*, 23–24.

48. J. C. Hurewitz, "The Historical Context," in Louis and Owen, *Suez 1956*, 20.

49. Kyle, *Suez*, 43. Kyle was explicitly told this by Julian Amery, a Conservative MP and member of the Suez Group in the 1950s.

50. Herbert Morrison, Sept. 27, 1951, in Kyle, *Suez*, 8.

51. Eden, *Full Circle*, 426.

52. Otto von Bismarck in R. W. Seton-Watson, *Britain in Europe 1789–1914: A Survey of Foreign Policy* (Cambridge, UK: Cambridge University Press, 1937), 553.

53. Eden, *Full Circle*, 313.

54. These comments are from, respectively, Rab Butler, Nigel Nicolson, and Lord Kilmuir. Carlton, *Eden*, 376. Carlton cautions against reading these accounts as fully representative of RAE's leadership, but there are so many similar descriptions that they cannot be entirely discounted.

55. Trevelyan, *Middle East in Revolution*, 64.

56. Nutting, *No End of a Lesson*, 17. Rhodes James, *Eden*, 431n; footnote disputes Nutting's account of that night. Nutting claimed he stayed up half the night persuading RAE not to sever relations with Jordan; James claims RAE had no memory of such a meeting. RAE's memory was not always reliable on Suez-related subjects, as his own memoirs repeatedly demonstrate.

57. Lawrence Tal, "Jordan," in Sayigh and Shlaim, *Cold War and the Middle East*, 112; Shlaim, *Lion of Jordan*, 97–98.

58. John Bagot Glubb in Nutting, *No End of a Lesson*, 30.

59. Eden, *Full Circle*, 348.

60. Lawrence Tal, "Jordan," in Sayigh & Shlaim, *Cold War and the Middle East*, 112. GAN sent Anwar Sadat and Abdel Hakim Amer.

61. GAN speaking to the BBC, in Moncrieff, *Suez Ten Years After*, 34. See also Heikal, *Cairo Documents*, 85–86.

62. Trevelyan, *Middle East in Revolution*, 71; see also Nutting, *No End of a Lesson*, 28.

63. Nigel Nicolson, "Diary of a Suez Rebel," London *Daily Telegraph*, Oct. 27, 1996.

64. Lord Home in Hennessy, *Muddling Through*, 131.

65. Rhodes James, *Eden*, 457.

66. Aswan High Dam press release from US Department of State, July 19, 1956. Aswan Dam, 1956: JFDP, Box 100, Reel 38; Public Policy Papers.

67. JFD to Herbert Hoover & embassies, Sept. 27, 1955, FRUS 1955–57, vol. 14, doc. 314, p. 526.

68. JFD, Memorandum of a conversation at the Department of State, Oct. 3, 1955, FRUS 1955–57, vol. 14, doc. 323, p. 543.

69. RAE in Nutting, *No End of a Lesson*, 23.

70. Eden, *Full Circle*, 420.

71. Cooper, *Lion's Last Roar*, 95.

72. Ibid., 92.

73. Otto Passman in Burns, *Economic Aid and American Policy Toward Egypt*, 48–49.

74. JFD telephone call to AWD, 3:40 p.m. Memoranda of Telephone Conversation, General, DDEP, box 10.

75. Eisenhower, *Strictly Personal*, 187. DDE had suffered stomach problems for years, but the pain became acute on June 7, 1956, and he was admitted to Walter Reed Army Medical Center in Washington, DC. Ileitis was diagnosed and he required an immediate operation. DDE had been expected to spend fifteen days in the hospital but, owing to a persistent infection after the surgery, he was not released until June 30 and was then sent to convalesce in his home in Gettysburg, PA.

76. Mohamed Heikal, informed apparently by Ahmed Hussein, denies that Hussein used this wording, in Heikal, *Cutting the Lion's Tail*, 115. Yet the well-informed CIA agent Wilbur Eveland confirms it in Eveland, *Ropes of Sand*, 194n. The substance of what was said chimes with the memorandum of the conversation written by William M. Rountree, assistant secretary of state. Rountree reports that Hussein said that the Soviets had made a "very generous offer" and warned that GAN might have to accept it if the US could not do a deal soon. See Burns, *Economic Aid and American Policy Toward Egypt*, 95.

77. JFD in Heikal, *Cutting the Lion's Tail*, 115.

78. In Mosley, *Dulles*, 403.

79. JFD news conference, Apr. 2, 1957. Aswan Dam, 1956: JFDP, Box 100, Reel 38.

80. JFD telephone call from Senator William F. Knowland, Thursday, July 19, 1956, 5:10 p.m. Memoranda of Telephone Conversation: General, DDEP, box 10.

81. William B. Macomber Jr., JFDOHP. When he gave this interview, Macomber was not absolutely sure whether he said "I hope so," as reproduced here, or something similar along those lines.

82. Miles Copeland in Eveland, *Ropes of Sand*, 193.

83. RAE via William Clark in Lapping, *End of Empire*, 262. See also Shuckburgh, *Descent to Suez*, June 20, 1956, p. 256: RAE had already decided Britain would pull out of funding the dam a month earlier, and Shuckburgh predicted the Soviets would finance it instead.

84. Copeland, *Game Player*, 200.

85. Ibid., 170.

86. Heikal, *Cutting the Lion's Tail*, 114. The point about the grape juice seems coy: according to CIA agent Wilbur Eveland, GAN served whisky to his guests, and it is implied he took some himself. See Eveland, *Ropes of Sand*, 101–2. Perhaps this was evidence for a story Christian Pineau told: "To understand the Arabs, it must be remembered that the Quran always carries two interpretations. So my [Moroccan] interlocuters refused the wine with dinner but accepted whisky in the evening, for if the sacred text forbade consuming alcohol as a drink, it did not prohibit it as a medication for exhausted diplomats." Pineau, *1956/Suez*, 29.

87. Jawaharlal Nehru in Heikal, *Cutting the Lion's Tail*, 116; see also Heikal, *Cairo Documents*, 74.

88. Heikal, *Cutting the Lion's Tail*, xiii. See also Laura M. James, "When Did Nasser Expect War? The Suez Nationalization and Its Aftermath in Egypt," in Smith, *Reassessing Suez 1956*, 149–55, on his reaction to JFD's statement.

89. Conversation in Mosley, *Dulles*, 404. Heikal, *Cutting the Lion's Tail*, 116, confirms that Nasser and Byroade talked and Byroade was upset, but does not detail the conversation.

90. The Indian historian Sarvepalli Gopal—who knew Nehru well—insisted that news of the nationalization came to Nehru "as an unpleasant surprise." Mohamed Heikal agreed: "Nehru had necessarily not been told in advance about nationalization and was in consequence both hurt and angry." Sarvepalli Gopal, "India and the Non-Aligned Nations," in Louis and Owen, *Suez 1956*, 157; Heikal, *Cutting the Lion's Tail*, 134. Conversely, Trevelyan also believed that GAN had been planning to nationalize the Canal Company in the event of American withdrawal for at least a month. Trevelyan, *Public and Private*, 78. See also James, *Nasser at War*, 22–23 on the question, which cannot precisely be answered, of when exactly GAN decided to nationalize the Canal Company.

91. Humphrey Trevelyan in Robertson, *Crisis*, 69.

92. Cooper, *Lion's Last Roar*, 45.

93. GAN in Lapping, *End of Empire*, 264. See also Heikal, *Cairo Documents*, 94; and Sayyid Mar'i, Political Papers, in Troen and Shemesh, *Suez-Sinai Crisis 1956*, 360–61.

94. Lucas, *Divided We Stand*, 139; Aburish, *Nasser*, 107–8.

95. Eden, *Full Circle*, 190.

96. NSK in Khrushchev, *Last Testament*, 340.

97. Kilmuir, *Political Adventure*, 268. The Earl of Kilmuir was present that night and his account of the proceedings, though skimpy on political detail, is precise on matters of dress. There is a better eyewitness account of the political aspects of the evening by Hugh Gaitskell in Gaitskell, *Diary*, July 26, 1956, pp. 552–53.

98. Eden, *Full Circle*, 426.

99. Stock, *Israel on the Road to Sinai*, 191, 264n.

100. Nutting, *No End of a Lesson*, 49–50. See Eden, *Full Circle*, 474–75 for his defense of his point of view.

101. Eden, *Full Circle*, 419.

102. Nuri es-Said as recalled by William Clark, in Lapping, *End of Empire*, 264. Similar version (without "hit him by yourself") in Heikal, *Cutting the Lion's Tail*, 130.

103. Nutting, *No End of a Lesson*, 47–48.

104. Cooper, *Lion's Last Roar*, 106.

105. Pineau, *1956/Suez*, 175.

106. Memorandum of Conversation, July 27, 1956, FRUS 1955–57, vol. 16, doc. 3, pp. 5–7.

107. Herbert Hoover to JFD, July 28, 1956, FRUS 1955–57, vol. 16, doc. 14, p. 25.

108. Winston S. Churchill, Address at Westminster College, Fulton, Missouri, Mar. 5, 1946.

109. Butler, *Art of the Possible*, 189.

Chapter 1: "We Must Keep the Americans Really Frightened"

1. Evans, *Algeria*, 88.

2. *Dictionary of African Biography*, ed. Emmanuel K. Akyeampong and Henry Louis Gates Jr., 429–30.

3. Guy Mollet, radio broadcast, Feb. 9, 1956, in Evans, *Algeria*, 151.

4. Note, Relations franco-égyptiennes, Direction d'Afrique-Levant, June 13, 1956, ADLC: 213QONT/510/EG-Politique française vis-à-vis de l'Egypte.

5. C. Douglas Dillon, JFDOHP.

6. Christian Pineau, Aug. 1, 1956, in Maurice Vaïsse, "France and the Suez Crisis," in Louis and Owen, *Suez 1956*, 137.

7. DBG, Diary, Oct. 23, 1956, in Troen and Shemesh, *Suez-Sinai Crisis 1956*, 310.

8. CIA NSC Briefing, Algeria, Aug. 28, 1956, USNA: CIA-RDP79R00890A000700080023–7.

9. CIA Office of National Estimates, "North African Reactions to Recent French Moves," Staff Memorandum No. 88–56, Nov. 2, 1956, USNA: CIA-RDP79T00937A000500020010–5.

10. *New York Times*, Oct. 24, 1956, 4.

11. Ibid., 1. Brady was released the next morning.

12. Ben Bella in Merle, *Ahmed Ben Bella*, 116–23.

13. Habib Bourguiba in "Rebel Chiefs Captured in Algeria," London *Times*, Oct. 23, 1956, 10.

14. Pineau, *1956/Suez*, 127.

15. Fullick and Powell, *Suez: The Double War*, 80.

16. See Trita Parsi, *Treacherous Alliance: The Secret Dealings of Israel, Iran, and the United States* (2007; New Haven, CT: Yale University Press, 2008), p. 23. Israeli leaders went to great lengths to keep the Tipline pumping after the Yom Kippur War of 1973, but the Iranians stopped its use altogether after the Iranian Revolution of 1979.

17. Gaitskell, *Diary*, July 30, 1956, 560.

18. Peres, *Battling for Peace*, 119.

19. Bar-Zohar, *The Armed Prophet*, 226–27; Shlaim, "Conflicting Approaches," 194. DBG had presented a plan to capture the Straits of Tiran to the Israeli cabinet on Dec. 5, 1955.

20. DBG in Bar-Zohar, *Armed Prophet*, 12.

21. H. H. Asquith in Barr, *Line in the Sand*, 35.

22. The story of the Sykes-Picot agreement and its influence on the Balfour Declaration is told brilliantly and in much more detail in Barr, *Line in the Sand*, 20–56.

23. Shuckburgh, *Descent to Suez*, 211.

24. Neville Chamberlain in Barr, *Line in the Sand*, 196.

25. DBG in *The Jewish Plan for Palestine: Memoranda and Statements Presented by the Jewish Agency for Palestine to the United Nations Special Committee on Palestine* (Jerusalem: Jewish Agency for Palestine, Sept. 1947), 310.

26. Shlaim, *Israel and Palestine*, xi.

27. DBG in Bar-Zohar, *Armed Prophet*, 172–73.

28. Kamal al-Din Hussein, in James, *Nasser at War*, 7.

29. David Tal, "The 1956 Sinai War: A Watershed in the History of the Arab-Israeli Conflict," in Smith, *Reassessing Suez 1956*, 136.

30. The British ambassador to Egypt in 1956 actively encouraged GAN to emulate Mustapha Kemal, in terms of having no ambitions toward territorial expansion. GAN had apparently red *Grey Wolf*, a biography of Mustapha Kemal by Harold Courtenay Armstrong, seven times. Trevelyan, *Middle East in Revolution*, 73.

31. Author's interview with Uri Avnery, Tel Aviv, Mar. 2015.

32. Moshe Sharett, diary entry for Mar. 12, 1956, in Black and Morris, *Israel's Secret Wars*, 130.

33. Copeland, *Game Player*, 201.

34. Trevelyan, *Middle East in Revolution*, 14.

35. *New York Times*, Oct. 23, 1956, 7.

36. Nutting, *No End of a Lesson*, 101.

37. Lloyd, *Suez 1956*, 4.

38. Kyle, *Suez*, 87.

39. Selwyn Lloyd's Personal Diary, Oct. 22, 1956, UKNA: FO 800/716.

40. Sir Donald Logan in Chris Brady, "In the Company of Policy Makers: Sir Donald Logan, Assistant Private Secretary to the Secretary of State for Foreign Affairs," in Kelly and Gorst, *Whitehall and the Suez Crisis*, 146.

41. Mordechai Bar-On, "David Ben-Gurion and the Sèvres Collusion," in Louis and Owen, *Suez 1956*, 157. Bar-On quotes his own diary from Oct. 22, 1956. He adds, "Having read, many years later, Lloyd's most honest, humble, and humane memoirs, I have realized that those earlier impressions must have reflected either my Israeli prejudice or Lloyd's own utmost embarrassment."

42. Sir Donald Logan in Hennessy, *Muddling Through*, 141.

43. Pineau, *1956/Suez*, 128.

44. Harold Beeley in Hennessy, *Muddling Through*, 140.

45. DDE, Diary, Jan. 6, 1953, in Bowie and Immerman, *Waging Peace*, 213.

46. DDE, Annual Message to the Congress on the State of the Union, Jan. 5, 1956.

47. Montague Brown, *Long Sunset*, 126.

48. Unnamed US diplomat, 1954, in Cooper, *Lion's Last Roar*, 62.

49. "Dulles Formulated and Conducted U.S. Foreign Policy for More Than Six Years," *New York Times*, May 25, 1959.

50. Eveland, *Ropes of Sand*, 95; see also Kinzer, *Brothers*, 16.

51. Charles E. Bohlen, JFDOHP.

52. Eveland, *Ropes of Sand*, 95.

53. For a fuller version of the story of the Guatemala affair, see Tunzelmann, *Red Heat*, 56–59.

54. Charles E. Bohlen, JFDOHP.

55. JFD, May 8, 1953. Immerman, *Empire of Liberty*, 180.

56. Sir Roger Makins to FO, July 30, 1956, UKNA: PREM 11/1098.

57. Selwyn Lloyd to Sir Gladwyn Jebb in Paris, July 30, 1956, UKNA, PREM 11/1098.

58. DDE to RAE, July 31, 1956, UKNA: PREM 11/1098.

59. Eden, *Full Circle*, 436. See Rhodes James, *Eden*, 471–73.

60. Record of a meeting held in the Secretary of State's room in the House of Commons on July 31 at 9:00 p.m., July 31, 1956, UKNA: PREM 11/1098.

61. Macmillan, *Cabinet Years*, Aug 1, 1956, 580.

62. Copeland, *Game Player*, 198.

63. DDE confirmed this personally; see Dwight D. Eisenhower, JFDOHP. See also Nutting, *No End of a Lesson*, 52–53.

64. Cooper, *Lion's Last Roar*, 63, 77 (see also Robert Murphy, *Diplomat Among Warriors*, 468); and Shuckburgh, *Descent to Suez*, 186. See also Lucas, *Divided We Stand*, 35–36.

65. Robert Murphy, JFDOHP.

66. JFD in Eden, *Full Circle*, 437.

67. Charles E. Bohlen, JFDOHP. See also William B. Macomber's oral history in the same series.

68. Maurice Couve de Murville to Ministry for External Affairs, Aug. 4, 1956, ADLC: 213QONT/493/EG-xiv-1.

69. Eden, *Full Circle*, 437.

70. See Gladwyn Jebb in Kyle, *Suez*, 178.

71. Memorandum of a Conference with the President, July 31, 1956, FRUS 1955–57, vol. 16, doc. 34, p. 64.

72. Sir Alec Clutterbuck, high commissioner to India, in 1954. See Sunil Khilnani, "Nehru's Evil Genius," *Outlook India*, Mar. 19, 2007. RAE in Kyle, *Suez*, 277; see also 280.

73. JFD, Memorandum of a Conversation with the President, Aug. 8, 1956, FRUS, 1955–57, vol. 16, doc. 71, p. 164.

74. RAE in Butler, *Art of the Possible*, 188.

75. RAE to Jawaharlal Nehru, Aug. 12, 1956, UKNA: PREM 11/1094; RAE to DDE, Aug. 5, 1956, UKNA: PREM 11/1098.

76. Eden, *Full Circle*, 431.

77. Macmillan, *Cabinet Years*, July 27, 1956, 578.

78. C. Douglas Dillon in Paris to JFD, July 31, 1956, State Department Central Decimal Files, Suez Crisis, 974.7301/7–1056, USNA: RG 59/250/44/4/4. Echoing Mollet, RAE wrote about GAN's "horrible little book called *A Philosophy of Revolution* [his Arabic was rusty: *The Philosophy of the Revolution* was the correct title], which is like a potted edition of *Mein Kampf*." Eden, *Full Circle*, 483.

79. Christian Pineau in C. Douglas Dillon to JFD, July 27, 1956, State Department Central Decimal Files, Suez Crisis, 974.7301/7–1056, USNA: RG 59/250/44/4/4; see also Record of Meeting Held at 1 Carlton Gardens at 6 p.m. on Sunday, July 29, 1956, UKNA: PREM 11/1098; and Selwyn Lloyd in Top Secret Record of a Meeting Held in the Foreign Secretary's Room, Foreign Office, at 12 noon on Wednesday, Aug. 1, 1956, UKNA: PREM 11/1098. Pineau later denied that he had made any comparison of GAN with Hitler and claimed that only Guy Mollet had done that—see Christian Pineau in Moncrieff, *Suez Ten Years After*, 35. Yet he is repeatedly on record in the US and UK archives making exactly that comparison. As a coda to all this, writing in 1995, Winston Churchill's private secretary Anthony Montague Browne noted that "Nasser can be compared to a less bloodthirsty Saddam Hussein" (Montague Browne, *Long Sunset*, 162). Though the ultimate villainous touch points change over time, it seems GAN can always be compared to them.

80. Report by Allan Evans, Aug. 14, 1956, USNA: Subject files of the Bureau of Intelligence and Research (INR), 1945–1960, Lot 58D776, RG 59/250/62/4/3, box 11.

81. Butler, *Art of the Possible*, 188.

82. James, *Nasser at War*, 31. The man sent was Ali Sabri.

83. Trevelyan, *Middle East in Revolution*, 98.

84. Robert Menzies to RAE, Sept. 1956, in Eden, *Full Circle*, 471.

85. Sir Robert Menzies in Kyle, *Suez*, 221. See also Eden, *Full Circle*, 469, on RAE's belief that this statement by DDE was decisive to GAN's thinking.

86. Galpern, *Money, Oil, and Empire*, 144–45.

87. Ivone Kirkpatrick to Roger Makins, Sept. 10, 1956, in Lucas, *Divided We Stand*, 199.

88. Christian Pineau via Gladwyn Jebb, Sept. 9, 1956, in Kyle, *Suez*, 228.

89. Kyle, *Suez*, 254.

90. See Kyle, *Suez*, 224–25; also Eden, *Full Circle*, 479, on British and French lack of enthusiasm for SCUA.

91. Macmillan, *Cabinet Years*, Sept. 9, 1956, 595–96.

92. Copeland, *Game Player*, 207.

93. DDE, Sept. 11, 1956, in Kyle, *Suez*, 243–44.

94. Eden, *Full Circle*, 463. This was in response to DDE's letter of Sept. 3, 1956, which again made his opposition to force clear.

95. Sir Roger Makins (Lord Shenfield) in Hennessy, *Muddling Through*, 136.

96. C. Douglas Dillon, JFDOHP.

97. Hansard, 5th series, vol. 558, House of Commons, Session 1955–56, Sept. 12, 1956, col. 11–12; see also Kyle, *Suez*, 244–45.

98. GAN, Sept. 15, 1956, in James, *Nasser at War*, 32.

99. Memorandum of a conversation, JFD to Sir Roger Makins, Sept. 11, 1956, 5:20 p.m., General: DDEP, box 10.

100. Kyle, *Suez*, 249–50. The British plan was known as Operation Pile-Up.

101. DDE, JFDOHP.

102. RAE to Iverach McDonald in Carlton, *Eden*, 427.

103. Trevelyan, *Middle East in Revolution*, 102.

104. UNSC Resolution 118 (1956), Oct. 13, 1956, S/3675.

105. DDE in Kyle, *Suez*, 288.

106. Telephone call from Henry Cabot Lodge to JFD, Oct. 22, 1956, 4:44 p.m., Memoranda of Telephone Conversation, General, DDEP, box 10.

107. JFD to American Embassy Paris, Oct. 22, 1956. Chronological—John Foster Dulles (1–3), Aug. 1956, DDEP, box 80.

108. DBG, Diary, Oct. 18, 1956, in Troen and Shemesh, *The Suez-Sinai Crisis 1956*, 304.

109. DBG, Diary, Oct. 22, 1956, in ibid., 309.

Chapter 2: The Hammer and Sickle Torn Out

1. Sebestyen, *Twelve Days*, 17; Gati, *Failed Illusions*, 9.

2. Some Hungarians continued to call the AVH by its pre-1948 name, the AVO (Államvédelmi Osztály, State Security Department), pronounced "AH-voe." Sebestyen, *Twelve Days*, 28n. The House of Terror museum in Budapest records stories of state repression in Hungary under successive Fascist and Communist regimes.

3. Lendvai, *Hungary*, 43.

4. Gati, *Failed Illusions*, 133–34. Gati suggests that the proportion was 75 percent. He notes that estimating the number of Hungarians with Jewish backgrounds is difficult because their names were often "hungaricized."

5. Georgy Malenkov and Lavrenty Beria in Gati, *Failed Illusions*, 30; see also Kramer, "Soviet Union and the 1956 Crises," 179; and Molnár, *Budapest 1956*, 27.

6. Méray, *Thirteen Days That Shook the Kremlin*, 13.

7. Gati, *Failed Illusions*, 38.

8. Nikita Khrushchev in Gati, *Failed Illusions*, 122.

9. Sebestyen, *Twelve Days*, 108–9.

10. Anna Akhmatova in Taubman, *Khrushchev*, 285.

11. Barnes in Budapest to Secretary of State, Oct. 23, 1956, USNA: Records of the State Department, RG 59; Central Decimal Files: 764.00/10–2356.

12. See Lomax, *Hungary 1956*, 135.

13. JFD in *New York Times*, Oct. 22, 1956, 1.

14. Mićunović, *Moscow Diary*, 123–24.

15. Fryer, *Hungarian Tragedy*, 43. See *New York Times*, Oct. 22, 1956, 1, 6, for reports on Hungarian protests of Oct. 21, 1956.

16. Molnár, *Budapest 1956*, 111.

17. Barnes in Budapest to Secretary of State, Oct. 23, 1956, USNA: Records of the State Department, RG 59; Central Decimal Files: 764.00/10–2356.

18. Sebestyen, *Twelve Days*, 112.

19. Nutting, *No End of a Lesson*, 101.

20. Ibid., 102.

21. TNA: CAB 128/30 CM (56) 72, confidential annex, Oct. 23, 1956; Hennessy, *Prime Minister*, 222–23.

22. Shimon Peres and DBG in Peres, *Battling for Peace*, 128.

23. Moshe Dayan in Sharon, *Warrior*, 142.

24. Gilbert, *Israel*, 310.

25. Sharon, *Warrior*, 144.

26. Peres, *Battling for Peace*, 129.

27. In Avi Shlaim, "The Protocol of Sèvres, 1956," in Tal, *The 1956 War*, 128–29. For DBG and the oil, see 133.

28. Aburish, *Nasser*, 90.

29. Dorril, *MI6*, 602; Scott Lucas and Alistair Morey, "The Hidden 'Alliance': The CIA and MI6 Before and After Suez," in Stafford and Jeffreys-Jones, *American-British-Canadian Intelligence Relations*, 97–98.

30. Eveland, *Ropes of Sand*, 97, 98n.

31. GAN in Jefferson Caffery to State Department, Mar. 23, 1954, FRUS 1952–54, vol. 9, doc. 1304, p. 2242.

32. Eveland, *Ropes of Sand*, 101.

33. Trevelyan, *Middle East in Revolution*, 27.

34. The $3 million bribe is confirmed both by GAN's confidant Mohamed Heikal and by CIA agent Wilbur Eveland, though Heikal thought it was offered to General Neguib and GAN intercepted it. Eveland does not give precise dates but tells the story so that the decision to provide the money was made under Neguib's leadership; it was, though, handed over to GAN's aide once GAN was leader of the country. Eveland, *Ropes of Sand*, 91, 98, 98n; Heikal, *Cairo Documents*, 54–55; James, *Nasser at War*, 7. Lucas and Morey agree that the bribe was offered to GAN in Scott Lucas and Alistair Morey, "The Hidden 'Alliance': The CIA and MI6 Before and After Suez," in Stafford & Jeffreys-Jones, *American-British-Canadian Intelligence Relations*, 99–100; see also Lucas, *Divided We Stand*, 38.

35. Kermit Roosevelt to GAN, Dec. 23, 1954, in James, *Nasser at War*, 9–10.

36. The American ambassador Raymond Hare, who was director general of the Foreign Service at the time, thought Dulles actively worked against it. "We got word that Iran wanted to join the Baghdad Pact," he remembered. "And that night a telegram was sent to the Ambassador in Tehran instructing him to dissuade Iran from joining the Baghdad Pact. I've never seen this any place. The message went, but the Ambassador never acted. I've forgotten now whether the timing wasn't right—perhaps it wasn't too welcome a task, on his part, anyway, but it was never acted on." Raymond Hare, JFDOHP.

37. "En marge de la conference du Baghdad," Dec. 1955, ADLC: 214QONT/537/PRO-iv-1.

38. "Note pour le président du conseil," Mar. 9, 1956, ADLC: 214QONT/537/PRO-iv-1.

39. See Kyle, *Suez*, 56–60.

40. Heikal, *Cairo Documents*, 79.

41. GAN in James, *Nasser at War*, 10.

42. Heikal, *Cairo Documents*, 80.

43. Ibid., 81.

44. Ralph Murray and GAN in Lapping, *End of Empire*, 258, 259.

45. Chaim Herzog in Gilbert, *Israel*, 322.

46. Kyle, *Suez*, 63.

47. Eveland, *Ropes of Sand*, 73.

48. Sharon, *Warrior*, 88, 90.

49. United Nations Security Council S/RES/101 (1953), S/3139/Rev. 2, Nov. 24, 1953. The resolution is known generally as Resolution 101. It was adopted by nine votes to zero with two abstentions (Lebanon and the USSR).

50. Eveland, *Ropes of Sand*, 74.

51. Uri Avnery interview with the author, Mar. 2015.

52. DBG in Sharon, *Warrior*, 91.

53. At the time, some Israelis suspected he tacitly supported the fedayeen. Yet documents that the Israelis themselves captured from Egyptian military intelligence in October and November 1956 proved that the Egyptian military and government had been attempting to restrain Palestinians from infiltration into Israel. Shlaim, "Conflicting Approaches," 188–89.

54. Black and Morris, *Israel's Secret Wars*, 127–28.

55. Filiu, *Gaza*, 87.

56. Copeland, *Game Player*, 199.

57. Kyle, *Suez*, 65; Filiu, *Gaza*, 87.

58. Shlaim, "Conflicting Approaches," 188.

59. CIA agent Miles Copeland argued that the Gaza raid was "perfect gameplay from the Israelis' point of view." In his analysis, the Israelis would rather have GAN in a fiercely anti-Israel position than a mild anti-Israel position, because it would decrease the chances of his allying with the United States. Copeland connected this to the Suez crisis and said it "played right into Israeli hands." Copeland, *Game Player*, 199. There is little evidence that the Israelis actually intended this chain of events to proceed from the raid, though, and it is extremely questionable whether the 1956 war ultimately helped their case or harmed GAN's internationally. It did result in some short-term gains, which are detailed in the epilogue to this book.

60. Shlaim, "Conflicting Approaches," 188–89.

61. Trevelyan, *Middle East in Revolution*, 31, 36.

62. Embassy in Tel Aviv to Department of State, Apr. 5, 1955, FRUS 1955–57, vol. 14, doc. 66, p. 139; Kyle, *Suez*, 66. See also Shlaim, "Conflicting Approaches," 189–90.

63. James, *Nasser at War*, 13.

64. Copeland, *Game Player*, 199; Lucas, *Divided We Stand*, 48.

65. Reported in Herbert Hoover to JFD, Sept. 19, 1955, FRUS 1955–57, vol. 14, doc. 284, p. 481.

66. Peres, *Battling for Peace*, 75–76.

67. Sir Harold Caccia, deputy undersecretary of state, on Evelyn Shuckburgh to Harold Macmillan, Sept. 23, 1955, FO 371/113674; Kyle, *Suez*, 75.

68. Copeland, *Game of Nations*, 134–35.

69. Heikal, *Cairo Documents*, 60.

70. Kermit Roosevelt to AWD, in Herbert Hoover to US mission at UN, Sept. 27, 1955, FRUS 1955–57, vol. 14, doc. 311, p. 521.

71. The letter from JFD to GAN (Sept. 27, 1955) is in FRUS, 1955–57, vol. 14, doc. 315, pp. 527–28.

72. Henry Byroade to State Department, Oct. 1, 1955, FRUS, 1955–57, vol. 14, doc. 321, pp. 538–39.

73. See Embassy in Egypt to State Department, Nov. 17, 1955, FRUS, 1955–57, vol. 14, doc. 416, p. 781.

74. Copeland, *Game Player*, 198.

75. Golda Meir speaking in New York, Dec. 18, 1955, in William Morris to Foreign Office, Jan. 6, 1956, UKNA: FO 371/121708, VR 1071/10.

76. Abba Eban, JFDOHP. Eban was obliged to defend Israel's action in the United Nations despite his strong opposition to it.

77. Message to the CIA, Feb. 22, 1956, in FRUS, 1955–57, vol. 15, doc. 112, pp. 206–7.

78. GAN, June 19, 1956, in James, *Nasser at War*, 18–19.

79. Filiu, *Gaza*, 92–93; Morris, *Israel's Border Wars*, 380–81.

80. Eveland, *Ropes of Sand*, 195.

81. Copeland, *Game Player*, 200.

82. "Cairo Mission in Amman," London *Times*, Oct. 24, 1956, 8.

83. "France Recalls Cairo Ambassador, London *Times*, Oct. 24, 1956, 10.

84. *New York Times*, Oct. 24, 1956, 1.

85. CIA Office of National Estimates, Staff Memorandum No. 88–56, Nov. 2, 1956, USNA: CIA-RDP79T00937A000500020010–5.

86. United Nations, *Problem of Hungary*, 148–49; Molnár, *Budapest 1956*, 116.

87. Barnes in Budapest to Secretary of State, Oct. 23, 1956, USNA: Records of the State Department, RG 59; Central Decimal Files: 764.00/10–2356.

88. Imre Nagy, spring 1957, in Rainer, *Imre Nagy*, 102.

89. Gati, *Failed Illusions*, 146.

90. Sebestyen, *Twelve Days*, 117–18.

91. Josip Broz Tito in Molnár, *Budapest 1956*, 117.

92. The story of the Cuban revolution's changing politics has been told at length in Tunzelmann, *Red Heat*.

93. Clement Voroshilov, Oct. 1956, in Taubman, *Khrushchev*, 295.

94. Gati, *Failed Illusions*, 5, 95, 166.

95. Kopácsi, *In the Name of the Working Class*, 122–23.

96. Lomax, *Hungary 1956*, 117–18; Molnár, *Budapest 1956*, 132–33.

97. Fryer, *Hungarian Tragedy*, 64–65.

98. Herman Phleger, JFDOHP.

99. JFD, speech, *US News & World Report*, Apr. 21, 1956, JFDP, Middle East, 1956, box 106, reel 41.

100. Khrushchev, *Khrushchev Remembers*, 431.

101. Working notes of the CPSU presidium, Oct. 23, 1956, Sebestyen, *Twelve Days*, 120–21.

102. See picture in Fryer, *Hungarian Tragedy*, vii. See also "Hour-by-Hour Chronicle from Budapest Radio," London *Times*, Oct. 25, 1956, 10.

103. Stephen Vizinczey in Sebestyen, *Twelve Days*, 119. See Kopácsi, *In the Name of the Working Class*, 127–29 for a memorable account of the statue falling.

104. Fryer, *Hungarian Tragedy*, 44–45.

105. Barnes in Budapest to Secretary of State, Oct. 23, 1956, USNA: Records of the State Department, RG 59; Central Decimal Files: 764.00/10–2356.

106. United Nations, *Problem of Hungary*, 151.

107. Ernő Gerő and Imre Nagy in Sebestyen, *Twelve Days*, 124–25. See also Molnár, *Budapest 1956*, 121.

108. Fryer, *Hungarian Tragedy*, 46.

109. Sebestyen, *Twelve Days*, 125.

110. DDE to WSC, Apr. 27, 1956. Dwight D. Eisenhower Presidential Library: DDE's Papers as President, DDE Diary Series, Box 14, Apr. 1956 Miscellaneous (1).

111. DDE in Hughes, *Ordeal of Power*, 203.

112. United Nations, *Problem of Hungary*, 49–50; Kopácsi, *In the Name of the Working Class*, 145.

Chapter 3: A Plan on a Cigarette Packet

1. Radio Kossuth, Oct. 24, 1956, in Sebestyen, *Twelve Days*, 127.

2. Kopácsi, *In the Name of the Working Class*, 150.

3. Avi Shlaim, "The Protocol of Sèvres, 1956," in Tal, *1956 War*, 129–30; Kyle, *Suez*, 328.

4. Bar-Zohar, *Armed Prophet*, 232; Peres, *Battling for Peace*, 129.

5. Moshe Dayan, 1976, translated in Shlaim, "Conflicting Approaches," 181.

6. Nuri es-Said in Gaitskell, *Diary*, July 26, 1956, 554.

7. Moshe Sharett in Shlaim, "Conflicting Approaches," 184–85.

8. Shlaim, "Conflicting Approches," 182.

9. Ibid., 200.

10. Sharon, *Warrior*, 135.

11. Eveland, *Ropes of Sand*, 78.

12. In Isaac Alteras, "Eisenhower and the Sinai Campaign of 1956: The First Major Crisis in US-Israeli Relations," in Tal, *1956 War*, 27.

13. Avnery, *Israel Without Zionists*, 113.

14. Shlaim, "Conflicting Approaches," 187; Aburish, *Nasser*, 65–66.

15. Bar-Zohar, *Armed Prophet*, 192–95.

16. Peres, *Battling for Peace*, 88.

17. See Shalom, *Ben-Gurion's Political Struggles*, 23–35, for a full account of the scandal in the 1960s.

18. Shlaim, "Conflicting Approaches," 187–88.

19. Uri Avnery, interview with the author, Mar. 2015.

20. DBG in Shlaim, "Conflicting Approaches," 191.

21. GAN and Kermit Roosevelt in Burns, *Economic Aid and American Policy*, 61; Lucas, *Divided We Stand*, 87.

22. Peres, *Battling for Peace*, 117.

23. Shlaim, "Conflicting Approaches," 198; Stock, *Israel on the Road to Sinai*, 184–85.

24. Uri Avnery, interview with the author, Mar. 2015.

25. Peres, *Battling for Peace*, 118.

26. Miklos Vásárhelyi in Sebestyen, *Twelve Days*, 133.

27. Gati, *Failed Illusions*, 150.

28. Kopácsi, *In the Name of the Working Class*, 154–55.

29. Pál Kabelács in Csete, *1956 Budapest*, 70.

30. "Insurrection in Budapest," London *Times*, Oct. 25, 1956, 10; Réthly, *Hungarian Revolution*, 16.

31. Pál Maléter in Sebestyen, *Twelve Days*, 130–31.

32. Report from Anastas Mikoyan and Mikhail Suslov to the CPSU presidium, out of sequence (Oct. 24, 1956); Archive of Foreign Policy, Russian Federation (AVP RF) F. 059a, Opis 4, Papka 6, Delo 5, Listy 1–7, translation by Johanna Granville, in *Cold War International History Project Bulletin*, no. 5, Woodrow Wilson International Center for Scholars, Washington DC, Spring 1995. See also Méray, *Thirteen Days That Shook the Kremlin*, 104.

33. Avi Shlaim, "The Protocol of Sèvres, 1956," in Tal, *1956 War*, 131.

34. Moshe Dayan in Kyle, *Suez*, 328.

35. Peres, *Battling for Peace*, 130.

36. It is widely believed that Israel built its first nuclear weapon ten years later, in December 1966. Israel has never officially confirmed that it has a nuclear weapons program. On Suez and Israel's nuclear industry, see Aronson, *David Ben-Gurion and the Jewish Renaissance*, 256–60.

37. Avi Shlaim, "The Protocol of Sèvres, 1956," in Tal, *1956 War*, 132.

38. Eden, *A Memoir*, 249.

39. Mordechai Bar-On, "David Ben-Gurion and the Sèvres Collusion," in Louis and Owen, *Suez 1956*, 158.

40. Kyle, *Suez*, 330.

41. Rhodes James, *Eden*, 532.

42. Avi Shlaim, "The Protocol of Sèvres, 1956," in Tal, *1956 War*, 136.

43. CIA NSC Briefing, "French Coup in North Africa," Oct. 25, 1956, USNA: CIA-RDP79R00890A000700100025–2.

44. CIA Office of National Estimates, "North African Reactions to Recent French Moves," Staff Memorandum no. 88–56, Nov. 2, 1956, USNA: CIA-RDP79T00937A000500020010–5. The figure for the dead in Morocco is from NSC Briefing, "French Coup in North Africa," Oct. 25, 1956, USNA: CIA-RDP79R00890A000700100025–2.

45. Ben Bella in Merle, *Ahmed Ben Bella*, 116–23.

46. Pineau, *1956/Suez*, 140–45.

47. *Jerusalem Post*, Oct. 25, 1956, 1.

48. Winthrop W. Aldrich to JFD, Oct. 23, 1956 (received Oct. 24, 1956), State Department Central Decimal Files, Suez Crisis, 974.7301/10–2356, USNA: RG 59/250/44/4/4.

49. JFD, Memorandum of a Conference with the President, Oct. 24, 1956, 11:30 a.m., United Kingdom—Misc. Paper—UK, 1956, 1960, DDEP, box 37.

50. Memorandum of a telephone call between JFD and Henry Cabot Lodge, FRUS 1955–57, vol. 25, doc. 104, p. 273.

51. Mr. Gomułka Acclaimed by Huge Warsaw Crowd," London *Times*, Oct. 25, 1956, 10.

52. NSK in Zhu, *1956*, 119.

53. Charles E. Bohlen in Moscow to Secretary of State, Oct. 24, 1956, USNA: Records of the State Department, RG 59, Central Decimal Files: 764.00/10–2456.

54. Sebestyen, *Twelve Days*, 136–37.

55. Mićunović, *Moscow Diary*, 127.

Chapter 4: Bloody Thursday

1. James, *Nasser at War*, 38.

2. *New York Times*, Oct. 25, 1956, 5.

3. Kyle, *Suez*, 333.

4. "The chief danger, especially for us, was that the conflict [between Israel and Egypt] would spread," RAE would claim in his 1959 memoir, which he wrote in denial of the reality of his collusion with Israel. "It is evident that [Anglo-French] intervention stopped it spreading." Eden, *Full Circle*, 526–27.

5. Alexander Schnee for the ambassador to Department of State, Oct. 25, 1956, State Department Central Decimal Files, Suez Crisis, 974.7301/10–2356, USNA: RG 59/250/44/4/4.

6. Abba Eban in *New York Times*, Oct. 26, 1956, 1, 4.

7. Sharon, *Warrior*, 141.

8. Heath, *Course of My Life*, 169–70.

9. Cabinet Meeting, Oct. 25, 1956, 10 a.m., CM (56) 74th conclusions, UKNA: PREM 11/1103.

10. Barnett, *Verdict of Peace*, 491.

11. Gaitskell, *Diary*, Mar. 9, 1956, 465.

12. Memorandum for the Record on Meeting at Greenbrier, White Sulphur Springs, WV, Mar. 27, 1956. White House Memoranda, 1953–59, DDEP, box 22. For other contemporaries questioning RAE's mental health and judgment at this point, see Trevelyan, *Public and Private*, 56; Dodds-Parker, *Political Eunuch*, 114; Richard Powell in Hennessy, *Muddling Through*, 142.

13. Cooper, *Lion's Last Roar*, 138.

14. Eden, *Full Circle*, 568; see also Rhodes James, *Eden*, 523–24. RAE and most of his biographers do not mention the reason Lady Eden was in the hospital. Randolph Churchill, *The Rise and Fall of Sir Anthony Eden*, 260, mentions that it was for a dental examination.

15. Carlton, *Eden*, 428.

16. Lucas, *Divided We Stand*, 55. The aide was William Clark.

17. Macmillan, *Cabinet Years*, Feb. 3, 1957, 612.

18. Horace, Lord Evans in Butler, *The Art of the Possible*, 194.

19. Eden, *Full Circle*, 549–50.

20. Anonymous bus driver in Eden, *Full Circle*, 546.

21. Selwyn Lloyd to Sir Norman Brook, Aug. 8, 1959, UKNA: FO 800/728.

22. Nutting, *No End of a Lesson*, 104–8.

23. Avi Shlaim, "The Protocol of Sèvres, 1956," in Tal, *1956 War*, 136.

24. Radio Kossuth, Oct. 25, 1956, in Sebestyen, *Twelve Days*, 138.

25. Anastas Mikoyan in Sebestyen, *Twelve Days*, 140.

26. Sebestyen, *Twelve Days*, 144.

27. Kopácsi, *In the Name of the Working Class*, 164.

28. Unsigned message from Budapest to Secretary of State, Oct. 25, 1956, USNA: Records of the State Department, RG 59, Central Decimal Files: 764.00/10–2556.

29. *New York Times*, Oct. 27, 1956, 2.

30. Gábor Jobbágyi, "Bloody Thursday, 1956: The Anatomy of the Kossuth Square Massacre," trans. Andy Clark, *Hungarian Review* 5, no. 1, Jan. 15, 2014.

31. Gati, *Failed Illusions*, 159.

32. Sebestyen, *Twelve Days*, 145.

33. Aldrich in London to Secretary of State, Oct. 26, 1956, USNA: Records of the State Department, RG 59, Central Decimal Files: 764.00/10–2656.

34. Imre Nagy in Rainer, *Imre Nagy*, 107.

35. Avi Shlaim, "The Protocol of Sèvres, 1956," in Tal, *1956 War*, 136.

36. "Fighting in Meknes," London *Times*, Oct. 26, 1956, 10.

37. Anwar Sadat in al-Gomhuria, Oct. 25, 1956, quoted in *Jerusalem Post*, Oct. 26, 1956, 1.

38. Anonymous Moroccan source quoted in *New York Times*, Oct. 26, 1956, 5.

39. Eden, *A Memoir*, 250; Earl Mountbatten of Burma to RAE, Nov. 2, 1956, UKNA: PREM 11/1090.

40. Winthrop W. Aldrich to JFD, Oct. 26, 1956, State Department Central Decimal Files, Suez Crisis, 974.7301/10–2356, USNA: RG 59/250/44/4/4.

41. Notes on the 38th Meeting of the Special Committee on Soviet and Related Problems, Washington, Oct. 25, 1956, FRUS, 1955–57, vol. 25, doc. 107, p. 277.

42. Memorandum of a telephone conversation between the President in New York and the Secretary of State in Washington, Oct. 25, 1956, 5:02 p.m., Eisenhower Library, FRUS vol. 25 (Eastern Europe), doc. 111, pp. 290–91; see also footnote of AWD's conversation with JFD.

43. *New York Times*, Oct. 26, 1956, 1, 18.

Chapter 5: The Two Musketeers

1. "Military Implications of Mounting Operation Musketeer," Chiefs of Staff to Egypt Committee EC (56) 63, Top Secret Annex, Oct. 25, 1956, UKNA: PREM 11/1103.

2. Eden, *Full Circle*, 430.

3. DDE, JFDOHP.

4. William Dickson in Kyle, *Suez*, 88.

5. Shuckburgh, *Descent to Suez*, Mar. 2, 1956, 340.

6. Kyle, *Suez*, 90; Anthony Gorst, "'A Modern Major General': General Sir Gerald Templer, Chief of the Imperial General Staff," in Kelly and Gorst, *Whitehall and the Suez Crisis*, 33.

7. Cloake, *Templer*, 342; Monroe, *Britain's Moment*, 188.

8. DDE in Lucas, *Divided We Stand*, 76.

9. Gerald Templer in Ziegler, *Mountbatten*, 528.

10. "Egyptian Nationalisation of the Suez Canal Company," Top Secret Report by the Joint Intelligence Committee, JIC (56) 80 (Final) (Revise), Aug. 3, 1956, UKNA: CAB 158/25.

11. Norman Brook in Keith Kyle, "The Mandarin's Mandarin: Sir Norman Brook, Secretary of the Cabinet," in Kelly and Gorst, *Whitehall and the Suez Crisis*, 70.

12. See Anthony Gorst, "'A Modern Major General': General Sir Gerald Templer, Chief of the Imperial General Staff," in Kelly and Gorst, *Whitehall and the Suez Crisis*, 36; Kyle, *Suez*, 172–79 has a much more detailed account of the first stage of political wranglings.

13. Viscount Montgomery of Alamein, Parliamentary Debates (Hansard), 5th series, vol. 238 (House of Lords), Mar. 28, 1962, col. 1002–3.

14. See correspondence between Hugh Gaitskell and RAE in Gaitskell, *Diary*, 570–88.

15. Anwar Sadat in Keith Kyle, "Britain's Slow March to Suez," in Tal, *1956 War*, 115n. See also pp. 95–96 on Gaitskell's objection to British arms sales to Egypt.

16. Eden, *Full Circle*, 445.

17. Barnett, *Verdict of Peace*, 493.

18. Kyle, *Suez*, 202.

19. Interview with William B. Macomber Jr., Sept. 19, 1993, Library of Congress: Foreign Affairs Oral History Collection of the Association for Diplomatic Studies and Training, http://hdl.loc.gov/loc.mss/mfdip.2004mac07.

20. Memorandum of a Conversation, Aug. 19, 1956, FRUS 1955–57, vol. 16, doc. 99, p. 235.

21. Macmillan, *Cabinet Years*, Aug. 24, 1956, 590.

22. Charles Keightley, Sept. 1956, in Kyle, *Suez*, 234.

23. Lord Hailsham in Kyle, *Suez*, 235.

24. Lord Mountbatten's account, 1956, in Eric Grove and Sally Rohan, "The Limits of Opposition: Admiral Earl Mountbatten of Burma, First Sea Lord and Chief of Naval Staff," in Kelly and Gorst, *Whitehall and the Suez Crisis*, 108. It is generally worth taking Lord Mountbatten's accounts with a pinch of salt: they tend to place him more firmly at the righteous center of events than others around him remember. This account, though written very close to the time, is considerably more believable than his memories of various events later in life.

25. Hugh Stockwell, "Report on Operation Musketeer, August to December 1956," UKNA: WO 288/77.

26. Top Secret Report by Air Marshal D.H.F. Barnett, Air Task Force Commander, on Operation Musketeer, Nov. 27, 1956, UNKA: AIR 20/10746.

27. David Lee in Hennessy, *Muddling Through*, 138.

28. Herman Phleger, JFDOHP.

29. CIA NSC Briefing, Consequences of UK-French Military Action (SNIE 30–4–56), Sept. 6, 1956, USNA: CIA-RDP79R00890A000700090002–9.

30. Aug. 24, 1956, in Keith Kyle, "Britain's Slow March to Suez," in Tal, *1956 War*, 103.

31. Cooper, *Lion's Last Roar*, 207; see also Kyle, *Suez*, 303 on how little Keightley and the chiefs of staff knew.

32. See Motti Golani, "The Sinai War, 1956: Three Partners, Three Wars," in Tal, *1956 War*, 174.

33. Pineau, *1956/Suez*, 162.

34. General Charles Keightley and Admiral Manley Power in Kyle, *Suez*, 341.

35. Foreign Office minutes, Aug. 3, 1956, in Christopher Goldsmith, "In the Know? Sir Gladwyn Jebb, Ambassador to France," in Kelly and Gorst, *Whitehall and the Suez Crisis*, 83–84. See also "Egyptian Nationalisation of the Suez Canal Company," Top Secret Report by the Joint Intelligence Committee, JIC (56) 80 (Final) (Revise), Aug. 3, 1956, UKNA: CAB 158/25: "Great resentment would undoubtedly be created by what would be interpreted as a plot between Israel and the West."

36. See Macmillan, *Cabinet Years*, Aug. 3, 1956, 583, and Aug. 4, 1956, 584; Kyle, *Suez*, 170.

37. Sept. 25, 1956, in Keith Kyle, "The Mandarin's Mandarin: Sir Norman Brook, Secretary of the Cabinet," in Kelly and Gorst, *Whitehall and the Suez Crisis*, 73.

38. Kyle, *Suez*, 174.

39. Peres, *Battling for Peace*, 122; Shimon Peres, "The Road to Sèvres: Franco-Israeli Strategic Cooperation," in Troen and Shemesh, *Suez-Sinai Crisis 1956*, 142.

40. Peres, *Battling for Peace*, 118.

41. Tayekh, *Origins of the Eisenhower Doctrine*, 114.

42. Pineau, *1956/Suez*, 132.

43. Eugene Gilbert to Christian Pineau, June 19, 1956, in Maurice Vaïsse, "France and the Suez Crisis," in Louis and Owen, *Suez 1956*, 135. For more on the French administration's affection for Israel at the time, see Shimon Peres, "The Road to Sèvres: Franco-Israeli Strategic Cooperation," in Troen and Shemesh, *Suez-Sinai Crisis 1956*, 143–44.

44. Eden, *Full Circle*, 476.

45. Kyle, *Suez*, 264–65.

46. Mr. Westlake in Tel Aviv to FO, Sept. 26, 1956, TNA: FO 371/121779.

47. R. M. Hadow to Mr. Westlake in Tel Aviv, Oct. 3, 1956, TNA: FO 371/121779.

48. Kyle, *Suez*, 293.

49. Sharon, *Warrior*, 137; Kyle, *Suez*, 293.

50. Anthony Gorst, "'A Modern Major General': General Sir Gerald Templer, Chief of the Imperial General Staff," in Kelly and Gorst, *Whitehall and the Suez Crisis*, 41.

51. Kyle, *Suez*, 282.

52. Nutting, *No End of a Lesson*, 90–96.

53. Moshe Dayan, *Diary*, Oct. 21, 1956, 61.

54. Eden, *Full Circle*, 511.

55. Avi Shlaim, "The Protocol of Sèvres, 1956," in Tal, *1956 War*, 122–23.

56. Shimon Peres in Mordechai Bar-On, "David Ben-Gurion and the Sèvres Collusion," in Louis and Owen, *Suez 1956*, 148.

57. DBG, Diary, Oct. 17, 1956, in Mordechai Bar-On, "David Ben-Gurion and the Sèvres Collusion," in Louis and Owen, *Suez 1956*, 149; Kyle, *Suez*, 299.

58. RAE in Kyle, *Suez*, 308–9. The UNSC debate was on Oct. 19, 1956.

59. Shimon Peres, "The Road to Sèvres: Franco-Israeli Strategic Cooperation," in Troen and Shemesh, *Suez-Sinai Crisis 1956*, 147.

60. Ferenc Donáth, István Pozsár, and unnamed student in Rainer, *Imre Nagy*, 108–11.

61. Imre Nagy and Ferenc Donáth in Gati, *Failed Illusions*, 153–54.

62. Anastas Mikoyan to Nikita Khrushchev, Oct. 26, 1956, in Sebestyen, *Twelve Days*, 153.

63. Gergely Pongrácz, in National Security Archive Cold War Interviews, George Washington University, June 17, 1996.

64. Sebestyen, *Twelve Days*, 156–57; Fryer, *Hungarian Tragedy*, 74–82.

65. Memorandum of Discussion at the 301st meeting of the National Security Council, Washington, Oct. 26, 1956, 9:00–10:42 a.m., FRUS 25 (Eastern Europe), doc. 116, pp. 295–99.

66. FRUS 25 (Eastern Europe), docs. 119–121.

67. Gati, *Failed Illusions*, 72. The United States distributed food packages in East Germany after the uprising in 1953, which annoyed the Kremlin, but that seems to have been its only involvement.

68. Adams, *First-Hand Report*, 196.

69. Christian Pineau, JFDOHP.

70. NSK in Hayter, *Kremlin and the Embassy*, 138–39. See also Eden, *Full Circle*, 356–61; Richard Crossman, *The Backbench Diaries of Richard Crossman*, ed. Janet Morgan (London: Hamish Hamilton and Jonathan Cape, 1981), 491; Richard Crossman in Taubman, *Khrushchev*, 357.

71. JFD in Hoopes, *Devil and John Foster Dulles*, 131.

72. Memorandum of a Telephone Call, JFD to AWD, Oct. 15, 1956, 4:45 p.m., General, DDEP, box 10.

73. Kyle, *Suez*, 338.

74. JFD to American Embassy London, Oct. 26, 1956, Chronological—John Foster Dulles (1–3), 1956 August, DDEP, box 80.

75. Nutting, *No End of a Lesson*, 110.

76. Bar-Zohar, *Armed Prophet*, 234.

77. Mosley, *Dulles*, 413–14.

78. Kyle, *Suez*, 339; FRUS 1955–57, vol. 17, doc. 314, p. 593 and note.

79. General Charles Cabell, JFDOHP.

80. Christian Pineau, JFDOHP.

81. John Colville, *The Fringes of Power: Downing Street Diaries 1939–1955*, rev. ed (London: Weidenfeld & Nicolson, 2004), 667.

82. Montague Browne, *Long Sunset*, 210.

83. Memorandum of a telephone call between DDE and JFD, Oct. 26, 1956, FRUS 1955–57, vol. 25, doc. 121, pp. 306–7.

84. JFD to American Embassy London, Oct. 26, 1956, USNA: Records of the State Department, RG 59, Central Decimal Files: 764.00/10–2656.

Chapter 6: The Omega Plan

1. Ariel Sharon and Moshe Dayan in Sharon, *Warrior*, 142.

2. Mordechai Bar-On, "David Ben-Gurion and the Sèvres Collusion," in Louis and Owen, *Suez 1956*, 160.

3. Dodds-Parker, *Political Eunuch*, 103.

4. Dorril, *MI6*, 601; Scott Lucas and Alistair Morey, "The Hidden 'Alliance': The CIA and MI6 Before and After Suez," in Stafford and Jeffreys-Jones, *American-British-Canadian Intelligence Relations*, 98.

5. In Mitchell, *Society of the Muslim Brothers*, 8.

6. Mohammed al-Ghazali, in Mitchell, *Society of Muslim Brothers*, 241.

7. J. Heyworth-Dunne in Mitchell, *Society of Muslim Brothers*, 28n.

8. Gordon, *Nasser*, 20; Mitchell, *Society of Muslim Brothers*, 98. The officer who met Nasser was Mahmud Labib.

9. Mitchell, *Society of Muslim Brothers*, 46.

10. Ibid., 89.

11. Sir Ralph Stevenson to RAE, Jan. 1, 1952, UKNA: FO 371/96870, JE 1018/1.

12. Sir Ralph Stevenson to Foreign Office, Jan. 26, 1952, UKNA: FO 371/96872, JE 1018/55.

13. CIA intelligence memorandum, "Terrorism, a Threat to Near Eastern Stability," July 26, 1951, USNA: CIA-RDP91T01172R000300290023–4.

14. Maurice Couve de Murville to Ministry for External Affairs, Aug. 28, 1954, ADLC: 213QONT/483/EG-v-6.

15. M. A. Hankey to Foreign Office, Aug. 31, 1953, UKNA: FO 371/102706, JE 1015/123.

16. Eden, *Full Circle*, 257.

17. Mitchell, *Society of Muslim Brothers*, 131.

18. GAN in Mitchell, *Society of Muslim Brothers*, 151.

19. See James, *Nasser at War*, 6–7.

20. Gordon, *Nasser*, 33–34.

21. Ian Black, "Osama bin Laden Was Blind in One Eye, Says al-Qaida Leader," *Manchester Guardian*, Sept. 27, 2012.

22. Eveland, *Ropes of Sand*, 103–4.

23. Copeland, *Game Player*, 201.

24. Sir Richard Hull in Dorril, *MI6*, 605.

25. Shuckburgh, *Descent to Suez*, Nov. 28, 1955, 305.

26. Harold Macmillan to Sir Humphrey Trevelyan, Nov. 26, 1955, UKNA: FO 371/113738, JE 1423/252G.

27. Harold Macmillan to JFD, Nov. 26, 1955, UKNA: FO 371/113738, JE 1423/252G.

28. Michael T. Thornhill, "Alternatives to Nasser: Humphrey Trevelyan, Ambassador to Egypt," in Kelly and Gorst, *Whitehall and the Suez Crisis*, 23.

29. Copeland, *Game Player*, 201.

30. James, *Nasser at War*, 19; Dorril, *MI6*, 610. The paid French hitman in 1954 was Jean-Marie Pellay; he is said to have just missed his target.

31. See Dorril, *MI6*, 613.

32. Herbert Hoover in Sir Roger Makins to Foreign Office, Nov. 27, 1955, UKNA: FO 371/113738, JE 1423/253G.

33. Foreign Office to Washington, Nov. 28, 1955, UKNA: FO 371/113738, JE 1423/253G.

34. Shuckburgh, *Descent to Suez*, Mar. 8, 1956, 345.

35. RAE in Shuckburgh, *Descent to Suez*, Mar. 12, 1956, 346.

36. George Young to BBC, 1985; in Dorril, *MI6*, 609; see also Kyle, *Suez*, 150–51.

37. Eveland, *Ropes of Sand*, 169–71. According to Eveland, George Young later joined the Society for Individual Freedom, which argued that white Europeans were inherently superior to Jews, Arabs, Asians, and Africans.

38. Memorandum from the Secretary of State to the President, Mar. 28, 1956, FRUS 1955–57, vol. 15, doc. 223, pp. 419–21.

39. CIA Briefing, "Egypt's Role in the Muslim World," n.d. (c. 1955–56), USNA: CIA-RDP78–02771R000500030002–9.

40. CIA NSC Briefing: Middle East Update, Mar. 20, 1956, USNA: CIA-RDP79R00890A000700030022–3.

41. Memorandum from the Secretary of State to the President, Mar. 28, 1956, FRUS 1955–57, vol. 15, doc. 223, pp. 419–21.

42. See Eveland, *Ropes of Sand*, 132–38, 143–51.

43. Eveland, *Ropes of Sand*, 182. See also 198–201 for more on American plotting against the Syrian government.

44. See Heikal, *Cutting the Lion's Tail*, 104–5; Lucas, *Divided We Stand*, 118.

45. Dorril, *MI6*, 631; West, *Friends*, 141.

46. Macmillan, *Cabinet Years*, Aug. 29, 1956, 592.

47. Hennessy, *Prime Minister*, 216.

48. Wright, *Spycatcher*, 160–61.

49. London *Times*, June 19, 1975, 1, 6; Scott Lucas and Alistair Morey, "The Hidden 'Alliance': The CIA and MI6 Before and After Suez," in Stafford and Jeffreys-Jones, *American-British-Canadian Intelligence Relations*, 106 and note.

50. Dorril, *MI6*, 639.

51. Ibid., 632; Bower, *Perfect English Spy*, 192.

52. Scott Lucas and Alistair Morey, "The Hidden 'Alliance': The CIA and MI6 Before and After Suez," in Stafford and Jeffreys-Jones, *American-British-Canadian Intelligence Relations*, 107; Kyle, *Suez*, 211; Lucas, *Divided We Stand*, 101, 193–94.

53. Memorandum of Conversation, Sept. 22, 1965, USNA: State Department Central Decimal Files, 774.11/9–2256.

54. Fisher Howe to the Under Secretary, Sept. 28, 1956, USNA: State Department Central Decimal Files, 774.11/9–2856.

55. DDE in Dorril, *MI6*, 636.

56. Memorandum of Conference, Oct. 6, 1956, DDE, Staff Notes, Oct. 1956; Ambrose and Immerman, *Ike's Spies*, 240.

57. Laurent Rucker, "The Soviet Union and the Suez Crisis," in Tal, *1956 War*, 77; Andrew and Mitrokhin, *Mitrokhin Archive*, vol. 2, p. 148. Rucker dates the dispatch of the KGB agents to around Oct. 1, 1956. The KGB agent, Vadim Kirpichenko, dates it to the end of July.

58. See Eveland, *Ropes of Sand*, 202–4 and 218–23 for more on Ilyan's financial request and plotting; Lucas, *Divided We Stand*, 140.

59. William Blum, *Killing Hope: US Military and CIA Interventions Since World War II* (2003; London: Zed Books, 2004), 86–87; Eveland, *Ropes of Sand*, 225. Blum gives the delayed date as October 30, but Eveland, who was on the ground, says it was October 29.

60. *Jerusalem Post*, Oct. 28, 1956, 1.

61. "Tunisians Clash with French Troops," London *Times*, Oct. 29, 1956, 7.

62. Christian Pineau, *Jerusalem Post*, Oct. 28, 1956, 3.

63. In CIA intelligence report, Oct. 31, 1956, USNA: CIA-RDP81–00280R001300040086–1.

64. Rainer, *Imre Nagy*, 111.

65. Molnár, *Budapest 1956*, 155.

66. Rainer, *Imre Nagy*, 111–13.

67. Mosley, *Dulles*, 415; Kyle, *Suez*, 339. Mosley's source for this story was Amory; Kyle's was a rival CIA agent, James Jesus Angleton.

68. Mosley, *Dulles*, 417.

69. Hughes, *Ordeal of Power*, 211.

70. Henriques, *One Hundred Hours to Suez*, 47.

71. Address by the Secretary of State Before the Dallas Council on World Affairs, Oct. 27, 1956, FRUS 1955–57, vol. 25, doc. 128, pp. 317–18.

Chapter 7: No Picnic

1. Cooper, *Lion's Last Roar*, 158–59.

2. Nutting, *No End of a Lesson*, 109.

3. Ben Bella in Merle, *Ahmed Ben Bella*, 123.

4. Maurice Bourgès-Maunoury in Pineau, *1956/Suez*, 133.

5. "State of Emergency in Aleppo," London *Times*, Oct. 29, 1956, 7; *Jerusalem Post*, Oct. 29, 1956, 1.

6. CIA Office of National Estimates, Staff Memorandum No. 88–56, Nov. 2, 1956, USNA: CIA-RDP79T00937A000500020010–5.

7. Gati, *Failed Illusions*, 162.

8. Imre Nagy in Rainer, *Imre Nagy*, 113; Anastas Mikoyan in Gati, *Failed Illusions*, 173–74.

9. Gati, *Failed Illusions*, 167. The tapes of RFE's broadcasts were made available only in the 1990s. For more on the impact of these broadcasts, see also pp. 183–86.

10. Vyacheslav Molotov and Kliment Voroshilov, Oct. 28, 1956, in Kramer, "Soviet Union and the 1956 Crises," 186.

11. NSK in Laurent Rucker, "The Soviet Union and the Suez Crisis," in Tal, *1956 War*, 84.

12. Bar-Zohar, *Armed Prophet*, 235.

13. DBG in Bar-Zohar, *Armed Prophet*, 239.

14. Hughes, *Ordeal of Power*, 212–13.

15. Hungary and Suez Crisis; 1955–1956, JFDP, State Department records, box 1, folder 1.

16. Telephone calls, Oct. 28, 1956, from DDE to JFD, 7:00 p.m.; from JFD to DDE, 9:00 p.m.; and from JFD to DDE, 5:35 p.m., Memoranda of Telephone Conversations, White House, DDEP, box 16.

Chapter 8: "Sandstorms in the Desert"

1. DDE to DBG, Oct. 28, 1956, FRUS 1955–57, vol. 16, doc. 394, p. 801.

2. Bar-Zohar, *Armed Prophet*, 237.

3. Kyle, *Suez*, 348.

4. Uri Avnery, interview with the author, Mar. 2015.

5. Dayan, *Diary*, Oct. 29, 1956, 74–75.

6. United Nations, *Problem of Hungary*, 23–24.

7. Ibid., 55.

8. Imre Nagy in Rainer, *Imre Nagy*, 116.

9. "Resurgence," London *Times*, Oct. 29, 1956, 9.

10. "New Offer to Algerians," London *Times*, Oct. 30, 1956, 6.

11. GAN via Amin Howeidy in James, *Nasser at War*, 40; see also Kyle, *Suez*, 350.

12. James, *Nasser at War*, 39–40; Moshe Shemesh, "Egypt: From Military Defeat to Political Victory," in Troen and Shemesh, *Suez-Sinai Crisis 1956*, 153.

13. Henriques, *One Hundred Hours to Suez*, 137–38.

14. GAN, in Nutting, *Nasser*, 75.

15. Clark, *From Three Worlds*, 197.

16. Robinson, Shira, *Citizen Strangers: Palestinians and the Birth of Israel's Liberal Settler State* (Stanford: Stanford University Press, 2013), 160–1.

17. Blumenthal, *Goliath*, 125–27.

18. Eyal Kafkafi, "Segregation or Integration of the Israeli Arabs: Two Concepts in Mapai," *International Journal of Middle East Studies* 30, no. 3 (Aug. 1998): 366n.

19. Kyle, *Suez*, 348–49; "Israel Explores Dark Pages of Its Past," *Washington Post*, Oct. 31, 1999; "Rivlin Condemns 'Terrible Crime' of Kafr Kassem Massacre," *Times of Israel*, Oct. 26, 2014.

20. Sharon, *Warrior*, 144.

21. Ibid., 145.

22. Kyle, *Suez*, 350.

23. GAN in Heikal, *Cutting the Lion's Tail*, 177.

24. Status Report on the Near East Given by the Director [AWD] at the White House to a Bipartisan Congressional Group, Nov. 9, 1956, USNA: CIA-RDP80B01676R004200050014–8.

25. Etienne Dennery, ambassador to Switzerland, to the Minister for Foreign Affairs in Paris, Oct. 15, 1956, ADLC: 213QONT/480/EG-iv-5.

26. "Report on the World Today: Washington," *Atlantic Monthly*, Aug. 1956.

27. Telephone call, JFD to Sherman Adams, Oct. 29, 1956, 11:28 a.m., Memoranda of Telephone Conversations, White House, DDEP, box 16.

28. C. Douglas Dillon to JFD, Oct. 29, 1956, State Department Central Decimal Files, Suez Crisis, 974.7301/10–2356, USNA: RG 59/250/44/4/4.

29. Kyle, *Suez*, 351; Eliezer Cohen, *Israel's Best Defense: The First Full Story of the Israeli Air Force*, trans. Jonathan Cordis (Shrewsbury, UK: Airlife, 1994), 107–8; Ehud Yonay, *No Margin for Error: The Making of the Israeli Air Force* (New York: Pantheon, 1993), 161–63.

30. Heikal, *Cutting the Lion's Tail*, 177–78.

31. JFD to American Embassies in Paris and London, Oct. 29, 1956, Top Secret, Chronological—John Foster Dulles (1–3), Aug. 1956, DDEP, box 80.

32. Immerman, *Empire of Liberty*, 169–70.

33. JFD in Kinzer, *Brothers*, 49; Immerman, *Empire of Liberty*, 175.

34. AWD in Kinder, *Brothers*, 48.

35. Kinder, *Brothers*, 53–4; Preussen, *John Foster Dulles*, 125.

36. Eveland, *Ropes of Sand*, 63.

37. Abba Eban, JFDOHP. See also, in the same collection, James Hagerty's interview.

38. Shuckburgh, *Descent to Suez*, Dec. 16, 1954, 243.

39. Raymond Hare, JFDOHP.

40. See Judah Nadich, *Eisenhower and the Jews* (New York: Twayne, New York, 1953) for rabbinical approval of DDE (Nadich was a rabbi). On George Patton's antisemitism and his attitude to displaced persons camps, see Richard Cohen, "What Bill O'Reilly Ignored About George Patton," *Washington Post*, Sept. 29, 2014.

41. Uri Avnery, interview with the author, Mar. 2015.

42. DDE, Address at Byrd Field, Richmond, VA, Oct. 29, 1956.

43. Clark, *From Three Worlds*, 197.

44. Barnes in Budapest to Secretary of State, Oct. 29, 1956, USNA: Records of the State Department, RG 59, Central Decimal Files: 764.00/10–2956.

45. Kyle, *Suez*, 399; Shlaim, *Lion of Jordan*, 118–19.

46. Memorandum of a Conference with the President by Andrew Goodpaster, Oct. 29, 1956, 7:15 p.m., United Kingdom—Misc. Paper—UK, 1956, 1960, DDEP, box 37.

47. DDE (according to his own recollection) in Love, *Suez*, 503.

48. Baeyens, *Un coup d'épée*, 18.

49. "United States Ready to Honour Middle East Pledge," London *Times*, Oct. 30, 1956, 8.

50. Hughes, *Ordeal of Power*, 214.

51. Memorandum of a Conference with the President, Oct. 29, 1956, FRUS 1955–57, vol. 16, doc. 412, p. 840.

52. Kyle, *Suez*, 354–55.

Chapter 9: Ultimatum

1. Michail Bey Ilyan in Eveland, *Ropes of Sand*, 227.

2. Dorril, *MI6*, 642, 646–47. Ilyan eventually ended up in exile in Britain.

3. JFD and AWD in Dorril, *MI6*, 642; Kyle, *Suez*, 367.

4. Heikal, *Cutting the Lion's Tail*, 179.

5. Oct. 31, 1956, Adams, *Suez and After*, 82.

6. Trevelyan, *Middle East in Revolution*, 116; Michael T. Thornhill, "Alternatives to Nasser: Humphrey Trevelyan, Ambassador to Egypt," in Kelly and Gorst, *Whitehall and the Suez Crisis*, 11.

7. *Jerusalem Post*, Oct. 30, 1956, 1.

8. "Aims of the Drive," London *Times*, Oct. 30, 1956, 8.

9. Stock, *Israel on the Road to Sinai*, 191.

10. Winthrop W. Aldrich to JFD, Oct. 30, 1956, State Department Central Decimal Files, Suez Crisis, 974.7301/10–2356, USNA: RG 59/250/44/4/4. In 1967, Aldrich published an account of his meeting in which he claimed that Lloyd had said Britain would name Israel as the aggressor before the Security Council. If true, this would have been a flat-out lie. Yet Aldrich's 1967 account is contradicted by his own cable of October 30 and by the British Foreign Office account of the meeting. See Kyle, *Suez*, 355.

11. Cabinet meeting CM (56) 75th Conclusions, Minute 1, UKNA: CAB 128/30/299.

12. Dodds-Parker, *Political Eunuch*, 105.

13. Kyle, *Suez*, 369.

14. Ibid., 373.

15. *Jerusalem Post*, Oct. 31, 1956, 1.

16. For instance, GAN complained to the British ambassador in Bahrain in March 1956 that "the Saudis had embarrassed him" by giving £50,000 to the Muslim Brotherhood and heaping rewards on Egyptian paratroopers training in Saudi Arabia. Sir B. Burrows to Foreign Office, Mar. 3, 1956, UKNA: PREM 11/1448.

17. See Anthony Cave Brown, *Treason in the Blood* (Boston: Houghton Mifflin, 1994); James Craig, "Philby, Harry St. John Bridger (1885–1960)," *Oxford Dictionary of National Biography* (Oxford University Press, 2004).

18. As of 2015, the United States Energy Information Administration estimated Saudi reserves at 268 billion barrels.

19. Franklin D. Roosevelt in Morton, *Buraimi*, 65.

20. Al-Rasheed, *History of Saudi Arabia*, 89–114.

21. The politician was former Egyptian prime minister Hussein Sirri Pasha. Report from G. Lewis Jones, Chargé in Cairo to Deparment of State, Feb. 23, 1955, USNA: State Department Central Decimal Files, Gamal Abdel Nasser, 774.11/2–2355, USNA: RG 59/250/43/5/5.

22. Harold Macmillan to RAE, Nov. 25, 1955, UKNA: PREM 11/1448.

23. Copeland, *Game of Nations*, 58–59; Citino, *From Arab Nationalism to OPEC*, 96–98.

24. Eden, *Full Circle*, 331–32; see also 334.

25. RAE to DDE, Jan. 16, 1956, UKNA: PREM 11/1448.

26. For a much more detailed account of the Buraimi dispute, see Morton, *Buraimi*.

27. JFD to DDE, July 7, 1953; WSC, FO memoir of conversation with Winthrop Aldrich, May 22, 1953; both quoted in Petersen, "Anglo-American Rivalry," 76.

28. RAE in Shuckburgh, *Descent to Suez*, 187.

29. Nutting, *No End of a Lesson*, 42.

30. Telephone call JFD to DDE in Augusta, Wed., Apr. 11, 1956, 1:10 p.m., Memoranda of Telephone Conversations, White House, DDEP, box 16.

31. RAE, "The Economic Situation," Jan. 5, 1957, TNA: CAB 129/84, CP (57) 8, cited in Simon C. Smith, Introduction, in Smith, *Reassessing Suez 1956*, 6.

32. Quoted in Simon C. Smith, Introduction, in Smith, *Reassessing Suez 1956*, 8.

33. Hughes, *Ordeal of Power*, 215.

34. Memorandum of a Conference with the President, Oct. 30, 1956, United Kingdom—Misc. Paper—UK, 1956, 1960, DDEP, box 37.

35. Barnes in Budapest to Secretary of State, Oct. 30, 1956, USNA: Records of the State Department, RG 59, Central Decimal Files: 764.00/10–3056.

36. Barnes in Budapest to Secretary of State, Oct. 30, 1956, USNA: Records of the State Department, RG 59, Central Decimal Files: 764.00/10–2556.

37. Mao Tse-tung in Taubman, *Khrushchev*, 297; see also Zhu, *1956*, 160.

38. Nikolai Bulganin and Nikita Khrushchev, Oct. 30, 1956, in Gati, *Failed Illusions*, 179.

39. Kramer, "Soviet Union and the 1956 Crises," 188.

40. Mićunović, *Moscow Diary*, 129–30.

41. Barnes in Budapest to Secretary of State, Oct. 30, 1956, USNA: Records of the State Department, RG 59, Central Decimal Files: 764.00/10–3056.

42. Imre Nagy in Rainer, *Imre Nagy*, 119–20.

43. Nutting, *No End of a Lesson*, 116.

44. Shuckburgh, *Descent to Suez*, Nov. 1, 1956, 362.

45. Reported in Verrier, *Through the Looking Glass*, 154. The swear word is blanked out in the original.

46. RAE in Parliamentary Debates (Hansard), 5th series, vol. 558 (House of Commons), col. 1281.

47. Denis Healey and RAE in Parliamentary Debates (Hansard), 5th series, vol. 558 (House of Commons), col. 1290–91.

48. Oct. 30, 1956, Benn, *Years of Hope*, 193.

49. James Reston in Isaac Alteras, "Eisenhower and the Sinai Campaign of 1956: The First Major Crisis in US-Israeli Relations," in Tal, *1956 War*, 30.

50. Cooper, *Lion's Last Roar*, 167. The aide appears to have been William Clark, who also remembered the story. See Rhodes James, *Eden*, 568.

51. RAE to DDE, Oct. 30, 1956, FRUS 1955–57, vol. 16, doc. 421, pp. 856–57.

52. Telephone call from JFD to DDE, 11:37 a.m., Oct. 30, 1956, Memoranda of Telephone Conversations White House, DDEP, box 16.

53. DDE to RAE, Oct. 30, 1956, FRUS 1955–57, vol. 16, doc. 424, pp. 860–61.

54. Hayter, *Kremlin and the Embassy*, 142.

55. Khrushchev, *Khrushchev Remembers*, 430.

56. Heikal, *Sphinx and Commissar*, 70–71. Heikal retells this story in *Cutting the Lion's Tail*, 192–93, and *Cairo Documents*, 111. DDE agreed, telling his advisers, "Look at the map.... Geography makes effective Soviet intervention in Egypt difficult, if not impossible." Murphy, *Diplomat Among Warriors*, 476.

57. Khrushchev, *Last Testament*, 342. See also Khrushchev, *Khrushchev Remembers*, 443.

58. Charles E. Bohlen to Secretary of State, Oct. 31, 1956, USNA: Records of the State Department, RG 59, Central Decimal Files: 764.00/10–3156.

59. Charles E. Bohlen in Moscow to Secretary of State, Oct. 20, 1956, USNA: RG 59, Records of the Department of State, Central Decimal Files, 684A.86/10–3056. See also FRUS 1955–57, vol. 25, doc. 145, p. 347, n. 3.

60. Sir William Hayter to FO, Oct. 30, 1956, UKNA: PREM 11/1170.

61. Sergei Khrushchev, *Khrushchev on Khrushchev: An Inside Account of the Man and His Era*, tr. William Taubman (Boston: Little, Brown, 1990), 57.

62. Heikal, *Cutting the Lion's Tail*, 179. See also Nutting, *No End of a Lesson*, 115–16.

63. GAN in Heikal, *Cairo Documents*, 108.

64. In James, *Nasser at War*, 41; see also Abd al-Latif al-Bughdadi, Diary, Oct. 30, 1956, in Troen and Shemesh, *Suez-Sinai Crisis 1956*, 338.

65. GAN in Moncrieff, *Suez Ten Years After*, 48.

66. *Jerusalem Post*, Oct. 31, 1956, 1.

67. Moshe Dayan's (unpublished) Diary, Oct. 30, 1956, in Motti Golani, "The Sinai War, 1956: Three Partners, Three Wars," in Tal, *1956 War*, 172–73.

68. Telephone call between DDE and JFD, FRUS 1955–57, vol. 16, doc. 427, p. 863.

69. Telephone call from JFD to DDE, 2:53 p.m., Oct. 30, 1956, Memoranda of Telephone Conversations, White House, DDEP, box 16. For DDE's letter to RAE and Guy Mollet, see FRUS 1955–57, vol. 16, doc. 430, p. 866.

70. *Paris Match*, Oct. 29, 1966, 84. There is an atmospheric firsthand account of this event by Pedrazzini's colleague Paul Mathias in the same edition of *Paris-Match*, 74–77.

71. Réthly, *Hungarian Revolution*, 28; Gati, *Failed Illusions*, 177; Kopácsi, *In the Name of the Working Class*, 196.

72. Fryer, *Hungarian Tragedy*, 63–64; see also Méray, *Thirteen Days That Shook the Kremlin*, 153–54.

73. Gati, *Failed Illusions*, 177n.

74. Hugh Gaitskell in Parliamentary Debates (Hansard), 5th series, vol. 558 (House of Commons), col. 1347–48.

75. Alfred Robens in ibid., col. 1371.

76. Selwyn Lloyd in ibid., col. 1375, 1378.

77. In Lucas, *Divided We Stand*, 263.

78. Sharon, *Warrior*, 146.

79. JFD telephone call to Lester Pearson in Ottawa, Oct. 30, 1956, 3:00 p.m., Memoranda of Telephone Conversations, General, DDEP, box 10.

80. RAE to DDE, Oct. 30, 1956, FRUS 1955–57, vol. 16, doc. 434, pp. 871–72.

81. Telephone calls from DDE to JFD 3;40 p.m., JFD to DDE 3:50 p.m., Oct. 30, 1956, Memoranda of Telephone Conversations, White House, DDEP, box 16.

82. Memorandum of a Conversation with the President, Oct. 31, 1956, FRUS 1955–57, vol. 16, doc. 435, pp. 873–74.

83. Galpern, *Money, Oil, and Empire*, 167.

84. Cooper, *Lion's Last Roar*, 169.

85. Nutting, *No End of a Lesson*, 121.

86. Eden, *Full Circle*, 530; Kyle, *Suez*, 364–65; Pineau, *1956/Suez*, 163.

87. See FRUS 1955–57, vol. 16, doc. 439, pp. 881–82.

88. DDE draft (unsent), Oct. 30, 1956, DDEP, box 16.

89. Hughes, *Ordeal of Power*, 216–17.

90. Telephone calls from DDE to JFD, 4:54 p.m., and JFD to DDE, 5:23 p.m., Oct. 30, 1956, Memoranda of Telephone Conversations, White House, DDEP, box 16.

91. Adlai Stevenson in *New York Times*, Oct. 31, 1956, 1, 24.

92. DDE and John Eisenhower in Eisenhower, *Strictly Personal*, 189–90.

93. Kyle, *Suez*, 376–77.

Chapter 10: Perfidious Albion

1. "Egyptian Warship Captured," London *Times*, Nov. 1, 1956, 10; Fullick and Powell, *Suez: The Double War*, 90; Gilbert, *Israel*, 321; Baeyens, *Un coup d'épée*, 63.

2. Gerald Templer in Cloake, *Templer*, 352.

3. Cooper, *Lion's Last Roar*, 170.

4. Sharon, *Warrior*, 146.

5. Rechavam Ze'evi in Sharon, *Warrior*, 147.

6. Sharon, *Warrior*, 148.

7. Ibid., 149.

8. Gen. Sir Charles Keightley to Chiefs of Staff, Oct. 31, 1956, in Keith Kyle, "Britain and the Crisis, 1955–1956," in Louis and Owen, *Suez 1956*, 128.

9. Secret Staff Summaries, State Dept., Nov. 1, 1956, Hungary and Suez Crisis, 1955–1956, JFDP, State Department Records, box 1, folder 1; Raymond Hare, JFDOHP; Current Intelligence Bulletin, Nov. 2, 1956, USNA: CIA-RDP79T00975A002800120001-7.

10. Barnes to Budapest, Oct. 31, 1956, USNA: Records of the State Department, RG 59, Central Decimal Files: 764.00/10–3156.

11. "Budapest Reported Free of Soviet Troops," London *Times*, Nov. 1, 1956, 8.

12. NSK in Taubman, *Khrushchev*, 296; see Khrushchev, *Khrushchev Remembers*, 418.

13. Kramer, "Soviet Union and the 1956 Crises," 189–90.

14. Zhu, *1956*, 168–77, has a much more detailed account of the complicated changing positions of Chinese policy on Hungary over the last few days in October.

15. Mićunović, *Moscow Diary*, 130.

16. NSK in Laurent Rucker, "The Soviet Union and the Suez Crisis," in Tal, *1956 War*, 84.

17. Maksim Saburov in Kramer, "Soviet Union and the 1956 Crises," 190.

18. Réthly, *Hungarian Revolution*, 30.

19. Cooper, *Lion's Last Roar*, 173.

20. Secret Staff Summaries, State Dept., Nov. 1, 1956, Hungary and Suez Crisis, 1955–1956, JFDP State Department Records, box 1, folder 1.

21. JFD to Richard Nixon, telephone call, Oct. 31, 1956, in Kunz, *Economic Diplomacy*, 125.

22. "India Condemns Anglo-French Action," London *Times*, Nov. 1, 1956, 9.

23. Moshe Sharett in "India Condemns Anglo-French Action," London *Times*, Nov. 1, 1956, 9.

24. "Menace to France," London *Times*, Nov. 1, 1956, 9.

25. Nutting, *No End of a Lesson*, 122–23. RAE denied having any memory of this meeting. See Rhodes James, *Eden*, 570. James believes RAE's denial; the present author is inclined not to on the grounds, first, that RAE's memories are often unreliable, and second, that Nutting's account is specific in its detail and captures the authentic ring of RAE's speech.

26. Dodds-Parker, *Political Eunuch*, 106.

27. Oct. 31, 1956. Benn, *Years of Hope*, p 193.

28. Hughes, *Ordeal of Power*, 218–19. Present at the meeting were Sherman Adams, Wilton Persons, James Hagerty, Andrew Goodpaster, Gabriel Hauge, and Emmet Hughes.

29. Memorandum of a telephone conversation between Abba Eban and Mr. Burdett, Oct. 31, 1956, FRUS 1955–57, vol. 16, doc. 448, p. 894.

30. "Cutting Off Gaza Strip," London *Times*, Nov. 1, 1956, 10.

31. Imre Nagy in Fryer, *Hungarian Tragedy*, 63.

32. János Kádár and Imre Nagy in Gough, *Good Comrade*, 87.

33. RAE in Eden, *Full Circle*, 532.

34. Hugh Gaitskell in Parliamentary Debates (Hansard), 5th series, vol. 558 (House of Commons), col. 1454, 1459.

35. William Yates himself told this story in 1996. Keith Kyle, "Britain's Slow March to Suez," in Tal, *The 1956 War*, 108–9.

36. Nigel Nicolson, "Diary of a Suez Rebel," London *Daily Telegraph*, Oct. 27, 1996.

37. DBG to Maurice Bourgès-Maunoury, 5:00 p.m., Oct. 31, 1956, in Kyle, *Suez*, 382.

38. Mosley, *Dulles*, 418.

39. Heikal, *Cutting the Lion's Tail*, 180.

40. Kyle, *Suez*, 383.

41. Flight-Lieutenant John Slater in London *Daily Mirror*, Nov. 1, 1956, 24.

42. *New York Times*, Nov. 1, 1956, 6.

43. Kyle, *Suez*, 384.

44. Abd al-Latif al-Bughdadi, Diary, Oct. 30, 1956, in Troen and Shemesh, *Suez-Sinai Crisis 1956*, 340.

45. Richard M. Bissell, JFDOHP.

46. In Mosley, *Dulles*, 148. Though Mosley does not attribute this to a specific interviewee, his sources included high-up CIA agents like Richard Bissell, who would certainly have had access to this information.

47. Sharon, *Warrior*, 150.

48. DDE in Robertson, *Crisis*, 171.

49. "Washington Charge of Collusion with Israel," London *Times*, Nov. 1, 1956, 10.

50. Harry S. Truman and Adlai Stevenson in Cooper, *Lion's Last Roar*, 175.

51. DDE to Senator William Knowland, in Ambrose, *Eisenhower*, vol. 2, p. 361.

52. "U.N. Assembly to Meet To-day," London *Times*, Nov. 1, 1956, 10.

53. Winthrop Aldrich in "U.S. Envoy on 'Very Grave Anxiety,'" London *Times*, Nov. 1, 1956, 9.

54. "Over the Brink," London *Times*, Nov. 1, 1956, 11.

55. Mordecai Bar-On in Motti Golani, "The Sinai War, 1956: Three Partners, Three Wars," in Tal, *1956 War*, 180.

56. Dayan, *Diary*, Nov. 3, 1956, 127.

57. DDE in "Washington Charge of Collusion with Israel," London *Times*, Nov. 1, 1956, 10.

58. Hughes, *Ordeal of Power*, 219–22.

Chapter 11: "There Is Something the Matter with Him"

1. NSK and Anastas Mikoyan in Taubman, *Khrushchev*, 298.

2. Abd al-Latif al-Bughdadi, Diary, Nov. 1, 1956, in Troen and Shemesh, *Suez-Sinai Crisis 1956*, 340.

3. Nutting, *No End of a Lesson*, 128.

4. Keith Kyle, "Britain's Slow March to Suez," in Tal, *1956 War*, 110.

5. *Egyptian Gazette*, Nov. 1, 1956, in Kyle, *Suez*, 380.

6. Abd al-Latif al-Bughdadi, Diary, Nov. 1, 1956, in Troen and Shemesh, *Suez-Sinai Crisis 1956*, 340.

7. GAN announcement and quote in London *Times*, Nov. 2, 1956, 8.

8. Heikal, *Cairo Documents*, 111.

9. Ali Abu Nuwar in Shlaim, *Lion of Jordan*, 120.

10. Sir C. Duke to Foreign Office, Nov. 3, 1956, UKNA: FO 371/121786, VR 1091/508.

11. *New York Times*, Nov. 2, 1956, 3.

12. Kyle, *Suez*, 399–400; Heikal, *Cutting the Lion's Tail*, 188.

13. Sir William Hayter to Foreign Office, Nov. 1, 1956, UKNA: PREM 11/1170.

14. Anastas Mikoyan and Mikhail Suslov in Gati, *Failed Illusions*, 190.

15. Cooper, *Lion's Last Roar*, 176.

16. London *Times*, Nov. 2, 1956, 8.

17. RAE to Guy Mollet, Nov. 1, 1956, UKNA: FO 800/727.

18. Luard, *History of the United Nations*, vol. 1, pp. 6–8.

19. Clark, *From Three Worlds*, 203.

20. Henry Durant in Moncrieff, *Suez Ten Years After*, 19.

21. Pineau, *1956/Suez*, 163.

22. Top Secret Staff Summaries, State Dept., Nov. 2, 1956, Hungary and Suez Crisis, 1955–1956, JFDP State Department Records, box 1, folder 1.

23. These bulletins can be read in TNA: PREM 11/1163.

24. Lord Charteris and a confidential interviewee in Ben Pimlott, *The Queen: Elizabeth II and the Monarchy* (1996; HarperCollins, London, 2002), 253–55.

25. Lord Charteris in Ben Pimlott, *The Queen: Elizabeth II and the Monarchy* (1996; HarperCollins, London, 2002), 253–55.

26. Lord Mountbatten, tour diaries, June 13, 1976, in Ziegler, *Mountbatten*, 546.

27. Lord Charteris in Ben Pimlott, *The Queen: Elizabeth II and the Monarchy* (1996; HarperCollins, London, 2002), 255.

28. UK High Commission in India to UK delegation at the UN in New York via Foreign Office, Nov. 1, 1956; UK High Commission in India to Commonwealth Relations Office, Nov. 1, 1956; UK High Commission in Pakistan to Commonwealth Relations Office, Nov. 1, 1956; all in UKNA: FO 371/118904.

29. King Hussein of Jordan in London *Times*, Nov. 2, 1956, 6.

30. Clark, *From Three Worlds*, 203.

31. *Jerusalem Post*, Nov. 2, 1956, 4.

32. The story of how Yuri Andropov deliberately deceived Nagy is told in Andrew and Gordievsky, *KGB*, 355–56, and in Andrew and Mitrokhin, *Mitrokhin Archive*, vol. 1, p. 327.

33. Jenő Szell in Gough, *Good Comrade*, 88. It has often been repeated at this point that János Kádár voiced his intent to fight the Soviets in the streets with his bare hands, but other evidence contradicts this; see Gough, *Good Comrade*, 90, for a debunking.

34. Molnár, *Budapest 1956*, 182.

35. Todor Zhivkov in Kramer, "Soviet Union and the 1956 Crises," 204.

36. Minutes of the Egypt Committee, EC (56) 36th meeting, Nov. 1, 1956, TNA: CAB 134/1216.

37. Clark, *From Three Worlds*, 203.

38. London *Times*, Nov. 3, 1956, 5 (report delayed from Nov. 1).

39. JFD telephone call to DDE, 8:40 a.m., Nov. 1, 1956, Memoranda of Telephone Conversations, White House, DDEP, box 16.

40. Imre Nagy in United Nations, *Problem of Hungary*, 25.

41. London *Times*, Nov. 3, 1956, 5 (report delayed from Nov. 1).

42. National Security Council meeting, Washington DC, Nov. 1, 1956, FRUS 1955–57, vol. 16, doc. 455, p. 906.

43. Telephone call from DDE to JFD, Thur., Nov. 1, 1956, 12:25 p.m., Memoranda of Telephone Conversations, White House, DDEP, box 16.

44. JFD telephone call to DDE, 11:05 a.m., Nov. 1, 1956, Memoranda of Telephone Conversations, White House, DDEP, box 16.

45. Cooper, *Lion's Last Roar*, 177.

46. Vice-Admiral Robin Durnford-Slater, Oct. 31, 1956, and Nov. 1, 1956, in Kyle, *Suez*, 411.

47. General Sir Charles Keightley in Kyle, *Suez*, 412.

48. Top Secret Staff Summaries, State Dept., Nov. 2, 1956, Hungary and Suez Crisis, 1955–56, JFDP State Department Records, box 1, folder 1.

49. Nutting, *No End of a Lesson*, 128–29; Kilmuir, *Political Adventure*, 273–74; journalist Iverach McDonald in Kyle, *Suez*, 388.

50. Parliamentary Debates (Hansard), 5th series, vol. 558 (House of Commons), col. 1625.

51. Clarissa Eden and Dora Gaitskell in Lucas, *Divided We Stand*, 274.

52. RAE in Parliamentary Debates (Hansard), 5th series, vol. 558 (House of Commons), col. 1627.

53. Rhodes James, *Eden*, 558–59.

54. Aneurin Bevan in Parliamentary Debates (Hansard), 5th series, vol. 558 (House of Commons), Nov. 1, 1956, col. 1710.

55. George Craddock MP (Bradford South, Labour) and Edwin Leather MP (North Somerset, Conservative), in London *Times*, Nov. 2, 1956, 5.

56. *New York Times*, Nov. 2, 1956, 9.

57. London *Times*, Nov. 2, 1956, 8. There is a photograph of the protest in London on p. 16.

58. Michael G. Fry, "Canada, the North Atlantic, and the UN," in Louis and Owen, *Suez 1956*, 307.

59. Luard, *History of the United Nations*, vol. 2, p. 33.

60. JFD Statement in the UN General Assembly, Nov. 1, 1956, and US Draft Resolution (UN doc. A/3256) in Department of State Bulletin, Nov. 12, 1956, in vol. July–Dec.1956, 751–55.

61. JFD in Carlton, *Eden*, 447. See also William B. Macomber Jr., JFDOHP: "And he [JFD] told me later—it was the next day that he was taken sick—that if he had died that next day that he would have been content to have that speech as his last words."

62. Lester Pearson in Luard, *History of the United Nations*, vol. 2, p. 34.

63. Herman Phleger, JFDOHP.

Chapter 12: "Love to Nasty"

1. Henriques, *One Hundred Hours to Suez*, 186.

2. Sir M. Wright to Foreign Office, Nov. 2, 1956, UKNA: FO 371/121786, VR 1091/509.

3. London *Times*, Nov. 3, 1956, 7.

4. Heikal, *Cairo Documents*, 112.

5. Nutting, *No End of a Lesson*, 132–33. AWD confirmed that the British had sunk the blockship in a meeting of the NSC on Nov. 1. National Security Council meeting, Washington DC, Nov. 1, 1956, FRUS 1955–57, vol. 16, doc. 455, p. 914.

6. Lapping, *End of Empire*, 274; Bulletin for HM the Queen, Nov. 4, 1956, UKNA: PREM 11/1163.

7. Copeland, *Game Player*, 203.

8. Cooper, *Lion's Last Roar*, 179–80.

9. Nutting, *No End of a Lesson*, 134.

10. Pineau, *1956/Suez*, 162.

11. General Keightley to Chiefs of Staff, Nov. 2, 1956, in Keith Kyle, "Britain and the Crisis, 1955–1956," in Louis and Owen, *Suez 1956*, 128.

12. Lord Mountbatten of Burma to RAE, Nov. 2, 1956, TNA: PREM 11/1090.

13. Bertrand Russell in *Manchester Guardian*, Nov. 2, 1956, 8.

14. Gerald Templer in Cloake, *Templer*, 355.

15. Arleigh Burke, JFDOHP.

16. Richard M. Bissell, JFDOHP.

17. James Hagerty, JFDOHP.

18. János Kádár in Gough, *Good Comrade*, 94.

19. Réthly, *Hungarian Revolution*, 34.

20. Current Intelligence Bulletin, Nov. 3, 1956, USNA: CIA-RDP79T00975A002800130001–6.

21. RAE in Parliamentary Debates (Hansard), 5th series, vol. 558 (House of Commons), col. 1754.

22. London *Times*, Nov. 3, 1956, 4.

23. Adams, *Tony Benn*, 122.

24. Eden, *Full Circle*, 541.

25. Nutting, *No End of a Lesson*, 135–36.

26. Eden, *Full Circle*, 540.

27. Ibid., 459.

28. London *Times*, Nov. 3, 1956, 5.

29. Richard Nixon in Eden, *Full Circle*, 541–42.

30. DDE to Alfred Gruenther, Nov. 2, 1956, in Ambrose, *Eisenhower*, vol. 2, p. 365; Kyle, *Suez*, 427.

31. Abd al-Latif al-Bughdadi, Diary, Nov. 1956, in Troen and Shemesh, *Suez-Sinai Crisis 1956*, 342–43. This conversation is also reported with a couple of key differences in Heikal, *Cutting the Lion's Tail*, 180. Heikal does not report the suicide threat. He also says Salah Salem asked GAN to surrender individually to the British embassy rather than suggesting a collective surrender for the entire Egyptian leadership. Baghdadi's account has been preferred here because it appears to have been a diary written at the time, even if it was subsequently edited.

32. Heikal, *Cairo Documents*, 110–11.

33. GAN via Mahmoud Hammroush in Aburish, *Nasser*, 119.

34. Heikal, *Cutting the Lion's Tail*, 181.

35. *New York Times*, Nov. 3, 1956, 2.

36. Sir C. Duke to Foreign Office, Nov. 2, 1956, UKNA: FO 371/121786, VR 1091/494.

37. CIA Office of National Estimates, "North African Reactions to Recent French Moves," Staff Memorandum No. 88–56, Nov. 2, 1956, USNA: CIA-RDP79T00937A000500020010–5.

38. London *Times*, Nov. 6, 1956, 8.

39. Top Secret Staff Summaries, State Dept., Nov. 2, 1956, Hungary and Suez Crisis, 1955–1956, JFDP State Department Records, box 1, folder 1.

40. Henriques, *One Hundred Hours to Suez*, 180–81; Kyle, *Suez*, 414.

41. Dayan, *Diary*, Nov. 3, 1956 (incident is Nov. 2), 117.

42. Voice of Britain in Kyle, *Suez*, 416–17.

43. Lucas, *Divided We Stand*, 272.

44. GAN in Moncrieff, *Suez Ten Years After*, 48.

45. GAN in Kyle, *Suez*, 418.

46. Heikal, *Cutting the Lion's Tail*, 200n.

47. Heikal, *Sphinx and Commissar*, 71.

48. JFD in London *Times*, Nov. 3, 1956, 6.

49. Memorandum of a telephone conversation between the Secretary of State in Washington and the Representative at the United Nations (Lodge) in New York, Nov. 2, 1956, 4:11 p.m., FRUS vol. 25 (Eastern Europe), doc. 156, p. 365.

50. Study Prepared for U.S. Army Intelligence, "Hungary: Resistance Activities and Potentials," Jan. 1956, National Security Archive, George Washington University, http://nsarchive.gwu.edu/NSAEBB/NSAEBB76/doc1.pdf.

51. Appendix to NSC 5608/1, July 18, 1956, Supplementary Statement of Policy by the National Security Council on US Policy Toward the Soviet Satellites in Eastern Europe. This document was not included in the relevant FRUS volume but has since been declassified.

It can be viewed online at the National Security Archive, George Washington University, http://nsarchive.gwu.edu/NSAEBB/NSAEBB76/doc4.pdf.

52. Minutes of 290th NSC meeting, July 12, 1956. These quotes were not included in the FRUS account of the meeting. They can be viewed online at the National Security Archive, George Washington University, http://nsarchive.gwu.edu/NSAEBB/NSAEBB76/doc2.pdf.

53. Top Secret Staff Summaries, State Department, Nov. 2, 1956, Hungary and Suez Crisis, 1955–1956, JFDP: State Department Records, box 1, folder 1, Public Policy Papers. See also: Barnes in Budapest to Secretary of State, Nov. 1, 1956, USNA: Records of the State Department, RG 59, Central Decimal Files: 764.00/11–156.

54. Khrushchev, *Khrushchev Remembers*, 421.

55. Mićunović, *Moscow Diary*, 131; on Malenkov's cold embrace, 144.

56. Khrushchev, *Khrushchev Remembers*, 421.

57. On János Kádár's alleged Titoism, see CIA information report, Nov. 2, 1956, USNA: CIA-RDP80T00246A031800590001–4.

58. Mićunović, *Moscow Diary*, 132–40.

59. United Nations, *Problem of Hungary*, 56.

60. Charles E. Bohlen to Secretary of State, Nov. 2, 1956, USNA: Records of the State Department, RG 59, Central Decimal Files: 764.00/11–256.

61. Harold Watkinson and Harold Macmillan in London *Times*, Nov. 3, 1956, 6.

62. London *Times*, Nov. 3, 1956, 6.

63. DDE in London *Times*, Nov. 3, 1956, 6.

64. Henry Cabot Lodge to Secretary of State, Nov. 2, 1956, USNA: Records of the State Department, RG 59, Central Decimal Files: 764.00/11–256.

65. William B. Macomber Jr., JFDOHP.

Chapter 13: "Help the Burglar, Shoot the Householder"

1. Mićunović, *Moscow Diary*, 140–41.

2. Cooper, *Lion's Last Roar*, 181–82.

3. Abba Eban, JFDOHP.

4. Scott Lucas and Alistair Morey, "The Hidden 'Alliance': The CIA and MI6 Before and After Suez," in Stafford and Jeffreys-Jones, *American-British-Canadian Intelligence Relations*, 110.

5. Cooper, *Lion's Last Roar*, 182.

6. Ibid., 182–83.

7. Eveland, *Ropes of Sand*, 228.

8. Sir Ivone Kirkpatrick, minute to Africa Dept., FO, Nov. 3, 1956, UKNA: FO 371/118904.

9. Carlton, *Eden*, 450.

10. Ministry of Defence, London, to GHQ, Middle East Land Forces, Nov. 3, 1956, UKNA: AIR 8/1940.

11. General Keightley to Chiefs of Staff, Nov. 3, 1956, UKNA: AIR 8/1940.

12. Quoted in Kyle, *Suez*, 434–35.

13. Montague Browne, *Long Sunset*, 212. Montague Browne quotes from Winston Churchill's and RAE's letters.

14. Réthly, *Hungarian Revolution*, 36.

15. Current Intelligence Bulletin, Nov 3, 1956, USNA: CIA-RDP79T00975A002800130001–6.

16. *Jerusalem Post*, Nov. 4, 1956, 3.

17. *Special Report of the Director of the United Nations Relief and Works Agency for Palestine Refugees in the Near East, Covering the Period 1 November 1956 to mid-December 1956* (New York: United Nations, 1957), UN General Assembly: Official Records, 11th Session, Suppl. 14A (A/3212/Add.1); see also Filiu, *Gaza*, 96–97; Sayigh, *Armed Struggle*, 65.

18. Abdel Aziz al-Rantissi in Joe Sacco, *Footnotes in Gaza* (London: Jonathan Cape, 2009), xi. Sacco's illustrated re-creation of the events of November 1956 in the Gaza Strip is one of the best available historical accounts.

19. Eden, *Full Circle*, 542.

20. RAE and Hugh Gaitskell in Parliamentary Debates (Hansard), 5th series, vol. 558 (House of Commons), col. 1866.

21. Denis Healey in Parliamentary Debates (Hansard), 5th series, vol. 558 (House of Commons), col. 1905.

22. London *Times*, Nov. 5, 1956, 7.

23. Foreign Office to Ralph Murray at AFHQ, Nov. 4, 1956, UKNA: FO 371/118904.

24. "A Foreign Office spokesman said last night that a British frigate, operating in the Gulf of Suez, had shot down an Israeli aircraft 'which interfered with her patrol.'" In "Navy Shoot Down Israeli Aircraft," London *Times*, Nov. 5, 1956, 8.

25. Sir M. Wright to Foreign Office, Nov. 3, 1956, UKNA: FO 371/121786, VR 1091/515.

26. London *Times*, Nov. 5, 1956, 7.

27. Luard, *History of the United Nations*, vol. 2, pp. 34–35.

28. Abd al-Latif al-Bughdadi, Diary, Nov. 3, 1956, in Troen and Shemesh, *Suez-Sinai Crisis 1956*, 345.

29. Nutting, *No End of a Lesson*, 137–38.

30. Memorandum of conversation between DDE, Herbert Hoover and Herman Phleger, Nov. 3, 1956, 11:10 a.m., Eisenhower Library, FRUS 25 (Eastern Europe), doc. 158, p. 369, footnote 11.

31. Charles E. Bohlen to Secretary of State, Nov. 3, 1956, USNA: Records of the State Department, RG 59, Central Decimal Files: 764.00/11–356.

32. Réthly, *Hungarian Revolution*, 36.

33. Hennessy, *Prime Minister*, 247; RAE's lines taken from London *Times*, Nov. 5, 1956, 4; Louis St. Laurent's words from London *Times*, Nov. 5, 1956, 6. Footage of the broadcast is available at the British Pathé archive.

34. Andrew and Mitrokhin, *Mitrokhin Archive*, vol. 1, p. 324.

35. UN General Assembly Resolution 998 (ES-1).

36. Keith Kyle, "Britain's Slow March to Suez," in Tal, *1956 War*, 113; Kyle, *Suez*, 437.

37. Abba Eban and Ceylonese ambassador in Kyle, *Suez*, 437.

38. Sir Pierson Dixon to Foreign Office, Nov. 4, 1956, UKNA: PREM 11/1105 ff 185–6.

Chapter 14: Reaping the Whirlwind

1. Andrews and Gordievsky, *KGB*, 356.

2. Imre Nagy in Rainer, *Imre Nagy*, 134.

3. Imre Nagy in Moncrieff, *Suez Ten Years After*, 15–16.

4. János Kádár in United Nations, *Problem of Hungary*, 37.

5. Mindszenty, *Memoirs*, 212.

6. Bibó, *Art of Peacemaking*, 356.

7. The witness was the wife of Zoltán Vas. Imre Nagy in Rainer, *Imre Nagy*, 138.

8. Abd al-Latif al-Bughdadi, Diary, Nov. 4, 1956, in Troen and Shemesh, *Suez-Sinai Crisis 1956*, 347.

9. Nutting, *No End of a Lesson*, 141–43.

10. Baeyens, *Un coup d'épée*, 82–87; Kyle, *Suez*, 435.

11. Baeyens, *Un coup d'épée*, 92: "il faut aller aussi vite et aussi loin que possible, saisir des gages."

12. Unnamed Hungarian combatant in Sebestyen, *Twelve Days*, 2–3; also in London *Daily Mirror*, Nov. 5, 1956, 2.

13. Julius Hay in Molnár, *Budapest 1956*, 198; see also United Nations, *Problem of Hungary*, 26.

14. "Eden," London *Observer*, Nov. 4, 1956.

15. Anthony Greenwood in London *Times*, Nov. 5, 1956, 4; Aneurin Bevan in Cooper, *Lion's Last Roar*, 187.

16. Cooper, *Lion's Last Roar*, 188.

17. Winston Churchill in Montague Browne, *Long Sunset*, 212.

18. Lord Mountbatten of Burma to Lord Hailsham, Nov. 4, 1956; Lord Hailsham to RAE, Nov. 5, 1956; Lord Hailsham to Lord Mountbatten of Burma, Nov. 5, 1956; all TNA: PREM 11/1090.

19. Kyle, *Suez*, 432–33.

20. Hugh Gaitskell, Nov. 4, 1956, in Gaitskell, *Diary*, 619–22.

21. Clark, *From Three Worlds*, 208–9.

22. Sir M. Wright to Foreign Office, Nov. 4, 1956, UKNA: FO 371/121786, VR 1091/523. The British ambassador to Lebanon agreed with him: "Unless it is soon made abundantly clear that Her Majesty's Government will apply the same severe criteria in judging Israeli aggression as have been used against Egyptian policy in the Canal issue, we shall inevitably forfeit both friendship and respect." Mr. Middleton to Foreign Office, Nov. 4, 1956, UKNA: FO 371/121786, VR 1091/524.

23. Harold Macmillan in Lloyd, *Suez 1956*, 206.

24. Eden, *Full Circle*, 551.

25. Carlton, *Eden*, 450.

26. *Manchester Guardian*, Nov. 5, 1956, 1.

27. Eden, *Course of My Life*, 173.

28. Butler, *Art of the Possible*, 193. RAE took issue with Butler's retelling of the story, in which Butler claimed RAE told the whole cabinet he was thinking of resigning, but it would appear to be in essence correct that he did bring this subject up even if not with the whole cabinet. According to Lady Eden, who was defensive of her husband's role and reputation, RAE took Butler, Macmillan, and Salisbury aside and said he would have to resign if the three of them would not support him. Rhodes James, *Eden*, 567.

29. Eden, *Memoir*, 253–54. See also the accounts in Carlton, *Eden*, 450–51; Kyle, *Suez*, 442.

30. Lloyd, *Suez 1956*, 207.

31. Cooper, *Lion's Last Roar*, 182.

32. DDE to Bulganin, Nov. 4, 1956, quoted in Mr. Coulson (Washington) to Foreign Office, Nov. 6, 1956, UKNA: PREM 11/1170.

33. Christian Pineau, London *Times*, Nov. 5, 1956, 6.

34. *Manchester Guardian*, Nov. 5, 1956, 6.

35. Herman Phleger, JFDOHP.

36. Ibid.

37. Thompson in Vienna to Secretary of State, Nov. 4, 1956, USNA: RG 59, Records of the Department of State, Central Decimal Files: 764.00/11–456.

38. Rabenold in Zagreb to Secretary of State, Nov. 5, 1956, USNA: RG 59, Records of the Department of State, Central Decimal Files: 764.00/11–556.

39. Clare Booth Luce, Eyes Only the President, in C. Douglas Dillon to Secretary of State, Nov. 4, 1956, USNA: RG 59, Records of the Department of State, Central Decimal Files: 764.00/11–456.

40. Robert Murphy, JFDOHP.

41. Mosley, *Dulles*, 421.

42. Eveland, *Ropes of Sand*, 229.

43. Averell Harriman, JFDOHP.

44. DDE in Gati, *Failed Illusions*, 19.

45. Gati, *Failed Illusions*, 112.

46. Luard, *History of the United Nations*, vol. 2, pp. 36–37.

47. Arkady Sobolev and Henry Cabot Lodge in London *Times*, Nov. 5, 1956, 8.

48. London *Times*, Nov. 5, 1956, 8.

49. Kyle, *Suez*, 445.

50. Heikal, *Cairo Documents*, 113.

51. Abd al-Latif al-Bughdadi, Diary, Nov. 5, 1956, in Troen and Shemesh, *Suez-Sinai Crisis 1956*, 348.

Chapter 15: "Hit 'Em with *Everything* in the Bucket"

1. Peter Woods in London *Daily Mirror*, Nov. 7, 1956, 9.

2. Leulliette, *St. Michael and the Dragon*, 198.

3. It would have been more correct, though not more polite, to say *"shuftini kushik"*—"show me your cunt." The author is indebted to Thomas Small for these Arabic translations.

4. *Jerusalem Post*, Nov. 6, 1956, 3.

5. Sir J. Nicholls to Foreign Office, Nov. 4, 1956, UKNA: PREM 11/1105 f 171.

6. Sir Pierson Dixon to Foreign Office, Nov. 5, 1956, UKNA: PREM 11/1105 f 123.

7. Ibid., ff 118–20. Dixon was at this point considering whether to resign himself, according to Hennessy, *Prime Minister*, 243.

8. Fullick and Powell, *Suez: The Double War*, 98; Kyle, *Suez*, 446–47.

9. Clark, *Suez Touchdown*, 79–80.

10. Dodds-Parker, *Political Eunuch*, 112.

11. Galpern, *Money, Oil, and Empire*, 179.

12. Cooper, *Lion's Last Roar*, 191.

13. Galpern, *Money, Oil, and Empire*, 175.

14. "Perhaps it is too Machiavellian to see Macmillan's role in Suez as a bid to oust Eden but it was Macmillan who became Prime Minister in 1957." Lewis Johnman, "The Economics of the Suez Crisis," in Gorst, Johnman, and Lucas, *Post-War Britain*, 179.

15. Keith Kyle, "Britain's Slow March to Suez," in Tal, *1956 War*, 114. See Lucas, *Divided We Stand*, 91–92, on RAE's clashes with Macmillan.

16. Nutting, *No End of a Lesson*, 133.

17. RAE to DDE, Nov. 5, 1956, FRUS 1955–57, vol. 16, doc. 499, pp. 984–86. RAE's extraordinary claims about GAN's ambitions seem to have come from MI6's faulty intelligence reports based on the fantastical stories of "Lucky Break." See Lucas, *Divided We Stand*, 109.

18. Quoted in United Nations, *Problem of Hungary*, 38.

19. Fryer, *Hungarian Tragedy*, 82.

20. United Nations, *Problem of Hungary*, 38; see also Hayter, *Kremlin and the Embassy*, 145. Peter Fryer also alleged that some of the rank-and-file Soviet troops had no idea they were in Hungary, but suggested they had been told a different story: "They thought at first they were in Berlin, fighting German fascists." Fryer, *Hungarian Tragedy*, 82.

21. Stephen Vizinczey in Lomax, *Hungary 1956*, 121.

22. USARMA Budapest to Secretary of State, Nov. 5, 1956, USNA: RG 59, Records of the Department of State, Central Decimal Files: 764.00/11–556.

23. Conant in Bonn to Secretary of State, Nov. 5, 1956, USNA: RG 59, Records of the Department of State, Central Decimal Files: 764.00/11–556.

24. Wailes in Budapest to Secretary of State, Nov. 5, 1956, USNA: RG 59, Records of the Department of State, Central Decimal Files: 764.00/11–556.

25. Violet Bonham Carter in London *Times*, Nov. 6, 1956, 11.

26. Memorandum of a conference with the President, White House Memoranda, 1953–1959, DDEP, box 22.

27. C. Douglas Dillon to JFD, Nov. 5, 1956, State Department Central Decimal Files, Suez Crisis, 974.7301/11–156, USNA: RG 59/250/44/4/4.

28. Hare in Cairo to JFD, Nov. 6, 1956, State Department Central Decimal Files, Gamal Abdel Nasser, 774.11/11–656, USNA: RG 59/250/43/5/5.

29. C. Douglas Dillon to Secretary of State, Nov. 5, 1956, USNA: RG 59, Records of the Department of State, Central Decimal Files: 764.00/11–556.

30. Selwyn Lloyd in Parliamentary Debates (Hansard), 5th series, vol. 558 (House of Commons), col. 1958.

31. Nutting, *No End of a Lesson*, 142–43.

32. Aneurin Bevan in Parliamentary Debates (Hansard), 5th series, vol. 558 (House of Commons), col. 1965.

33. Victor Collins in Parliamentary Debates (Hansard), 5th series, vol. 558 (House of Commons), col. 1951.

34. Kyle, *Suez*, 450–52.

35. Taubman, *Khrushchev*, 359. Taubman notes that NSK was jealous of the international attention this letter and his others brought Bulganin.

36. Bulganin to RAE, Nov. 6, 1956, UKNA: PREM 11/1170.

37. Harold Macmillan in Memorandum of a Conversation with JFD, Aug. 1, 1956, FRUS, 1955–57, vol. 16, doc. 46, p. 108.

38. Nikolai Bulganin to RAE, Sept. 11, 1956, in Thomas, *Suez Affair*, 186–87.

39. Sir William Hayter to Foreign Office, Nov. 6, 1956, UKNA: PREM 11/1170.

40. Nikolai Bulganin to DBG, Nov. 5, 1956, in Laurent Rucker, "The Soviet Union and the Suez Crisis," in Tal, *1956 War*, 80.

41. DBG, Diary, Nov. 7, 1956, in Troen and Shemesh, *Suez-Sinai Crisis 1956*, 318.

42. Kyle, *Suez*, 454–55.

43. Nikolai Bulganin, in London *Times*, Nov. 6, 1956, 10.

44. Khrushchev, *Khrushchev Remembers*, 434.

45. NSK in Taubman, *Khrushchev*, 359.

46. Hughes, *Ordeal of Power*, 222–24; Memorandum of a Conference with the President, Nov. 5, 1956, White House Memoranda, 1953–59, DDEP, box 22.

Chapter 16: Back Down

1. Wright, *Spycatcher*, 85–86.

2. Sergei Khrushchev in James G. Blight, Bruce J. Allyn, and David A. Welch, *Cuba on the Brink: Castro, the Missile Crisis, and the Soviet Collapse* (Lanham, MD: Rowman & Littlefield, 2002), 130.

3. See evidence of John Erickson in Moncrieff, *Suez Ten Years After*, 23.

4. Cooper, *Lion's Last Roar*, 197.

5. C. Douglas Dillon, JFDOHP; see also Cooper, *Lion's Last Roar*, 194.

6. Ralph Murray at AFHQ to Foreign Office, Nov. 6, 1956, UKNA: FO 371/118904.

7. Leulliette, *St. Michael and the Dragon*, 203.

8. Kyle, *Suez*, 463.

9. Allied Forces Headqarters to Ministry of Defence, Nov. 6, 1956; Chiefs of Staff to General Keightley, Nov. 6, 1956; both UKNA: AIR 8/1940.

10. Allied Forces Headquarters to Commander in Chief Mediterranean et al., Nov. 6, 1956, UKNA: AIR 8/1940.

11. Cooper, *Lion's Last Roar*, 199–200.

12. Murphy, *Diplomat Among Warriors*, 476.

13. Heikal, *Sphinx and Commissar*, 72.

14. Verrier, *Through the Looking Glass*, 156–57.

15. Brendan Bracken in Carlton, *Eden*, 458.

16. Eden, *Full Circle*, 557.

17. Kunz, *Economic Diplomacy*, 133.

18. Nutting, *No End of a Lesson*, 148.

19. Alec Home in Hennessy, *Prime Minister*, 236.

20. HM the Queen in London *Times*, Nov. 6, 1956, 5.

21. Conversation in Kyle, *Suez*, 467. Kyle took the phrasing of this conversation from a BBC television interview with Christian Pineau. There is a similar account of it in Pineau, *1956/Suez*, 176 but, as Kyle points out, Pineau seems to have confused some parts of it in his book with another conversation later that day.

22. Copeland, *Game Player*, 203.

23. Konrad Adenaur in Pineau, *1956/Suez*, 191.

24. Clark, *From Three Worlds*, 211.

25. Dayan, *Diary*, Nov. 6, 1956, 179.

26. DBG in Bar-Zohar, *Armed Prophet*, 249.

27. Memorandum of a conference with the president, Nov. 6, 1956, FRUS 1955–57, vol. 16, doc. 518, p. 1014.

28. Status Report on the Near East Given by the Director [AWD] at the White House to a Bipartisan Congressional Group, Nov. 9, 1956, USNA: CIA-RDP80B01676R004200050014–8.

29. Status Report on the Near East Given by the Director [AWD] at the White House to a Bipartisan Congressional Group, Nov. 9, 1956, USNA: CIA-RDP80B01676R004200050014–8.

30. Anonymous secretary in Hughes, *Ordeal of Power*, 225.

31. DDE and RAE in Transcript of a Telephone Conversation, Nov. 6, 1956, 12:55 p.m., FRUS 1955–57, vol. 16, doc. 525, pp. 1025–27.

32. Clark, *From Three Worlds*, 212; Eden, *Full Circle*, 561.

33. London *Times*, Nov. 7, 1956, 10.

34. Rhodes James, *Eden*, 576.

35. Sir Gerald Templer in Cloake, *Templer*, 355.

36. London *Times*, Nov. 7, 1956, 10.

37. Kenneth Darling in Hennessy, *Muddling Through*, 146.

38. Leulliette, *St. Michael and the Dragon*, 207–8.

39. General Keightley to Chiefs of Staff, Nov. 6, 1956 (KEYCOS 49 & 51), UKNA: AIR 8/1940.

40. Clark, *Suez Touchdown*, 103–4.

41. Washington correspondent and James Reston in London *Times*, Nov. 6, 1956, 10.

42. London *Times*, Nov. 7, 1956, 10.

43. Wailes in Budapest to Secretary of State, Nov. 6, 1956, USNA: RG 59, Records of the Department of State, Central Decimal Files: 764.00/11–656.

44. *Jerusalem Post*, Nov. 7, 1956, 1.

45. Béla Lucza in Csete, *1956 Budapest*, 102.

46. Fryer, *Hungarian Tragedy*, 12.

47. Mićunović, *Moscow Diary*, 144–45.

48. Ibid., 148

49. Sergei Khrushchev, NSK and Taubman in Taubman, *Khrushchev*, 359–60.

50. Abd al-Latif al-Bughdadi, Diary, Nov. 6–18, 1956, in Troen and Shemesh, *Suez-Sinai Crisis 1956*, 350–54.

51. E.L.M. Burns in Stephens, *Nasser*, 239.

52. *New York Times*, Nov. 8, 1956, 3.

53. RAE to Guy Mollet, Nov. 6, 1956, UKNA: PREM 11/1105, f 71.

54. Thomas, *Suez Affair*, 164.

55. DDE in Hughes, *Ordeal of Power*, 224–29.

Epilogue: "The Curse of the Pharaohs"

1. Heikal, *Sphinx and Commissar*, 73–4.

2. Status Report on the Near East Given by the Director [AWD] at the White House to a Bipartisan Congressional Group, Nov. 9, 1956, USNA: CIA-RDP80B01676R004200050014–8.

3. Heikal, *Sphinx and Commissar*, 73–74.

4. Lucas, *Divided We Stand*, 305.

5. Eden, *Memoir*, 256.

6. Adams, *First-Hand Report*, 209.

7. Cooper, *Lion's Last Roar*, 215.

8. William B. Macomber Jr., JFDOHP.

9. DBG Nov. 7, 1956, in Isaac Alteras, "Eisenhower and the Sinai Campaign of 1956: The First Major Crisis in US-Israeli Relations," in Tal, *1956 War*, 34–35.

10. DDE to DBG, Nov. 7, 1956, FRUS 1955–57, vol. 16, doc. 550, 1064.

11. In Henriques, *One Hundred Hours to Suez*, 252.

12. DBG to DDE, Nov. 8, 1956, FRUS 1955–57, vol. 16, doc. 560, p. 1095.

13. Sharon, *Warrior*, 155–56.

14. Mahgoub, *Democracy on Trial*, 87.

15. Moshe Shemesh, "Egypt: From Military Defeat to Political Victory," in Troen and Shemesh, *Suez-Sinai Crisis 1956*, 158.

16. Sir Richard Powell in Hennessy, *Muddling Through*, 134.

17. Arleigh Burke, JFDOHP.

18. Andrew Goodpaster, JFDOHP.

19. DDE, JFDOHP.

20. Denis Healey quoted in Nutting, *No End of a Lesson*, 147.

21. Nigel Nicolson, "Diary of a Suez Rebel," London *Daily Telegraph*, Oct. 27, 1996. The chief whip was Edward Heath.

22. Nutting, *No End of a Lesson*, 148.

23. Peter Thorneycroft in Parliamentary Debates (Hansard), 5th series, vol. 560 (House of Commons), col. 402.

24. Status Report on the Near East Given by the Director [AWD] at the White House to a Bipartisan Congressional Group, Nov. 9, 1956, USNA: CIA-RDP80B01676R004200050014–8.

25. Coulon, *Soldiers of Diplomacy*, 24.

26. Pineau, *1956/Suez*, 93.

27. C. Douglas Dillon, JFDOHP.

28. Montague Browne, *Long Sunset*, 209.

29. Murphy, *Diplomat Among Warriors*, 478–79.

30. Dwight D. Eisenhower, JFDOHP.

31. Winthrop Aldrich in Carlton, *Eden*, 456. No communications passed between the American government and RAE between November 7 and 23, when RAE left for his vacation, except for a short exchange on November 11 about a summit. Lucas, *Divided We Stand*, 300.

32. Krozewski, *Money and the End of Empire*, 155.

33. Farnie, *East and West of Suez*, 734.

34. Galpern, *Money, Oil, and Empire*, 167, 184–85.

35. RAE in Parliamentary Debates (Hansard), 5th series, vol. 562 (House of Commons), Dec. 20, 1956, col. 1493; Denis Healey in Hennessy, *Prime Minister*, 207.

36. Copeland, *Game Player*, 203.

37. Lloyd, *Suez 1956*, 219. Lloyd's memory is corroborated to some extent by a telegram he sent to Eden after this meeting. Then, he wrote that JFD "had no complaint about our objectives in our recent operations. In fact they were the same as those of the United States but he still did not think that our methods of achieving them were the right ones. Even so, he deplored that we had not managed to bring down Nasser." Selwyn Lloyd to RAE, in Rhodes James, *Eden*, 577n. Christian Pineau also told a self-aggrandizing story alleging that JFD regretted his Suez stance, in Pineau, *1956/Suez*, 195.

38. Douglas MacArthur II to Herbert Hoover [Jr.], Nov. 20, 1956, USNA: State Department Central Decimal Files, 774.11/11–2056.

39. Cooper, *Lion's Last Roar*, 270.

40. Status Report on the Near East Given by the Director [AWD] at the White House to a Bipartisan Congressional Group, Nov. 9, 1956, USNA: CIA-RDP80B01676R004200050014–8.

41. Eden, *Full Circle*, 559.

42. Douglas MacArthur II to Herbert Hoover [Jr.], Nov. 20, 1956, USNA: State Department Central Decimal Files, 774.11/11–2056.

43. See Clea Lutz Bunch, "Supporting the Brave Young King: The Suez Crisis and Eisenhower's New Approach to Jordan, 1953–1958," in Smith, *Reassessing Suez 1956*, 107–21.

44. DBG, Diary, Dec. 13, 1956, in Troen and Shemesh, *Suez-Sinai Crisis 1956*, 326.

45. On the repairing of the special relationship in 1957, see G. Wyn Rees, "Brothers in Arms: Anglo-American Defence Co-operation in 1957," in Gorst, Johnman, and Lucas, *Post-War Britain*, 203–20.

46. Cooper, *Lion's Last Roar*, 269.

47. Mária Tamáska and colleagues in Gough, *Good Comrade*, 102–3.

48. Kramer, "Soviet Union and the 1956 Crises," 211.

49. Csaba Varró in Csete, *1956 Budapest*, 166.

50. Kramer, "Soviet Union and the 1956 Crises," 196–98. There were also protests from students at the Moscow Institute of Railroad Engineering and the All-Union State Institute of Cinematography.

51. NSK in Taubman, *Khrushchev*, 300.

52. Mao Tse-tung in Taubman, *Khrushchev*, 339.

53. CIA Information Report, Nov. 9, 1956, USNA: CIA-RDP80T00246A031800590001–4.

54. Laurent Rucker, "The Soviet Union and the Suez Crisis," in Tal, *1956 War*, 84.

55. Ann Fleming in Parker, *Goldeneye*, 213.

56. See Rhodes James, *Eden*, 587–89.

57. Eden, *Memoir*, 259.

58. Ian Fleming to Sir William Stephenson, in Parker, *Goldeneye*, 212.

59. RAE in Parliamentary Debates (Hansard), 5th series, vol. 562 (House of Commons), Dec. 20, 1956, col. 1493; Denis Healey in Hennessy, *Prime Minister*, 207.

60. Kilmuir, *Political Adventure*, 278.

61. Heath, *Course of My Life*, 177.

62. Guy Mollet in Jean-Paul Cointet, "Guy Mollet, the French Government and the SFIO," in Troen and Shemesh, *Suez-Sinai Crisis 1956*, 138.

63. Christian Pineau, JFDOHP.

64. Maurice Vaïsse, "Post-Suez France," in Louis and Owen, *Suez 1956*, 339. Charles de Gaulle was believed to have discreetly approved of the Suez intervention but was unhappy with the British commanding it instead of the French.

65. Cooper, *Lion's Last Roar*, 233.

66. *Le Monde*, Nov. 8, 1956, 8.

67. Mohamed Heikal and GAN in Heikal, *Cairo Documents*, 117–18.

68. GAN in Lacouture, *Nasser*, 181. He was speaking to Kennett Love.

69. Copeland, *Game Player*, 204.

70. Eveland, *Ropes of Sand*, 240–41.

71. Copeland, *Game Player*, 204.

72. Amin Howeidy in James, *Nasser at War*, 46.

73. JFD in Kunz, *Economic Diplomacy*, 159.

74. Galpern, *Money, Oil, and Empire*, 194.

75. Copeland, *Game Player*, 204–5.

Fates

1. Eden, *Full Circle*, 423.

2. Shlaim, *Lion of Jordan*, 160.

3. Scott Lucas and Alistair Morey, "The Hidden 'Alliance': The CIA and MI6 Before and After Suez," in Stafford and Jeffreys-Jones, *American-British-Canadian Intelligence Relations*, 112–13; Andrew and Mitrokhin, *Mitrokhin Archive*, vol. 2, p. 196.

4. Khrushchev, *Khrushchev Remembers*, 423. There is a full account of Nagy's arrest in Méray, *Thirteen Days That Shook the Kremlin*, 252–54.

5. Andrew and Gordievsky, *KGB*, 357.

6. Sharon, *Warrior*, 151.

7. McNamara, *Britain, Nasser and the Balance of Power in the Middle East*, 1, 7n.

8. Nutting, *No End of a Lesson*, 159.

9. See Macmillan, *Cabinet Years*, 607n.

BIBLIOGRAPHY

Published works

Abdel Nasser, Tahia Gamal. *Nasser: My Husband*, trans. Shereen Mosaad. Cairo: American University in Cairo Press, 2013.

Aburish, Saïd K. *Nasser: The Last Arab*. London: Duckworth, 2004.

Adams, Jad. *Tony Benn*. London: Macmillan, 1992.

Adams, Michael. *Suez and After: Year of Crisis*. Boston: Beacon Hill Press, 1958.

Adams, Sherman. *First-Hand Report: The Inside Story of the Eisenhower Administration*. London: Hutchinson, 1962.

Al-Rasheed, Madawi. *A History of Saudi Arabia*, 2nd ed. Cambridge: Cambridge University Press, 2010.

Ambrose, Stephen E. *Eisenhower*, vol. 2, *The President*. London: Allen & Unwin, 1984.

Ambrose, Stephen E., with Richard H. Immerman. *Ike's Spies: Eisenhower and the Espionage Establishment*. Garden City, NY: Doubleday, 1981.

Andrew, Christopher, and Oleg Gordievsky. *KGB: The Inside Story of Its Foreign Operations from Lenin to Gorbachev*. London: Hodder & Stoughton, 1990.

Andrew, Christopher, and Vasili Mitrokhin. *The Mitrokhin Archive*, vol. 1, *The KGB in Europe and the West*. London: Allen Lane, 1999.

———. *The Mitrokhin Archive* vol. 2, *The KGB and the World*. London: Penguin Books, London, 2006.

Aronson, Shlomo. *David Ben-Gurion and the Jewish Renaissance*, trans. Naftali Greenwood. 1999. Cambridge: Cambridge University Press, 2011.

Avnery, Uri. *Israel Without Zionists: A Plea for Peace in the Middle East*. London: Macmillan, 1969.

———. *Israel's Vicious Circle: Ten Years of Writing on Israel and Palestine*, ed. Sara R. Powell. London: Pluto Press, 2008.

Baeyens, Jacques. *Un coup d'épée dans l'eau du Canal: la seconde campagne d'Egypte*. Paris: Fayard, 1976.

Bar-Zohar, Michael. *Suez Ultra-Secret*. Paris: Librairie Arthème Fayard, 1964.

———. *The Armed Prophet: A Biography of Ben-Gurion*, trans. Len Ortzen. London: Arthur Barker, 1967.

———. *Ben-Gurion*, tr. Peretz Kidron. London: Weidenfeld & Nicolson, 1978.

Barnett, Correlli. *The Verdict of Peace: Britain Between Her Yesterday and the Future*. London: Macmillan, 2001.

Barr, James. *A Line in the Sand: Britain, France and the Struggle That Shaped the Middle East.* London: Simon & Schuster, 2012.

Ben-Eliezer, Uri. *The Making of Israeli Militarism.* Bloomington: Indiana University Press, 1998.

Benn, Tony. *Years of Hope: Diaries, Letters and Papers 1940–1962,* ed. Ruth Winstone. London: Hutchinson, 1994.

Bibó István. *The Art of Peacemaking: Political Essays,* trans. Péter Pásztor. New Haven, CT: Yale University Press, 2015.

Black, Ian, and Benny Morris. *Israel's Secret Wars: The Untold History of Israeli Intelligence.* London: Hamish Hamilton, 1991.

Blackwell, Stephen. *British Military Intervention and the Struggle for Jordan: King Hussein, Nasser and the Middle East Crisis, 1955–1958.* New York: Routledge, 2009.

Blumenthal, Max. *Goliath: Life and Loathing in Greater Israel.* New York: Nation Books, 2013.

Bohlen, Charles E. *Witness to History: 1929–1969.* New York: Norton, 1973.

Bower, Tom. *The Perfect English Spy: Sir Dick White and the Secret War 1935–90.* London: Heinemann, 1995.

Bowie, Robert R., and Richard H. Immerman. *Waging Peace: How Eisenhower Shaped an Enduring Cold War Strategy.* New York: Oxford University Press, 1998.

Boyle, David. *With Ardours Manifold.* London: Hutchinson, 1959.

Brand, Laurie A. *Official Stories: Politics and National Narratives in Egypt and Algeria.* Stanford, CA: Stanford University Press, 2014.

Brendon, Piers. *Ike: The Life and Times of Dwight D. Eisenhower.* London: Secker & Warburg, 1987.

Brown, Anthony Cave. *Treason in the Blood: H. St. John Philby, Kim Philby, and the Spy Case of the Century.* Boston: Houghton Mifflin, 1994.

Burns, William J. *Economic Aid and American Policy Toward Egypt, 1955–1981.* Albany: State University of New York Press, 1985.

Butler, Richard Austen, Lord. *The Art of the Possible.* London: Hamish Hamilton, 1971.

Cannadine, David. *Ornamentalism: How the British Saw Their Empire.* (London; Allen Lane/Penguin Press, 2001.

Carlton, David. *Anthony Eden: A Biography.* New York: Viking, 1981; London: Allen & Unwin, 1986.

Childers, Erskine B. *The Road to Suez: A Study of Western-Arab Relations.* London: MacGibbon & Kee, 1962.

Citino, Nathan J. *From Arab Nationalism to OPEC: Eisenhower, King Sa'ud, and the Making of U.S.-Saudi Relations,* 2nd ed. Bloomington: Indiana University Press, 2010.

Clark, D.M.J. *Suez Touchdown: A Soldier's Tale.* London: Peter Davies, 1964.

Clark, William. *From Three Worlds: Memoirs.* London: Sidgwick & Jackson, 1986.

Cloake, John. *Templer—Tiger of Malaya: The Life of Field Marshal Sir Gerald Templer.* London: Harrap, 1985.

Cooper, Chester L. *The Lion's Last Roar: Suez, 1956.* New York: Harper & Row, 1978.

Copeland, Miles. *The Game of Nations: The Amorality of Power Politics.* New York: Simon & Schuster, 1969.

———. *The Game Player: Confessions of the CIA's Original Political Operative.* London: Aurum Press, 1989.

Coulon, Jocelyn. *Soldiers of Diplomacy: The United Nations, Peacekeeping, and the New World Order.* Toronto: University of Toronto Press, 1999.

Coward, Noel. *The Noel Coward Diaries*, ed. Graham Payn and Sheridan Morley. London: Weidenfeld & Nicolson, 1982.

Csete Örs. *1956 Budapest: arcok és sorsok/faces and stories*. Magyar Napló Kiadó, Budapest, 2001.

Dayan, Moshe. *Diary of the Sinai Campaign 1956*. London: Sphere, 1967.

———. *Story of My Life*. London: Weidenfeld & Nicolson, 1976.

Dodds-Parker, Douglas. *Political Eunuch*. Ascot, UK: Springwood Books, 1986.

Dorril, Stephen. *MI6: Fifty Years of Special Operations*. London: Fourth Estate, 2001.

Dutton, David. *Anthony Eden: A Life and Reputation*. London: Arnold, 1997.

Eayrs, James. "Canadian Policy and Opinion During the Suez Crisis. *International Journal: Quarterly of the Canadian Institute of International Affairs* 12, no. 2 (Spring 1957): 97–108.

Eban, Abba. *Voice of Israel*. London: Faber & Faber, 1958.

Eden, Anthony. *Full Circle: The Memoirs of the Rt. Hon. Sir Anthony Eden, K.G., P.C., M.C.* London: Cassell, 1960.

Eden, Clarissa. *A Memoir: From Churchill to Eden*, ed. Cate Haste. London: Weidenfeld & Nicolson, 2007.

Eisenhower, John S. D. *Strictly Personal*. Garden City, NY: Doubleday, 1974.

Evans, Martin. *Algeria: France's Undeclared War*. Oxford: Oxford University Press, 2012.

Eveland, Wilbur Crane. *Ropes of Sand: America's Failure in the Middle East*. New York: Norton, 1980.

Farnie, D. A. *East and West of Suez: The Suez Canal in History, 1854–1956*. Oxford: Clarendon Press, 1969.

Filiu, Jean-Pierre. *Gaza: A History*, trans. John King. London: Hurst, 2014.

Fryer, Peter. *Hungarian Tragedy and Other Writings on the 1956 Hungarian Revolution*. London: Index Books, 1997.

Fullick, Roy, and Geoffrey Powell. *Suez: The Double War*. London: Hamish Hamilton, 1979.

Gaitskell, Hugh. *The Diary of Hugh Gaitskell, 1945–1956*, ed. Philip M. Williams. London: Jonathan Cape, 1983.

Galpern, Steven G. *Money, Oil, and Empire in the Middle East: Sterling and Postwar Imperialism, 1944–1971*. Cambridge: Cambridge University Press, 2009.

Gati, Charles. *Failed Illusions: Moscow, Washington, Budapest, and the 1956 Hungarian Revolt*. Washington, DC: Woodrow Wilson Center Press; Stanford, CA: Stanford University Press, 2006).

Gilbert, Martin. *Israel: A History*. New York: Doubleday, 1998.

Goold-Adams, Richard. *The Time of Power: A Reappraisal of John Foster Dulles*. London: Weidenfeld & Nicolson, 1962.

Gordon, Joel. *Nasser: Hero of the Arab Nation*. Oxford: Oneworld, 2006.

Gorst, Anthony, Lewis Johnman, and W. Scott Lucas, eds. *Post-War Britain, 1945–64: Themes and Perspectives*. New York: Pinter Publishers, 1989.

Gough, Roger. *A Good Comrade: János Kádár, Communism and Hungary*. New York: I. B. Tauris, 2006.

Hayter, William. *The Kremlin and the Embassy*. London: Hodder & Stoughton, 1966.

Heath, Edward. *The Course of My Life: My Autobiography*. London: Hodder & Stoughton, 1998

Heikal, Mohamed. *Nasser: The Cairo Documents*. London: New English Library, 1972.

———. *Sphinx and Commissar: The Rise and Fall of Soviet Influence in the Arab World*. London: Collins, 1978.

————. *Cutting the Lion's Tail: Suez Through Egyptian Eyes* London: André Deutsch, 1986.

Hennessy, Peter. *Muddling Through: Power, Politics and the Quality of Government in Postwar Britain*. London: Victor Gollancz, 1986.

————. *The Prime Minister: The Office and Its Holders Since 1945*, rev. ed. London: Penguin, 2001.

Henriques, Robert. *One Hundred Hours to Suez: An Account of Israel's Campaign in the Sinai Peninsula*. London: Collins, 1957.

Hoopes, Townsend. *The Devil and John Foster Dulles*. London: André Deutsch, 1974.

Hughes, Emmet John. *The Ordeal of Power: A Political Memoir of the Eisenhower Years*. London: Macmillan, 1963.

Immerman, Richard H. *John Foster Dulles: Piety, Pragmatism, and Power in U.S. Foreign Policy*. Wilmington, DE: SR Books, 1999.

————. *Empire for Liberty: A History of American Imperialism from Benjamin Franklin to Paul Wolfowitz*. Princeton, NJ: Princeton University Press, 2010.

James, Laura M. *Nasser at War: Arab Images of the Enemy*. Basingstoke, UK: Palgrave Macmillan, 2006.

Kandil, Hazem. *Soldiers, Spies, and Statesmen: Egypt's Road to Revolt*. New York: Verso, 2012.

Kelly, Saul, and Anthony Gorst, eds. *Whitehall and the Suez Crisis*. Portland, OR: Frank Cass, 2000.

Khrushchev, Nikita Sergeyevich. *Khrushchev Remembers*, trans. Strobe Talbott. London: André Deutsch, 1971.

————. *Khrushchev Remembers: The Last Testament* trans. Strobe Talbott. London: André Deutsch, 1974.

Kilmuir, David Patrick Maxwell Fyfe, Earl of. *Political Adventure: The Memoirs of the Earl of Kilmuir*. London: Weidenfeld & Nicolson, 1964.

Kinzer, Stephen. *The Brothers: John Foster Dulles, Allen Dulles, and Their Secret World War*. New York: St. Martin's Griffin, 2013.

Kopácsi Sándor. *In the Name of the Working Class (1979)*, trans. Daniel and Judy Stoffman. London: Fontana, 1986.

Kramer, Mark. "The Soviet Union and the 1956 Crises in Hungary and Poland: Reassessments and New Findings." *Journal of Contemporary History* 33, no. 2 (Apr. 1998): 163–214.

Krozewski, Gerold. *Money and the End of Empire: British International Economic Policy and the Colonies, 1947–58*. Basingstoke, UK: Palgrave, 2001.

Kunz, Diane B. *The Economic Diplomacy of the Suez Crisis*. Chapel Hill: University of North Carolina Press, 1991.

Kyle, Keith. *Suez: Britain's End of Empire in the Middle East*, rev. ed. London: I. B. Tauris, London, 2011.

Lacouture, Jean. *Nasser: A Biography*, trans. Daniel Hofstadter. New York: Knopf, 1973.

Lapping, Brian. *End of Empire*. London: Granada, 1985.

Lendvai, Paul. *Hungary: The Art of Survival*, trans. Noel Clark. London: I.B. Tauris, London, 1988.

Leulliette, Pierre. *St. Michael and the Dragon: A Paratrooper in the Algerian War*, trans. Tony White. London: Heinemann, 1964.

Lewis, William Roger. "Dulles, Suez, and the British," 133–58 in *John Foster Dulles and the Diplomacy of the Cold War*, ed. Richard H. Immerman. Princeton, NJ: Princeton University Press, 1990.

Lewis, William Roger, and Roger Owen, eds. *Suez 1956: The Crisis and Its Consequences.* Oxford: Clarendon Press, 1989.

Lloyd, Selwyn. *Suez 1956: A Personal Account.* London: Jonathan Cape, 1978.

Lomax, Bill. *Hungary 1956.* London: Allison & Busby, 1976.

Love, Kennett. *Suez: The Twice-Fought War.* London: Longman, 1970.

Luard, Evan. *A History of the United Nations*; vol. 1, *The Years of Western Domination, 1945–1955*; vol. 2, *The Age of Decolonization, 1955–1965.* London: Palgrave Macmillan, 1982, 1989.

Lucas, W. Scott. *Divided We Stand: Britain, the US and the Suez Crisis.* London: Hodder & Stoughton, 1991, Sceptre, 1996.

McDermott, Anthony. *Egypt from Nasser to Mubarak: A Flawed Revolution.* London: Croom Helm, 1988.

McHugo, John. *Syria: From the Great War to the Civil War.* London: Saqi, 2014.

Macmillan, Harold. *The Macmillan Diaries: The Cabinet Years, 1950–1957*, ed. Peter Catterall. London: Macmillan, 2003.

McNamara, Robert. *Britain, Nasser and the Balance of Power in the Middle East, 1952–1967: From the Egyptian Revolution to the Six Day War.* London: Frank Cass, 2003.

Mahgoub, Mohamed Ahmed. *Democracy on Trial: Reflections on Arab and African Politics.* London: André Deutsch, 1974.

Mansfield, Peter. *Nasser.* London: Methuen Educational, 1969.

Menzies, Robert. *Afternoon Light: Some Memories of Men and Events.* London: Cassell, 1967.

Méray Tibor. *Thirteen Days That Shook the Kremlin*, trans. Howard L. Katzander. London: Thames & Hudson, n.d. (1959).

Merle, Robert. *Ahmed Ben Bella.* Paris: Éditions Gallimard, 1965.

Mićunović, Veljko. *Moscow Diary*, trans. David Floyd, intro. George Kennan. Garden City, NY: Doubleday, 1980.

Mikardo, Ian. *Back-Bencher.* London Weidenfeld & Nicolson, 1988.

Mindszenty József. *Memoirs*, trans. Richard Winston, Clara Winston, Jan van Heurck. London: Weidenfeld & Nicolson, 1974.

Mitchell, Richard P. *The Society of the Muslim Brothers.* London: Oxford University Press, 1969.

Molnár Miklós. *Budapest 1956: A History of the Hungarian Revolution.* London: Allen & Unwin, 1971.

Moncrieff, Anthony, ed. *Suez Ten Years After: Broadcasts from the BBC Third Programme.* London: British Broadcasting Corp., 1967.

Monroe, Elizabeth. *Britain's Moment in the Middle East, 1914–1971*, rev. ed. London: Chatto & Windus, 1981.

Montague Browne, Anthony. *Long Sunset: Memoirs of Winston Churchill's Last Private Secretary.* London: Cassell, 1995.

Moran, Charles, 1st Baron. *Winston Churchill: The Struggle for Survival, 1940–1965.* London: Constable, 1966.

Morris, Benny. *Israel's Border Wars, 1949–1956: Arab Infiltration, Israeli Retaliation, and the Countdown to the Suez War.* Oxford: Clarendon Press, 1997.

Morton, Michael Quentin. *Buraimi: The Struggle for Power, Influence and Oil in Arabia.* London: IB Tauris, 2014.

Mosley, Leonard. *Dulles: A Biography of Eleanor, Allen, and John Foster Dulles.* London: Hodder & Stoughton, 1978.

Murphy, Robert. *Diplomat Among Warriors*. London: Collins, 1964.

Neguib, Mohammed. *Egypt's Destiny*. London: Victor Gollancz, 1955.

Nichols, David A. *Eisenhower 1956: The President's Year of Crisis, Suez and the Brink of War*. New York: Simon & Schuster, 2012.

Nutting, Anthony. *No End of a Lesson: The Story of Suez*. London: Constable, 1967.

———. *Nasser*. London: Constable, 1972.

Orde, Anne. *The Eclipse of Great Britain: The United States and British Imperial Decline, 1895–1956*. New York: St. Martin's Press, 1996.

Pappé, Ilan. *A History of Modern Palestine*. Cambridge: Cambridge University Press, 2004.

Parker, Matthew. *Goldeneye: Where Bond Was Born: Ian Fleming's Jamaica* London: Hutchinson, 2014.

Peres, Shimon. *Battling for Peace: Memoirs*, ed. David Landau. London: Weidenfeld & Nicolson, 1995.

Petersen, Tore Tingvold. "Anglo-American Rivalry in the Middle East: The Struggle for the Buraimi Oasis, 1952–1957." *International History Review* 14, no. 1, Feb. 1992.

Pickles, Dorothy. *Algeria and France: From Colonialism to Cooperation*. London: Methuen, 1963.

Pineau, Christian. *1956/Suez*. Paris: Éditions Robert Laffont, 1976.

Preussen, Ronald W. *John Foster Dulles: The Road to Power*. New York: Free Press, 1982.

Pudney, John. *Suez: De Lesseps' Canal*. London: J. M. Dent, 1968.

Rainer János M. *Imre Nagy: A Biography*. London: I. B. Tauris, 2009.

Raviv, Dan, and Yossi Melman. *Every Spy a Prince: The Complete History of Israel's Intelligence Community*. Boston: Houghton Mifflin, 1991.

Réthly Akós, with Eörsi László. *The Hungarian Revolution 1956*. Budapest: Premier Press, 2006.

Rhodes James, Robert. *Anthony Eden*. London: Weidenfeld & Nicolson, 1986.

Robertson, Terence. *Crisis: The Inside Story of the Suez Conspiracy*. London: Hutchinson, 1965.

Sadat, Anwar el. *Revolt on the Nile*, foreword by President Nasser. London; Allan Wingate, 1957.

Sayigh, Yezid. *Armed Struggle and the Search for State: The Palestinian National Movement 1949–1993*. Oxford: Clarendon Press, 1997.

Sayigh, Yezid, and Avi Shlaim, eds. *The Cold War and the Middle East*. Oxford; Clarendon Press, 1997.

Sebestyen, Victor. *Twelve Days, Revolution 1956: How the Hungarians Tried to Topple Their Soviet Masters*. London: Weidenfeld & Nicolson, 2006.

Shalom, Zaki. *Ben-Gurion's Political Struggles, 1963–1967: A Lion in Winter*. New York: Routledge, 2006.

Sharon, Ariel, with David Chanoff. *Warrior: An Autobiography*. New York: Simon & Schuster, 1989; Touchstone, 2001.

Shlaim, Avi. "Conflicting Approaches to Israel's Relations with the Arabs: Ben-Gurion and Sharett, 1953–1956," *Middle East Journal* 37, no. 2, Spring 1983.

———. *Lion of Jordan: The Life of King Hussein in War and Peace*. London: Allen Lane, 2007.

———. *Israel and Palestine: Reappraisals, Revisions, Refutations*. New York: Verso, 2010.

Shuckburgh, Evelyn. *Descent to Suez: Diaries 1951–56*. London: Weidenfeld & Nicolson, 1986.

Sirrs, Owen L. *A History of the Egyptian Intelligence Service: A History of the Mukhabarat, 1910–2009*. London: Routledge, 2010.

Smith, Jean Edward. *Eisenhower in War and Peace*. New York, Random House, 2013.

Smith, Simon C., ed. *Reassessing Suez 1956: New Perspectives on the Crisis and Its Aftermath.* Aldershot, UK:Ashgate, 2008.

Srodes, James. *Allen Dulles: Master of Spies*, Washington. DC: Regenery, 1999.

Stafford, David, and Rhodri Jeffreys-Jones, eds. *American-British-Canadian Intelligence Relations, 1939–2000.* London: Frank Cass, 2000.

Stephens, Robert. *Nasser: A Political Biography.* London: Allen Lane/Penguin Press, 1971.

Stock, Ernest. *Israel on the Road to Sinai, 1949–1956: With a Sequel on the Six-Day War, 1967.* Ithaca, NY: Cornell University Press, 1967.

Szulc, Tad. *The Secret Alliance: The Extraordinary Story of the Rescue of the Jews Since World War II.* New York: Farrar, Straus & Giroux, 1991.

Tal, David, ed. *The 1956 War: Collusion and Rivalry in the Middle East.* London: Frank Cass, 2001.

Taubman, William. *Khrushchev: The Man and His Era.* London: Free Press, 2003.

Tayekh, Ray. *The Origins of the Eisenhower Doctrine: The US, Britain and Nasser's Egypt, 1953–57.* New York: St. Martin's Press, 2000.

Thomas, Hugh. *The Suez Affair.* London: Weidenfeld & Nicolson, 1967.

Thornhill, Michael T. *Road to Suez: The Battle of the Canal Zone.* Stroud, UK: Sutton, 2006.

Trevelyan, Humphrey. *The Middle East in Revolution.* London: Macmillan, 1970.

———. *Public and Private.* London: Hamish Hamilton, 1980.

Troen, Selwyn Ilan, and Moshe Shemesh. *The Suez-Sinai Crisis 1956: Retrospective and Reappraisal.* London: Frank Cass, 1990.

Tudda, Chris. *The Truth Is Our Weapon: The Rhetorical Diplomacy of Dwight D. Eisenhower and John Foster Dulles.* Baton Rouge: Louisiana State University Press, 2006.

Tunzelmann, Alex von. *Red Heat: Conspiracy, Murder and the Cold War in the Caribbean.* London: Simon & Schuster, 2011.

United Nations. *Report of the Special Committee on the Problem of Hungary.* General Assembly Official Records, 11th session, suppl. 18 (A/3592). New York: United Nations, 1957.

Unwin, Peter. *Voice in the Wilderness: Imre Nagy and the Hungarian Revolution.* London: Macdonald, 1991.

Verrier, Anthony. *Through the Looking Glass: British Foreign Policy in an Age of Illusions.* London: Jonathan Cape, 1983.

West, Nigel. *The Friends: Britain's Post-War Secret Intelligence Operations.* London: Coronet Books, 1990.

Wright, Peter. *Spycatcher: The Candid Autobiography of a Senior Intelligence Officer.* Toronto: Stoddart, 1987.

Wynn, Wilton. *Nasser of Egypt: The Search for Dignity.* Cambridge, MA: Arlington Books, 1959.

Yergin, Daniel. *The Prize: The Epic Quest for Oil, Money and Power.* New York: Simon & Schuster, 1991; with new epilogue, 2008.

Young, George K. *Masters of Indecision: An Inquiry into the Political Process.* London: Methuen, 1962.

Zhu Dandan. *1956: Mao's China and the Hungarian Crisis.* Ithaca, NY: East Asia Program, Cornell University, 2013.

Ziegler, Philip. *Mountbatten: The Official Biography.* London: Collins, 1985.

INDEX

ABOUT THE AUTHOR

Alex von Tunzelmann is the author of two previous history books, *Indian Summer* and *Red Heat*. She lives in London.